Music Legends on Maui

Conversations with Icons of Rock, Country, Jazz, Blues, Hawaiian, Soul & Reggae in Paradise

Jon Woodhouse

Arkadia Maui

ISBN: 978-1-64184-807-7 (Hardcover)
ISBN: 978-1-64184-806-0 (Paperback)
ISBN: 978-1-64184-805-3 (Ebook)

Book design by JETLAUNCH
Front cover photo Jimi Hendrix on Maui by Brian Byrnes
All other photos by Jon Woodhouse unless specified
First Edition

TABLE OF CONTENTS

INTRODUCTION

My Moment with Bob

"I hear you're a writer," says Bob Dylan peering up at me. Stunned that one of the greatest music icons is addressing me, I manage to mumble, "yes."

Dylan is backstage after a brilliant concert in Kaanapali on Maui, sitting next to my girlfriend Brook at the time.

"What do you write about?" he asks. "Music," I respond.

And that was about it for MY MOMENT WITH BOB, although it's worth mentioning that when he flew into the old Kaanapali airport with his band, we didn't have enough room in the two vans I had hired to transport everyone to the hotel.

So what does Dylan do? Leave the roadies behind?

"I'll wait," he announces.

One would be hard-pressed to imagine any other luminary choosing to hang for around 45 minutes outside an airport, sitting on a bench (with my girlfriend), with passengers coming and going; even if it was a balmy Maui day with an azure ocean beckoning through the palm trees.

The Lure of Maui

Tell people you live on Maui and they light up. The magical appeal of this unique Hawaiian island is known around the world. The elemental energy is powerful. It's in the land ('āina in Hawaiian), in the ocean (moana/kai), and in the streams (kahawai) and waterfalls (wailele). The mana is strong. It emanates in sacred places. "Each island has its mana, or its spiritual essence," explains revered Hawaiian musician Keola Beamer."

It All Began in London

Born in war-recovering London in 1948, I was mad about music from an early age, devouring British TV pop shows like the *Six-Five Special* in the late 1950s and *Ready Steady Go!* in the mid-'60s. Glued to Radio Luxembourg at night (like teen Jeff Beck, who remembered it as "the absolute oxygen of life"), I was entranced by the Beatles' first singles and EPs (I couldn't afford the albums).

My primary school days were inconsequential except that it bore the name of the nearby historic church where Captain James Cook was married in 1762, some 16 years before he first landed in Hawai'i.

Early significant events included David Bowie (as Davy Jones and The Lower Third) playing my high school dance in Brentwood, and Paul Simon serenading us after classes one afternoon. And Jimi Hendrix blew my mind one night playing a small venue soon after he arrived in England.

Basking in the flowering of Britain's psychedelic movement included trips to UFO (London's first underground club), where Pink Floyd was the de-facto house band at all-nighters. College week- end highlights ranged from The Doors and Jefferson Airplane at the Roundhouse, and helping organize a Ten Years After concert. I saw supergroup Blind Faith's debut and the Rolling Stones before 500,000 fans in Hyde Park, later hailed as "a major event in English social history."

The British music magazine *Q* once ran a story on "The Best Gigs Ever." It included The Doors' Roundhouse show, Cream's debut at the 1966 Windsor Jazz & Blues Festival, Pink Floyd and the Rolling Stones in Hyde Park, and Led Zeppelin at Bath's Festival of Blues & Progressive Music in 1970 – all shows I attended.

I had the pleasure of shaking hands with Jimi Hendrix backstage one night, and I assisted German artist Gustav Metzger with his liquid crystal light show for The Who at the Roundhouse. Metzger was the auto-destructive artist who had inspired The Who's stage mayhem.

Initially trained as a teacher, I briefly taught social studies at London's Ealing Art College (formerly attended by Pete Townshend, Ron Wood, and Freddie Mercury), and I only dipped my toes into journalism after moving to Maui in 1980.

First writing a weekly music column for the Maui Bulletin, I gravitated to our daily paper, The Maui News. With the News since 1983, I've been blessed with the opportunity to interview so many legends who were lured to perform on our island in the middle of the Pacific.

Synthesizing hundreds of interviews conducted over the decades, loosely arranged by genre, *Music Legends* opens with a section devoted to acclaimed artists who live, have lived or have been impacted by Maui. In a way, it's a history of influential artists who have shaped the course of music in the 20th century - through the lens of Hawai'i.

As music has profoundly influenced my life, it has been one of the greatest joys to connect with so many amazing artists and shine a light on their creativity and accomplishments.

With deep gratitude to The Maui News, and thanks to On Maui! magazine, the Maui Bulletin, and the Maui Arts & Cultural Center and CEO Art Vento, which presented concerts with many of the musicians represented here.

I would also like to thank Anita Hallard, Maria Knauer, Ben Verdery, Donna Mosher, Arnie Kotler, and Annie Woodhouse, who all helped with editing advice.

MAUI NO KA OI

"SOFT-HEARTED HANA"

George Harrison

"Everything else can wait, but the search for God cannot wait."

After a mind-expanding mushroom trip, while vacationing on Maui, George Harrison was inspired to write the playful "Soft-Hearted Hana." Singing about Kipahulu's seven sacred pools and the island's majestic Haleakalā volcano, he dedicated the song to his friend Bob Longhi, who had guided George's first hike in Hana's pastoral wonderland and ran a famous Lahaina restaurant.

During this fertile time, a full moon rising over the ocean inspired George to compose the dreamy "Here Comes the Moon," a sublime sequel to "Here Comes the Sun." Other Maui composed songs included "Your Love Forever," "Love Comes To Everyone," and the bluesy "Rocking Chair in Hawaii," which was released posthumously.

In an introduction to George's memoir *I, Me, Mine*, Olivia Harrison described how they had relished an idyllic time staying in a small cottage in Hana. George told producer Ted Templeman about his love for Hawai'i in the book *George Harrison: Behind the Locked Door.* "You get the feeling you're high all the time," he marveled.

George had briefly first visited Hawai'i in 1964, when he landed on Oahu with John Lennon, during a stopover before heading to Tahiti. The Beatles would later include the Hawaiian word aloha in the coda of their hit song "Hello Goodbye," and the accompanying video featured faux hula dancers adorned with leis and grass skirts.

Desiring a peaceful life, Harrison bought a secluded estate in the tropical setting of Nahiku, up the road from Hana. He filmed a video for his song "This is Love" at his Maui home in 1987, where you can see him strumming a guitar at the ocean edge.

One of his old friends, drummer Mick Fleetwood, suggests he gave George the idea to check out Hana. "I like to think I turned George on to Maui years ago," Mick explains. "I said, you need to go to Maui. There's a place called Hana. He had never heard of it."

With the rest of the Beatles, George studied Transcendental Meditation with the Maharishi Mahesh Yogi at an ashram in the Indian town of Rishikesh. Former Maui resident Beach Boy Mike Love also attended the retreat. "It was enormously influential on all of us, most especially George," Love says of their time in India.

Passionate about the 'ukulele, his love for the instrument endeared him to folks in Hana, where he was affectionaly known as Keoki. He would sometimes stop in at Bounty Music in Kahului and leave with 'ukuleles to share with friends. Owner Paul Weinstein recalls: "George came in about half a dozen times. Sometimes his wife Olivia would come in, 'George is heading for the airport, he wants a Kamaka 'uke to take to back with him.' He was on Maui for solitude, not to be bothered. I had a small office where he would sit and play different 'ukes. A lot of them he would give away."

In the liner notes to 'ukulele virtuoso Jake Shimabukuro's *Walking Down Rainhill,* Olivia Harrison wrote: "George felt liberated playing the uke and loved it because it made everyone smile." Jake had become famous covering "While My Guitar Gently Weeps." "I especially love Jake's versions of George's songs," she wrote.

One of George's friends, part-time Maui resident Emil Richards would visit the Nahiku estate. A virtuoso percussionist, Emil practiced TM and had stayed at the Maharishi's Rishikesh ashram right after the Beatles left. He performed on the 1974 *Dark Horse* tour and introduced George to Olivia. George would sometimes call him up when he was on island and hire a helicopter to bring him over from Maui's west side. "He was a consummate musician, always playing and singing and writing," Richards remembered. "We both practiced Transcendental Meditation, and this brought us closer."

2

"I feel fortunate to have realized what the goal is in life," George told *Rolling Stone* in an April 19, 1979 interview. "There's no point in dying having gone through your life without knowing who you are, what you are, or what the purpose of life is."

After George passed in 2001, his family released a statement. "He left this world as he lived in it, conscious of God, fearless of death, and at peace, surrounded by family and friends. He often said, 'everything else can wait but the search for God cannot wait, and love one another.'"

"WORLD TURNING"

Fleetwood Mac

"Mick has always loved Maui. That's why the rest of us went to Maui."

Stevie Nicks recalls a magical time on Maui hanging out with George Harrison in the late 1970s, on the day he began composing the song "Soft-Hearted Hana." In a photo that captures that moment, George is looking up playing his guitar, Stevie is immersed in writing, and the late restaurateur Bob Longhi is smiling in the left corner.

The two musicians were having fun coming up with lyrics together in Hana. "We were writing a sort of parody of 'Here Comes the Sun,'" Stevie explains. "We were writing 'Here Comes the Moon,' because by then, we were all such night birds. We just hung out and wrote and sang and talked for two days. I had been famous for not even quite three years, and we were talking with George about being famous and what it meant and what you had to give up. I had met George before at a record party in Mexico in Acapulco for *Rumours*. We were really young then. We were rocking and beautiful and crazy, and that was all going down on Maui."

The photo of the trio hanging out in Hana has special significance for Nicks. "The photo was taken by my best friend Mary (DeVitto). I had it made into an 8 x 10 and put in a little frame. When I go on the road, it goes right on my makeup mirror. So before I go on stage, whether it's with Fleetwood Mac or in my solo career, the three of us are looking back at me, and that has been my inspiration every single night.

"There are lots of nights where you kind of go; I wish I didn't have to go on stage tonight. I'm tired, I don't feel like doing it, and I look at George Harrison and look at Longhi and look at me, and I go, well, you just have to because it's important. It's important to make people happy, so get out of your chair, put on your boots, and go out there and do your thing."

The island has played a significant role in the lives of most of Fleetwood Mac's members. "Mick has always loved Maui," says Stevie. "That's why the rest of us went to Maui. Because Mick was always there, whenever there was a vacation, all of us followed suit."

After completing their debut *Buckingham Nicks* album in 1973, Stevie and Lindsey Buckingham flew to Maui for a vacation. "When I met Stevie and Lindsey, they had completed *Buckingham Nicks*," Mick Fleetwood recalls. "They stayed at the Napili Kai hotel (on Maui's west side) when they finished the album, and we did likewise. The whole band got on a plane and stayed at the Napili Kai, and that was our first entree. It was a band treat, and that was it for me and John. We fell in love with the island."

Mick Fleetwood has made the island his home for many years, and John McVie had a house there. Stevie owns a home on the west side, and she met one of her closest friends, Sharon Celani, performing at Lahaina's old Blue Max.

"I ended up buying land in Olinda where I planned to retire, and he bought the house that I'm in now (in Napili)," Mick continues. "Then the dream crashed in the Fleetwood Mac deluge with all our relationships falling apart. I often behaved like a bad rock star. I was suitably anesthetized to everything, and like an idiot, I didn't realize I had sold the land in Olinda."

After Christine McVie left Fleetwood Mac to retire in England in 1998, it took a trip to Maui in 2013 to coax her into performing again, at a historic concert at the Maui Arts & Cultural Center (MACC).

"There's no doubt that Maui was part of the story of her returning to Fleetwood Mac," Mick explains during a 2014 interview. "Chris said the first time she walked on stage was at the MACC, and it was magical. Chris had come up to the house and watched us rehearse, and the next morning she called and said, 'would you like me to play?' I said, are you kidding me? This island worked some magic.

"Chris never got on an airplane again after moving back to England from L.A., until she came to Maui. I traveled with her, and that's the beginning of the story. She woke up, 'what am I doing? I miss playing,

I miss my friends, I miss part of my life,' but she was petrified about getting on a plane. She got help, and the chap she was working with on it said, 'where would you book a ticket if you could?' She said, 'I would like to visit John (McVie) and Mick, and I love Maui.'

I broke the story that Fleetwood Mac's classic lineup was reportedly set to begin recording together for the first time in 27 years. A UK *Guardian* newspaper article noted: "Word of the studio reunion emerged through a tiny item in *The Maui News*, following Mick Fleetwood's gig at a small festival in Wailuku, Hawaii. Chatting after performing at Willie K's BBQ Blues Festival, Mick Fleetwood confirmed the rumor that Christine McVie will rejoin Fleetwood Mac, wrote columnist Jon Woodhouse."

The composer of some of the group's biggest hits, including "Don't Stop," "You Make Loving Fun," and "Little Lies," McVie was a little anxious about returning to the fold. "It's a lot to reconnect and be part of a process; it's like getting back on the bike," Mick notes. "She was nervous. She had pulled away from the seething mass of Fleetwood Mac politics and lifestyle. Her criteria was very simple, 'this has to be happy, and it has to be alive and vibrant.'"

When Fleetwood Mac made their official debut at the Windsor National Jazz & Blues Festival on August 13, 1967, Christine Perfect performed at the fest with the Chicken Shack blues group. The historic lineup at the Royal Windsor Racecourse included Cream, Jeff Beck, and John Mayall's Bluesbreakers.

"Chicken Shack with Christine was playing in the tent, and we were on the main stage," Mick recalls. "John McVie was not actually in Fleetwood Mac, although it was called Fleetwood Mac. He was standing at the side of the stage, waiting to play with John Mayall. That gig was very prophetic. John ended up marrying Chris, and she ended up joining Fleetwood Mac. She would follow us around whenever she could, and she ended up being a massive part of our history."

Before he joined the legendary band that would bear his name, Mick drummed briefly with British blues icon John Mayall's band, which included guitarist Peter Green and bassist John McVie. "A lot of people thought it was an internal preordained conspiracy, but it was never even thought about," says Mick about their exodus. "I left, and then Peter left, and he had no intention of forming a band. He was going to go off and wander around Morocco and do what Eric Clapton and Brian Jones did, just be a wandering minstrel. But then he phoned me up and said, 'let's put a band together.' We didn't leave John Mayall to do it."

London was a fertile creative vortex in the late 1960s. "It was a great time," Mick enthuses. "There were The Yardbirds and the Stones and early Fleetwood Mac, and then you had the side headed up by the Beatles."

Fleetwood Mac began, like a number of leading British bands, with its roots firmly planted in the blues. "There were all these funny little English guys selling themselves to the company store known as the blues greats," he explains. "We did our version, and we were blessed that Jeremy (Spencer) was basically Elmore James incarnate, and Peter (Green) had this burning quest, an emotive need.

"We were part of this little tidal wave that gave longevity and notice to an art form that was all but wiped out. We were part of a chapter that was a crossbreed where we had borrowed and re-invented American blues. There was Eric and Cream and bands that became more famous, and we were at the real grassroots of that whole thing, and that makes me feel real good."

A unique confluence of British and American cultural influences would eventually propel Fleetwood Mac into the mega-star strato-sphere. The English blues-rockers fused with the California-based duo of Lindsey Buckingham and Stevie Nicks in 1975, to create one of the world's most popular bands.

"It was an unlikely partnering of the styles of Christine, John, and myself that came straight out of the pubs of England with Freddie King and B.B. (King) and John Lee Hooker, and that became this musical bed that was triggered with Stevie and Lindsey's sense that came from country and the Everly Brothers and the Kingston Trio," he says. "All these things that made an unlikely combo came together. A song like 'World Turning' is basically Lindsey and Stevie meeting us on our side of our music, and then on the other side of the spectrum, you have things like 'Rhiannon.'

By the release of *Rumours*, the popularity of the Anglo-American version of Fleetwood Mac exploded. Rated number four in *Rolling Stone*'s list of the 100 Greatest Albums of All Time, *Rumours* has sold more than 40 million copies worldwide since its release in 1977.

"We didn't have any inkling of what would happen," he says about its phenomenal success. "It was way out of anyone's aspirations. We had made *Fleetwood Mac* with Stevie and Lindsey, and it had sold four or five million, so we felt we had a chance. It was a very hard album to make with everyone lovesick. We spent a year making it, a lot of blood, sweat, and toil, and internal upsets. You had the anguish and emotive poignancy that came out of *Rumours*, with Lindsey and Stevie basically talking to each other through their songs. The huge success of *Rumours* caused problems. It became a sort of mutant. People talked about the numbers of how much the album sold, and the music got somewhat forgotten. Whereas with an album like *Tusk*, we shoved out a double album, which we were told, don't do."

The costly experimental *Tusk*, which record label executives warned was a suicidal move, allowed the members to stretch creatively like the Beatles with the *White Album*. "*Tusk* was a very important album for us to do," Mick emphasizes. "Everyone was getting a little frustrated, and it relieved a lot of stuff. If we hadn't done *Tusk,* I think the band would have broken up. People said we were crazy doing it, but it was a success, selling five million copies, and it saved the band."

With homes in Kula and Napili, Mick had long felt a desire to move to Maui. "I've planned to roost here since about 1973," he says. "I knew when I first came here that after the madness calmed down, this was where I wanted to be. It was mysteriously written in some book that we ought to be here. In the early years, I used to arrive in pieces from the lifestyle I was leading. I came here to heal myself, and Maui was where I turned around.

"I was drinking a hell of a lot, and the party was forever. The whole downtime from Fleetwood Mac, I got away from playing because of my lifestyle. Then before I moved here, I was on track to playing again because I was not completely out of my gourd all the time. This is where I turned the corner. I knew I had to rein myself in. This is where I did it, and it held."

When he first opened his Fleetwood's on Front St. restaurant in Lahaina, Mick was reminded of the stressed-out comedy character Basil Fawlty, played by Monty Python's John Cleese. "I did feel like Basil Fawlty sometimes," he says, laughing. "At the beginning, I really didn't know what I was doing."

Besides occasionally performing at Fleetwood's, hands-on involvement for the drummer includes pop-in times for meet and greets. "I talk shop. It is the John Cleese, how are you, guy? It's my pleasure. Then I disappear and go on tour with Fleetwood Mac and then come home."

Since moving to Maui, he formed the Island Rumours Band, which included former Mac guitarist Rick Vito, renowned falsetto singer Raiatea Helm, local virtuoso Willie K, and Eric Gilliom fusing rock and Hawaiian influences. Renamed House of Rumours, Mick reformed the group in late 2021, with the addition of former New York session guitarist Joe Caro in the role of music arranger.

He also founded the Mick Fleetwood Blues Band with Vito and Maui musicians Lenny Castellanos and Mark Johnstone, releasing the Grammy-nominated recording *Blue Again.* "I don't function as a musician unless I'm able to play with people," he notes. "I don't sit in my living room strumming a guitar or playing the piano. Ultimately I'm most comfortable playing blues. I'm a blues drummer."

In recent years he developed a fondness for the ʻukulele. "I've got about 20 now," he enthuses. "They're always in my car. It's like a pacifier for me. I love it." At his House of Fleetwood store in Paia, which opened in late 2021, Mick sells his own signature brand of ʻukuleles, hand-made on Maui, as well as ʻukuleles designed by George Harrison's son Dhani.

Was he inspired by his former brother-in-law George Harrison? "Inadvertently he turned me on to it," he says. "I truly loved him. Technically, family-wise, I was George's brother-in-law when he was married to Pattie (Boyd), and I was with Jenny (Boyd), my first wife. He never traveled anywhere without a ʻukulele. He loved turning people on to the ʻukulele.

"George's lovely wife Olivia still has a home here. We were at her home three years ago, and I had my ukulele with me. It was Ringo's birthday. I was playing on the porch, and I went out in the garden, and she basically forced me to play, and we both sang a song to him on Maui."

Reflecting on their five-decade career, Mick notes: "Considering we're a funny old franchise and the disorganized, funny trip we've been on, everything eventually comes together. We're the junior elder statesmen of this business. Bob Dylan or Willie Nelson are the elder statesmen, and at some point, they will be done or leave us. Who is to say when this stops?"

Ten months after the release of *Lindsey Buckingham/Christine McVie,* the band's mercurial guitarist was dismissed from Fleetwood Mac. With the addition of Tom Petty band guitarist Mike Campbell and Crowded House's Neil Finn, the new version of the group all convened to begin rehearsals - on Maui.

"Maui has had this connection to Fleetwood Mac," marvels Mick. "There are all the early stories of Fleetwood Mac when we came here after *Rumours* and for the first time with *Fleetwood Mac* when we stayed in Napili. And the (MACC show) was the first time Christine had been on a stage in 16 years.

"It's always been amazing how lots of things happen that are connected, like with the last lineup of the band. We rehearsed at the MACC with Neil and Mike coming into the band, and it was all done here. Stevie has a house here, and Neil flew in from New Zealand. It was a Hail Mary of I think this could work. It worked, and the seed was here. The journey with Fleetwood Mac, whether it's over or not, has been amazing, and my mission statement is one way, or another anything that's less than healed I hope is healed."

"ON THE ROAD AGAIN"

Willie Nelson

"Most everything I do, I do off the top of my head without any long-range planning and very little thinking. It looks good when it works."

"Of all the places I've been on earth, Maui is the most spiritual," Willie Nelson wrote in his book *The Tao of Willie*. Touring Hawai'i with Bonnie Raitt in the early 1980s, the country icon fell in love with the island and bought a beach house near the town of Paia.

"Maui has this spiritual quality," Willie explained in his 2015 autobiography *It's A Long Story: My Life*. "It's in the air, the mountains covered in mist, the exotic plants, the wildlife, the sea, the sky, the wise kupuna who tell stories that connect the mysteries of nature to the mysteries of man."

An old soul known for dispensing Zen-like wisdom, Willie was once proclaimed "the Hillbilly Dalai Lama" by musician friend Kinky Friedman. "I think we all get the energy from the same guy, and it's important to spread it around," he says during an interview at his Maui home. "As I get older, I realize it more. I began to realize that we were feeding off each other, and we're all feeding off the big dynamo in the sky. It's what makes us all get out and have energy. I think that's why Hawai'i is so good and Maui in particular, because it is the place to come and get what you need, for your spirit or your body, whatever's wrong - physical, mental, or spiritual."

With an astrology chart that reflects a mystical nature, Willie was influenced early on by Norman Vincent Peale's *The Power of Positive Thinking*. He wrote about the profound impact of reading *The Aquarian Gospel of Jesus the Christ* and the search for enlightenment in *It's a Long Story*. After experiencing a collapsed lung swimming off Maui in the summer of 1981, he addressed reincarnation and sang about "Little Old Fashioned Karma," on his *Tougher Than Leather* album.

Dividing time between Maui and Texas, when he's on the island, "electric" Willie sometimes used to perform at Charley's in Paia. With Trigger, his favorite acoustic guitar left on the mainland; he would serenade the packed restaurant with his signature gems, playing electric guitar.

"I don't have Trigger over here, so I play electric, and it's a little more blues and rock," Willie explains. "After a couple of weeks here, I get rested and sunburned, and I'm ready to move around a little bit."

A very generous artist, over the years, he has donated his time for a range of island benefits, from Paia's Tibetan Buddhist center and the Montessori School of Maui to the renovation of Wailuku's old Iao Theater and Ka Lima O Maui. "I like to every now and then give a little back," he continues. "It's a good feeling. If I can do something, I will. It's that simple."

Born on April 30, 1933, in the small Texas town of Abbott, times were hard in those rural depression days, but young Willie doesn't remember an impoverished scenario. "Probably in some people's opinion, it was sort of 'Grapes of Wrath'/'Tobacco Road' type living, but I didn't realize it being that bad," he says. "My grandparents raised me and my sister, and we were happy. I worked on all the farms around. I saved my way through school working on farms."

In the late '50s, Willie taught guitar lessons at the Buskirk Music Studios in Pasadena, Texas. One night over dinner, he sang a song he had been working on. Buskirk offered to pay for the meal for the rights to the song, which turned out to be the "Family Bible," a Top 10 hit in 1960. "I was living in Houston, and I sold him the rights for $50," Willie recalls. "It took him and two more guys to raise the money."

In time his gift for composing distinctive songs was noticed in Nashville, and within a few months of arriving in the country capital, he had sold three top-10 hits for Patsy Cline, Faron Young, and Billy Walker.

The release of *Crazy: The Demo Sessions*, in 2003, featured a collection of sparse recordings not intended for commercial release but for pitching songs to other artists - including "Crazy," the country and pop hit for Patsy Cline in 1961. Ironically, the restrained style demonstrated on the demo tapes brought Nelson his greatest commercial success in the 1970s. "Finally, they were out there and the way I wanted them to be in the beginning because I thought they were good enough to be masters then," he says.

Willie's ascent was hard-fought. He didn't fit the mold of how country artists were supposed to sing or dress. "I've always been hard-headed," he suggests. "My grandmother raised me, and she said, 'Hugh (his middle name), remember a hard head always makes a sore ass.' She was right."

Record producers would try to bury his singing and tell him it's not commercial. "In Nashville, they didn't consider me a singer," he laughs. "They still don't. My songs and my singing and playing, it wasn't commercial. When I ran into a few rules, I ignored them because I knew I had to in order to keep doing what I was doing. I tried doing it their way, but I'd rather be a failure on my own. So I left town (Nashville) and tried to prove you didn't have to do it that way. It took a while for anybody to realize I could sell records. To a great extent, I've proved you can do it anyway you want to."

Sensing a new audience for his kind of music, Willie moved back to Texas in the early '70s. Country music was about to experience a major shift with a new progressive form - what became known as outlaw country. "I saw in Austin when I first moved back a movement, a lot of young, long-haired hippie kids sneaking into places like Big G's, where it was mostly redneck cowboys. Things started changing. It was an exciting time. A lot of people knew there was something new happening."

When he walked into Columbia Records with his *Red Headed Stranger* album, label executives couldn't comprehend the idea of a country concept album. He was told it sounded like an underproduced demo session. "The first thing I asked was let me do it the way I want to. There was a little resistance. I went in and did *Red Headed Stranger* for $20,000, and that didn't make a lot of producers happy because it showed everybody you didn't need to spend six months and a million dollars to make music. They thought it was a demo, and Waylon (Jennings) told them, as only Waylon could do, what he thought about it.

They weren't hearing it, but when they saw it made money, they quit arguing about it."

Characteristically low-key, humble, and unpretentious, this living legend says, "I'm sort of impulsive. Most everything I do, I do off the top of my head without any long-range planning and very little thinking. It looks good when it works."

Whatever genre of music he tackles, somehow Willie always manages to make each song sound uniquely his own. "It's called plagiarism," he laughs. "You rip off everybody and then mix it up, so nobody will know. Kris (Kristofferson) wrote a song, 'Let's All Get Together and Steal Each Other's Songs.' I like that. The songs that I do are always songs that I like. I have to really like them."

Selling around 75 million records throughout a six-decade career, he seems to release more albums than any other artist ("one a week," he jokes), that sometimes he reports he's not sure what's even out there.

By 1978, Willie changed musical course once again with his *Stardust* collection of pop standards that spent more than a decade on the country charts. The notion of a country singer recording an album of pop chestnuts was totally alien to the country music establishment. Industry insiders predicted he faced musical suicide, and his label resisted issuing it.

"The arguments were these are a bunch of old songs that everybody's heard and nobody's going to buy them again," Willie recalls. "My argument was good songs are good songs, and people will like to hear new versions. They're going to love 'Stardust' and 'Georgia,' and all the standards. I just believed in the material."

Stardust remained on the country charts for almost ten years and sold more than four million copies. "Like *Red Headed Stranger*, they didn't think it would do anything at all. 'He's crazy. He's blowing money, he's ruining his career.' If it starts working, then they agree what a brilliant idea it was," he adds, laughing.

Willie earned the biggest recording success of his career in 1982, with a moving, top-10 charting version of Elvis Presley's "Always on My Mind." During the '80s, he recorded duets with such diverse stars as Julio Iglesias, Bob Dylan, Leon Russell, Dolly Parton, Neil Young, Carlos Santana, and Ray Charles.

Willie recalls fond times with Ray Charles and how the blind singer would always beat him at chess. "He used Braille pieces that were all the same color so he could feel them, and I couldn't," Willie explains with a characteristic laugh. "We were doing a special in Austin, and he invited me to come over and play. I laughed a little bit, Ray Charles inviting me to play chess. He comes to the door, and I walked in, and there was a big foyer and a lot of lights, and we walked into his living room to sit down, and there was no lights. He brings out these chess pieces, and they're all the same color and no lights. So how does a blind man beat a hillbilly? That's the way you do it."

For *Across the Borderline*, in 1993, Willie composed the song "Heartland" with Bob Dylan. He says they once talked about recording a unique project. "We were going to write an album, and we had this plan where one of us would write the first song and send it to the other one, and listen to it, and write a song to follow it, and send it back. A kind of a concept album. It might have been fun."

Three years later, *Spirit*'s powerful contemplation on love and spirituality captured Willie with a simple production backed by his sister Bobbie Nelson on piano, Johnny Gimble on fiddle, and Jody Payne on guitar. "I wanted the similar sound of the *Red Headed Stranger*, and even a little more because we don't use bass or drums anywhere," he explains. "It's kind of like country chamber music."

Opening and closing with Spanish flavored instrumentals, the album tracked the elevation of the human spirit from low to high. "The concept of the album is to raise the spirits," he explains. "Starting out on a low level with 'She is Gone' and 'Your Memory Won't Die in My Grave,' it starts a slow climb upward, and there's "Too Sick to Pray' and 'I'm Waiting Forever,' and then it goes into the more positive side of the album. It ends with an instrumental, which is the spot where words are not necessary."

We have all come to love Willie's unique voice so much it's easy to overlook his skills as a guitarist. Watching him perform with Kris Kristofferson one night at Charley's in Paia, one could marvel at his dexterity and thoughtful style. "I was a guitar player long before I was a singer," he notes.

This gifted guitarist released the instrumental album *Night and Day* in 1999, which showcased his appreciation for jazz. "I love to play instrumentals," he says. The album included "Nuages," a tune by his favorite guitarist, gypsy jazz icon Django Reinhardt. "He's the greatest guitar player ever," Willie enthuses. "Every guitar player I know will agree; this guy was the best. I try to learn his songs, and it's a challenge."

So has he got it down? "No. I listen to me playing it, and then I go back and listen to him playing it. Sorry Django, I didn't want to screw it up for you. Norah Jones told me one of her band players said that I play like Django with one finger."

Having been raised around rural farms, Willie began championing the plight of small farmers, teaming with Neil Young and John Mellencamp to present benefit Farm Aid concerts. "I really don't believe that the general public realizes the importance of keeping the small family farmer on the land," he emphasizes. "The big corporate farmers couldn't care less about an acre of ground. They'll drain it of all its nutrients, fill it full of chemicals and pesticides, and move on to the farm next door. We're pushing genetically altered food on everybody. We're in a hell of a mess. If you're looking for a light at the end of the tunnel, there might be one, but there could be a freight train. I've always said if you don't take care of the farmers, the country is never going to improve. Every civilization that has gone under in the past has gone under because of its inability to feed its people."

Never shying from controversy, he released the Iraq war protest song, "Whatever Happened to Peace on Earth," and followed it with "Peaceful Solution," made available at no charge on the web to anyone wishing to use his vocals and create their own version. "We were on the way to the Coachella Festival, and my daughter Amy was traveling with me, and we'd been up all night," Willie explains. "It was about three in the morning, and she said she had had this dream where I had written a song called 'Peaceful Solution' and was singing it on stage. I went back and tried to lie down and go to sleep, and I couldn't. So I got up, and she had a little recording device, and we recorded it a capella. I thought the easiest way to get it out is to give it away."

Besides the raw a capella version, Willie recorded a jazz version with the Maui's Gypsy Pacific group and a reggae version featuring

Marty Dread, Willie's son Lukas Nelson, and actor Woody Harrelson on backing vocals.

Willie has collaborated on several songs with Maui's Marty Dread, including the anti-war song "Take No Part," "Lend a Hand to the Farmers," and "Laws of Nature." "He wrote 'Laws of Nature' on a napkin and said this is a song for you to record," Marty reports. "I came up with a melody and brought it back to him, and he played Trigger and sang on half of it. There's a poignant line about his sons becoming the bearer of his torch."

Supporting Maui musicians over the years, at island concerts backed by the Planetary Bandits, he championed the late Willie K, inviting him to play a Fourth of July Picnic in Luckenbach, Texas. "I got to know him pretty good," says the country star. "I think he's really great."

Willie released the critically-acclaimed album *To All the Girls* in 2013, showcasing new duets with a range of female artists, including Dolly Parton, Loretta Lynn, Wynonna Judd, Rosanne Cash, and Maui's Lily Meola. "It was incredible, some of the best singers in the world," he says. "It's something I have long wanted to do."

For his 89th birthday in 2022, he released *A Beautiful Time*, which included his profound original song "Energy Follows Thought," about mindfulness, the metaphysical power of mental creation, and opening to spirit guidance.

Loved by so many, Willie never disappoints in concert. "We're not pushing anything but music," he says. "I don't preach to them. I know music can have healing effects. All we try to do is put on a good show and get some good positive energy exchange going. When that happens, it's a perfect day."

Touring and recording for decades, committed to promoting earth-conscious projects and donating his time generously to so many causes - how does he do it all? "I just think I'm mischievous," he suggests laughing. "I wake up in the morning and say, what can I get into today."

Willie Nelson, Spreckelsville - "Maui has this spiritual quality"

Mick Fleetwood photo exhibit, Wailea -
"Maui has had this connection to Fleetwood Mac"

Mick Fleetwood, Steven Tyler & Willie K,
opening of Fleetwood's on Front St. in Lahaina

Christine McVie, Mick Fleetwood & Rick Vito - "Maui was part of the
story of her returning to Fleetwood Mac"

Carlos Santana at the MACC -
"We play to accelerate the spiritual vibration of this planet"

Beach Boys' Mike Love, Kahului Airport -
"We have a lot of fond memories of Hawai'i"

The Doobie Brothers' Pat Simmons & Michael McDonald at the MACC -
"I got into slack key real heavy, and I still love it"

The author & Willie Nelson, Spreckelsville, photo by Annie Nelson

Donald Fagen & Boz Scaggs at the MACC - "I feel very fortunate to be able to do what I do and have a career"

Michael McDonald on 'uke, Mulligan's on the Blue -
"It's something I picked up to relieve the boredom on the road"

"WHEN DOVES CRY"

Prince

"Every night I thank God for my life and my music."

"I'm much happier and open now," said Prince. "All of which I attribute to God." The one-time reclusive star, who for years refused to conduct any interviews, began opening up to the media in the late 1990s. Freed from his old contract with Warner Bros., the Artist Formerly Known as Prince talked with Oprah about his new life and granted me a brief interview in 1997, before a Honolulu show.

When Prince announced in 1993 that he was changing his name to a glyph that merged the male and feminine, the move symbolized the death of an old persona and the birth of a more spiritually attuned being, resulting in albums like *Emancipation*. Roaming through musical genres and moods, he addressed a range of themes while emphasizing spiritual redemption and the joy of loving partnership.

Emancipation included a radiant rendering of Joan Osborne's hit "One of Us." "The words have a very deep meaning," Prince said. "People of all races shouldn't shy from the statement, what if God was one of us."

So what inspired his new openness? "Freedom," Prince answered. "I own all the rights to *Emancipation*. Any work I do for this project is so much more rewarding than the past."

Encompassing a cycle of 36 songs, *Emancipation* was influenced by Prince's studies of ancient Egypt. Ever since his wife began sharing books with him about the pyramids, he felt a strong affinity with this mysterious world. "The connection is intense for me," he emphasized. "My wife and I believe we lived there as one individual in another life."

Following his marriage on Valentine's Day in 1996 to Mayte Garcia, Prince and his wife spent their honeymoon in Hawai'i. Prince credited his wife with helping bring profound changes to his life. "She's changed my mind about a lot of things," he said. "She's given me the reason to have hope for the human race."

A vegetarian, he was inspired by John Robbins' book *A Diet for New America*. "The rampant cruelty to animals astounds me," he said. "I am a vegetarian – now and forever."

Producing a body of work which remained unmatched by almost any other contemporary artist, he knew some folks had a hard time keeping up with his changes. "If they can't follow, they weren't meant to," he said. "My real support comes from the daring cliff divers in life."

Having amassed such an extensive, diverse palette of songs, I wondered if he sometimes felt like he was just warming up for some incredible projects. "Always," he responded. "It's what I live for; to continue using my gifts makes every day incredible for me. Every night I thank God for my life and my music."

Spiritual growth primarily differentiated the old Prince from his new self. Asked if he felt divinely inspired, he answered, "Indeed I do. Many creative people speak of their talent as a gift. I'm no different." And as to the greatest gift Prince felt his music offered, he simply stated - "love."

In the forward to *Prince in Hawaii: An Intimate Portrait of an Artist*, photographer Afshin Shahidi wrote: "The magic and beauty of the Hawaiian Islands compliment Prince, his music and his being." It included photos of Prince sailing off Maui's west side.

Prince's concert in 2003 at the MACC, was one of the most memorable events ever presented on Maui. "We've been looking around this island for some funky music," he announced during his spectacular show. "Willie K, he's funky," he proclaimed about one of Hawaii's most talented musicians.

From the opening intro of "Let's Go Crazy," the audience rose en masse and never sat. Creating a frenzy among the hordes of women in the venue, after a couple jumped on stage, Prince declared, "I need more dancers." The damn broke as upwards of one hundred women swarmed around the rock star, creating havoc for security. Obviously relishing the attention, he jumped up on a speaker and began playfully wielding a whip above them.

The jam of the year followed with an after-show party at a Kihei club with Prince and his phenomenal band roaring on instrumental jams until two a.m. The jam included "All The Critics Love U in Maui," available on the boot *Complete Hawaii Tapes Vol.2: Maui.* Near the close, Prince invited Willie K on stage to add his fire to the mix. "It was surreal," Willie recalled. "We became friends, and every once in a while, we'd hang out. He was very shy and always positive about everything, especially music. Music was his Bible."

"He loved listening to Willie K," says percussionist Estaire Godinez, who toured with Prince in 1999. "He told me Willie was one of his favorite musicians on the island." Spending time on Maui during the Christmas and New Year's holidays, Prince was known to sneak into movie screenings at the MACC.

Prince loved visiting Maui, especially when George Benson was on island. "He could jam with George Benson," says Godinez. "That was one of his connections because he was a Jehovah's Witness. He really loved Maui, loved the people, and the energy of Maui. It was his favorite island."

"DIAMONDS ON THE SOLES OF THEIR SHOES"

Paul Simon

"I'm very fortunate that my voice stayed clear."

When Paul Simon announced that he was retiring from touring in early 2018, no one expected that a year later, this music icon would present his first-ever concerts on Maui as a way of offering thanks to the island that had become a home.

"I thought this was a perfect opportunity to say a big thank you to our new home," says Simon, who performed two sold-out benefit concerts at the MACC in August 2019. "How grateful we are that we are living there and are able to make some kind of contribution to the people and the land and show our respect and our affection for Maui."

Drawing more than 8,000 fans over two nights, it was undoubtedly one of the most extraordinary assemblies of musical talent on a Maui stage, with up to 14 superb musicians, including acclaimed South African bassist Bakithi Kumalo from the celebrated *Graceland* sessions, backing Simon.

A snapshot overview of his artistic evolution the repertoire ranged from the sublime masterpiece of "Sound of Silence" to the complex orchestration of "Can't Run But," from his *In the Blue* album. The concerts benefitted the Auwahi Forest Restoration Project, which is helping reforest Maui with native trees, and Kuaʻaina Ulu ʻAuamo (KUA), which helps protect our ocean and land.

It was not the first time that Simon sang on Maui. On New Year's Eve in 2018, he hopped on stage at the MACC with part-time Maui resident Woody Harrelson at Bill Maher's comedy show. He has also been a long-time fan of Maui-based Hawaiian legend Keola Beamer. "He's an exceptional musician, a very good player, and beautiful singer," says Simon, who invited Beamer to sing on stage with him at the Maui concert, where they performed the Beamer

Brothers' classic "Honolulu City Lights" together.

Right before the coronavirus crisis hit Hawai'i, in early March 2020, Keola Beamer conducted an Aloha Music Camp on Kauai, which included Simon's surprising presence. "We had kept it a secret, and everyone was in shock when he walked in the room," Beamer explains. "He did a wonderful job sharing acoustic songwriting techniques and relating it to slack key guitar. It was very cool. He's very interested in slack key."

Over seven decades, Simon has contributed immensely to popular culture. Named one of the 100 Greatest Songwriters of All Time and one of the 100 greatest guitarists by *Rolling Stone*, he has earned 16 Grammy Awards, including three for Album of the Year (*Bridge Over Troubled Water, Still Crazy After All These Years*, and *Graceland*).

Before heading out solo, Paul Simon and Art Garfunkel were one of the best-selling music groups of the 1960s. Prior to the release of the duo's *Wednesday Morning, 3 A.M.* debut, Simon had spent time in England, settling in the town of Brentwood, where I went to school. One afternoon, we were informed a young folk singer from America wanted to entertain us after classes. It was Simon. His set included "Homeward Bound," which he told us he had just composed.

After the breakup of Simon & Garfunkel, for any fans wonder- ing if Simon's solo work could live up to the duo's greatness, his *Paul Simon* album blew out any doubts. It would have been hard to imagine Garfunkel singing the funky reggae of "Mother and Child Reunion" (partly recorded in Jamaica with Jimmy Cliff's backing band), or the exuberant samba flavored "Me and Julio Down by the Schoolyard" (with Brazilian legend Airto Moreiro on percussion).

The dazzling *There Goes Rhymin' Simon* cemented his genius status with many standouts, from the jubilant gospel of "Loves Me Like a Rock" and the feel-good "Kodachrome" to the delicate beauty of the "St. Judy's Comet" lullaby.

As much as Simon was admired, no one expected the landmark *Graceland,* which sold around 16 million copies worldwide. Inspired by his fascination with the South African mbaqanga musical style, Simon once suggested Graceland's title song was his best composition. "It probably was at one moment in time," he says.

"It certainly would be up there. I don't really have one constant favorite song. That's a good one. I like the track a lot. The story has enough elements of biography to be emotionally resonant for me personally and enough imagination for it to go and take you off, hopefully into some other sonic place. That song is fun to do and reexamine from time to time. That's what happens with these songs. I go back over them, and I kind of fix things that maybe I missed the first time, or I was unaware of, or players in the band change."

While most of his peers have creatively peeked, into the 21st century Simon kept innovating. At the age of 74 in 2016, he delivered the superb experimental work *Stranger to Stranger*. Spelling out the consequences of economic inequality on "Wristband," he painted a chilling tribute to the victims of the Sandy Hook Elementary School shooting on "The Riverbank," and sounded dire warnings of impending calamity on the masterful "The Werewolf."

Simon's most recent album, *In the Blue Light*, re-imagined some of his lesser-known songs that are personal favorites. Highlights included an intriguing orchestral arrangement of "Can't Run But," by Bryce Dessner from The National band. "Bryce's arrangement is really clever," says Simon. "The arrangement on 'Magritte' ("René and Georgette Magritte with Their Dog after the War") by Bob Sirota was also a beauty. Both of those songs were not really familiar songs from my repertoire, but I always thought they were really interesting. Once I started performing them in my show with (New York ensemble) yMusic they became almost favorites."

Into his 70s, Simon has continued to craft remarkable, imaginative songs. "I'm very fortunate that my voice stayed clear," he says. "Usually, just by this decade (in his 70s), your voice starts to become frayed. As long as I get a lot of sleep and rest it my voice is pretty clear. Part of the reason I stopped touring is that when I went on tour I had to go to sleep so much to get my voice ready for the shows. I had nothing to do in-between shows except go to sleep. I'll sleep very comfortably in Maui. I'll be in my own bed."

"GOOD VIBRATIONS"

The Beach Boys

"I never get tired of singing the songs because they brought so much joy to multiple generations all around the world."

"We have a lot of fond memories of Hawai'i," says 'Beach Boys' co-founder Mike Love, who had a home on Maui for many years.

The Hawaiian islands held an almost mythical fascination for the iconic Californian group. Beginning with "Hawaii" in 1963, their affection continued with the *Smiley Smile* album, where Carl Wilson played 'ukulele on the quirky "Little Pad." Then came the trippy instrumental "Diamond Head" on the *Friends* album.

Years later, they recorded "Kona Coast," where they watched for shooting stars off Lahaina. Their 1992 *Summer Paradise* album, included the romantic remembrance "Lahaina Aloha," and *Ultimate Christmas* in 1998, included "Melekalikimaka" (not a cover of the well known "Mele Kalikimaka"), where they imagined spending Christmas in Hawai'i.

Once owning the old Lindbergh estate (the former home of the famous aviator) in remote Kipahulu on Maui, Love recalls how "I used to take the back road to my place in Kipahulu. I bought the Samuel Pryor place, and for a while, I had both spots. I'd been to the Samuel Pryor place in 1975, near a beautiful waterfall. I love Maui. The only problem was I wasn't there enough, and there were too many issues."

The Beach Boys first played Hawai'i in 1963 - as a backing band. "It was three nights in a row," Love recalls. "Dee Dee Sharp was the headliner, and we backed her up. We were second on the bill. 'Surfin' Safari' had come out in '62, and 'Surfin' USA' in '63, and we came back with Jan & Dean in 1964." The nine-date tour included a show on Maui at Wailuku's Baldwin Auditorium.

Planning to record a live album and a possible film called *Le'id in Hawaii*, the group flew to Oahu for concerts in August 1967. Ads in Honolulu papers suggested fans bring leis and 'ukuleles. But back in Los Angeles, they discovered the tapes were unusable. Released in 2017, rehearsal and concert recordings from the Oahu shows surfaced on *Live Sunshine - 1967*.

In one of their last concerts together, all three Wilson brothers performed with the rest of the Beach Boys on Maui in February 1983, at Wailuku's War Memorial Stadium. Tickets were $10. I interviewed Carl Wilson over lunch in Lahaina after the show, but I lost my only copy.

Brian Wilson would return to his Hawai'i fascination on his Grammy-winning solo album *Brian Wilson Presents Smile*. He sang about waterfalls and luaus on "In Blue Hawaii." The quirky pirate's tale "On a Holiday," referenced old Waikiki and Queen Lili'uokalani, while "Roll Plymouth Rock" addressed the loss of American Native lands and colonization of the Sandwich Islands (what Captain Cook named Hawai'i) with Wilson adding his impression of a Hawaiian chant.

One of the most successful and important American bands in rock history, the Beach Boys' massive popularity began with a stream of hit teen anthems espousing the joys of California's surf, sun, and hot rods. "I wrote all the lyrics to 'California Girls," Love explains, quoting lyrics which also referenced Hawai'i girls. "We sang originally about our environment in Southern California, and then we progressed."

That progression included their *Pet Sounds* masterpiece, initially conceived as an effort to top the Beatles' *Rubber Soul*. The album included the sublime "Caroline, No," and the complex, harmonically sophisticated "God Only Knows," constructed with 23 studio musicians. Paul McCartney would later praise it on *BBC Radio 1* as his favorite song of all time - "one of the few songs that reduces me to tears every time I hear it," he said.

In a 1996 interview about *Pet Sounds*, Brian Wilson reported, "God was with us the whole time we were doing this record. We were trying to capture spiritual love that couldn't be found anywhere else in the world." He also felt he was on a mission "to spread the gospel of love through records."

Unfortunately, it was way too innovative for their record label. "Capitol hated it," Al Jardine recalled in 2000 *Goldmine* interview. "They wanted some hit records."

Then came the tour de force of "Good Vibrations," widely acclaimed as one of the greatest songs of all time. "*Pet Sounds* was more introspective and reflective," says Love, who co-wrote many of the band's hits including "Good Vibrations." "'Good Vibrations' is the one you have to say you're most proud of. Brian did the amazing track over a few months' time. I came up with lyrics to compliment the work he had done – *he begins singing about good vibrations.* It was avant-garde with great chord progressions and lyrics. I felt 'Good Vibrations' was the Beach Boys' psychedelic anthem or flower power offering. It was unique and creative and successful."

The epic "Good Vibrations" was featured on *Smiley Smile*, released in 1967, which included songs from the abandoned *SMiLE* project, and offered a glimpse of their experimental trajectory way beyond the surf. Resplendent with quirky songs about "Wind Chimes," "Vege- tables" (with Paul McCartney munching on raw veggies), and "Fall Breaks and Back to Winter," it was later described by author Nick Kent in *The Dark Stuff* as "one of the best chill-out albums to listen to during an LSD comedown." Scorned by most music critics at the time, *Melody Maker* in 1971 praised *Smiley Smile* as "The Great Undiscov- ered Pop Album."

Love suggests the Beach Boys in California and the Beatles in England had a shared appreciation. "It was like a mutual admiration society," he says. "I remember when George Harrison was being inter- viewed with Paul and Ringo, and he said, 'We were just trying to keep up with the Beach Boys.' There was a creative competition. It was like *Rubber Soul* was really great, Ok here's this one called *Pet Sounds*. I think the competition enriched both sides of the Atlantic."

Around the time of the groups' *Friends* album, Love became initi- ated into Transcendental Meditation. Invited by the Maharishi Mahesh Yogi to travel to India to study TM, Love joined the Beatles and Don- ovan in 1968 at an ashram retreat overlooking the Ganges. While celebrating his birthday in Rishikesh, Paul and George composed and sang to him the Beach Boys' flavored song "Spiritual Regeneration/ Happy Birthday Mike Love."

"It was the most phenomenal time that I've ever experienced," he recalls. "I was the first person to hear 'Back in the U.S.S.R.' on acoustic guitar. Paul McCartney came to the breakfast table one morning playing 'Back in the U.S.S.R.' I said, what you should do in the middle is talk about all the girls in Russia. It was like a Beach Boys prototype thing. It was a fascinating time.

"I went to many lectures with the Maharishi and the Beatles," he continues. "We had long hours of meditation, six, ten, or twelve hours. It was a teacher training course, and I had just learned meditation. The Beatles had learned it in Wales."

It was actually the Beatles who turned the Beach Boys on to TM. Al Jardine recalled in the *Goldmine* interview that when the band was in London, John Lennon and George Harrison knocked on his hotel room door. "There's John and George standing there. They were proselytizing on behalf of TM. They suggested that we get involved and that they would see us later in Paris."

"We had been taught in Paris where we played a UNICEF show," Love explains. *"The curtain opened, and on one side of the Maharishi in the middle of the first row was George Harrison, and on the other side was John Lennon. It was kind of intimidating.*

"Paul McCartney once told me later backstage at a show, 'I don't think it was the lads' cup of tea,' meaning to become a teacher of TM. I did eventually become a TM teacher, and so did Al Jardine. There are a lot of profound benefits from meditating all these years."

Released in the summer of 1968, *Friends* reflected the impact of TM. Pastoral themes and reverence for nature included tranquil songs like the Dennis Wilson gems, "Little Bird" and "Be Still." Brian Wilson would later call it his favorite Beach Boys' album.

Into the late '60s and early '70s, the band enjoyed a creative renaissance releasing a series of stellar albums beginning with the critically-acclaimed masterpiece *Surf's Up*, featuring the stunning title track, proclaimed by music magazine *Mojo* as the Beach Boys' greatest song. Then came *Carl And The Passions - So Tough*, which Elton John praised for its "moments of breathtaking genius and experimentation."

This adventurous period could be termed the Cosmic Beach Boys, equalling the Beatles' similar metaphysical explorations. Take the profound rumination on mortality and impermanence in "Til I Die," with its gorgeous closing harmony cascade, composed by Brian Wilson in the depths of depression. Bruce Johnston called it "the last great Brian Wilson song," and author Dave Perkins in *God Only Knows: Faith, Hope, Love, and The Beach Boys*, deemed it an "existential masterpiece."

"Long Promised Road" pondered the soul's journey/struggle to find deeper meaning, and the surreal imagery of "Surf's Up," temporarily closed the door on their sunny songs with its impressionistic tale of spiritual awakening.

With lyrics about cosmic consciousness, "Feel Flows" transcendent psychedelia (with jazz legend Charles Lloyd on sax and flute) was another divine musing - one of the "best inner quest songs" praised *Melody Maker* at the time. The sublime "All This is That," from *Carl and The Passions,* encouraged inner journeying, buoyed by chanting the Jai Guru Dev mantra (which the Beatles employed on "Across The Universe"), and the joyful gospel groove of "He Come Down," paid homage to the Maharishi and wisdom teachers.

On *15 Big Ones* in 1976, they would return to meditation with the "TM Song," and venerate the Maharishi on "Everyone's In Love With You" (with Lloyd again on flute). Dennis Wilson, the other creative genius in the band, recorded the moving "Holy Man," which was finally released on the 2008 Legacy Edition of his marvelous solo album *Pacific Ocean Blue*. The original *Blue* album art included photos shot on Maui.

The original member's final complete album together, *LA (Light Album)* in 1979, included the vocal gem "Good Timin'" and Dennis Wilson's soulful "Angel Come Home."

After Dennis Wilson's death, the musicians flew to London to record *The Beach Boys*. It featured Ringo Starr drumming on one track and one tune each composed by Stevie Wonder and Boy George. "Ringo playing on drums on 'California Calling' was a lot of fun," Love recalls, adding that Culture Club's producer called Wonder, and "asked him if he had something which you would like the Beach Boys to record. So Stevie came in, and we did it."

The creative genius behind the group, whose influence had been limited for several years because of persistent emotional and mental problems, returned with a number of songs that co-credited his controversial therapist, Eugene Landy. "I think he edits what Brian does and makes suggestions," Love reported in 1985. "Brian is quite well equipped to do the music." Love added Brian was working on a solo album. "Brian could use this expression at this stage of his life because of his problems."

During this lengthy recovery period, often in seclusion in Hawai'i near Kona, Brian spent a month on Maui in 1987. He released his debut solo album, *Brian Wilson*, highlighted by the majestic, eight-minute "Rio Grande" suite, a year later. Including sounds of a Native American rain dance, this complex, *SMiLE*-flavored opus has been acclaimed as a brilliant psychedelic western saga.

The album also featured the soulful "Love and Mercy," partially recorded in Honolulu. "'Love and Mercy' is probably the most spiritual song I've ever written," Wilson reported in the liner notes for the reissued album.

To mark their 50th anniversary, the surviving original members reformed for a historic tour in 2012 and produced the remarkable recording *That's Why God Made the Radio*, which became their highest-charting studio album of new material since 1965.

"It was pretty darn nice," says Love about re-teaming for the album. "Brian and I were in the studio listening to a playback of the song 'That's Why God Made the Radio,' and we remarked that it's still like 1965 all over again. Getting back in the studio together in Hollywood felt like déjà vu, and more importantly, sounded like déjà vu."

As for their enduring popularity over six decades, Love notes: "These songs have created so much happiness for so many people for so many years. When we started making music, it wasn't to be famous. It was for the sheer love of singing those harmonies. Brian and I would sing Everly Brothers' songs, and we'd get my sister to sing along with us, to make two parts and three parts. Brian became obsessed with the group The Four Freshmen, who sang real close four-part harmony. That's the unique feature that distinguishes the Beach Boys from many other groups, the sophisticated, beautiful harmonies. And there's no one better than Brian at structuring chord progressions and harmony."

In August 2021, the iconic band released *Feel Flows: The Sunflower and Surf's Up Sessions 1969-1971*, a box set collection exploring their most adventurous period. Previously unreleased songs included an early piano demo of Brian Wilson's transcendent "Til I Die" and Dennis Wilson's soulful "Hawaiian Dream."

"I think it's the quality of the heart in the music," says Love about their continuing popularity, "along with the beautiful harmonies and the sheer joy that some of the themes bring. I never get tired of singing the songs because they brought so much joy to multiple generations, all around the world."

"SOUL SACRIFICE"

Carlos Santana

*"We don't play music to pay the rent, we play to accelerate
the spiritual vibration of this planet.
That's why people come."*

"It's like heaven on earth," Carlos Santana enthuses about Maui. "It's whipped cream." Making Maui his home for a few years and marrying his wife, Cindy Blackman-Santana, on the island, the legendary guitarist continues, "We feel really grateful connecting with the visible and invisible rainbows. I feel like I'm sucking up all kinds of glorious energy. There's something extremely divine.

"The very last day I lived on Maui, a rainbow the size of the island would not go away. We rode from Kapalua to the airport, and the rainbow followed us. I thought this was the gods telling me, thank you for spending time with us."

Santana recalls feeling blessed the first time he arrived in Hawai'i with his original band in 1970. "We were in a limousine for the first time, and we went to this house close to the (Diamond Head) crater. They were playing George Harrison's 'My Sweet Lord' and Edwin Hawkins' 'Oh Happy Day.' It was an incredible time to come to Hawai'i because God was on the Top Ten. So every time I come to Hawai'i, all those memories flood my brain. It was a whole experience I'll never forget."

A musical alchemist, Santana can be counted on to uplift his audience wherever he plays. Exploring various permutations of Latin, rock, blues, and jazz for decades, this guitar icon has fueled hearts and souls with one of the most distinctive sounds in contemporary music.

"When we come into any venue, and we hit the first note, the sound reminds a person on a molecular level that you have more in your inner bank than you think you do, and you're capable to create miracles and blessings," he says. "Those things are just not for Jesus or the Dalai Lama or Mother Theresa."

Santana likes to inject a little consciousness-raising after a few songs in his shows. "Everyone needs to be reminded, gently as an invitation, not as an imposition, that everyone has the capacity, the power to create blessing and miracles," he says. "John Lennon got in trouble for saying what he needed to say, imagine there's no this or that. There are certain things that need to be updated, like in the Constitution or the Bible. They were written in a certain consciousness, and we have evolved from the pen and paper to high definition TV. We have evolved as humans and spirits, so I hope I present it in the right frequency, not as a divisive or threatening thing."

Whatever style of music he embraces, one always feels moved by the pure tone of his guitar. The incredible passion that distinguishes his playing at times almost feels like painful ecstasy, I suggest. "I've never heard anyone quite put it like that," he responds. "But it's a good word. Someone called me the other day and said, 'bro, you play with the intensity of a demon and the accuracy of an angel.' Painful ecstasy or the intensity of a demon and the accuracy of an angel that's just me where I belong and who I am. I'm like Bob Marley and John Lennon and Marvin Gaye and Stevie Ray (Vaughan). I'm one of them, and I'm still here.

"We don't play music to pay the rent," he emphasizes. "We really play to accelerate the spiritual vibration of this planet. It's not just 'Oye Como Va,' 'Black Magic Woman,' or 'A Love Supreme,' it's what's inside the vibration. My tools are sound and colors. With that, like a surgeon, I go really deep inside people. When you play from your heart you sound like an ambassador of light and life for the planet."

So what does he think has aided his remarkable longevity? "Gg," he says. "God's grace because I don't believe in chance, fortune, or fate. I believe in God's grace, and that never fails me."

The son of a noted mariachi violinist, Carlos Santana grew up in Tijuana, in a neighborhood with no electricity or running water. Hearing B.B. King perform at San Francisco's Fillmore Auditorium in 1966 proved one of the pivotal events that shaped his early music. "B.B. King made me realize I had to leave my home and my mother and father, and I had to stop washing dishes. After I saw him at the Fillmore, I realized you go way inside your heart, come up with a note, and people just stand up."

Santana's instantly recognizable sound was formed absorbing the music of many of our greatest artists. "I listened for many years to all the Kings - B.B., Freddie and Albert, and Miles and Aretha and Dionne Warwick," he recalls. "You put all that into a funnel, and by the time it gets to the floor, you've got your tone. It's a combination of a lot of things.

"I tried for the longest time to sound like B.B. King and Freddie King and Albert King, and Otis Rush and Buddy Guy and Eric Clapton, all the people I loved. I used to hide in the closet in the dark and just play, so I could get closer to those I loved in sound. Then I realized no matter how much I tried, I just sound like me. Why am I fighting it?"

Santana's potent music has long been distinguished by its spiritual dimension. A one-time devotee of Sri Chimnoy, as Devadip (the lamp, light, and eye of God) Santana, he performed and recorded with fellow followers John McLaughlin ("Love Devotion Surrender") and Alice Coltrane ("Illuminations"). He later embraced Jesus as a guide in the early '90s. "Jesus - the ultimate, multidimensional, multicolor, nothing-but-love hippie," he wrote in his autobiography *The Universal Tone*.

"Everyone has pretty much the same mission to uplift humanity, bring people closer, and to celebrate our differences and not be afraid of them," he says. "Anything else is a waste of time. I think you are always dynamic, just like Mother Theresa was if you do things for other people. If you just do things for yourself, you don't need to get out of bed. It turns me on to turn people on to the same principles that inspired John Coltrane and Bob Marley, that is to heal one another and heal this planet and move forward to the next millennium. If we all start seeing God in each other, we're home."

After topping the charts at the turn of the century with phenomenally successful albums like *Supernatural*, *Shaman*, and *All That I Am*, Santana teamed with an array of guest vocalists to interpret a bunch of rock classics on *Guitar Heaven*. The project was initially daunting for him. "I love conquering fear," he reveals. "I was scared to death to do an album like that. You're always scared when you start thinking, well, what will people think? And if you say I don't give a beep, then I'm going to have confidence that my light will complement the songs."

Receiving a call from George Harrison's widow, Olivia Harrison, congratulating him on his cover of "While My Guitar Gently Weeps," certainly helped. "She said, 'I listened to the song, and I started jumping up and down and crying and laughing,'" he reports. "That's incredible in itself, an affirmation from George Harrison through his wife that he loves what I did."

Teaming with producer Rick Rubin, Santana released the remarkable *Africa Speaks* in 2019 to wide acclaim. "As passionately exciting as anything in the classic Carlos canon," praised the U.K.'s *Mojo,* and *Rolling Stone* affirmed: "Woodstock was 50 years ago; this is Santana now."

Having performed worldwide, the guitarist fondly remembers a couple of shows that hold special significance for him. "Playing in Jerusalem, we saw Palestinians and Hebrews dancing together for four hours, and they forgot about whatever it is they're fighting about before Jesus was here," he marvels. "We also played in San Quentin for some of the most hard-core, vicious, angry criminals. It took three songs for them to dance together, to melt the hate ice and convert it into love rain.

"The warden told me when B.B. King played there, only the blacks stayed; the Latinos and American Indians went back to their cells. 'But when you guys played, nobody went back to their cells. They all danced and celebrated.' People were screaming like they were at a Grateful Dead concert. It was not an easy thing to melt the heart and bring out the soul. I would call that the crown of success."

"BREEZIN'"

George Benson

"All of sudden, I had money in my pocket, and I'm buying a Mercedes Benz, and I moved to Maui."

One of several famous musicians who made Maui a home in the early 1980s, you could often catch guitar virtuoso George Benson jamming in Lahaina clubs with local jazz players. He ended up building a studio in the town, and as a Jehovah's Witness, he would knock on doors offering copies of *The Watchtower*.

"It represents a great part of my life, a very satisfactory part of my life," Benson says about his time on Maui. "I didn't know life could be so good until I moved to Kā'anapali."

Passionate about absorbing various guitar styles, Benson spent time studying Hawaiian steel guitar with local legend Henry Allen. "I wanted to learn one of my favorite songs, 'Blue Hawaii,'" he explains. "It was a great satisfaction to learn it. Hawaiians have a very unique style of playing steel guitar with a bar. It's been copied, but no one has done it quite as well as the Hawaiians. I think it's one of the most pleasant sounds there is."

One of the greatest jazz guitarists of our time, Benson has been lauded for his melodic guitar style, and his soulful singing on hits such as "This Masquerade," "Turn Your Love Around," and "The Greatest Love of All."

An eloquent, fluid player, Benson typically injects a funky groove into his music. "When I first heard jazz music, people like Charlie Christian and Benny Goodman, you could dance to it," he explains. "Later on, when music got to be cool, Miles Davis brought a whole different attitude to the music. I think we lost an audience. People like to get involved in music. It's not just mental, and they like to get physical with the beat. That kind of attracted me, and I wanted to bring more of that back into the music."

41

Benson was enthralled as a child the first time he heard a guitar played. "I was fascinated, especially when I saw a wire going across the room to a box, and I saw the sound was going through that wire and coming out of the box. I sat down right in front of the speakers, and the vibration was hitting me in the back. I guess it put something in my bones because ever since then, I've loved the guitar. I was seven years old when that happened."

A talented child, he was known as Little Georgie Benson. "I had my own radio show and made my first record at ten," he explains. "I was a singer who happened to play 'ukulele with a little strumming on the guitar. I had a singing group at 15 years old, and I had to sing, play guitar, and dance at the same time. By the time I was 17, I was one of the few guitar players in my town. I was the cat they called, and I started going to jam sessions."

Influenced by legendary guitarists such as Charlie Christian, Wes Montgomery, Kenny Burrell, and Django Reinhardt, Benson was first turned on to jazz by the saxophone artistry of Charlie Parker. "More than anything else, Charlie Parker is my greatest influence," he says. "I became a fan of jazz. At first, it destroyed my constituents because people didn't want me to play that, they wanted me to sing. All the girls in the audience would say, 'Georgie, don't play, sing.' I was in trouble."

Before he took on the pop world, Benson had earned a reputation as the premier jazz guitarist of his time. Back in the '60s, he played with many jazz luminaries, including Miles Davis, Freddie Hubbard, Herbie Hancock, Hubert Laws, and Ron Carter.

Releasing critically acclaimed albums, on his unique interpretation of the Beatles' *Abbey Road* album – *The Other Side of Abbey Road* in 1970, he transformed songs like "Oh Darling" into a swinging blues and added a deep jazz funk groove to "Come Together."

"Producer Creed Taylor called me in one day and said, 'take this album home and tell me if there's anything you like,'" Benson recalls. "It was the Beatles' *Abbey Road*. The next day I came back and said, everything on there is good, meaning pick one (song) and let's do it. He said, 'good, we'll do the whole album.' I couldn't believe it.

"It was not well received by the jazz world when it came out. I got all kinds of splashback. But it was classy and had some of the baddest musicians around New York on it and a great arranger. I said if I never cut another record in my life I'm glad I did this one. It didn't sell at first, but when *Breezin'* came out, people went back to see what I had done, and *The Other Side of Abbey Road* and *White Rabbit* gave legs to my pop career."

Did he ever hear from any of the Beatles what they thought about it? "When it came out, they sent me messages how they loved what I did with their music," he says. "I was very proud of that because I thought maybe I had destroyed their songs. We became friends by proxy over the years. Finally, I did a TV show in England, *Top of the Pops*, and Paul McCartney teases me about that. He tells people, 'I used to open for George Benson. I opened on *Top of the Pops,* and he closed the show.'" McCartney later teamed with Benson for a cover of Sam Cooke's "Bring it on Home to Me," on the album *Givin' It Up.*

When he first broached the idea of adding vocals to jazz recordings in the early 1970s, he was met with disdain. "I told the producer I wanted to try something, so I started vocal scatting with the guitar and the band booed," he says. "They didn't want me to do it. But when I got to Warners (Bros. Records) with a different producer (Tommy LiPuma), we did one take of 'This Masquerade.' When it was over, he said, 'we could be here all night, but it's never going to get better than that.'"

It was Benson's voice that brought him mainstream attention. His Record of the Year Grammy-winning *Breezin'* featured the hit remake of Leon Russell's "This Masquerade." "The producer had sent me the song, and he called me up and asked what I thought, and I said what song is that? I couldn't find it, so he sent it to me again. I played it for one of the guys and his wife, and she said it was her favorite. I'd never heard of the song or Leon Russell. I said maybe I'd better learn it. When we got to the studio at the last minute, the producer decided maybe we don't need any vocals on the album because everything was going so good. I said, wait a minute man, you made me go through all this trouble to learn this tune, let's do it at least one time. So that's the one and only take of 'This Masquerade.'"

Breezin' became the best-selling jazz album of all time. "I knew it was going to be bigger than any other previous record," says Benson, "but we had no idea it was going to be that big. To most people, the *Breezin'* album came out of nowhere. But I was an established artist who had already reached the number one spot in jazz polls. I knew it would be successful because it was on Warner Bros. I figured we'd sell two or three hundred thousand records, but it went gold in six weeks and then platinum. There was no such thing as a platinum jazz album. All of a sudden, I had money in my pocket and I'm buying a Mercedes Benz, and I moved to Maui. It was an incredible transition."

Once Benson became widely known, he continued to release gold and platinum-selling recordings, such as *Give Me the Night, Weekend in L.A.,* and *20/20,* that showcased his dazzling technical mastery and the fluidity and emotional range of his guitar playing. And always, he would find a tight groove. "Coming up, all I heard were records that swung hard," he notes. "Like Count Basie and the king of swing Benny Goodman, and Charlie Christian showed how to put those notes in the middle and make it move along. When I tackle a song, it always has to have some feeling and movement to it."

Having recorded a version of Sam Cooke's "A Change is Gonna Come" and Donny Hathaway's "Someday We'll All Be Free," had he ever thought of making an album of classic social activist songs? "I stay out of politics," he says. "Two reasons, first my religion doesn't allow me, and I don't like anything that divides people. Don't pick a side; just stay neutral. That way, you can talk to both sides. Once you take a stance, people are not reasonable. I know what music can do, and I'd rather go that route that makes people like each other."

Covering songs over the years by artists ranging from Miles Davis and the Beatles to Charlie Parker and Stevie Wonder, Benson paid tribute to the great Nat King Cole in 2013. "He inspired my whole career when I heard him sing," he explains. "I wanted to be like that. When I was coming up, he was the star African American in the world. When I was a kid, I used to win singing contests singing his songs. Way later in life, he was still my favorite."

Along with lush, orchestrated tunes like "Walking My Baby Back Home" and "I'm Gonna Sit Right Down and Write Myself a Letter," *Inspiration: A Tribute to Nat King Cole* included a terrific version of "Unforgettable," featuring a striking trumpet solo by Wynton Marsalis.

"He was worried about his solo," Benson reveals. "I said, Wynton, you couldn't play a bad solo if you tried. You gave me a New Orleans feel, and you didn't jazz it up to the degree where you couldn't enjoy it. He made it interesting with some highlights and curved notes. I said, man you don't have to worry about this solo; it's historic."

The album opened with an excerpt of Little Georgie Benson strumming a 'ukulele and singing Cole's "Mona Lisa" at the age of eight. "My mother found that tape," he marvels. "She saved it all those years. My producer heard it and said, 'this is going on the album.' I said you can't put that on the album. He said, 'it's going on George.' We put it in there, and everybody likes it."

"BABYLON SISTERS"

Steely Dan

*"Ironically, as the band started to get good, we decided we
were killing ourselves traveling, and we wanted
to do more sophisticated music."*

"Hawai'i is just a great place to live, and those of us who
are lucky enough and discerning enough to have
enough sense to live here, it's very well appreciated,"
enthused Steely Dan's Walter Becker in 1996, talking in his home studio. "Almost every time you walk out of your door, you're looking at
some beautiful site. Even more than that, there's a feeling of being in
Hawai'i, the minute you step off the plane, you get it. It's pretty much
incomparable. This is one of the treasures. There's something about
Hawai'i that after you've lived here, you never feel quite as relaxed any
place else."

Making Maui his home for many years after Steely Dan initially
folded, Becker occasionally focused on producing and built his own
recording studio in Upcountry Maui. Very unassuming and the antithesis of the rock star (we once shared an evening listening to live jazz
at Longhi's in Lahaina), he was blessed with a dry wit which he would
sometimes display in entertaining letters to *The Maui News*.

Becker met Steely Dan's Donald Fagen in college in upstate New
York, where they bonded over a love for jazz. Then, as their official bio
notes - *"In 1971, with the city degenerating into a vile Gomorrah of debt
and porn, the lads relocated to sunny Los Angeles."*

The band's debut, *Can't Buy a Thrill*, set the bar high. With its
hypnotic, sinewy rhythm and oblique lyrics about corrupting addictions, their first hit, "Do It Again," became an instant favorite and a
classic rock staple.

With Becker on bass and guitar, Fagen had accepted the lead vocalist role by default. "Donald never wanted to be the singer," Becker recalled. "We always had this idea that we were going to find some singer, but we never did."

"We discussed getting an actor to do it," says Fagen, who experienced an intermittent panic disorder. "It was more important to have someone who could act rather than be a great singer, and we had to have a frontman to talk to the audience. Neither of us was interested in doing it. We hired Dave Palmer, who sang on the first album, but he wasn't able to express the attitude we were looking for. Since I didn't have to twist myself into a pretzel to have this attitude, that was my whole life, I became the singer. The first time I ever sang on a record, aside from demos, was 'Do It Again,' which became a hit. So I was stuck."

Record success meant they had to tour. Unfortunately, the duo wasn't so keen on playing live. "You'd get on stage, and nobody could hear anybody, or the audience couldn't hear you," Becker explained. "It was the habit in those days for headliners to use up the entire available time in the afternoon doing their soundcheck, and you wouldn't have any soundcheck. They wanted to sound their best, and they didn't want to be embarrassed by some upstart rock and rollers from L.A. There were a number of shows after which Donald and I would discuss the quickest ways of getting the hell out of there, get a cab to the airport, and call it quits.

"We'd go out and play all these gigs and come back, and everybody would be trashed, and we had no new songs. Nerves were frayed, and we were in worse shape. We just decided writing songs and making records was more important, and it more or less worked out."

Deciding to quit touring in 1974, Fagen explains, "A traveling rock and roll band is basically a jock experience, and we were just not cut out for that. Traveling around with ten young, wild boys with just too bodacious. In the early days, we were opening for heavy metal bands, so we armed ourselves with two drummers, two guitarists, two of everything except lead singers. We hired Mike McDonald as a backup singer, so we figured we couldn't fail because we had such a monstrous setup. Ironically, as the band started to get good, we decided we were killing ourselves traveling, and we wanted to do more sophisticated music. So we started working only in the studio."

Along with crafting an innovative blend of rock, jazz, and funk, Steely Dan was known for smart, cryptic lyrics. "We were trying to do something a little different," Becker noted. "We were trying to find ways to give our songs a certain amount of depth and not cave in to the temptation to just write trivial stuff. It's hard with songs because there are so few words. There are many cases where there is embedded in some of these songs a narrative of a sort, but because it's just a couple of lines, it has to be a sketch or impressionistic thing. A lot of times, things we were doing seemed a little obscure. I think it's valid. It's not important that the rational meaning be right on the surface."

And there was often a twist of wry humor. "Both of us were very focused on humor and different ways of using humor in songwriting," he continued. "The trick is not to be too funny. There's a line you don't want to cross, and early on, we crossed it many times.

"It was a similar balancing act to the one we had to employ vis-à-vis jazz harmonies and elements from jazz. We learned that jazz being the ever unpopular musical form in America that it is; once people pegged that what you were doing was jazz, they didn't like it anymore. They tended to dismiss what you were doing as no longer appropriate to the musical milieu of the '70s. We had to use the humor elements and some of the pop music and jazz harmonies very sparingly."

By the time of *Gaucho*, the musicians faced a creative cul-de-sac. "We were very much part of our culture, and there was a very depressing time towards the very end of the '70s," says Fagen. "The energy and glamour of the '60s had turned into a nightmare. A lot of creative people stopped making records. There was a real depletion of energy, and we were having a lot of personal problems."

And then, according to their official bio - *"Walter moved to the island of Maui. Donald wrote and recorded his first solo album. Then, he more or less cracked up."*

Two years after *Gaucho*, Fagen released his first solo album, and then there was silence - for ten years. He credits the CD boom with keeping him from needing a day job after Steely Dan's initial demise and the long gap between solo albums. "The invention of CD made it possible for me to make a living," he says. "If it weren't for that, I would have had to have taken some handyman jobs or work in a bookstore.

"After *The Nightfly*, it was a very confused time," he continues. "I put everything I knew into that record, and it was the most personal thing I've ever done. I think it frightened me a bit that I had exposed myself. I shocked myself into a sort of paralysis. I had to grow up more during the '80s before I had anything else to say."

The musicians attempted a reunion in the late '80s. "We got together here (on Maui) in 1988, for about a year working on songs," Becker revealed. "We finished a couple of songs and started many, but we didn't really succeed in what we intended to do to make an album. It wasn't in the cards at that moment."

Interviewed on Maui in 1992, Fagen was in the midst of collaborating with Becker on his second solo album, *Kamakiriad*. He felt grateful to be collaborating in such a relaxed environment. "I went through therapy and was involved in a relationship that ended," he says. "Walter was going through a parallel experience, so when we started working together again, after a couple of false starts, we fell into a very easy working relationship. We had both changed a lot, but we went back in the same mode, having fun and joking around. Walter is very funny and has a lot of energy which keeps everything buoyant."

The Grammy-nominated *Kamakiriad* included the Dan-ish "Snowbound," co-composed with Becker. "I wrote all the songs except for one with Walter some years ago," he says. "After going through personal transformations in the '80s, I started getting this idea for this other thing. I was still having trouble getting started. I didn't have the enthusiasm to start recording because I wasn't sure how to go about it, so I called Walter and asked him to produce it, and since then, it's been easy.

"Much like *The Nightfly*, it's a concept album in the sense all the songs are related. In *The Nightfly*, the songs came from the viewpoint of someone in the late '50s and early '60s and were pretty much autobiographical. The music's maybe a little simpler than I've written in the past, and there are fewer instruments. The music has a lot of influence from soul music, the music I listened to in my young adulthood."

So can we dance to it? "I hope so," he says. "The kind of music people dance to now seems so horrific to me. I like everything to have

49

a great-sounding groove. I couldn't work on anything that didn't have a swing to it."

Seeking some satisfying grooves, Fagan embarked on a series of shows with some friends in 1991. The New York Rock and Soul Revue included Michael McDonald, Boz Scaggs, and Phoebe Snow, who all shared lead vocals on the *Live at the Beacon* album.

"There were these artists who were not working a lot, were out of the public eye," he explains. "The record sold about 200,000, which for that kind of marginal project is great. A few people have knocked it as a bunch of white people singing soul music. The spirit we did it in was to have a good time. It's essentially just for fun and if they take it too seriously, fuck them."

While Steely Dan fans loved hearing Fagen singing classics like "Pretzel Logic" and "Chain Lightning," he initially felt uneasy about singing on stage again. "The only thing I've been apprehensive about is my voice," he reveals. "I got stuck with a job (in Steely Dan), not considering myself a singer in the first place. It was a loud band to sing over, and I have a small voice."

When Fagen and Becker finally decided to hit the road again as Steely Dan in 1993, fans rejoiced. "For the most part, the fans who bought our records had never seen us play live," Becker explained. "A lot of the stuff we had never played live. People were very enthusiastic, and it was very uplifting generally."

With seven albums to draw from, they ignored early hits like "Do It Again" and "Rikki Don't Lose That Number." "Donald had a pretty potent veto on some of the earlier songs that he no longer chooses to be associated with," Becker noted. "Generally, we wanted to play things that would be the best grooves to be riding along on that still seemed harmonically sophisticated. It was appealing to play songs that we hadn't played before on stage like 'Babylon Sisters' or 'Deacon Blues.'"

When work began on Steely Dan's *Two Against Nature* on Maui in the winter of 1997, it was as though the duo simply picked up where they'd left off with *Gaucho*. And as one might expect from such masters of their craft, the album boasted superbly sophisticated melodies and arrangements. "They certainly know what they're looking for," says Dave Russell, the Maui engineer on the project. "They work until they get it exactly the way they want it. When you see the final picture, the result is amazing."

The duo's triumphant return elicited four Grammy nominations in 2001, and having never tasted a win before (besides for engineering), the musicians were stunned to win the evening's top honor - Album of the Year – along with Best Pop Vocal Performance and Best Pop Performance by a Duo or Group with Vocal. They were also elected into the Rock and Roll Hall of Fame in 2001. "We're persuaded it's a great honor to be here tonight," said Becker before walking off stage with Fagen, leaving their Hall trophies on the podium.

The co-founder of Steely Dan died in 2017 at the age of 67. In a statement, Fagen said, "Walter Becker was my friend, my writing partner and my band mate since we met as students at Bard College in 1967. I intend to keep the music we created together alive as long as I can with the Steely Dan band."

"DREAM ON"

Aerosmith

"If you looked up stability in the dictionary, there wouldn't be a picture of us."

"We were lucky to play the HIC (Honolulu International Center) in 1976, and growing up in the Bronx and New Hampshire, I always had this affinity for hula dancing and palm trees," recalls Aerosmith's Steven Tyler.

"Joe (Perry) was up on stage doing a soundcheck, ripping it up. I was backstage checking my clothes out and contemplating my navel, and I heard him playing really loud by himself (he starts singing a famous Aerosmith riff). It so grabbed me I went running out of the dressing room up on stage, sat down on the drums, and just started jamming with Joe. What the fuck is that? My original thoughts for 'Walk This Way' was there. I wrote the lyrics and melody after that. But to me, it's Maui, it's Honolulu, it's the whole mana vibe here."

Dreaming for years about making Maui a home, Tyler continues: "While we were there (on Oahu), I said, Joe, why don't we go over to Maui. We stayed in Kaanapali, and I immediately started looking at houses. Someone mentioned the nude beach, and we drove from Kaanapali all the way over here (Makena) and got stuck in the sand.

"Then I got married in '88, and we had kids, and we always came to Maui for the Christmas break. To keep in shape, I'd jog down to La Perouse (Bay), and there was a house down there. It was what the fuck is that? It was the most Maui-ish house I'd ever seen. I fell in love with it. Then I took *American Idol*, which was a great payday. I made an offer, and I had cash, and I got it. It's a dream come true. I live in a very magical house with whales and sunsets in a state park on a lava flow."

A familiar, friendly presence on Maui when he's not touring, Aerosmith's charismatic lead singer is often seen around our island. He hung with our late resident spiritual teacher Ram Dass, attended a one-day silent retreat "to decompress," drummed at Makena's Little Beach, and shared his sobriety wisdom at Maui's drug court.

"My hats off to you," he told the graduates. "You're my heroes because you have come from somewhere that I lived myself. I'm so proud of you, each and every one."

Tyler has also been passionately involved with the eradication of an extremely invasive plant - non-indigenous Miconia, "which is taking the fucking island over if we don't do something about it," he warns. "It's everywhere. I'm in a helicopter with no doors with Dr. James Leary, and we go way the other side of Hana, and I shoot paintball herbicide at the root of the plant. It's a herbicide created to only kill Miconia."

Born for rock stardom, Taylor's intriguing astrology chart reflects many dynamic aspects, indicating magnetic energy coupled with an optimistic outlook, a generous spirit, and self-confidence. (FYI - Aires sun, Sagittarius rising, Scorpio moon, with major aspects including Sun trine Mars and the Ascendant)

Born Steven Tallarico in 1948, the son of a classical musician, he grew up ready to rock - first as a drummer. "I started playing drums in 1964, in school, a snare drum, and I got the feeling of being in front of people," he says. "I could see how everybody was attracted to the rhythm. Then I was a singing drummer in a band."

At the age of 17, he spent time in New York's Greenwich Village, "when The Mamas and the Papas, Bob Dylan, the Lovin' Spoonful, it all broke. I was playing at the Cafe Wah? That's where I got my chops in '67 and '68, and then I went to Woodstock." Attending the historic festival in 1969, he led an impromptu drum circle.

A fan of early Peter Green-era Fleetwood Mac, Tyler told Mick Fleetwood: "He wouldn't be doing what he's doing if he hadn't heard 'Rattlesnake Shake,'" Fleetwood reports. "That was the beginning of Aerosmith. He said, 'Mick, we were the guys who used to sit in the front row in Boston looking at you doing this stuff, going oh my God if only we could.'"

Before forming Aerosmith, Perry and bassist Tom Hamilton played in the Jam Band, and their cover of Mac's "Rattlesnake Shake" so impressed Taylor he wanted to join. "We were high school age and had a series of bands," recalls Hamilton. "I remember the first time I heard Steven play; he was a legend. He had these unbelievable bands in New York and would come and play during the summer, and everyone would fight to get to see them. I went one night, and it was mesmerizing. Why was he not famous yet? Every summer, he would come up with different bands. Then he was ready to do something really different. That's why he was attracted to playing with Joe and I."

"We started playing clubs (in Boston) where no one came," says Tyler. "I swear to fuck I'd go to the owner; nobody's here. But then there was one club where there was a couple of hundred people, and a month later, we played there again, and people were all over the roof and breaking in the windows in the bathroom, which was our dressing room. And you kind of get the inkling that maybe you are doing something right.

"We had finally written our first song, and we were getting ready to put our first album out. We were a tight, bad-ass band, and it just took off. Joe was a madman, and I wrote five songs on the first album, a couple on the piano, 'Dream On' and 'One Way Street.' Once Joe and I wrote songs, it was all over because we had never really been in a band where you write songs.

"Joe's mom got us a bus and gave us money for rent for an apartment, and we all lived together. I said, if we live, eat, and wake up together before we drive each other crazy, we might have something. Fucking A if I wasn't right. It was beautiful. We all started getting high together and jamming at night. It was great. It was magic. Our vibe just took off."

By the time of their third album, *Toys in the Attic*, Aerosmith had conquered the charts, and their first five albums eventually attained multi-platinum status. One of the most famous rock bands in the world, serious substance abuse would later contribute to their decline, and Joe Perry and Brad Whitford left the group.

Reforming, resolving old differences and ultimately overcoming their addictions, Tyler notes: "We had a second coming in '87. We started writing again and got tight with each other, and we had the whole explosion of *Pump* and *Get a Grip*, some great albums, and we had so much fun writing songs with other people."

Into the 21st century, Aerosmith returned to their raw roots, releasing the terrific *Honkin' on Bobo*, featuring eleven covers of vintage blues songs. "We had been thinking about doing a blues album for a long time, and we were just waiting for the right time," Hamilton explains. "It was just a matter of picking music that everyone thought would be fun to play."

Sounding refreshed and reinvigorated, *Honkin'* included an earth-shattering version of the Big Joe Williams' standard "Baby Please Don't Go." "We like to think of it as one of our new standards," says Hamilton. "It's a classic thing that we've been about since we first got together and played songs by The Yardbirds, that had a portion of a song that we called a rave-up, where everything is really quiet, and it builds up to a frenzy."

Various health issues in recent years have derailed the group. "If you looked up stability in the dictionary, there wouldn't be a picture of us," Hamilton notes. "For some reason, we're still here, and there's still a lot of people who want to hear us. If that wasn't there, I don't think we would be as inspired.

"I think about parallels and how we're a microcosm. It can get pretty chaotic in our band, and there's a lot of chaos in the world, a lot of intense stuff happening. It's like a wave, and you've just got to be able to stand up and keep going."

Aerosmith rocked Maui's War Memorial Stadium in 2009, with the biggest production in the island's history. "Tonight get to fulfill a lifelong dream to play Maui," Joe Perry tweeted. "Jimi played here. This area is absolutely no doubt an energy center, even the whales know it."

The Maui show included such unique moments as an opening with dancing and Tahitian-style drumming from Hālau Kulia Ika Nuʻu, Tyler strumming an ʻukulele, serenading with a snippet of "Little Grass Shack," and Perry sharing how he was married in ʻIao Valley.

Living on Maui since 2012, Tyler has joined Mick Fleetwood on stage at his Fleetwood's restaurant, jammed with Willie K at his Blues Fest, and performed at the annual New Year's Eve charity show in Wailea, hosted by Shep Gordon. When he began recording and touring with the Nashville-based Loving Mary Band, he brought them to Maui in late December 2018, including a show at Fleetwood's on Front St. with proceeds benefiting Janie's Fund.

Created by Tyler in partnership with Youth Villages to help abused young women, Janie's Fund was inspired by his Grammy-winning hit "Janie's Got a Gun." "I wrote the song on the piano, and as I'm sitting there diddling the keys, the first thing that came to mind was Janie's got a gun. I thought, what the fuck is that? It's like the exercise when you wake up in the morning and grab a pen, and crazy shit comes out. I wrote the lyrics, and Tom Hamilton had this bass lick, and it was perfect for the introduction.

"Every time Tom played it I started singing like an American Indian (*he begins imitating Native chanting*) having fun with it. He thought I was taking the piss out of him, but I wasn't. I slowed it on to the front of the song, and it was beautiful. When I was done, I just thought I had painted a picture of a girl who was abused.

"I happened to take this course about how to attract more flies with honey than vinegar or how to get along with your fucking band, and I found out that Ringo Starr had gone there too. So I called him and up and said, hey man, is it a co-dependency course? Is it a place where you learn how to get along with people and talk good instead of fuck you, I'm not doing that," he continues laughing. "I went there and found out how many women in America are abused. All the shit that goes along with being a woman.

"I have always been asked to do things for charities, and I figured it was time. We got hold of Youth Villages, and they adopted Janie's Fund. A good friend said, 'Steven, you're talking about abuse, you don't want to talk about guns, how about Janie's got a fund.' I thought that's beautiful. Everything from there was a gift from God, and we're opening up the second house in Memphis."

Interested in exploring country music, Tyler began collaborating with the Loving Mary Band. "I went down to Nashville and had a thought of doing a country record," he explains. "The vibe down there was different from anything I had experienced. A dear friend, Marti Frederiksen, who wrote some great songs with Aerosmith, lives in Nashville and knows all these musicians. It's great to be in a country band, to have three people singing with you, it's insane. We sing so good together."

Frederiksen first landed in Aerosmith's camp in 1997, when he began composing with Tyler and Perry. The voice of Stillwater's lead singer in Cameron Crowe's cult hit movie *Almost Famous*, he lived on Maui off and on for five years, contributing to a handful of Aerosmith songs composed on the island. "We worked on a lot of stuff, including a lot of songs that have not been released," he notes. "They were definitely Maui inspired. The first time I went to Maui was in 2002, with Joe and Steven, and we wrote 'Girls of Summer' and 'Lay it Down.'"

Released in 2016, Tyler's *We're All Somebody From Somewhere* found him crafting some of his most engaging songs in years. He dipped into a country pool flavored with bluesy southern rock and even lively Cajun on "Sweet Louisiana." "I love the country vibe, particularly outlaw country music," he enthuses. "The hook is huge, and it makes you pine for your girl and your dog."

Loving chilling on Maui, Tyler emphasizes how grateful he feels to finally have a home here. "Maui was always where my mind went," he says. "It's otherworldly. The life I have I love the attention and I love playing shows and going places, and everybody knows your name, but it's a bit much. There are times when you just have to clear your mind out. So the times I get to come here, it's been outrageous. I come here and drop to my knees and thank God."

"BLACK WATER"

The Doobie Brothers

"I always in my heart felt we were emulating a Bay Area kind of sound."

When Michael McDonald joined The Doobie Brothers and helped catapult the band to Grammy-winning superstar status, the shift in their sound caused some consternation at their record label.

"We played a gig in L.A. with Michael and afterwards had a label party," founding lead guitarist/vocalist Pat Simmons recalls. "Cher and Greg Allman, and Rod Stewart were there, and everybody said this new lead singer is fantastic. But the head of promotion at Warner Bros. came up and said, 'who's this guy Mike McDonald, he sucks, you'll never make it with this guy.' I was almost in tears. He's the head of promotions, and he's going to kill us. So we did the record thinking it was going to be our last, and the rest is history."

With worldwide record sales of more than 48 million (including three multi-platinum, seven platinum, and 14 gold albums), before The Doobie Brothers became famous, the legendary rockers honed their skills as the house band at Chateau Liberté. A Santa Cruz biker hangout, they earned $60 a night. It was a tough crowd to please - "only if you took a lot of breaks," says Simmons. "And if they wanted you to play a song twice in a row, you did it. In a sense, it was a badge of honor that you could actually get up and entertain these guys, and they weren't booing you."

Making Maui his home for many years, Simmons has performed with the Doobies since their formation in San Jose in 1970. He remembers feeling some trepidation when producers Ted Templeman and Lenny Waronker from the Warner Bros. Records label showed up at the Chateau to check them out.

"They were wearing slacks and sweater vests and button-down collars, kind of conservative, and there's a dozen Hells Angels parked in front, and everyone was smoking weed and drinking heavily. We're blasting away with our amps all the way up, and the bikers were crazy and stomping around. I looked back at Ted and Lenny, and their eyes were as big as silver dollars, and they signed us after that."

Blending acoustic and electric guitars with tight harmonies and often adventurous arrangements, the Doobies created an exhilarating sound rooted in rock and embracing influences from folk and country. "Part of what got us together was Skip Spence of Moby Grape," he explains. "He took us in to make our first demo. All of us had loved Moby Grape. I thought their debut album was the best things to come out of the San Francisco scene. I loved the Beatles harmonies and the Beach Boys. The Grape was blues-influenced, but they had this great harmony thing. When I met Tom (Johnston) and John (Hartman) they said we want to put a band together like Moby Grape. So from the get-go, we had in mind we were going to be a three-part harmony band."

Aligned with the spirit of leading Bay Area bands, Simmons says: "I always in my heart felt we were emulating a Bay Area kind of sound. Originally, we started out with Tommy's rhythmic, soulful guitar thing and my more country blues-based picking. We were Southern in our musical influences with a lot of R&B and Delta blues and harder blues, as were a lot of Bay Area bands like the Dead and Santana, and the Steve Miller Blues Band."

Relocating from California to Maui, Simmons fell in love with his new tropical home. "Living here has really inspired me. I listen to lots of Hawaiian music, and it's given me another viewpoint. You can get so hung up on what's popular and trying to remain contemporary. It's been really good for me living here."

The Doobie Brothers' early albums often included cool little solo instrumentals by Simmons. "I was fooling around in the studio one day playing an instrumental, and our producer said, 'let's record it.' We recorded a part of one, 'Busted Down Around O'Connelly Corners' for *The Captain and Me* as a segue. After we did the first one, Ted (Templeman) always wanted me to come up with some little guitar instrumentals as a signature."

59

The release of the band's second album, *Toulouse Street*, rocketed them into the national spotlight, but it was an unusual song from their *What Were Once Vices Are Now Habits* album that solidified their popularity.

"We had scored some success with songs from *Toulouse Street* and *The Captain and Me*, then we put out *What Were Once Vices Are Now Habits*, and we couldn't get arrested," he notes. "We put out a couple of singles, and we couldn't get played. 'Black Water' had been released as a B side, and suddenly it started getting played. Then the record company reprinted it as an A-side, and it took off."

Composed and sung by Simmons, "Black Water" defied convention with its unusual arrangement and a capella vocal. "I've always been a proponent of folk blues," he explains. "I've been really influenced by a lot of Southern acoustic players like Doc Watson, Reverand Garry Davis, and John Hurt, and Chet Atkins was a huge mentor to me in terms of the kind of music I listen to. That's where that style of music started. I had spent some time in New Orleans, and the lyrics pretty much apply directly to the music scene in New Orleans."

The sing-along a capella breakdown in the middle was "something I had talked about with Ted, and I was thinking about a sort of gospel blues thing with a Dixieland breakdown where everybody was singing something a little different."

The song's chart success came as a complete surprise. "I never would have thought it was commercial," he says. "It was an off-the-wall thing we had no intention of putting out as a single. It was a happy accident. It was lucky for us. We were having a hard time actually."

The band's first number one hit, "Black Water," sold two million copies and was the fastest-selling single in Warner Bros.' history at the time. Its success inspired the band to explore more adventurous material. "It made us realize we could do other things and broaden our horizons," he says. "It was a different type of song and a different singer. Tommy had been the lead singer. It was a real turning point for us. We had been mostly a rock and soul kind of thing, and that record enabled us to do some softer ballads."

Even in their formative days, the Doobies sought to expand the frontiers of rock, drawing on a variety of musical genres. Simmons created some of the band's more daring compositions, including the epic outlaw ballad "I Cheat the Hangman" on the band's *Stampede* album, which featured an unusual string arrangement influenced by Mussorgsky's "Night on Bald Mountain," and the brilliant "Clear as the Driven Snow" on *The Captain and Me.*

"We were always trying to be more than a rock band," he says. "I like to be challenged by music and come up with things that are difficult and interesting to play. At the same time, some of the best music we do are simplistic three-chord songs which you could play in your sleep, and so you can really let loose and put more energy into them."

Reflecting an influence of English guitarist John Renbourne, "Clear as the Driven Snow" warned about the pitfalls of substance abuse. "I loved all the guitar instrumental things Renbourne was doing, and I ended up writing a song about getting past cocaine and drinking, doing substances, and straightening out your life. The lyrics reflect that indirectly. It starts almost as a ballad, and then it gets to rock, reflective of the cacophony of my brain. We were influenced a bit by The Who and our drummer John Hartman loved Keith Moon, and I wanted to give John a chance to kick it hard."

An admirer of Eckhart Tolle's transformative book *The Power of Now: A Guide to Spiritual Enlightenment*, a friend tried to coax him into joining Scientology in his early days. "I used to play with a guy who was a Scientologist, when it first became a thing in the '60s, in California," he recalls. "He played pedal steel on (Grateful Dead's) *Aoxomoxoa*. He tried to get me into it, and I went to the center in San Jose. I was a psych major in college, and I wasn't buying it."

As far as Tolle's influential work, "it's probably one of the most impactful books I've ever read," he says. "It was what I already believed, so it enforced that with much more clarity. I still try to relate to people on that level. All we have is this moment. We have no control over the future or the past."

Before he moved to Hawai'i, Simmons had discovered the beauty of Hawaiian slack key guitar and introduced the beguiling style on a track on *Stampede*. "I got into slack key real heavy, and I still love it," he continues. "The Beamer Brothers were an inspiration. The concept is basically similar to a ragtime approach to music, the difference being an open tuning and slacking the strings."

He later contributed the sweet instrumental "Mele Pau'ole," co-composed with his son Pat Simmons Jr., to the album *It's A Slack Key World* by popular contemporary Hawaiian music band Hapa.

In the mid-1970s, the Doobies almost folded when founding member Tom Johnston quit, but the discovery of Michael McDonald's gift as a composer and lead vocalist dramatically altered their future. "When Tom went home, I thought we were really screwed in a number of ways," Simmons recalls. "At one point, I was ready to just go home. Jeff Baxter is the one who talked me into going on. He felt we should give it a try before we throw in the towel.

"We wrote a bunch of songs, and at that time, Mike McDonald was just our background singer. We had a date to record, and we waited and waited for Tommy to put something together for us, and he never showed. At that point, we asked Mike if he had any songs. He came down and sat at the piano and started playing a few songs. We were all knocked out. We had no idea. So we went with a new direction, and it worked."

With the addition of the soulful singer-keyboardist, almost overnight the band refined their rock sound with more sophisticated jazz and funk arrangements. McDonald had introduced a funky pop sound on *Takin' it to the Streets*, but their follow-up, *Livin' on the Fault Line*, found limited acceptance.

Highlights included Simmons' Steely-Danish "Chinatown," the cool jazzy groove of the title song (with Victor Feldman on vibes), and the instrumental gem, "Larry the Logger Two-Step." "*Fault Line* was very experimental, a lot funkier and jazzier with outrageous arrangements," he says. "It's one of my favorites, but commercially it didn't do that well. It was disappointing. I thought it was some of the best playing we had ever done in the studio."

Then came the landmark *Minute by Minute*, which sold more than three million copies and earned four Grammy Awards. "When we went back into the studio again for *Minute by Minute,* everybody was nervous, particularly Mike because he had put so much into the album before that. He wanted this record to really count, so we took a lot of takes of different songs. It ended up being our most successful record."

After McDonald's departure, the band dissolved and then reformed in the late 1980s, modeled on the early lineup with the return of

Tom Johnston and drummers Michael Hossack and Keith Knudsen. The resulting album *Cycles* heralded a return to the vintage rocking guitar-dominated sound. "Everybody was playing well, and everybody was pretty straight, no one strung out, so it was a joy," says Simmons.

They closed their 2000 recording *Sibling Rivalry* with the Hawaiian flavored acoustic instrumental "Five Corners." Co-composed by Simmons with a title derived from a well-known intersection in Haiku, the tune reflected his affection for Hawaiian music. "Hawaiian music is subtle, and subtleties of music appeal to me," he explains. "I love the sound of the guitar in Hawaiian music. The tunings and voicing are different, and for me musically, it's been a challenge to hear those voicings and absorb them. I feel like with 'Five Corners,' I was able to incorporate some of those voicings and some of that feeling."

The Doobie's *World Gone Crazy*, in 2010, recalled early classic albums like *The Captain and Me*. It reunited the band's primary composers Johnston and Simmons with producer Ted Templeman, who had helped shape their early seminal works.

One of the standout tracks featured a Maui friend, country legend Willie Nelson making a surprise appearance. He co-composed and sang with Simmons on the wonderful "I Know We Won," which also featured Maui-based Bonnie Raitt Band bassist "Hutch" Hutchinson.

"Willie has done so much for so many people on Maui," Simmons notes. "We were his backing band at the MACC and also at a show on the mainland. We've talked about writing a song together for a long time. I had a track I was working on with a first verse about looking back at life and what it was like when I was a kid. I gave it to Willie, and he wrote a second verse and chorus, and it was very cool. I was going for a positive vibe, and he took it beyond into life being a game to win."

Backing the country star in concert "was a bit of a challenge," says Simmons. "We learned the songs just like the records, and of course, he never does them that way. He started doing songs that we had not rehearsed, and everyone turned and looked at each other."

Simmons was pleased when The Doobie Brothers were finally elected in 2020 to the Rock & Roll Hall of Fame. The iconic band had been eligible for more than 20 years. "We're pretty thrilled," he says. "For Tommy (Johnston), it's particularly meaningful because he wasn't there when we got Grammy Awards. He deserves a lot of credit for the songs he's written and his performances on records, and his general dedication to music. Speaking for myself, I don't live my life looking for accolades or awards. My reward is in the music and having the opportunity to do what I've done with the band and outside the band. Having fun doing what I'm doing is a huge reward for me."

When the 2020 pandemic derailed their planned 50th-anniversary tour with Michael McDonald and the release of new music, the musicians began collaborating remotely, producing occasional music videos, including teaming with Peter Frampton for an inspired cover of Eric Clapton's song "Let It Rain."

The Doobies with McDonald also released a video in July 2021 of a terrific gospel-infused version of "Takin' It to the Streets." They played against a backdrop of protest images of Martin Luther King, Jr., Gandhi, and Nelson Mandela, along with various films of women's suffrage, the Vietnam War, workers' rights, and Black Lives Matter marches. "It's taking it to the streets with more social relevance that Mike was thinking about in the first place, and so there are images of civil rights marches from the '60s and more recent marches," he explains.

The Doobies also covered the Staples Singers' civil rights anthem, "Freedom Highway." "Our arrangement is so amazing," he says. "It started out as a typical Staples' thing and ended up going into almost progressive jazz."

Heading out in the summer of 2021 for a tour with McDonald, the band released a four-track EP in August, followed by the *Liberté* album in October. One of the standout tracks, the country-flavored road tale "Cannonball," sounded like a new classic.

"I had just got done with the Cannonball endurance race for antique motorcycles," Simmons explains. "You get up at the crack of dawn and ride to the sun goes down. It focuses your psyche, and it takes you back in time as you're on these old country roads. We thought of that as a template and wanting a song that people can relate to. We started thinking of it as a journey of life. Every day we all have our burden to bear. It became an archetype of what we all have to go through in our lives."

"SCHOOL'S OUT"

Alice Cooper

*"Rock and roll needs the ultimate villain.
They needed their Darth Vader."*

"Alice Cooper here, we're in Maui tonight, and we have an audience." It's a Tuesday evening in Wailuku, and legendary rocker Alice Cooper is commanding the airwaves recording his syndicated show *Nights With Alice Cooper* at Maui's KAOI-FM.

Spinning classic rock favorites by The Who, Pink Floyd, and Lynyrd Skynyrd, interspersed with nuggets from less known acts like Humble Pie and The Sorrows, Alice explains: "The radio show is the easiest thing I've ever done. People like that I'm playing different music, not just playing the same old AC/DC and Led Zeppelin. I tell the stories behind these guys, and I can tell them because I was there."

Celebrity guests frequently pop up on his show, like Question Mark from the '60s garage rock band Question Mark & The Mysterians of "96 Tears" fame. "The craziest interview I ever did was Question Mark," Alice reports. "After 20 minutes, he started telling me that he doesn't live on Mars, he lives in Mars, and that the air is food, and they don't wear clothes, and Elvis really likes it. All I could say was, uh-huh, uh-huh. It was insane, he was dead serious."

After 45 years of performing and 27 studio albums, Alice was finally inducted into the Rock and Rock Hall of Fame in 2011. The rock legend who crafted classic rebellious anthems such as "School's Out," "I'm Eighteen," and "No More Mr. Nice Guy" had been passed over 16 times before being inducted.

"There's no chronological order to it," he suggests. "Bands like the Moody Blues should have been in 15 years ago. Alice Cooper was eligible 16 years ago, and we just got in, yet there are newer bands that get in. No one quite knows how the nominations work. When I got in, I was expecting a secret handshake and a dossier on what was really going on at Area 51, who killed Kennedy, and where Hoffa was buried. But none of it happened."

While in London on tour in 2011, Alice was invited to the U.K.'s Houses of Parliament to have tea with Conservative Party MP Mike Weatherley, who announced: "I first got involved in politics as a result of an MP in 1973, trying to ban him from getting into the country. It is wonderful that now in 2011, we embrace the creativity of such a unique artist as Alice Cooper."

Back in the early '70s, British morality crusader Mary White-house campaigned to ban "School's Out" on the BBC, and a politician attempted to ban Alice from entering England. "Cooper is peddling the culture of the concentration camp," MP Leo Abse had railed at the time. "Pop is one thing, anthems of necrophilia are another."

Decrying "filth" on TV, Whitehouse had previously protested the Beatles classic "Please Please Me" as a pornographic corrupting influence. She had also complained that Jimi Hendrix's performance in a 1968 television documentary was, "the most obscene thing I, at any rate, have ever seen on television."

About Alice's performance on the British TV show *Top of the Pops,* she complained "It is our view that if there is increasing violence in the schools during the coming term, the BBC will not be able to evade their share of the blame." She also protested that the show, "has given gratuitous publicity to a record which can only be described as anti-law and order. This record is subversive."

Alice's manager, Maui resident Shep Gordon, reported in his book *They Call Me Supermensch,* "We made all the papers, all the evening news shows. Everyone was shocked and outraged. There wasn't enough money in the world to pay for press like that."

"School's Out" shot to Number One in the U.K. "We couldn't thank her (Mary Whitehouse) enough," Alice recalls. "We were sending her flowers and cigars to Leo Abse because he wanted to ban us. When you get banned, the record went right to number one, and we sold out Wembley Arena without anybody having seen us before. Luckily we had a great show and really good music, songs like 'Eighteen' and 'Schools Out.' We broke in England before America. We kept thanking the British government for banning us."

The multi-platinum selling artist who pioneered spectacular, theatrical rock, spawning endless imitators, and shaped the future of heavy metal, began his professional career in Phoenix, imitating the Beatles in a high school band. "Everybody did the Beatles' songs, and then we started with the Rolling Stones, and more obscure British bands," he explains.

Relocated to L.A., Alice was introduced to Shep Gordon, by Jimi Hendrix. "He was living in the same apartment building as Shep," Alice explains. "He also knew the Chambers Brothers, and we were living in the basement of the Chambers Brothers' house.

"Jimi Hendrix would come over and see the Chambers Brothers and say, 'who's this band in the cellar?' He liked us and he went to Shep and said, 'I know a band that could use a manager,' and he introduced us. The very next day, Frank Zappa saw us and loved us, and we had a record contract signed, and that's after years of trying."

Unleashed at the close of the 1960s, Alice's trailblazing mix of glam and increasingly shocking stage theatrics starkly contrasted with the peace-loving hippy movement of the time. The shadow had emerged.

"We went the exact opposite way," he says. "We had long hair and played the hippy festivals, but I saw a lot of rock heroes, a lot of rock Peter Pans, and where's Captain Hook? I would gladly be Captain Hook. I would be Mr. Hyde. I would be Jack the Ripper. Rock and roll needs the ultimate villain. They needed their Darth Vader. I was ripe to be that character. I created Alice to be rock's villain, and who has more fun?"

Leading legends of the time like Salvador Dali and Groucho Marx flocked to his shows. "They saw through what it was," he says. "Groucho Marx would bring Fred Astaire and Mae West and Jack Benny, and Salvador Dali and all they saw was vaudeville, very loud, rock 'n' roll, really demented vaudeville. People called it shock rock, but to us, it was vaudeville."

Bad Alice would need punishing, and his shows routinely featured mock executions by electric chair, guillotine, and hanging rope. Dancing on the edge, at a London show in 1988, Alice almost hung himself.

"I insisted on it being realistic, and when you're doing the gallows, it's a trick, a way of doing it, so it looks real," he says. "The more real it looks, the more dangerous it is. There was a piano wire that literally stops you from hanging. It got stressed, and at one show, it snapped and the rope caught me by the neck. Luckily I snapped my head back so the rope went over my chin. My hands were handcuffed behind me. I didn't have any control. I like the idea of my audience realizing there's a possibility that something could go wrong, like the circus with a trapeze guy without a net. It gets exciting. It's showbiz."

Another trap brought him to his knees. Serious alcohol abuse threatened his life, and, as he wrote in his book, *Alice Cooper, Golf Monster: A Rock 'n' Roller's 12 Steps to Becoming a Golf Addict*, he found sanctuary in golf.

"I reached a point where I was drinking a bottle of whiskey a day, and I was getting up in the morning and throwing up blood, and all my friends were dying or dead," he reveals. "You get to a crossroads where you decide to live or die. I went into hospital and stayed 30 days or so, and when I came out, I was healed. It was a very spiritual healing. At that point I never had another urge to drink. The doctors were saying, 'you need to go to A.A.' I never had to go to A.A. once.

"So now what was I going to do? I used to get up and drink and watch TV. I went to a golf seminar and took lessons and ended up becoming pretty much an addicted golfer. My wife laughs and says, I traded one bad habit for a worse one. She's kidding."

The mascara-daubed godfather of shock rock, who used to chop up baby dolls on stage, surprised some of his former detractors by openly expressing his Christian faith. He's championed a Christian teen center in Phoenix and been awarded an honorary doctorate by a Christian college for his philanthropic work.

"I grew up in a Christian home," he says. "I was a prodigal son. My dad was a pastor, and my grandfather was a pastor. I went out and did everything I could to destroy myself, then when I quit drinking, I became more focused and realized I was looking for something with deeper meaning, something to fill the hole, and it wasn't another car, it wasn't a mansion, and it wasn't another hit record. I was longing spiritually to get back to my home, which was the Christian church. I go to Bible studies and church on Sundays, and I have an organization that tries to persuade gang kids into a different life. But I still do my show and play Alice Cooper to the hilt. I'm still the villain of rock 'n' roll.

Sober, he finds it easier to transition between his villainous alter ego and regular Vincent Furnier. "Alice will always be my favorite rock star," he continues. "It's fun to play him. I don't have to be him all the time. Onstage I can be this really over the top, Allan Rickman-type villain. I never get tired of it, and apparently, the audience never gets tired because we sell out every show. When I was drinking, I never knew where Alice began, and I stopped. Now it's easy to clearly understand that *that* Alice belongs on stage and doesn't belong walking the streets. I look forward to playing him now."

On Maui for the Christmas holidays, where he has a home, Alice annually rings in the New Year at a benefit show, which typically features other legends like Aerosmith's Steven Tyler. It's become an annual rite at the close of the year for a number of our famous full-time and part-time residents to rock out in a fundraiser for the Maui Food Bank and the Maui Arts & Cultural Center.

As our interview comes to a close, I ask Alice about the time he was coaching his son's Little League team, and the kids had no clue about his rock star status, only that he had somehow shown up in the *Wayne's World* movie and was idolized by "we're not worthy" Wayne and Garth.

"I didn't realize that the kids on my team had no idea who Alice Cooper was," he reports. "But when they saw *Wayne's World*, they were, how did coach Cooper get in *Wayne's World?* The parents knew who I was, but not the kids. And now with *Guitar Hero,* every nine-year-old kid knows 'School's Out' and listens to my albums."

So after so many years, do fans still "I'm not worthy" him? "Every day, at least three times a day," he says, laughing. "And they all think they're the first ones who thought of it."

"THERE'S ONLY ONE WAY TO ROCK"

Sammy Hagar

"I'm probably the most misunderstood cat in rock and roll."

I t's likely a surprise to discover that rocker Sammy Hagar credits contact with extraterrestrials for aiding his success. "I had a dream when I was about 19, and I felt I was programmed, and it changed my life," he explains during a Maui vacation in 1992.

"It was the middle of the night. I started waking up, and there was a feeling these guys are going; he's waking up. I opened my eyes, but I couldn't move the rest of my body. My whole room was lit up, so light you couldn't even see the walls. It was scary though I wasn't being hurt. Then all of a sudden, it went black, and I could move again. Ever since then, my life has changed. From the next day on, everything started happening. I started writing songs, and reading certain kinds of books. I was put on a quest, and I'm still on it."

Sammy is feeling relaxed hanging out on Maui with his future wife, Kari (who produced the documentary *Ram Dass, Going Home*). As the lead singer of Van Halen at the time, he had just performed three record-breaking, sold-out nights at Oahu's Blaisdell Arena. Following the shows, the band members descended on Maui for a little R&R, and that's when Sammy revealed his contact encounter.

Since this remarkable event, Sammy reports contacts have continued. "It's happened four or five times since then with the same guys, but I don't remember it as much. I'm into astronomy and metaphysics, anything you could possibly do to maybe make contact. You start finding out about different ones. They're from all over the universe, and some of them are from different dimensions. Some are people living right here, the walk-ins, like Ruth Montgomery writes about. There's a lot of walk-ins around."

Around 20 years later, he revealed some of this alien saga in his book *Red: My Uncensored Life in Rock*. He wrote how he would devour illuminating books like Alan Watts' *This Is It,* and Russian mystic Peter Ouspensky's *A New Model of the Universe* and *The Fourth Way.*

Feeling directed since that fateful first encounter, Sammy relays how relevant things started popping into his life. "I was working on a garbage truck, and I picked up an old suitcase and there was a book in it on numerology. I read the book and got so into the number nine. I named my publishing company Nine Music. Then I got into the color red. Numerologically, red is the number nine."

This early metaphysical exploration led him to the power of thought manifestation. "People are telling me you've got to be careful what you wish for. One night before a show, I said, I think I'll start wearing a cross. I walk out on stage, and bang a cross hits me. For the next three or four shows, they start coming up. Nine months of this stuff, it's almost this is getting ridiculous. I'm being more careful about what I say, think, and do. You can also attract the wrong stuff, thinking negative, being mad at your companion."

All this cosmic talk from a rock 'n' roller many have perceived as a boozing, cruising, party animal might seem somewhat odd. Didn't Sammy compose the rebellious anthem "I Can't Drive 55" and such hedonistic grinders as "Source of Infection" and "Black and Blue?"

"There's no question about it; I'm probably the most misunderstood cat in rock and roll," Sammy exclaims. "I've always been criticized by the rock press as a guy who thinks he's 16 years old, and goes out there and corrupts teenagers - just party, party, party. My song 'I Can't Drive 55,' everyone's going, he's trying to get kids to drink and drive and speed. I'm just talking about getting busted for it when everybody speeds. No one drives 55. If they do, they get beeped at. That's all I get thought of, and I thought it was a legitimate gripe."

Feeling at home on Maui, Sammy bought ten acres in Haiku, and spent more than 20 years on the island. He opened Sammy's Beach Bar & Grill at the Kahului Airport and donated all restaurant profits to local children's charities. He also set up the Blessings in a Backpack program, which provides meals to elementary school kids, funded by a percentage of touring profits. Sammy sold his Haiku retreat in 2018.

Sammy would later memorialize one of Maui's famous products on the hidden instrumental track "Maui Wowie," on *Ten 13,* where he played 'ukulele one night in Haiku, and later released on the collection *This is Sammy Hagar: When the Party Started, Vol. 1.*

During this time, Sammy developed a friendship with Maui-based artist Loren Adams. The famous rocker established a close bond with the acclaimed visionary artist and his wife. An avid fan of Adams' classic surrealist work, Sammy remembers when he first set eyes on one of his extraordinary paintings - *Telos Mu*, which depicts the ancient civilization of Mu, centered in the Pacific that is believed to have flourished around 24,000 B.C. The painting tells of a visitation by advanced extraterrestrial intelligence.

"I'm not a guy who goes around looking for art," Sammy suggests. "My ex-wife took me to Loren and Patty's gallery in Carmel. She wanted to show me a painting of a cow. I'm going; I don't want to buy no picture of a cow. I look up, and *Telos Mu* was hanging on the wall. I went, wow, this is incredible. So I commissioned a piece *Naacal Temple*. It's the land of Mu out here (off the Hawaiian islands)."

Sammy discovered the musician and artist shared a similar mystical interest. "I knew a lot about the same kind of stuff," he notes. "I've read about Atlantis and Mu, and I've always been interested in aliens and UFOs."

Sammy's now deep in conversation while headed to a limo waiting to whisk him to the airport. His girlfriend encourages haste because of an imminent flight departure, but Sammy has an important task at hand. He's collected some Maui rocks, and he's hip to the local custom that you don't take rocks home. So he's taking time to wend his way back to the beach to throw them in the ocean. Not exactly the action of a dedicated hell-raiser.

Which leads Sammy to point out: "Take a song like 'Right Now,' off the last record, and the video we made, which is very much higher consciousness. If U2 had written this song, it would have been, oh, the answer. Nothing against them; they're wonderful. We write, and it's like, yeah, Van Halen's recorded some trivial stuff about here and now. That's old Zen philosophy. That's one of the heaviest things you can say. I felt I nailed it lyrically. We've written some great songs, 'Dreams' and 'Love Walks In,' which is about a walk-in."

So does he get a little ticked off about the lack of respect? "None," he responds, laughing. "It used to bug me a lot because I always considered myself a lyricist. It's Van Halen; they're the party band.

"We're really sensitive and conscientious," he continues. "I just read an article on Bono, and he said he's tired of being taken so seriously, they want to have more fun. So now on stage, the article said he seems more like Sammy Hagar shaking up a bottle of champagne and spraying the audience."

He pauses for a moment digesting the irony of the description. "I'm thinking here I am wanting to be taken seriously, and he wants have some fun."

"TAKIN' IT TO THE STREETS"

Michael McDonald

*"I went from playing little dives in L.A. to playing
'Long Train Running' in front of 20,000 people."*

One of the most distinctive and popular vocalists to emerge from California's late 1970s rock scene, Michael McDonald has lately been passionate about playing an instrument long associated with Hawai'i - the humble 'ukulele.

A former Maui resident, he's recorded with Hawai'i's 'ukulele wizard Jake Shimabukuro and he popped up at a Wailea club strumming an 'ukulele backing Gail Swanson. "It's something I picked up a couple of years ago to relieve the boredom on the road," McDonald explains. "When I'm sitting in a hotel room, I play this game thinking of songs that I've never heard on 'ukulele. What would they sound like on 'ukulele? So I'll play old Nat King Cole and Brenda Lee songs, and surprisingly many of them fit the instrument well."

His love for the 'uke led him to play it in concert on a *PBS* Christmas special. "It was kind of terrifying," he recalls. "It's one thing to play it in your room and another to play it when it's actually plugged in." On his *Season of Peace* album in 2018, he strummed along with Jake Shimabukuro, and he teamed with the Hawai'i star on the duets album *Jake & Friends* in 2021. Recorded in Paia on Maui, they revamped the Moody Blues' classic "Go Now." "He's a real solid 'uke player," Jake reports. "He just grooves."

McDonald's appealing blend of soul and soft rock has earned him five Grammy Awards and a string of hit songs from "Takin' It to the Streets" and "What a Fool Believes" with The Doobie Brothers to "I Keep Forgettin'" and "On My Own" with Patti LaBelle.

Into the 21st century, he successfully mined the Motown catalog. On *Motown*, he delivered impassioned covers of Marvin Gaye's timeless classic "I Heard it Through the Grapevine" and Stevie Wonder's

74

"Signed Sealed Delivered." "I really wanted to do a project like that," he explains. "But then fear set in - what would make you think you're the guy to do some kind of retrospective Motown album? And there are a million Black singers who could probably do it so much better.

"In that moment, I decided not to make a big deal out of it, just to do it for the love of the songs with my own approach that was respect-ful of the originals. And find some great obscure songs that people in America maybe weren't so aware of, say like the English audience were, so we did (the Four Tops') 'Loving You Is Sweeter Than Ever.' I just thoroughly enjoyed the whole project from start to finish."

Motown Two continued his soul homage covering more classics like Smokey Robinson's "The Tracks of My Tears" and Marvin Gaye's "What's Goin' On." Then in 2008, he released the marvelous *Soul Speak*, an eclectic covers collection including Van Morrison's "Into the Mystic," Bob Marley's "Redemption Song," and Stevie Wonder's "Liv-ing for the City." Guest artists on the album included Wonder, who played his distinctive harmonica on his own compositions as he had done on the *Motown* recordings. "He was really gracious," McDonald notes. "We were thrilled the first time and amazed the second time he agreed."

Raised in St Louis, Missouri, as a young boy, he realized his des-tiny lay in his voice. "My aunt lived in an old apartment building that had a big hallway, and on my way out, I'd tap my feet on the tile floor and make up melodies. I remember one time when I was about ten, stopping and thinking I'm pretty good at making up my own songs. I could probably do this for a living. I've always enjoyed singing, and I never stopped to think I wouldn't do it or would quit doing it.

"I started playing rock 'n' roll around 12, and we were a little neighborhood band. My sister Kathy managed us. She got us our first paying gig - we got $9 playing at an Episcopal church. They asked us to stop early. I don't think we sounded all that great."

First coming to national attention as a backing vocalist with Steely Dan, beginning with 1975's *Katy Lied*, he sang on *The Royal Scam, Aja*, and *Gaucho* and played keyboards on some tracks. For a musician playing L.A. clubs, it was a gig from heaven.

"I had turned 25, and I was playing in a club band, and I'm starting to wonder if I was ever going to get a decent gig," he says. "I got a call from (drummer) Jeff Porcaro, and he told me Steely Dan were auditioning to go on the road. I jumped at the chance, threw my Wurlitzer (organ) into the Pinto, and drove to Hollywood.

"They weren't nuts about my keyboard playing, but I could sing all the high parts. I got the job. It was a dream come true. Being with Steely Dan was one of those rare moments. That was my absolute favorite music being recorded at that point. It was the most interesting stuff I had heard since the Beatles or early James Brown. "

The next job teleported McDonald to stardom. Former Steely Dan guitarist Jeff Baxter called, "me out of the blue and by then I've learned never to say no," and inquired whether he might like to join The Doobie Brothers. "He said, 'Tom Johnston had taken ill in the middle of the tour, and would I feel like meeting them in New Orleans?' I got on a plane with my Wurlitzer and flew to New Orleans, and that was the start of my 10-years with them.

"I'd written a really offbeat thing ("Losin' End"), and the producer liked it. So it was, 'do you have any more tunes?' The next thing I wrote was 'Takin' It to the Streets,' then 'It Keeps You Running.' The whole thing just materialized. It was remarkable."

McDonald's participation was initially greeted with skepticism by record executives. The resulting *Takin' It to the Streets* album, featured McDonald's title track and "It Keeps You Runnin,'" both hits for the band.

"When the album came out, I went down to Burbank, and there was a Doobie Brothers' billboard for the album Takin' It to the Streets, and I'm sitting there looking at my song as the title of The Doobie Brothers' album. I couldn't believe it. Two years before, I was playing at the Trojan Room in Glendale."

"I went from playing little dives in L.A., to playing 'Long Train Running' in front of 20,000 people," he marvels. "It was very surreal. I remember feeling like an imposter, that someone was going to discover I didn't belong there. But it was a great experience working with those guys. They're still some of my greatest friends."

When Pat Simmons, the only remaining original Doobies' member, decided to quit, it was time for a solo career. "I kept thinking at some point I might leave the band," he says. "Once Pat quit I didn't want to be The Doobie Brothers. It was obvious I wasn't going to walk out and have a five-million selling record. It was one thing to write two or three songs for a band; to write ten songs on your own was a big task.

"It was very scary and awkward," he continues. "It was probably one of the most nerve-wracking experiences of my life. I remember being so afraid it was almost paralyzing. I'd always been a piano player in a band who sang some songs. All of a sudden, I was singing all the songs and I was supposed to somehow engage the audience. A friend of mine from Maui, Scotty Rotten, put it best; the stage presence I have is more, please don't beat me!"

McDonald need not have worried as his debut solo album, *If That's What It Takes*, featuring the hit "I Keep Forgettin,'" consolidated his broad appeal. A duet with James Ingram on "Yah Mo B There," won a 1985 Grammy, and another duet with Patti LaBelle, "On My Own," brought him a number one hit.

Of his many stellar collaborations, he's most proud of working with Ray Charles on *Genius Loves Company*. "We all have that one artist we idolize, and if there was one guy that really got me into the music business, it was Ray Charles," he enthuses. "So to actually perform with him and stand in front of a 40-piece orchestra, to sing a song together, was just the thrill of my life."

In 2019, he was among a diverse group of artists like Joss Stone and Angélique Kidjo, contributing to the rousing contemporary gospel collection *Oh Happy Day: An All-Star Music Celebration*. "There's probably no more exciting music than gospel," he says. "When it comes to power and passion, there's something about gospel that transcends all other styles of music, a limitless kind of energy. To me, it's one of the purest forms of American music. I think of gospel and jazz as the more progressive American genres. They're constantly pushing the limits."

McDonald usually celebrates New Year's Eve on Maui at benefit shows where he often channels his love for gospel in rousing versions of "Takin' It to the Streets" and Marvin Gaye's "Grapevine." In August 2019, he joined Paul Simon on stage at the MACC to perform a mashup of "Cecilia" and Billy Preston's "Will It Go Round in Circles."

His connection with Hawai'i includes collaborating with Henry Kapono on the *Same World* album and teaming with Hawai'i Island 'uke star Brittni Paiva, singing one of his hits on her *Tell U What* album. And in July 2020, he joined some fellow Maui mates, dubbed The Quarantines, for a virtual, pandemic version of Dave Mason's classic "Feelin' Alright."

As far as songwriting, McDonald says he sometimes struggles creatively and can battle self-doubt. "I'm always wrestling with it. Some songs come in an evening, and some you work on for months, looking for two words. Songs can drive me crazy. I get jazzed on some lyric ideas, and nine out of ten of them the next day they sound so silly. It's amazing how I can be almost two different people, one going this is a great idea, and the next day going, that's the most pretentious, ridiculous idea. I'm always trying to stay one step away from being too serious with my lyrics and pontificate. It's so easy to fall into thinking I've got the answer here, and that's kind of suicidal."

"LOVE IS A BATTLEFIELD"

Pat Benatar

"We were the first group of children of the feminist movement."

When Pat Benatar moved to remote Hana with her guitarist/husband Neil "Spyder" Giraldo, some of her advisors were worried that she might enjoy living in paradise so much she could drop off the radar. "A lot of our business people said, 'you'll never play again, you'll get over there and be making leis and never come out'," says Benatar during a 2006 interview. "They said we would have amnesia. They were busting us so bad that we would never make music again." Hence the title of her *Polyamnesia Off The Rock '06 Tour.*

Having fallen in love with Maui in the early 1980s - she was married in Hana in 1982 – Benatar and her husband knew they would one day plant roots there. "Ever since we got married, we spent any time that we could here," she continues. "Once we went there the first time, we were hooked."

The couple even named their youngest daughter Hana. "We had a bunch of names picked out," she explains, "but my husband said, 'let's just call her Hana'. I said, what? But when we saw her little face, she was Hana."

Benatar's affection for the islands led her to study 'Ōlelo Hawai'i and embrace the music. "I love it so much, and Spyder and I learned songs to do when we're at luaus with friends," she reports. "He can certainly incorporate it more into his playing than I can into my singing. You can't talk about two kinds of music further apart from each other than singing Hawaiian music and singing rock 'n' roll. I love the falsetto, and I love to do it. I studied Hawaiian for three years, so I'm pretty fluent now. I can speak it pretty well, but I'm not doing so great writing it out." Benatar and her husband said goodbye to Hana when they sold their house in 2017.

Growing up on Long Island, she reports, "I did theatrical and classical music when I was young because there wasn't really a place in the small town I grew up in to do pop music. I needed to sing so bad, I didn't care I was singing Puccini and doing *Camelot*. Spyder, on the other hand, was so far left of how I cut my musical teeth. He was into the Dead Boys and all that stuff. We're completely opposite, which kind of makes for a good mix together."

So does she ever launch into a Puccini aria in the kitchen? "Actually, more to Spyder's dismay, it's more if I'm breaking into 'Bali Hai' from *South Pacific*. He says, 'I can't believe I married a woman who's a total rocker freak who sings *South Pacific* in the house and in the car.'"

Trained as an opera singer, she studied with a voice coach from the prestigious Julliard School of Music. "I was preparing to go to Julliard, but at the last minute, I decided I really didn't want to sing classical music as my career," she says.

After discovery in a local talent contest, stardom beckoned. A commanding performer with a powerhouse voice and sexy presence, Benatar hit big with her debut album, *In the Heat of the Night*, and the hot singles "Heartbreaker" and "I Need a Lover."

"You spend your life preparing for that moment, but no matter what you do, you're not prepared," she recalls. "It's so overwhelming. It's the momentum of a huge train, and you can't catch up. It doesn't happen until maybe the second or third record that you get the reins of what's happening. It's exhilarating and fun, and overwhelming. I would never go back to those days. I prefer this so much more."

MTV played a pivotal role in establishing her early prominence. She was hot and rocking just as the fledgling video channel birthed. Her video for "You Better Run" was the second music video ever aired by MTV. "I don't think anyone anticipated how it was going to change everything," she says. "We were in a dumpy motel in Oklahoma when it first aired. They only had five videos, and there was nothing else on. They literally played these things 24 hours a day, over and over. By the next week, we couldn't go anywhere because people had seen our faces so much."

As a young woman in the 1980s, fronting a rock band in a male-dominated world, Benatar faced many challenges. "It was a nightmare," she reveals. "We were the first group of children of the feminist movement. I used to call it the gauntlet because every day there was some horrible thing like with (radio) station managers – 'you come here and sit on my lap.' I was so militant. I always had my fists up, ready to go. I was so aggressive because it was so necessary. I was a little pit bull. Nothing made me happier than making men in suits cry."

The decade belonged to Benatar, who scored hit after hit, won Grammy Awards for Best Female Rock Performance four years in a row, and sold tens of millions of albums worldwide. These hits included "Hit Me With Your Best Shot," "You Better Run," "Love is a Battle-field," and "Hell Is For Children," about the ravages of child abuse.

"I had no idea it would have such an impact," she says. "We got bags and bags of mail from children that were old enough to write and from adults who had lived through it. Unbelievably we had opposition from people who did not understand what the song was about. We had religious groups picketing and protesting at concerts because it was called 'Hell Is For Children.'"

Over the years, Benatar's music has impacted legions of fans, including many female performers. The liner notes of her greatest hits package included testimonials by artists such as Sarah McLach-lan, Tori Amos, and Joan Jett. "She exuded sensuality and vulnerability with great strength and passion - a true rock & roll goddess," wrote McLachlan.

Acclaimed as a rock goddess, she suggests: "I don't know if I'm viewed as a rock goddess, but if anyone had told me we'd still be doing this, I'd be laughing. I'm so happy because I'm enjoying it so much more now. I'm controlling it as opposed to it controlling me. I've man-aged to have a life and a professional life, which I'm extremely grateful for, and I love singing and writing more than I ever have. I'm incredi-bly blessed and happy."

"TURN OFF THE NEWS
(BUILD A GARDEN)"

Lukas & Micah Nelson

"Working with Neil has reminded me how important rock and roll is and how powerful it can be."

"Every time I'd drive through Hana, I used to listen to 'Pali Gap' because it was a Hawai'i-inspired song," Lukas Nelson recalls. "He did it around the time of *Rainbow Bridge*. I felt like it perfectly expressed the energy of the winding road out to Hana. It's like a magical journey through the forest of a psychedelic wonderland. That song was part of my childhood, the feelings of the wonder and mystery of Maui."

Lukas paid tribute to Hendrix with his band Promise of the Real on their debut album with a medley of "Pali Gap" and "Hey Baby (New Rising Sun)," showcasing his electric guitar virtuosity.

Micah Nelson also paid homage to Hendrix and his Maui connection on his *Particle Kid* album, with the densely layered track "The River." Reflecting Indian raga, electronica, and psychedelia influences, it culminated in a spoken voice coda about peace sampled from the *Rainbow Bridge* movie. "The whole intro is this voice talking about New Age concepts," Micah explains. "I grabbed a moment I resonated with a lot, as a powerful thing to close the record. Jimi has been a huge influence on me forever. I thought it was a nice tribute and a cool Maui connection."

Willie Nelson's sons were enveloped in music from their earliest days. Some of Lukas' earliest musical memories include "seeing Paul Simon and Ray Charles with my dad as a young kid, and being out on the road with Johnny Cash and The Highwaymen, Waylon Jennings and those guys." The stage first lured Micah as a three-year-old playing harmonica alongside Mickey Raphael in his dad's band. "I did that for a long time," he recalls. "Then on Maui when my brother picked up the guitar, I said, I guess I'll start playing the drums."

Willie recalls: "Lukas and Micah fooled around when they were really little. I kept drums around and guitars, and they'd take them up every now and again. I didn't push it. Micah wound up being the drummer, and Lukas took to the guitar."

Lukas credits his mom, Annie Nelson, with opening his world to the rock guitar greats. "My mom turned me on to Jimi and Stevie Ray," he notes. "I used to listen to the oldies station with my mom. On my dad's side, there was country and Dylan and Neil Young. I've played with Dylan a couple of times at shows we did with my dad. At one point, he was letting go of one of his guitar players and needed another one, and he asked me. I was just so busy at the time, I couldn't."

Both brothers would later tour and record with Neil Young, who invited Promise of the Real to become his backing band in 2015. Playing on his albums *The Monsanto Years, Earth, Paradox,* and *The Visitor,* Micah enthuses, "Neil has been our hero forever. Working with Neil has reminded me how important rock and roll is and how powerful it can be. It's supposed to be dangerous. A lot of music that calls itself rock has a big condom over it. It's so safe with no sense of danger at all."

Adopting the Particle Kid performing moniker, Micah creates innovative hybrid music. He described his self-titled debut album as "a love letter to the cosmos." The follow-up, *Everything Is Bullshit,* included the Dylanesque "Gunshow Loophole Blues."

A gifted artist, Micah's paintings and illustrations appeared in a booklet accompanying his brother's debut album with Promise of the Real. Lukas described the album as "a kind of a neo-hippie western." It included a cover of Neil Young's "L.A." and the original "Four Letter Word," which sounds like a lost track from Dylan's seminal *Highway 61.*

By the time of their third album, *Something Real,* you could understand why Neil Young felt the future of rock 'n' roll was in good hands, as they unleashed primal rock that recalled the might of legends like Led Zeppelin and Cream.

Released in 2019, POTR's *Turn Off the News (Build a Garden)* reflected influences of "Tom Petty and the Wilburys and JJ Cale," Lukas reports, while on the opening track, "there was a very Byrdseque kind if vibe that we were trying to capture."

Besides Willie Nelson, the album featured guest spots by Margo Price, Sheryl Crow, Kesha, and Neil Young. One of the highlights, "Civilized Hell," "was my tribute to badass women in my life," he explains. "It was based on a book I read called *The Monkey Wrench Gang,* by Edward Abbey. I wrote it originally based on that and this woman who goes out and burns billboards with a group of characters. They try and halt progress."

As for the title track, Lukas says: "We were trying to get people to connect with their local community more. It was less about the news itself and more about the actions you can take when you are not debilitated by the fear of the news. You can get so anxious sitting on your couch or on your phone, but there are so many things you could be doing in the moment. That was the point."

Reflecting on his path so far, Lukas says, "I'm not trying to be famous. I'm just trying to make music. When it's all said and done, I'd rather at my death bed look back and say, wow, what an authentic life, rather than what a successful life."

"PALI GAP"

Jimi Hendrix

"Driving up to the crater, Jimi said, 'I would love to live here and grow grapes.' That was his dream."

Jimi Hendrix flew to Maui on July 28, 1970, to participate in a film project, released a year later as *Rainbow Bridge*. It was his last filmed concert in America before his tragic death less than two months later.

Primarily shot on Maui and featuring a concert by the rock icon as an audience lure, it was envisioned as a more positive antidote to *Easy Rider*. "The idea of the film is a sort of space age 'Candid Camera,'" Hendrix's manager, Mike Jeffries, suggested in a U.K. *Record Mirror* interview. "We're going to shoot a lot of film and just see what comes out."

Called the "Rainbow Bridge Vibratory Color Sound Experiment," the free show on July 30 was staged to a few hundred folks in an Olinda meadow above the Seabury Hall private school.

While filming, Hendrix spent time at the school (which was closed for the summer), jamming, relaxing, and eating vegetarian meals. He loved hanging out in the school's serene surroundings at what he dubbed the "Cosmic Sandbox." "Everybody was staying there," says Linda Wilkes, who lived close by. "He loved Maui."

With scenes of surfing at Ma'alaea and trekking through Haleakalā crater, *Rainbow Bridge* offered a time capsule of the stoned, cosmic hippie days, with Hendrix musing about pyramids and past lives. About 48 minutes into the movie, he appeared on stage blasting Upcountry Maui with classics like "Foxey Lady" and "Voodoo Child."

Living on Olinda Road at the time, Wilkes recalls walking down to the school and hanging out with Hendrix. "My boyfriend Tab did the titles for the movie, and we'd go down there. I remember being in a tiny room with Jimi and the band jamming, with a big hookah in the middle. We later went to L.A. and lived in a house with Chuck Wein and Barry De Prendergast, the film's director and producer."

Wilkes recalls the concert as an extraordinary experience. "They made us all sit with our astrology sign. You can see in the movie people holding up banners for Aires and Scorpio. At the concert's opening, Hendrix played a note for each sign of the zodiac." Maui filmmaker Brian Kohne recalls encountering Hendrix's performance in Olinda as a six-year-old. "It just blew my mind. I was mesmerized."

With a strong wind blowing, the concert echoed around Upcountry. A *Maui News* headline on August 1 announced: "Camelot Comes to Haleakala." The scene "looked as though preparations were underway for a jousting tournament in King Arthur's day...and the colorful zodiacal banners lent an air of festivity. More than 800 of the long-haired set walked about a mile up the mountain slope to enjoy the music of Jimi Hendrix."

A *Honolulu Advertiser* review was headlined "Hendrix concert on Maui hummms." It quoted Seabury Hall headmaster, Reverand Roger Melrose: "This phenomenon taking place today is the first for Hawaii."

Fifty years later, the documentary, *Music, Money, Madness... Jimi Hendrix In Maui* explored his time on the island. "It's amazing how sleepy Maui was in 1970," reports the film's director John McDermott. "The idea of a rock concert on Maui was such an enormous deal." Interviewed in the doc, photographer Brian Byrnes, who took pictures of the concert (including the cover of *Music Legends on Maui*), reported: "To see Jimi Hendrix in this setting, it was like a gift from God."

Hendrix looked happy performing for blissed-out fans in the new concert footage, backed by bassist Billy Cox and drummer Mitch Mitchell. Two weeks earlier, he had played to an audience of more than 200,000 at the Atlanta International Pop Festival. A month later, he appeared before 600,000 at the U.K.'s Isle of Wight Festival.

"It was one of the greatest concerts," Billy Cox recalled. "I think Jimi enjoyed it, as you could see Jimi at his best."

Veteran Maui surfer/musician Les Potts hung out with Hendrix during the filming of *Rainbow Bridge*. "The book popular back then was *Chariot of the Gods* by Erich von Daniken, and we talked about that a lot," he says. "In the film footage that we shot, there was a (space) ship in the clouds."

Hendrix's fascination with space and science fiction began as a young boy watching the *Flash Gordon* movie serials. He started calling himself Buster after the actor Buster Crabbe, who played Gordon, and he was convinced of life on other planets. One afternoon playing with his brother in a field, a giant disk was reported to have appeared hovering in the sky.

This interest in extra-terrestrials and other worlds informed lyrics such as the star fleet in "Third Stone From the Sun," the Milky Way express in "The Stars That Play with Laughing Sam's Dice," and the giant space boat of "House Burning Down." On the eve of his death, he wrote a poem, "The Story of Life," where he mentioned flying saucers and angels.

A musician friend, Curtis Knight, who wrote the book *Starchild*, reported Hendrix said he felt certain a UFO had come down to put its spiritual stamp of approval on the Maui show. It was not uncommon to hear reports in the early 1970s of flying saucers seen near Haleakalā, known as the house of the sun in Hawaiian. An article in Oahu's *Sunday Star Bulletin & Advertiser* on August 2, 1970, was headlined, "film crew expecting spaceships on Maui." "Spaceship sightings these days are as normal as airplanes sightings," it quoted director Chuck Wein.

The day before the concert, Hendrix visited Lahaina and ended up jamming with a jazz pianist at the old Maui Belle nightclub on Front Street.

Spending time on Maui was a healing balm for Hendrix, needed space for spiritual and physical cleansing. The island has a long tradition of leaving stars alone, and he reveled in the opportunity to temporarily drop career demands. Interacting with like-minded souls, he could share metaphysical ideas and his passion for *The Urantia Book* and luxuriate among the island's many natural wonders.

Rainbow Bridge's director shared some spiritual books with Hendrix, including the ancient Chinese divination text the *I Ching* and *The Tibetan Book of the Dead*. The film's artistic director Melinda Merryweather recalls how "Chuck gave him two or three books which he carried everywhere, which were all about the spiritual age and looking at your higher self and looking at something more than the material world. He really loved that, and I think that's why he liked *Rainbow Bridge*. He's been quoted as saying it was like a spiritual candy store. It was a great gift for him."

Merryweather was with him when they drove up to the top of Haleakalā's 10,000-foot peak, and Hendrix told her he wanted to move to Maui. "When we were driving up to the crater for the first time, Jimi said, 'I would love to live here and grow grapes.' That was his dream that he would love to have a studio there and grow grapes. He loved Maui so much."

Before leaving Hawai'i, he wrote and recorded the song "Scorpio Woman" for Merryweather. "I said you have to write a song for me. He goes, 'what do you like?' I said, can you play flamenco? He looked at me like, can I play flamenco. I was shocked that he could. Then just to tease him, I said do you know anything about the masters, Bach and Beethoven?" Posthumously released on the compilation *Morning Symphony Ideas,* at 21 minutes long, "Scorpio Woman" features Hendrix singing and playing electric guitar.

"In the concert, he wanted to write his notes in colors which is something Beethoven did," Merryweather explains. "We found him an American Indian girl who could transfer his notes into colors. At the concert, we said you will participate in a color vibratory sound experience. Every (astrology) sign had a different color, and he went down the sounds of every sign and did it again. Then he took all the notes and merged them together, and people were crying, going, what is going on? People really felt it in their bodies. It was incredible. The experiment worked. Jimi told me he was sure they were going to cure cancer with sound."

In one *Rainbow Bridge* scene, Hendrix is seen sitting in a room at Seabury Hall talking about cosmic subjects, his origin on Mars, and a dream about being Cleopatra. "All of a sudden, he holds his throat, and he's choking to death," says Merryweather. "That's exactly what happened to him."

"He didn't want to leave Hawai'i," Chuck Wein recalled in the biography *Room Full of Mirrors*. "But there was a point where he had to go back to being Jimi Hendrix." As he was leaving the island, flying out of the old Kaanapali Airport, Les Potts remembers Hendrix saying, "You people are so lucky, you get to stay here."

Gypsy blues guitarist Beau Short reports Hendrix inspired him to move to Maui after he worked briefly as one of his assistant roadies ("I was just a sub") in England. Hendrix had just returned from the island and told him, "'if you ever get lost in life, go to Maui. It's the center of the universe.' He was going off about *Rainbow Bridge* and the crater and the (UFO) mother ship he saw. Jimi couldn't stop talking about Maui."

While he was on Maui, Hendrix called his journalist/friend Sharon Lawrence and told her that he had some reservations about the project. "I have mixed feelings about this movie. It's kinda weird, to say the least."

Confounding some audiences when it was released, *Rainbow Bridge* had originally been conceived with a much longer running time, which would have reduced its commercial appeal. The released film was severely edited, which made it almost incomprehensible. Still, United Nations General Assembly President Adam Malik praised it as "A new generation making a new world, but many people may not understand it yet." And the prestigious British Film Institute's *Monthly Film Bulletin* said, "Rainbow Bridge stands as one of the few films to be adequately representative of its time."

Interviewed before a Maui concert, Band of Gypsys' drummer Buddy Miles talked about Hendrix's premature death at the age of 27. "I don't think it was totally his choice being in a depressed mood, especially if you had the creative forces that James Marshall had," Miles suggested. "I think the man was just really hungry for love, and he wasn't getting what he rightfully deserved, and it killed him. He was so far ahead of everybody. Nobody could come close. His spirit will always live on."

In a May 1989 *Guitar Player* interview, Billy Cox reported: "Jimi's Spirituality, his whole psyche, was that of someone from another planet. Most of the time, he spoke about the Supreme Being. He was spiritual, and it came across in his personality."

Two weeks before his death, Hendrix was interviewed by the U.K. weekly *Melody Maker.* He talked about his desire to create more spiritually uplifting music in the future. "The music will paint pictures of earth and space, so that the listener can be taken somewhere," he said. "We are going to give them something that will blow their minds. I dig Strauss and Wagner, and I think they are going to form the background of my music."

Before Hendrix left Maui, he indicated to Merryweather that his time on earth was coming to a close. "Just before Jimi left, he asked me to decorate his Electric Lady Studio offices in New York because he loved my art direction for the film. I said I'd be happy to do that, and I said, I'll see you there then. He went, 'no, because I won't be here.' I went, what do you mean you won't be here? He looked me right in the eyes, and he said, 'I will not be here in my body.' I knew it was the truth because of the way he said it. He somehow knew he wasn't going to be here."

The documentary *Music, Money, Madness . . . Jimi Hendrix In Maui,* along with the album *Live In Maui,* was released in November 2020. "Seven weeks later, he was dead," notes McDermott. "He sadly died in London in September. Jimi only really had four years in the public eye releasing this amazing body of work."

ROCK & ROLL MUSIC

"HEY! BO DIDDLEY"

Bo Diddley

"I was there at the very beginning. I was the beginning."

E d Sullivan introduced Bo Diddley to America on November 20, 1955, marking the first rock and roll performance on national TV. "The Originator" beamed out his revolutionary, syncopated rhythm - the "Bo Diddley Beat" - that would influence legions of musicians from Elvis Presley, Buddy Holly, and the Rolling Stones to Jimi Hendrix, The Who, The Animals, The Clash, and even U2 ("Desire").

While Diddley's notorious debut captivated American teenagers - five months before Elvis Presley made his famous Sullivan debut - he was subsequently permanently banned from *The Ed Sullivan Show*. "I did two songs, and he got mad," Diddley recalled before a Maui concert.

Sullivan had requested Diddley to perform Tennessee Ernie Ford's song "Sixteen Tons" and was incensed when he opened with his new hit single, "Bo Diddley." In his book *Station to Station,* author Marc Weingarten writes how the show, which also included LaVern Baker, the Five Keys, and "honking" tenor saxophonist Willis "Gator" Jackson, was groundbreaking, "the first time a popular mainstream variety show had devoted an entire broadcast to race music."

"I was there at the very beginning," emphasized Diddley about his place in the history of rock. "I was the beginning, but I've been overlooked."

Unlike many of his peers, Diddley never received the wide respect and fame he deserved until way later in his career. "It's just the way America is," he continued. "There's no sense in trying to lie and hide it. It's wrong. I was just overlooked."

Born Elias Bates in McComb, Mississippi, in 1928, Diddley's first instrument was a violin. Then after years of classical training (including composing two violin concertos), he picked up the guitar. "I was studying to be a classical musician, but then I just started fooling around with the guitar," he recalled. "I'm basically self-taught. I figured out my own thing."

Moving to Chicago, he trained as an amateur boxer while exploring blues, gospel, and R&B. His big break came in the spring of 1955, when the fledgling Chicago blues label, Chess Records, launched Diddley's career alongside fellow Chicago musician Chuck Berry.

"He came up with the oddest beat I'd ever heard," Leonard Chess reported in the 1966 documentary *The Legend of Bo Diddley*. Recalling Diddley's genius, George Thorogood told *Rolling Stone*, "'Maybellene' is a country song sped up. 'Johnny B. Goode' is blues sped up. But you listen to 'Bo Diddley,' and you say, 'What in the Jesus is that?' You sit there, and you get numb listening to it."

While Berry quickly captured a pop career, Diddley's harder, blacker style kept him out of the mainstream, although he would later prove profoundly influential, particularly in Britain. It took almost a decade for most to wake up to the power of his music.

"You run out and jump over the cliff, and everybody gets tired before they get to the cliff, and you've already jumped over," said Diddley about being ahead of his time. "Everybody else, they're coming, but it just takes a little time for them to get there."

It was common in the late 1950s and early '60s for white musicians to cover Black artists' material to have a so-called "wider appeal." In the process, the white artists received more credit and remuneration. There are reports that Elvis had watched Diddley play at the Harlem's Apollo Theater and copied his moves.

Elvis Presley reported in a 1956 interview: "The colored folks been singing it and playing it just like I'm doing now man, for more years than I know. I got it from them."

"It upset me, but I couldn't worry about that," said Diddley. "I was just glad to be where I was at, but we were overlooked in many areas."

Diddley was part of the "Biggest Rock N Roll Show of '56" tour, headlined by Bill Haley, the only white artist among acts like The Platters and Big Joe Turner. With huge crowds attending, the *A Rock n' Roll Historian* blog noted: "Several shows are cancelled because of racial troubles including bomb threats, protests, pickets, and violence." In Birmingham, Alabama, the show was picketed by the White Citizen's Council urging white folks to stay away. In Greenville, South Carolina, a second show was cancelled after a bomb was found in the concert hall.

Often confronting racism, one day in 1959, Diddley and his band jumped into a Las Vegas hotel swimming pool. All the white swimmers immediately got out, and an attendant put up a "Contaminated Water" sign. At a South Carolina show, a Diddley band member jumped into the audience, and as white girls danced around him, the police charged in with clubs.

While rock 'n' roll's early days were mostly a male preserve, Diddley made a point of hiring female musicians in his band, including "Lady Bo" (Peggy Jones), hailed as the Queen Mother of Guitar, who played on "Hey! Bo Diddley," "Mona," and "Road Runner."

She was replaced by "The Duchess," Norma-Jean Wofford. *AllMusic* reviewer Bruce Eder noted, "on stage, they made a combination more overpowering than Brian Jones and Keith Richards." Wofford played on such albums as *Bo Diddley & Company* and *The Originator*. In later years, bassist Debby Hastings played with him up to his death. Hastings credits also included Chuck Berry, Little Richard, and Jerry Lee Lewis.

Diddley's powerful, primal songs like the provocative "Who Do You Love," "Road Runner," and "I'm A Man" provided the repertoire for a whole generation of British R&B bands, and following them, a new wave of American garage groups. The early British R&B bands were particularly enamored of Bo's beat. The Stones recorded "Mona" on their debut album, The Animals immortalized him on "The Story of Bo Diddley," and the Pretty Things took their name from a Diddley song.

He toured Britain for the first time in 1963, on a package with Little Richard, The Everly Brothers, and opening act, the Rolling Stones. The Stones would feature five Diddley songs in their repertoire in their early days, including "Road Runner" and "Pretty Thing." Brian Jones once reported Diddley was one of the Stones' biggest influences, and they backed him on a session he recorded for BBC radio.

"I went there to play one song ("Pretty Thing") which was a hit in America, and I got over there, and it was something else in England," he recalled. "The English kids like the Rolling Stones; they're the ones who gave Bo Diddley an everlasting push."

In 2018, the Stones released the live album *Voodoo Lounge Uncut*, which included a concert performance (from 1994) with their pioneering idol on his song "Who Do You Love?"

A wave of American psychedelic rockers later embraced Diddley's beat. Bands such as Quicksilver Messenger Service, The Seeds, Blues Magoos, The 13th Floor Elevators, and Captain Beefheart & His Magic Band took on "Mona," "Diddy Wah Diddy," and "Who Do You Love."

In 1967, Diddley recorded the classic *Super Blues Band* with Muddy Waters, Little Walter, and Buddy Guy, followed by *Super Super Blues Band* with Waters and Howlin' Wolf. Five years later, the Grateful Dead backed him at a show at the Academy Of Music in New York City. It was released on *Dick's Picks Volume 30* in 2003.

A decade later, The Clash invited Diddley to open during their first American tour, playing for punk rock fans. "I didn't worry about who it was," Diddley said nonchalantly, "they could have been church people." "In the flesh, he was more awe-inspiring than we could possibly imagine," the Clash's Joe Strummer marveled in a *Q* magazine interview.

Diddley was eventually bestowed with a Hall of Fame Award at the 1998 Grammy Awards. "It felt real good to have that slot," he said about his role as a founding father of rock and roll. "But it was a long time coming."

After Diddley died in 2008, aged 79, Mick Jagger paid tribute. "He was a wonderful, original musician who was an enormous force in music and a big influence on The Rolling Stones. He was very generous to us in our early years and we learned a lot from him. We will never see his like again."

"JOHNNY B. GOODE"

Johnnie Johnson

*"I always helped find the music that would go
with the lyrics Chuck wrote."*

Rock and roll history was made the night pianist Johnnie Johnson invited a young guitarist named Chuck Berry to play a New Year's Eve party at the close of 1952. The teaming of Berry's hillbilly guitar style with Johnson's blues-based boogie piano soon launched one of the most influential sounds in popular music.

"One of my musicians had an illness, and I called Chuck, and he was available," Johnson explained the fortuitous teaming, having met Berry earlier in the year.

Originally billed as the Johnny Johnson Trio, that one night led to a 28-year collaboration. Beginning with "Maybelline" in 1955, Berry released a stream of hits that would influence almost every rock 'n' roller who followed in his footsteps. All those primal hits featured Johnson's piano. "I never did write any lyrics," he said in a 1994 interview on Maui. "I always helped find the music that would go with the lyrics Chuck wrote."

Influenced by seminal piano players like Art Tatum, Earl Garner, Earl Hines, and Oscar Peterson, he grew up playing piano at an early age. "My parents bought me a piano when I was about five or six years old," he recalled. "I grew up around blues."

While most are familiar with such landmark rock tunes as "Sweet Little Sixteen," "Roll over Beethoven," and "Johnny B. Good," few folks know the name of Berry's pianist who helped define the classic rock beat. Memorialized by Berry in "Johnny B. Good," it was Johnson who influenced generations of piano players.

Into the 1990s, the spotlight began illuminating this pioneering hero, with Eric Clapton and Keith Richards singing his praises. In the liner notes to Johnson's album *Johnnie B. Bad*, the Stones' guitarist

95

reported, "when I first heard Chuck Berry's records the first thing I wanted to know was, who's this guy singing 'Johnny B. Good,' and the second thing was, who is playing that goddamn piano?"

Johnson's brilliant performance in the documentary *Hail! Hail! Rock 'n' Roll* led to some influential friendships. "We did a movie together, and Keith was overwhelmed with my playing," he explained. "Right after the rehearsals for the movie, he had me come to New York, and I got on his record *Talk is Cheap*. In the meantime, he was on my album *Johnnie B. Bad*. Ever since we've been tight together."

The New York Times praised Johnson's *Johnnie B. Bad* as "a long-overdue tribute to one of rock-and-roll's most talented unsung heroes."

Eric Clapton was equally impressed with Johnson's playing on the movie sessions. Not only did Clapton add his guitar to *Johnnie B. Bad*, but he also invited the veteran pianist to perform during a series of sold-out shows at London's Royal Albert Hall, captured on *24 Nights*.

Raised in the Blue Ridge Mountains of West Virginia, Johnson taught himself how to play piano listening to old blues records. During World War II, he played in service bands and settled in Chicago in 1946, where he sat in with blues greats like Muddy Waters. Moving to St. Louis in 1952, he played for a while with guitar legend Albert King and formed his own trio, which soon included Chuck Berry.

While Johnson recalls fond memories of playing rock 'n' roll in the 1950s and 1960s, he would rather forget the racism Black musicians often confronted touring in the South. "The only problem was segregation when we'd go to certain states where Blacks didn't have too much opportunity," he remembered. "We had to play two jobs, one for the white man and one for the colored. Some places, we couldn't get a hotel room, so some of the Black residents of the neighborhood would take us in, or we would go back to the bus we were traveling in and sleep in the bus."

Having toured around Europe and in Japan, Johnson made his Maui debut in 1994. "Hawai'i is more exciting than any of them because I've never been there," he enthused. "I hear it's God's country."

Pleased to finally get the recognition he deserved, he concluded: "Musicians with big names have come up to me and said we enjoyed your music for ages. It's coming out into the light now."

Johnson sued Berry in 2000, claiming he was an equal collaborator on early rock classics like "Roll Over Beethoven," "No Particular Place to Go," and "Sweet Little Sixteen." The lawsuit claimed Johnson was owed half of the "tens of millions of dollars in royalties, license fees and other payments" the songs have earned. The case was dismissed because the statute of limitations had passed.

Johnson was inducted into the Rock and Roll Hall of Fame in 2001. His final album, *Johnnie Be Eighty. And Still Bad!* was recorded in St. Louis in late 2004. He died in 2005. In an interview with the *Associated Press*, Chuck Berry praised Johnson as "the man with a dynamite right hand" and "my piano player who no one else has come near."

He was posthumously awarded the Congressional Gold Medal for breaking racial barriers in the military. During World War II, his African-American unit endured racism and inspired social change while integrating the previously all-white Marine Corps.

A documentary on his life was in production in 2021. In a trailer for *Johnnie Be Good*, Keith Richards points out, "Without Johnnie Johnson, there would probably have been no Chuck Berry." And Bonnie Raitt notes, "He's as close to being a founding father of rock and roll as we have, and they ought to put him on a stamp."

"BLUE SUEDE SHOES"

Carl Perkins

"When we played on shows many times, Elvis would be at the side of the curtain hollering, 'go cat.'"

At the musical oasis of Sun Records in Memphis, Tennessee, Sam Phillips gathered together a group of eager young men who would revolutionize popular music. They included Elvis Presley, Jerry Lee Lewis, Johnny Cash, Roy Orbison, and Carl Perkins.

Life seemed fairly uncomplicated for these Southern pioneers of rock 'n' roll. Their early days were characterized by minimal pressures, the absence of cut-throat competition, and genuine enthusiasm for crafting a new form of music.

"The simple music we played at Sun Records, from Elvis on down, we didn't realize what we were doing," Carl Perkins explained before a Maui show. "We just knew that the audience was liking what we were doing. We were influenced by Southern black gospel and blues, and we just speeded up some of the blues licks. I always thought rockabilly was nothing more than a white man's lyrics with a black man's rhythm. That's what we were doing."

Recalling the allure of Sun Records, Perkins continued: "There was some magic in that little studio. There was no clock on the wall. Sam Phillips was a very smart man. He didn't tell us how to play. He had the knack of knowing when you were really into your song.

"Several times I'd say, Mr. Phillips, I think I can sing it better. He'd say, 'but you can't play any better.' He did the same thing with Elvis and Jerry Lee. He made you relax. He'd say, 'you're getting hot. Let's go and get it, knock me out behind this glass.' That's what you tried to do. You'd say, I'll fix him, I'll burn my guitar up. He took away all the fear."

Revered as the King of Rockabilly, Perkins recalled how a sense of supportive comradeship fueled the young musicians. "That was another thing that I've not found since," he noted. "There was no animosity or jealousy. We all knew Elvis closed the show and we all pulled for each other. One of the first things you did was if Sam thought you had a hit record, he'd make arrangements for you to get a new Cadillac. That was every country boy's dream. He'd say, 'you guys have to pull up looking like stars.'

"Of course, we wound up paying for those Cadillacs with our royalty checks," he added, laughing. "We were proud of each other. When we played on shows many times, Elvis would be at the side of the curtain hollering, 'go cat.' It was more of a family. It was nothing to be recording, and one of them would walk in and play."

Often consulting each other for career advice, Perkins explained: "Elvis would say, 'what you think of this song Carl?' I'd say, man, I love that thing. I remember 'Mystery Train' was one of them. I'd say you're crazy if you don't do that."

The rock 'n' roller's stage routines were rarely manufactured, usually derived spontaneously or, as in the case of Elvis' shaking, the result of nervous tension. "Elvis didn't go to school or stand in front of the mirror to learn how to move on stage; that boy couldn't help that," Perkins said. "He'd turn to Scotty (guitarist Moore) and say, 'what are they screaming about?' Scotty would say, 'I don't know, but do it again.' He was shaking his leg. It was not a planned thing."

Besides his sensual gyrations, Elvis was also known for performing with his collar up. Perkins reveals the sartorial effect resulted from a bad skin condition. "He had some pimple problems on the back of his neck. He'd turn his collar up and say, 'can you see them?' I'd say, no, can't see them. He didn't want fans to see the little pimples."

Jerry Lee Lewis also benefited from Perkins' advice. Before "Whole Lotta Shakin' Going On" hit, Lewis was known as a shy musician who hid behind his piano. One night, Perkins suggested a move that transformed The Killer's career. "Jerry was very shy, believe it or not," he reported. "It doesn't make sense that Jerry Lee was shy, but he was. He was always cocky. You'd be in the studio and say, can you do so-and-so on piano? He'd say, 'no,' and do it the way he wanted to, and it was pretty much always right.

"On one of the first tours he went on, he said, 'you guys have got it made over me. I got to sit down at the dumb piano stool, and you're all up jumping around rocking. I ain't got a chance to get the crowd like you all do.' I said, can't you stand up and play this thing? The next show, he went out, and when he stood up, he accidentally turned the stool over. The crowd roared, and he swung his head, and that blond hair went in every direction, and his feet were kicking the piano, and they went wild.

"I turned to Johnny Cash and said, John, I might have told him wrong. I had to follow him, so my opening line was, I'm sorry, I don't have a piano stool to turn over, and I can't raise my foot high enough to kick his guitar, so I'm just going to have to pick and sing for you all."

Born into impoverished conditions, by age six, Perkins spent his days picking cotton until sunset, humming along to the gospel songs of field workers. His first guitar was fashioned out of a cigar box and a broomstick.

Especially in the South, the salacious shaking and rocking on stage angered Christian fundamentalists who cursed rock 'n' roll as the devil's music. Records were publicly smashed and boycotts organized.

Alabama's White Citizens Council warned, "Rock and roll is the basic heavy beat music of negroes. It brings out animalism and vulgarity." New Jersey Senator Robert Henrickson fumed, "Not even the Communist conspiracy could devise a more effective way to demoralize, confuse, and destroy the United States." Frank Sinatra even denounced rock in an interview as, "the most brutal, ugly, degenerate, vicious form of expression." That prompted Elvis to respond: "It's the greatest music ever, and it will continue to be so."

"In the late 1950s, there were a lot of DJs breaking records," Perkins recalled. "I never felt it was bad or influencing kids in the wrong way. I never saw nothing wrong with kids jitterbugging at a sock hop. They were just getting high on the music. I'm not ashamed of what I did or still do."

The Sun musician's popularity threatened segregation policies in the South, and sometimes Perkins feared for his life. The only white on a tour with Chuck Berry and Little Richard, he became a Ku Klux Klan target. Berry told him that they might be doing "as much with our music as our leaders are in Washington to break down the barriers."

Perkins' greatest claim to fame was the rockabilly classic "Blue Suede Shoes," which catapulted him into the limelight in 1956. Recorded in

October 1955, "Blue Suede Shoes" became Sun's first million-selling record and the first song ever to score high in the country, R&B, and pop charts at the same time.

A young couple had caught his attention while playing one night in a small club with a stage lit by a Wurlitzer jukebox. "I was watching them dance, and they were right in front of the little bandstand. He cautioned her, 'don't step on my suede shoes.' I'd seen those around but didn't have the money to buy any. I thought that it was probably a waste of money because you can't polish them, and if you stepped in mud, they were ruined. When the young man said that, it bothered me because she said she was sorry. I couldn't get it out of my mind. I went home and at about three in the morning thought of the old nursery rhyme, 'one for the money, two for the show.'"

He ran downstairs and began picking out the famous opening only to wake up his wife, who told him to keep it down. She said, 'you're going to wake the babies.' She said, 'whose song is it?' I said it's ours. She said, 'you can go back and finish it, and we'll rock them back to sleep.'"

Perkins scribbled out the lyrics on a paper sack which he framed, complete with spelling mistakes. "I spelled it swade," he chuckled. "I didn't know how to spell it. I didn't have a telephone, so I went across the street to an old man who had a phone and called Sam Phillips. I told him I wrote a new thing and I'll call it 'The Blue Suede Shoes.' He said, 'is it anything like 'Oh, Dem Golden Slippers?'" We cut the song three times, and the first cut is the one the record is today. The single's B-side was "Honey Don't," which was later covered by the Beatles."

"Blue Suede Shoes" was selected by the Rock and Roll Hall of Fame one of the songs that helped shape rock 'n' roll, and *Rolling Stone* would later rate Perkins among the 100 Greatest Artists of All Time.

Perkins seemed almost embarrassed by the adulation he received from fans and didn't quite understand why stars such as George Harrison and Eric Clapton revered him. "I can't imagine anything I've done musically that would warrant anybody of their stature remembering me," he said. "It's a very humbling thing for me. Guitar players like Eric Clapton and George Harrison listened to my old records and learned some lyrics."

Perkins association with the Beatles stretched back to their formative days. George Harrison was so enamored with Perkins he adopted the stage name Carl Harrison in 1959. As his records were tough to find in England in those early days, when a ship from America docked in Liverpool, John Lennon and Paul McCartney would try to borrow copies of Perkins' records from the crew.

"There have only been two great albums that I listened to all the way through when I was about 16," Lennon recalled in a 1980 interview. *"One was Carl Perkins' first or second. I really enjoyed every track."*

When Perkins toured Britain with Chuck Berry in 1964, he met his famous admirers, and they asked permission to record three of his songs. "They'd say, 'Carl, how did you do the guitar break on 'Right Spring, Wrong Yo-Yo'?' I was amazed to find out they knew every record I had made."

Perkins joined the Beatles in the studio and recorded his songs "Honey Don't," "Matchbox," and "Everybody's Trying to Be My Baby" with them. The session also included a version of "Blue Suede Shoes." "There are a few other songs we kicked around," he remembered. "I've been told by Paul McCartney that George Martin had the tape on."

John Lennon later performed Perkins' version of "Blue Suede Shoes" with Eric Clapton in Canada on the *Live Peace in Toronto 1969* album. Also, in 1969, Perkins teamed with Bob Dylan and Johnny Cash for some Nashville sessions, which included recording "Matchbox." Dylan co-wrote the bluesy song "Champaign, Illinois" with Perkins, released on his 1969 album, *Carl Perkins On Top*. "I figured Carl needed a song," Dylan reported in an interview.

Two years before his death at the age of 65, Perkins released *Go Cat Go!*, which featured him performing his songs with three former Beatles, plus Bono, Willie Nelson, and Paul Simon, and Jimi Hendrix's version of "Blue Suede Shoes."

Harrison sang at his funeral, playing "Your True Love," the B-side of "Matchbox." Bob Dylan sent a tribute note, which Wynonna Judd read. "He really stood for freedom," Dylan wrote. "That whole sound stood for all the degrees of freedom. It would just jump right off the turntable. We wanted to go where that was happening."

"THE BALLAD OF JOHN AND YOKO"

Yoko Ono

"When we were going to go on a tour after Double Fantasy, John said, 'let's do your freak stuff. Let's not do any pop stuff.' It would have been a very unsuccessful tour."

It's likely surprising to discover that John Lennon doubted his vocal ability. Yoko Ono revealed in a 1987 interview that he disliked his voice and would request it be mixed down during recording sessions.

"While he was going to the washroom, I'd push it up a bit," Yoko recalls while on Maui to curate a gallery show of John's drawings. "I had to finally confront him. I said, John, all you've got is your voice. That's the only commercial thing we've got here for our album. John said, 'I don't like my voice. It should be buried.' John has a clear, powerful voice that really cut through everything."

When Yoko Ono stepped into John Lennon's life, she provided the famous Beatle with an indispensable ally encouraging his avant-garde artistic dreams. Together they devised a series of experimental records and films, political events, and art happenings that delighted some and mystified many. "She changed my life completely," Lennon told the *New Musical Express* in 1972. "Yoko was like an acid trip."

After sponsoring Yoko's *Half-Wind Show* in London, John mounted the *You Are Here (To Yoko from John Lennon, With Love)* art exhibit. It included a collection of charity collecting boxes he had designed, a round white canvas, and a helium machine that blew up white balloons, releasing 365 over the city.

Wary of the intense media scrutiny that accompanied any Beatle activity, John had shied from revealing this facet of his artistry until Yoko's encouragement. "He was a good artist, and I felt it was very important that he have a show," says Yoko. "He said, 'I'm a Beatle; I can't do it.' In a way, he was right. He did his first art show in the

Robert Fraser Gallery. There was a strange atmosphere. The people enjoyed it, but the critics ignored it."

After the Beatles broke up, Ringo Starr mounted an art exhibition of steel furniture he had helped design at Liberty, one of London's most fashionable stores. The show included such utilitarian artifacts as a Rolls Royce grill table. While I wandered around the exhibit one afternoon, Ringo strolled in, trailed by a film crew. Seizing the moment, I approached him, and we chatted for a bit, with Ringo confirming that his bandmates were never going to reform.

John later mounted a *Bag One* art show of lithographs as a wedding gift to his wife. British police seized eight sketches of the couple making love, declaring them obscene, "the work of a sick mind." Police files released in 2001 disclosed that the real reason for the raid was the "great influence of John Lennon as a Beatle."

"We were in Canada at the time, and we couldn't believe it," says Yoko. "Then we started laughing. This was the middle of the '60s, revolution and all that."

Another controversy erupted with the infamous *Unfinished Music No. 1: Two Virgins* record cover, where John and Yoko posed naked in 1968. A symbolic gesture, it would create a fierce reaction.

"The cover was the mind-blower," Ringo recalled in *The Beatles Anthology* book. "He showed me the cover and I pointed to the *Times*: 'Oh, you've even got the *Times* in it…' as if he didn't have his dick hanging out."

John's record label refused to distribute the album, and it could only be purchased in a plain brown paper bag. Reportedly only 5,000 copies were released in the U.K. at the time. I was a proud owner. In America, 30,000 copies were seized by police at New Jersey's Newark Airport on the grounds that the cover was pornographic.

"It was just a natural process," Yoko explains. "Here we are. We're going to be naked to the world. In the artistic community, a nude model is nothing, so to consider that obscene was obscene to us. It was very strange that people took it so differently. We didn't want just the right light and angle and make it like a Playboy Bunny. We wanted to say, here we are. I'm sorry everything is hanging out."

"EMI killed our album *Two Virgins* because they didn't like it," John told *Red Mole* in 1971. "With the last record, they've censored the words of the songs printed on the record sleeve. They have to let me sing it, but they don't dare let you read it. Insanity."

Experimental recordings like *Two Virgins* and the *Wedding Album*, the naked album cover, the peace campaign bed-ins, and the *War is Over* billboards all emerged from the creative vortex of Lennon/Ono.

"We were doing something that we just felt like doing," says Yoko. "We didn't know we were going to get so much flack at the time and we were surprised. Both John and I had a very severe background. John was separated from his mother and father, and both of us were war children - that maybe had a lot to do with our daringness."

In August 1971, John and Yoko led a protest march in London (which I attended) against censorship and the assault by the British government on the underground magazine Oz. The couple also released the fundraising single "God Save Oz," teamed with the blistering, primal rock of "Do the Oz" on the B-side.

Having cut the chord with the Beatles and emboldened by Yoko's support, John embarked on releasing a remarkable series of protest songs, adopting the role of a contemporary reporter in the minstrel tradition. Interviewed in the British music paper *Melody Maker* in 1971, John asserted he was a revolutionary artist dedicated to change and revolution, writing songs for people to help express themselves.

With some lyrical assistance from Yoko, he decried the murder of prisoners and dehumanizing incarceration on the chilling "Attica State," and skewered misogyny with the '50s rocker "Woman is the Nigger of the World." He denounced tyranny with the universal plea "Bring On The Lucie (Freeda Peeple)," and propelled by a martial beat, condemned religious oppression in Northern Ireland on "Sunday Bloody Sunday."

He railed against the repressive establishment on "Working Class Hero," highlighted the demonization of Black Panther member Angela Davis on the rousing "Angela," and championed the plight of an imprisoned activist with the bluegrass-flavored "John Sinclair."

He urged revolutionary action with the impassioned "Power to the People," and expressed frustration with deceptive politicians on the smoldering "Gimme Some Truth." On the joyous "Happy Xmas (War is Over)," he embedded a powerful anti-war message, and he painted a glorious utopian future on his masterpiece "Imagine."

Yoko revealed John sometimes felt frustrated by rock's restrictive boundaries. "There was a point in his life where he started to feel that he could no longer express himself in the limits of rhyming. I said, express yourself as a stream of consciousness, and he said, 'it won't go with the music.' I said maybe the music should follow that, and it becomes extremely avant-garde, and that would be going into a new dimension. He said, 'maybe, that would be interesting.'

"When he said maybe, it wasn't because he was a redneck rocker who didn't know the value of that dimension. When we were going to go on a tour after *Double Fantasy*, and John said, 'let's do your freak stuff. Let's not do any pop stuff.' It would've been a very unsuccessful tour," she adds, laughing. "He was the king of rock and roll, and he didn't want to go into being an esoteric artist who's got 20 people to listen to him."

How did John influence Yoko? "He inspired me a lot," she reports. "He was very good at encouraging me, and he understood my work so well. Being appreciated is one way of really being encouraged. I was influenced by his warmth. He had a very warm side. I was doing very complicated kinds of harmonics, classical music harmonics, and he said, 'sometimes simple is better.' That really helped me."

Their willingness to push boundaries and make their private lives public earned them intense media censure. Yoko dealt with the negative onslaught by remaining silent. "It's an Oriental thing, being passive like in judo you don't fight, that's how I was. When they started to attack me, I didn't answer back. If I kept fighting back, it might have made me tired. Sometimes I think maybe I should have stood up for myself, but I didn't."

When John and Yoko first got together, she would join him in the studio during Beatles' recording sessions, which created conflict. "I'd be in the studio with the Beatles, and while 1 was waiting, the idea was I should be putting some ideas on tape. I'd be whispering into a tiny recorder. Later, John told me he was totally nervous because he thought, 'what is this girl doing?' It never occurred to me it would be intimidating for them."

Completing work on his *Rock 'N' Roll* album in late 1974, John took a five-year retirement, only returning to the studio in August 1980. When he dropped from public view to devote time to his new child and family, Yoko says this chapter has been too narrowly defined. "Most people think he was just devoting his time to the family, but there was a lot of dialogue. Are we going to go in this direction or that? It's too bad a lot of bad books are written about it. A lot we were exploring at the time was a kind of alternate reality and some very valid stuff."

They reversed traditional male-female roles in their relationship, with John staying at home with Sean while Yoko took on the business world. "We were hoping that people would get the message. *Double Fantasy* is a record that's the result of it in a way. We felt society would benefit more by tapping into the feminine energy, and also, the society itself became so masculine. So because of the yin-yang balance, it was time for that."

At the dawn of 1980, they felt the time was ripe to rekindle the creative fire and embrace the world with their art. Ready to make music again, "at first we were going to do an EP," she explains. "You've got two songs, I've got two songs, why don't we just put out a summer EP. Because of that suggestion, it opened his mind up, and he immediately wrote the rest of the songs.

"John used to love radio plays," she says. He had wanted to subtitle their *Double Fantasy* album *An Ear Play*. Yoko suggested *A Heart Play* instead, and that's what it became. Yoko recalls John "did mention in one interview that it's a heart play, a heart play with an ear in it."

Released in November 1980, three weeks before John's death, *Double Fantasy* won a Grammy for Album of the Year. One of Yoko's songs on the album, "Every Man Loves a Women," was reworked in 2004 with a dance mix that topped Billboard's dance chart and the *Everyman... Everywoman...* collection of 11 remixes followed in 2009.

"It's like a play and we're acting in it," John told *Newsweek* about *Double Fantasy*. "It's John and Yoko - you can take it or leave it. Being with Yoko makes me whole. We're like spiritual advisors."

During the so-called silent period, "John was writing music, primary for a musical called John and Yoko. There were a lot of different songs. Most of them were not sung from beginning to end."

I was fortunate enough to hear a cassette of these songs that Yoko lent me for a night, promising that I would not make a copy. The cassette included what would become "Free as a Bird."

Over lunch, at the old Kapalua Bay Hotel on Maui, we had reminisced about London and discovered a mutual appreciation for ancient Egypt and a particular temple in the desert where they and I had profound experiences.

Before the Beatles' *Anthology I* collection rocketed to the top of the charts, carried by a new recording featuring Paul, George, and Ringo performing with John on "Free as a Bird," the living Beatles had to seek Yoko's cooperation for the project.

"When the three of them approached me about it I had to go through a soul search about whether I should be doing this because these are cassette tapes that John recorded in his own private space," she explains during a 1996 interview. "I felt maybe it would be tampering, but then I felt it's like them reuniting. I started to look for a few appropriate songs."

Released in 1995, the Beatles' version of "Free as a Bird," included George Harrison strumming an 'ukulele at the end. Years later, Paul McCartney told *The Observer* that the musicians felt John's presence during the recording. "We even put one of those spoof backwards recordings on the end of the single for a laugh to give all those Beatles nuts something to do."

"'Free as a Bird' is an incredibly beautiful message to go around the world," says Yoko. "The world is getting a bit more violent, and people are getting depressed and a little frightened. Hopefully, this song can give people some inspiration and encouragement and awaken some love. I think John is a very good message. It's an easy message to understand for this generation than, say, reading the Buddhist scriptures or something. This is not to compare John with Buddha," she quickly adds, "but John is saying a lot of things that are very practical for this generation, and his vocabulary is more understandable for this century.

"He's really trying to honestly tell you through his experience. I think in that sense, it's very important that his message communicates. It's a very valid message that people can benefit from, and the message takes the form of pop songs that are easier to digest. He's a bigger power now, and this world needs that."

As to the essence of John's message? "Love," she says. "It's very simple, but there's nothing more."

As Russia's invasion of Ukraine escalated in March 2022, Yoko Ono promoted John's "Imagine" message, with large "Imagine Peace" LED billboards in major metropolitan areas, including London's Piccadilly Circus, New York's Times Square, and Seoul's K-Pop Square. With the message translated locally, other cities included Berlin, Los Angeles, Melbourne, and Milan. "Imagining is something that we can all do, even when we have different opinions about how to get there," Yoko said in a press statement.

"TALES FROM TOPOGRAPHIC OCEANS"

Yes

"'Close to the Edge' was close to the edge of realization."

"Hi, it's John Lennon," announced the Liverpool-accented voice on the phone to Alan White. Thinking it was a friend taking the piss, the future Yes drummer hung up. "He called back about 10 minutes later," recalls the British musician, "and said, 'it really is John Lennon. I saw you play in a club, and I think you'd be great for this gig I have to do in a couple of days in Toronto.' That's when I dropped the phone and fell off my chair."

"A limo picked me up, and there was Yoko and John at the airport, and then he says, 'I forgot to tell you Eric Clapton is playing guitar.' That's when Eric walked in."

The musicians headed to Canada for a legendary concert captured on the *Live Peace in Toronto 1969* album. "We didn't know what to play because we had never played together before," Lennon recalled in *John Lennon: Listen To This Book*. "We rehearsed on the plane," White continues. "I had a pair of drum sticks and played on the back of the seat." Capitol Records reluctantly released the concert album. According to Lennon, "they said, this is garbage.'" It sold gold.

That memorable gig led to the drummer recording at John and Yoko's Tittenhurst Park countryside estate in late May 1971, playing on the "Instant Karma!" single and *Imagine* album, featuring one of the most famous anthems of the 20th century. Lennon's best-selling single, it just featured backing by White and bassist Klaus Voorman, with added strings. "I didn't know it at the time, but it became the song of the millennium," he marvels. "The lyrics still stand up today."

After *Imagine*, Harrison subsequently snagged White to play on *All Things Must Pass*. White's Beatles' association led to Ringo Starr referring to him as "that other drummer." Then after touring Europe with

Joe Cocker and the Mad Dogs & Englishmen, he got a call to join Yes. "They said, 'we've got a gig on Monday, so you've got three days' (to learn all the material). Night and day, I listened to Yes music. All of a sudden, I was playing in front of 10,000 people in Dallas, Texas."

Acclaimed as a revolutionary pioneer of progressive rock, Yes was known for its electrifying musicianship, mystical lyrics, lengthy songs, and elaborate staging. The seeds of the group were sown in 1968 when lead singer Jon Anderson explains, "I was working in a bar above the Marquee Club, the famous rock 'n' roll club in London. I met Chris (Squire) in the bar, and we started rehearsing. People like Pete Townshend and Jimi Hendrix would wander in. I would be cleaning glasses and say hello, and the next minute I was touring with them with Yes.

"Our first major tour was with The Who, Rod Stewart, and the Small Faces, and we opened. We did about ten songs together around England, and Pete Townshend came over said, 'I think you have a great future. You're a great band.' All I could think was Pete Townshend is talking to me. In a year or two, we were getting great success."

The Who's guitarist was a major fan of the band, and as reported in *Close to the Edge: The Story of Yes,* he announced at London's Revolution Club, "this is the best fucking band you're gonna see. They've got a great singer and a great guitarist."

Beginning as a cover band devising elaborate versions of the Beatles' "I'm Only Sleeping" and the Byrds' "I See You," the innovative prog group first dazzled audiences with *The Yes Album* in 1971. Resplendent with virtuosic musicianship, it combined Anderson's striking falsetto vocals, complex, multi-part harmonies, layered guitar and bass parts, and swirling keyboards to launch classic songs such as "Starship Trooper," "I've Seen All Good People," and "Yours Is No Disgrace."

With the induction of flamboyant keyboardist Rick Wakeman, Yes found a virtuoso wizard who employed an entire bank of upwards of a dozen instruments, including Mellotron, various synthesizers, organ, two or more pianos, and electric harpsichord.

Fragile followed with more extended gems, including "Roundabout" and "Long Distance Runaround." "We wanted to do something a bit different," Anderson recalls. "We invented ourselves as we went along. I started listening to classical music, Stravinsky and Sibelius, and that's what inspired me to want to work along those lines. Steve Howe could play Spanish guitar, and Rick Wakeman was classically trained, and it all jelled together. Then we made *Close to the Edge,* which I think was the best of them. Since then, we've been up and down like a yo-yo."

The ambitious *Close to the Edge* comprised only three long tracks, including "Siberian Khatru," a rock adaptation of Stravinsky's "Rite of Spring," and the 19-minute title track, which mixed classical, psychedelic rock, pop, and jazz elements. *Time* magazine hailed it as "the most provocative album of the year."

Anderson was the primary composer of some of their most ambitious compositions like "Close to the Edge" and "Gates of Delirium." "We were lucky because in those days bands would play their music and do a lot of soloing, whereas we would do long pieces of music that were very structured like 'Close to the Edge,' 'And You and I,' 'Topographic,' and 'Gates of Delirium.' We created a style of music that was kind of unique, and we were so thankful that the fans enjoyed it."

The band was captured in all their glory on the brilliant, triple live *Yessongs,* featuring White drumming for the first time. Success continued with *Tales From Topographic Oceans,* another opus of four extended 20-minute-plus tracks, which topped the British charts and rose to number six in the U.S.

Tales from Topographic Oceans, with tracks like "Revealing Science of God," was inspired by Indian master Paramahansa Yogananda. "The percussionist with King Crimson gave me the book Autobiography of a Yogi," Anderson explains. *"It just spun my head around. It made me wake up."*

In the album notes, he detailed the influence of Yogananda's book. "It described the four-part Shastric Scriptures which cover all aspects of religion and social life as well as fields like medicine and music, art and architecture."

The acclaimed singer's emphasis on mystical elements in the band's music was initially inspired by meeting a spiritual teacher from Oahu. "It's so bizarre because most of it came from Hawai'i," he notes. "I was very lucky to meet a lovely lady from Honolulu who was known as the Divine Mother (Audrey Kitagawa). I was able to sit with her in Los Angels. I wasn't really interested in meeting gurus, and I really didn't feel close to any God-like energy until I met this lady from Honolulu. The first thing she said to me was, 'you know Jon, God is free,' and this light went on in my head.

"She's the most wonderful person, and me and my wife and children have been with her for 20 years. It's a wonderful connection with the divine. She taught me meditation, and I've been loyal to that energy ever since. There are so many different levels of connections to the divine, and I've always written about it in a more searching way. 'Close to the Edge' was close to the edge of realization."

Outside of Yes, Anderson released a number of mystically inclined solo albums. After spending time on Maui, where he got married, he translated his love for nature into a collection of songs on *Earth Mother Earth*, released in 1997. "My wife and I decided to spend a few months on Maui in order to write this album," he says. "It's acoustic music with me singing with the sounds of birds, insects, and the ocean. I had microphones out in the garden, me with just an acoustic guitar and Jane, my wife, singing about nature. We've just fallen in love with Maui, there's a beautiful energy there. It's a very special part of the world, being in the heart chakra. They say the Hawaiian islands are the heart chakra of the planet."

Feeling divinely inspired, he talks about contacts he has had with the fairy kingdom, native spirits, and angels. In 1977, he experienced a powerful mystical event that set the tone for his music and life. "I had a vision and met angels," he reveals. Visiting Las Vegas, he had just left a Frank Sinatra concert when a little girl came up to him and inquired, "are you ready Jon?" A mysterious man then joined him in a hotel room, which literally opened up to the heavens.

"The wall disappeared, and these people started slowly walking towards me. It was the light, and I started crying. They said I'd still be singing in the '90s about the light, just carry on singing about the light, and it will come through. It was a very powerful moment."

Among his memorable solo albums, he released *Survival & Other Stories* in 2010. Including tracks like "Unbroken Spirit," it was inspired by a close brush with death. "I went through this very serious illness," he reports. "My wife Jane saved my life twice in one year. I nearly died in Kaua'i."

Performing as a solo artist, Anderson delights audiences by presenting a spectrum of his music from Yes favorites to his solo work and mixing in covers like the Beatles' "A Day in the Life." "We used to do 'Every Little Thing' by the Beatles, and somebody said, 'why don't you do more Beatles' songs,' so I started doing 'A Day in the Life' on 'ukulele. I used to go almost every year to Kaua'i, and I bought a 'ukulele there for $25. I still play it, and it's still in tune.

"I love doing my solo shows. I got pretty sick on the last Yes tour, and after a few months, I thought maybe I should do a solo show. I went on stage and sang the songs I wrote for Yes, virtually the same way I wrote them. I was lucky I had so many fans everywhere. There's something magical as I can hear myself singing. With the band, you never knew if you could hear yourself."

Anderson released his latest album, *1,000 Hands: Chapter One* in 2020. Featuring some tracks originally recorded in 1990, the astonishing array of guest musicians included Chick Corea (on the title track), Ian Anderson, Jean-Luc Ponty, Billy Cobham, Edgar Winter, the vocal group Zap Mama, and the Tower of Power horn section, plus Yes band members Alan White, Steve Howe, Rick Wakeman, and Chris Squire. A spectacular video for his song "Ramalama" on the album included scenes of ancient Hawaiian hula kahiko.

So what was it like for him to be in a band with a massive international appeal? "It was a strange feeling," he says. "Everybody treats it differently. A couple of guys in the band were happy to be rock stars. I just wanted to work more, and I was interested in learning more about new styles of music and how world music was very important. And in the '80s, we had this incredibly big album *90125*. We toured the world, and we were number one.

"Right at the beginning of that tour, I went to see the movie *Spinal Tap*, and that changed my whole perception of what we were doing. You can't take it seriously. You can't be serious about being a rock star - you just enjoy it and put on a good show for the people because that's why you are there. Into the '80s, we were putting on some of the greatest shows that people had seen, and I'm really proud of that."

"DOWN BY THE RIVER"

Neil Young

"It is the heartbreaking story of one man who fought the corporate behemoth Monsanto."

When thousands of people around the world marched against the biotech giant Monsanto in May 2015, Neil Young participated on Maui, igniting Charley's Restaurant and Saloon in Paia, with a surprise gig backed by Lukas Nelson & Promise of the Real.

Blasting out songs from his incendiary *The Monsanto Years* agit-prop album, Young performed new compositions like "Big Box," which denounced monolithic corporations, and "Rules of Change," which decried the privatization of seeds.

Lukas and Micah Nelson, and the rest of the band seemed inspired backing the rock icon, and Young appeared especially energized playing with the young musicians. Micah reported, "Neil has been our hero forever."

Proceeds from the event were donated to local groups trying to halt GMO cultivation on the island. Monsanto (now Bayer) has a major presence on Maui growing GMO seeds.

Monsanto was busted for allegedly illegal spraying the banned nerve agent methyl parathion in 2014, just a short walk from beachside resorts in Kihei. "A teaspoon of methyl parathion would kill you," reported a U.S. government expert, "and several other people as well." Monsanto pled guilty and paid a $10 million fine in 2019.

Kaua'i-born activist Andrea Brower authored a revelatory doctoral thesis, "Hawai'i: GMO Ground Zero" which exposed the "agrochemical-seed-biotechnology industry's occupation of Hawai'i." She wrote: "For capitalist plantation agriculture to become the established norm in Hawai'i and displace the sophisticated production systems that preceded it, it took both imperial nations enforcing their commercial demands on the islands and the backing of a local state."

Neil Young played an acoustic version of "The Monsanto Years" with Promise of the Real at an "Outgrow Monsanto" protest event in Lahaina, while he was on Maui. Accompanied by Daryl Hannah, he joined residents planting sweet potatoes, taro, pumpkin, and tomatoes.

Talking about *The Monsanto Years,* before its release, Micah Nelson explained: "It's a concept album focusing on how corporations have essentially hijacked the American government. Neil is stating hard facts on this record. I hope it will spark public conversations about what's going on, at least get folks talking about it."

Young released a 10-minute short, *Seeding Fear,* about farmer Michael White, who took Monsanto to court. "It is the heartbreaking story of one man who fought the corporate behemoth Monsanto, and it illustrates why I was moved to write *The Monsanto Years,*" he said in a statement on *Facebook.*

The legendary rocker's connection to Hawai'i stretches back to the early '70s, when he joined his CSNY bandmates in Lahaina, composing new music, including "Hawaiian Sunrise." He later owned a three-acre estate on Hawai'i Island. In his autobiography, *Waging Heavy Peace: A Hippie Dream,* Young enthused, "there is a magical healing to the Big Island. Living in Hawai'i, with the horizon of the ocean meeting the sky, is soothing."

"MIDNIGHT RIDER"

Gregg Allman

*"Everybody was out with their bands, and I thought I can't
let them outdo old dad here, so I'll show them.
I don't know what I was thinking."*

When Duane Allman formed the Allman Brothers Band in
1969, his younger brother Gregg was the last member to
join. "My brother called me last," Gregg Allman recalled.
"I was in L.A. at the time, and he said, 'I've got this band, two drummers and two lead guitar players, and a bass player. I need you to come
back East and round this thing up and send it somewhere.'

"He said, 'nobody in the band writes or sings much, and by the
way, I need you to play a Hammond organ.' I'd sat down behind a
Hammond exactly two times in my life. I played a little bit of piano.
But when I got back, there was a brand new Hammond sitting there."

Growing up in Daytona, Florida, Gregg initially learned to play
guitar at 11 and gave Duane his first lessons. "I taught my brother just
how to get around the (guitar) neck, and he learned it in about two
weeks, being a natural musician," he said.

By 1960, they had formed the Kings, and a succession of groups
followed. "Somewhere down the line, you get tired of playing top 40
jive in some roadhouse," he continued. "So I started writing, and that's
what really hooked me on music."

His passion was sparked by attending some memorable shows by
greats such as Otis Redding, B.B. King, and particularly Ray Charles.
"I went to see Ray Charles live, and I almost went home and sold
everything I had. It was that good. He had about 14 horns and eight
Raylettes with him."

As far as significant influences growing up, he also singled out
R&B star Little Milton. "I met him two or three years before he died,
and we became real good friends. That was Little Milton Campbell.

117

I listened to Bobby Bland a lot and Johnny Guitar Watson, and of course Ray (Charles) and Curtis Mayfield, and obscure people like Garnett Mimms, who wrote the song 'Cry Baby.'"

Gregg Allman's shift from guitar to keyboards "had to do with my brother excelling so fast. He used to play rhythm guitar and sing, and we did a switch."

After graduating from high school, he had pondered a career in dentistry before he dived into music. "There were so damned many bands, the competition was crazy," he recalled. "So I kind of stuck to the idea I'd always wanted to be a dentist."

Gregg's powerful lead vocals, songwriting talent, and keyboard prowess perfectly complemented Duane's guitar virtuosity. The massively influential Allman Brothers Band ignited the entire genre of Southern rock. With their unique amalgam of rock, blues, country, and jazz flourishes, they expanded the boundaries of rock with legendary, extended onstage jamming.

The Brothers produced a number of superb albums, including the live *Allman Brothers Band at Fillmore East, Eat a Peach*, and *Brothers and Sisters*. "I like the live album a lot," he said. "I always have, and I think we all do. It's so spontaneous, the real thing, right there."

Along with playing with the Brothers, Gregg began releasing solo albums beginning in 1973, with *Laid Back*, which featured one of his most well-known songs, "Midnight Rider."

Feeling the need to express himself outside of the band, he explained: "The two deaths we had (Duane and bassist Berry Oakley) and everything. I'd come in off the road, and we had a hiatus almost. So I wanted to get it back together. It was my chance to do something with horns. I just love to play."

Allman's *Laid Back* displayed a mellower, soulful side than the Brothers' formidable rock jamming. Other solo works included the critically-acclaimed *Playin' Up a Storm* and *Searching for Simplicity* in 1997.

When the Allman Brothers Band took a break in 2007, Gregg decided to round up a bunch of friends to hit the road for a lengthy tour that made its way to Maui. "If you do it right, you can totally balance your life out," he said. "One good balance about this thing is coming out to Hawai'i."

At his Maui concert, he was impressed with local musician Vince Esquire, who opened the show. He subsequently invited the Maui guitarist to play with the Brothers at a Beacon Theater show in New York. A review of the historic night noted: "Thursday's show featured a cavalcade of guest guitarists, including Vince Esquire, who more than held his own with Warren Haynes and Derek Trucks on 'One Way Out' and 'Statesboro Blues.'"

The New York show led to an invitation to open some dates for Allman and play on his solo album *Low Country Blues*. During the recording sessions, Allman told Esquire how his guitar playing reminded him of Duane. "He said, the way I play reminded him a lot of his brother," Esquire reports. "He said the emotion and thought process behind it was very similar."

With his Friends band, audiences were treated to more of an R&B flavored approach with songs spanning his solo career, as well as funkier versions of Brothers' standards like "Whipping Post" and "Midnight Rider." "It's more of a real groove thing," he emphasized. "It's bluesy with songs from my six or seven records and some Allman Brothers' songs with re-arrangements.

Allman found it creatively enriching to explore different avenues of expression. "It's wonderful if you do it right, but if you do it wrong, you can work yourself to death," he suggested. "Everybody was out with their bands, and I thought I can't let them outdo old dad here, so I'll show them. I don't know what I was thinking."

Over the years many artists' voices become ravaged by time and abuse, but somehow Allman's voice remained remarkably untainted. A customized electronic device in his ears that blocked out sound helped preserve his voice. "I used to just use an earplug," he explained. "I got it from Muddy Waters. He said, 'I don't need no monitor, I put this cigarette butt in my ear, and I can hear my voice in the bone in my head.' I have this very expensive affair. The good thing is you can get through a week of gigs, and you wonder why your throat's not sore. It's because you're not screaming over all those damned guitars."

Allman said he was feeling happier in general. "I've got rid of my chemical problem. That's a lot to do with it. You just can't do that stuff, and I tried every way possible to make it work. That stuff started doing me, especially alcohol."

Since the early days of the Allman Brothers Band, the keyboardist has remained an avid fan of the traditional sound of the Hammond B-3 organ. "I love it to death," he enthused. "I've got six of them. Two are in the (Rock and Roll) Hall of Fame, two travel with me in this band, and two I leave with the Allman Brothers. You always have to have a backup."

And for a final question, one wonders if he's surprised that he's still going strong, having survived years of heroin and alcohol addiction and many rehab attempts? "Very," he answered. "I'm surprised I'm still going, and I'm so grateful for it."

Gregg Allman died in 2017 at the age of 69. Before his death, he recorded *Southern Blood* at the Muscle Shoals studio, where he and Duane recorded one of their first songs together before forming the Allman Brothers. "It's not often anyone has the (albeit heartbreaking) luxury of being able to map out their own memorial, and Allman leaves us with his head held high and a record of rare beauty," praised *Classic Rock*.

"ROCK AND ROLL ALL NITE"

KISS

"There's a myth perpetuated by journalists that real rock 'n' roll has to be lived dangerously."

"It was frightening in some ways," reports KISS co-founder Paul Stanley about the band's rapid ascent. "It's like being on the beginning of a roller coaster ride where you're being pulled to the top, and the only way you get out is when the ride is over. The momentum is going, and it's going to take its course. You better hold on tight, or you'll burn up real quickly, and there's no shortage of people around who want to become your friend by poisoning you with drugs or lies. I saw real quickly it was going to be my ticket to a great life or my demise. The idea of being a dead legend had no appeal."

It was Stanley who came up with both the band's distinctive name and logo. "You have these epiphanies, and I remember thinking it's probably a universal word that could be recognized everywhere," he recalls. "The logo is the exact one I did in my parents' house when I was 20 years old. We never had it redone."

A graduate of New York's prestigious High School of Music and Art, Stanley has tapped the lucrative celebrity art market, joining fellow musicians like Ron Wood, Ringo Starr, and Grace Slick, who have seen their artistic endeavors reap huge dividends.

Attending an exhibit of his work on Maui at Wailea's Celebrities Gallery, he took some time to talk about his artistic passion and his colorful life as a member of one of the world's most popular rock bands.

Besides art endeavors, Stanley and KISS co-founder Gene Simmons opened a Rock & Brews restaurant in Paia on Maui's north shore in 2014. It closed in July 2020 because of the pandemic. Simmons and his wife, Shannon Tweed, renewed their marriage vows on Maui at the sumptuous, tropical Haiku Mill setting in 2013.

From their inception, Simmons and Stanley had an ingenious concept for their band - performing in full theatrical regalia, including white pancake makeup with elaborate facial markings, platform boots, and outrageous black and silver outfits.

Fully costumed each member assumed an archetypal identity. Simmons was the tongue-flicking Bat Lizard, Peter Criss was the Cat, Ace Frehley was the Spaceman, and Stanley portrayed the Star Child. "It grew out of this idea of being larger than life and flamboyant," he says about his persona. "I wanted to project something that was glam and had real impact and said I'm the star."

KISS' ability to embody archetypal energies mesmerized legions of young kids. "There's something about KISS that's clearly timeless in the same way as Superman can apply any time," he muses. "I still remember so vividly in 1975, being in a New York City clothing store that had a little sticker of the *Destroyer* album cover, and a little boy went past it and said, 'Kiss.' I thought this is good. The legend grows larger as time goes on. It's so interesting because in the beginning, people wanted to believe that nothing this perfect could happen on its own, that somehow it was put together by some Madison Avenue team. It was just four guys who wanted to be the band they never saw, to be what we saw lacking in other bands, and to combine that."

Early in KISS' career, Gene Simmons realized that there was profit in aligning with their fan's longing for connection. "When we started, words like brand and marketing weren't in the common lexicon," he explains. "We just knew we wanted to go where no band had gone before. We were disappointed in rock bands, so why don't we put together the band that we never saw live on stage. We were clear the live concert was the be-all and end-all. Like a champion boxer, you get there by knocking everyone else in the way out. As soon as we started, we noticed fans started painting their faces like us, and they would make homemade T-shirts. It was like the football thing in England where it's not just a game; it's a gathering of tribes. You feel like you belong, and you want to wear your colors on the street and proclaim your allegiance. So the fans told us what they wanted."

Choosing to only appear in public adorned in their elaborate costumes and makeup had both advantages and disadvantages. "It was a blessing, but it was a disappointment in the beginning because we believed we would exist as KISS on stage, but also be around out of makeup," Stanley says. "It was our manager who came up with the idea that we should never been seen out of makeup.

"That was a little stunning because how were we going to get the accolades and recognition that we wanted. I can remember award shows where I would be at home watching on television because I wasn't going to sit in the audience with all the gear. And it was very interesting to go to a magazine stand and see all these covers with you on it, but it doesn't look like you. The idea that we had anonymity was mistaken because in or out of makeup, I was six feet tall with blue back hair down to my chest and platform boots. If you saw me on the street, I was either in KISS, or the circus was in town."

In 1983, Stanley insisted the band finally unmask. "I felt we had no choice," he says. "We had reached a point where it was becoming, if not a parody, it was losing its sense of identity. When we started losing members and coming up with new characters, it became like a menagerie. Should he be squirrel boy or turtle man?

Those who never idolized the band as fervent members of the KISS Army and the church of KISStianity, may not have grasped their phenomenal popularity. Iconic in stature, over their lengthy career, the band has sold more than 100 million albums worldwide, and they hold the record for the most albums charting simultaneously in the Top 100. Selling more gold records than any other American group in history, they created one of the best ever marketed rock brand.

KISS has more merchandise items and has generated more money from merchandise than any other artist in the history of music, with their ubiquitous logo emblazoning more than 3,000 products, from comic books, colognes, and credit cards to condoms and caskets.

"We'll get you coming, and we'll sure get you going," says Simmons, who was on Maui to promote the Paia Rock & Brews restaurant. "It (their brand) outsells the Beatles and Elvis combined. We have literally anything you could imagine."

At this point in the interview, Simmons opens up his iPhone to proudly regale me with pictures of all things KISS. "There isn't anything that we can't do because we refuse to follow anybody else's rules about who and what we are. We march to the beat of our own drummer. At the end of the day, we're like a wild animal that feeds on the ground and says, this is my territory, and fuck all of you."

"The truth of the matter is we would be idiots to put out anything that people didn't want," adds Stanley. "There are no marketing geniuses here, although one of us has a penchant for calling himself one. I think that the people who look down their noses at what we do are envious most of the time."

One wonders after so many years if rock stars ever tire of the all-consuming world of sex, drugs, and rock and roll? "There's a stereotype," he suggests. "Even when I was immersed in it, I said, you keep the drugs, I just want the sex and rock 'n' roll, and I was handed a ticket to a buffet. The drugs - I want to remember what I did. I think the whole stereotype when it becomes an ongoing lifestyle is pathetic. I see so many guys trying to live the life, but there's a big price to pay for it. There's a myth perpetuated by journalists that real rock 'n' roll has to be lived dangerously. I don't think that's the lifeblood of what makes good rock 'n' roll. It makes for a lot of sad stories and a lot of fans trying to emulate a myth. For every Keith Richards, there's a hundred Jimi Hendrixs."

"COME TO MY WINDOW"

Melissa Etheridge

"They couldn't say any longer – 'oh, we just played one woman on the radio.' It was impossible."

Having ascended to stardom with her double-platinum-selling debut album, Melissa Etheridge's memorable career highlights include an impassioned performance of Janis Joplin's classic "Piece of My Heart" at the 2005 Grammy Awards. Despite losing her hair from chemotherapy for breast cancer, she took the courageous step of performing live, even though she was exhausted from her debilitating treatment.

"I had the opportunity to stand up in front of the world," says Etheridge in a 2012 interview. "It was a personal thing for me, and it became quite a big statement for the rest of the world. When I was diagnosed with breast cancer months before, it was really a journey of crazy things over what does this mean? What's my life? What's my work? What's everything?

"Towards the end of my treatment, I got the call that I was nominated for a Grammy for *Lucky*, and so they asked if I would do this tribute to Janis Joplin. At first, I was, it just couldn't be done. I would be so weak. I am bald. But I thought I've got to jump back up on the horse. This is an opportunity for me to do a song that I have done half of my life, which I could do in my sleep, and I'm paying tribute to one of the artists I love. If I didn't do it, I would just sit there and be pissed at whoever was doing it, so I better go do it. It was exhausting, but it was cathartic."

Faced with life-threatening maladies, many experience transformation, forging new ways of being and a spiritual opening for Etheridge shifted aspects of her life. "That's what happened definitely," she reports. "There were moments of being completely alone and still. It hurt to watch television or to listen to anything. The chemotherapy was so hideous that those moments of quiet brought me great peace and understanding about life and what this is."

Citing authors like Don Miguel Ruiz and Ken Wilbur, she says, "I started to read some amazing philosophies and spiritual journeys, and I've been on one. That's what you're seeing in my music too."

The first album after her healing crisis, *The Awakening*, distilled her new insights. Addressing a diverse range of subjects from war and politics to religion and spirituality, she sang about deeper reality on the neo-psychedelic opening mantra "All There Is," the search for truth on "Message to Myself," and finding the divine within on "Kingdom of Heaven."

The Awakening closed with a trilogy of songs that touched on concepts such as the power of intention and the law of attraction. "I wanted people to understand," she explains. "It was sort of my life story in a little nutshell. I came out to California and found fame and fortune, but then life happened, and now I get it. Now I understand, and I believe. My path has changed, and I wanted to lead people to that."

A passionate, long-time activist for LGBTQ issues, breast cancer awareness, and alternative medical approaches, Etheridge continued her inner explorations on *Fearless Love*, a cumulative synthesis of her varied life experience and influences. "It's sort of my hopes, my dreams, my thoughts, my philosophy, my anguishes, the shadows, and musically a lot of my musical influences," she explains.

Mixing the personal and political, *Fearless Love* focused on the power of love vanquishing fear. "That's the philosophy part that I try to be living by day-to-day," she continues.

Among the highlights, one of the most intriguing tracks, the anthemic "We Are the Ones," was infused with Indian instrumentation. "In the last two years, I made friends with Salmon Ahmad, who was the lead singer with the Pakistani rock group Junoon," she explains. "I got very turned on by a lot of the music coming out of there. I realized how similar it is to our own blues melodies and our own music, so I wanted to put both of these together."

Born in Leavenworth, Kansas, in 1961, Etheridge began performing around the age of ten and later studied at Boston's Berklee College of Music. "I never wanted to do anything else," she recalls. "Even when I was a kid, one of my first memories was when I was about three years old dancing in front of the grown-ups and making them look at me. I did something, and they all applauded, and I was hooked. I thought this is it. This is what I want to do."

Often citing Bruce Springsteen as a primary inspiration, she initially fell in love with the Beatles. "It was the Beatles and the music of the '60s that really got me into it. I started playing when I was about 10 or 11 years old, covering country and Top 40 songs. I was playing in bands when I was about 13 or 14. Then Bruce came along when I was about 15. I didn't really hear him until *Born to Run*. He didn't reach Kansas until then, and it really changed my direction. It was like, wait a minute; I want to do it like that."

Etheridge eventually got to perform with Bruce Springsteen in 1995. They sang "Thunder Road" together on an episode of *MTV Unplugged*. "It's one of my favorite things I've ever done," she says. Springsteen had agreed to the duet after watching her perform "Piece of My Heart" at Joplin's induction at the Rock Hall of Fame in 1995.

A young female rocker working in a male-dominated business sometimes proved challenging. "Being a woman, the record company and myself ran into a few difficulties, but they were quickly overcome," she says. It helped that some strong women artists such as Tracy Chapman, Sinead O'Connor, k.d. lang, and Edie Brickell were also releasing potent music. "It was lovely. It was great that they couldn't say any longer – 'oh, we just played one woman on the radio.' It was impossible."

Coming out publicly as a lesbian at an LGBT ball following President Bill Clinton's inauguration in January 1993, she broke through to multi-platinum success with her fourth release, *Yes I Am*. "I think sometimes things line up," she says. "I think people were curious enough about the gay thing. They had heard the music, the grunge movement was in, and people were definitely giving time to real songwriters and their music. It was the times and the moment, and I just did what I loved. To me, I was going back to what I was doing on the first album, and it worked pretty well."

In 2019, she released *The Medicine Show*, which covered issues of health, wellness, and the benefits of medical marijuana (she has her own cannabis line - Etheridge Farms brand). It included the ballad "Here Comes the Pain" about the opioid crisis and "The Last Hello" about the Parkland School shooting survivors.

Asked about some of her career highlights over the years, she cites winning an Oscar for best original song in a motion picture for her composition "I Need to Wake Up," featured in the global-warming doc *An Inconvenient Truth*.

"Al Gore called me up and said that he had done this slide show and they were making a little documentary of it and would I like to do the music," she explains. "I had no idea it was going to be a major motion picture. I certainly had no idea I was going to win an Oscar for it. When I saw the path was leading to that (the Oscar), I was like, wow, cool."

TROUBADOURS

"DAY-O (THE BANANA BOAT SONG)"

Harry Belafonte

*"The role of art isn't just to show life as it is,
but to show life as it should be. I like to use my art to try
and help end injustice."*

Famous for introducing the lilting tones of Caribbean calypso to the American public, legendary musician, actor, and civil rights activist Harry Belafonte initially experienced tremendous opposition from his record company.

"There was huge resistance in the beginning at RCA because nobody in America knew about that kind of music," Belafonte recalls. "I went to the head of the company and explained the difficulty, and I was able to make the album. Then they shelved it for a while. But when another artist came out with exactly the same material, RCA released it, and it took off like a rocket. I was stunned by the inordinate success it achieved."

With the calypso craze dominating the charts in 1957, Belafonte became so popular he sold more records that year than Frank Sinatra and Elvis Presley. His smash *Calypso* album topped the charts, on and off, for an unheralded 31 weeks.

This renowned artist also captivated the American public as an actor in such 1950s films as *Carmen Jones*, *The World, The Flesh, and the Devil*, and *Island in the Sun*. But not all of America felt so enamored.

The theme of racial integration and the suggestion of a kiss between Belafonte and the film's white star in *Island in the Sun* aroused the ire of the Ku Klux Klan, which threatened to burn down any theater in the South which screened the movie. A South Carolina politician condemned it as "a sickening, repulsive, indecent spectacle," and the film was withdrawn from distribution in the South.

"The Ku Klux Klan existed, and America was legally segregated," he says, recalling the incident. "It was beyond just personal acceptance; segregation was a matter of law. For this film to play in a place which talked about integration in an affirmative way and to invite audiences to integrate and look at the film was hugely upsetting to Southern forces. But we prevailed."

Prejudice also trailed this American icon in the North. Married to a white woman, Belafonte could only rent an apartment in Manhattan after Eleanor Roosevelt wrote a syndicated column detailing his repeated accommodation denials.

Working with Martin Luther King, Jr., Belafonte endeavored to open up America and particularly the entertainment world to racial tolerance. "I saw very clearly that Hollywood was reflective of the mood and wishes of the nation," he says. "To try to change these institutions independently of what was going on in America was not a workable formula. We had to turn America around to turn these institutions around. When the civil rights movement did take off, Hollywood opened up, television, the music industry, and concerts halls all opened up."

During the McCarthy era, he was blacklisted as a Communist sympathizer, harassed by the House Un-American Activities Committee, and spied on by the F.B.I., who tapped his phone. Once secret documents revealed his manager was a government informant who claimed Belafonte "is a Communist and undoubtedly Peking controlled," and that "Belafonte, Martin Luther King and Mrs. King have for years been the willing tools of Peking." Legendary TV show host Ed Sullivan declined to honor the blacklist, and Belafonte appeared on his *Toast of the Town* program.

In 1968, during an appearance on Petula Clark's NBC special, while singing a duet of the anti-war song "On the Path of Glory," the British singer placed her hand on Belafonte's arm. It outraged an executive for the show's sponsor, Plymouth Motors, who demanded the song be re-shot. Clark insisted that it be aired intact or not be aired at all.

In a celebrated career that has spanned seven decades, Belafonte devoted his life and art to exposing injustice and helping those in need. "The role of art isn't just to show life as it is, but to show life as it should be," he emphasizes. "I can't stand injustice, and though I don't look for it, if it's there, I respond to it. I like to use my art to try and help end injustice."

Appointed by President John F. Kennedy as the first entertainer to act as cultural advisor to the Peace Corps, Belafonte began a long association with third world nations, which led to him initiating the famine-relief record "We Are the World" project, and USA for Africa, which poured funds into war-ravaged and drought-stricken lands.

Attending the Havana Film Festival in 1999, in a meeting with Fidel Castro, over dinner, he described meeting Cuban rappers who weren't officially recognized by the government and couldn't perform in Havana's clubs. Belafonte's enthusiasm, viewing hip-hop as an essential source of social change, inspired Castro to recognize hip-hop as a legitimate art form. Establishing the Cuban Rap Agency, Cuba's leader later described rap as the "vanguard of the revolution."

Born in Harlem in 1927 and raised during his formative years in Jamaica, Belafonte signed up for acting classes at New York's School of Drama after duty in the Navy during World War II. Walking into his first class, he met Marlon Brando, Rod Steiger, Walter Matthau, and Tony Curtis.

Impressing classmates with his singing voice, he was encouraged to audition as an intermission singer at Manhattan's legendary Royal Roost jazz club. His backup band included Charlie Parker, Miles Davis, and Max Roach.

During his rise to stardom, Belafonte experienced many charmed moments. His classic *Calypso* recording, which included the famous "Day-O" (the "Banana Boat Song"), became the first album ever to sell more than a million copies within a year. His 1959 live album, *Belafonte at Carnegie Hall*, spent the most time in the top 10 of Billboard's album chart until Michael Jackson's *Thriller*. Working in television, he became the first African American to win an Emmy and the first to produce a TV show.

"There's no question about it, my life has been replete with marvelous coincidences and a lot of luck," he says. "I have been very fortunate. Most people who have attained my level of success or bigger, who look on themselves as specially anointed, have deluded themselves. There are great artists who have not made it and are far better than I have ever aspired to be. It has nothing to do with talent or intelligence. A lot of it has to do with good fortune and luck."

Belafonte left Hollywood in the 1970s after starring with Bill Cosby and Sidney Poitier in the comedy *Uptown Saturday Night*. "I couldn't find anything I wanted to do, and much of the material was either mindless or extremely violent," he explains. "I think Hollywood has too much power, very little art, and is deeply insensitive to hues and significant social issues. As long as the greed and avarice, deceit and chicanery that makes that town what it is prevails, it's never going to be a happy place to be in."

A career renaissance in the 1990s saw him return to the screen in *White Man's Burden*. He won critical praise for his performance as the ruthless gangster Seldom Seen in Robert Altman's *Kansas City*, and in 2018, he played an elderly civil rights pioneer in Spike Lee's *BlacKkKlansman*.

Belafonte initially balked at playing a gangster in *Kansas City*. "My persona is so very different with the public," he notes. "To play this ruthless, immoral, violent, hateful character took me by surprise. Bob (Altman) said to me, 'Well, tell me Belafonte, who started this rumor that you're an actor?' That did it. I said, OK, from now on, it's your banana boat."

Interviewed before making his Maui debut fronting the multi-ethnic band Djoliba, he was asked about an *Ebony* magazine article, which posed the question, what he would like to be remembered for?

Belafonte answered with the quote, which he suggested be included here. He hoped "that others will learn that the exclusive acquisition of power and money is a remarkable waste of the journey of life. I would like in the end for it to be understood that he put his life in service."

"WE SHALL OVERCOME"

Joan Baez

"The most courageous thing I did for years was walk out on stage because I had such stage fright."

Joan Baez vividly recalls the pivotal day in 1956, when, as a 16-year-old, she first heard Martin Luther King, Jr. speak on nonviolence and civil rights at a youth conference. It ignited a fire that never dimmed.

"It was one of those life changes," Baez recalls. "Two hundred kids from all over the country came together to discuss what was going on in the world and what to do about it. When Martin Luther King, Jr. started to speak, I started to weep, and I couldn't stop. This man was doing what I had been reading about and talking about. I was basically blown away."

Seven years later, the folk music icon delivered an extraordinarily moving performance at the historic March on Washington for Jobs and Freedom - the pivotal day when King delivered his "I Have a Dream" speech - singing "We Shall Overcome" before more than 200,000 protestors. "I have a photo of myself from that day, and I look like a lion going into battle, ferocious," she says. "That's how I would get."

A lifelong social activist, raised by Quaker parents, Baez participated in the Selma-to-Montgomery march for voting rights in 1965 and protested the Vietnam War, releasing the 22-minute ballad "Where Are You Now My Son." She wrote "China" to condemn the massacre in China's Tiananmen Square and released the Spanish language album *Gracias a la Vida* in solidarity with those oppressed by Chile's dictatorship.

An influential member of Amnesty International since the 1970s, she sang to Occupy Wall Street protesters in 2011 and journeyed to the Standing Rock Sioux Reservation to protest the Dakota Access Pipeline.

When she was inducted into the Rock and Roll Hall of Fame in 2017, Baez announced: "My voice is my greatest gift. The second greatest gift was the desire to use it the way I have since I was 16 and became a student of and practitioner of nonviolence."

"I never considered myself to be a rock and roll artist," she says about the honor. "But as part of the folk music boom which contributed to and influenced the rock revolution of the '60s, I am proud that some of the songs I sang made their way into the rock lexicon."

Baez embraced the American folk music movement of the late '50s at the perfect moment. "The stars lined up," she says. "It was the right time at the right place and the right voice."

While playing Boston coffee houses, a musician friend invited her to join him on stage at the 1959 Newport Folk Festival. The performance generated praise for the "barefoot Madonna" with the extraordinary soprano voice. It wasn't long before she became the most popular folk singer in America. Appearing on the cover of *Time* magazine in 1962, she starred at the Monterey Folk Festival with her soon-to-be boyfriend, Bob Dylan, singing "With God on Our Side" to a cheering crowd of 20,000 folk fans. Headlining Newport in 1963, she closed the festival with Dylan, singing his epic song.

It was all a bit of a whirlwind, she says about her early star crowning. "When you are young, the idea of the future is the following Wednesday. I didn't see beyond where I was. I was living in Big Sur in a shack with my boyfriend. The only phone was down a hill in a lodge, and someone would yell, 'hey, your manager's on the line.' I had money but didn't understand it. One day I went to town to buy a flashlight and the kind of milk you mix with water to save money, and I ended up buying a Jaguar. The store was closed, so let's go round the corner and look at British Motors, and we drove out in an XKE. So it was a bit of a whirlwind."

Attaining almost mythical status as the Queen of Folk, one wonders if the mantle ever became a hindrance. "It was, but I didn't know it," she responds. "I had been so poor up to the switch that Madonna's looking pretty good."

While primarily known as a folk artist, Baez ventured into wider territory, including singing the Rolling Stones' "No Expectations" at the 1969 Woodstock Festival at six months pregnant, transforming The Band's "The Night They Drove Old Dixie Down" into a worldwide hit, recording the country-flavored *David's Album* in Nashville, and rocking with Steve Earle on her 2003 album *Dark Chords on a Big Guitar*.

Some of the stellar artists Baez has recorded with range from Bob Dylan and Kris Kristofferson to John Mellencamp and the Grateful Dead, while songs she has sung have been recorded by Led Zeppelin and Judas Priest. Jimmy Page and Robert Plant were inspired to cover "Babe I'm Gonna Leave You" on their debut album after hearing her folk version on *Joan Baez in Concert,* and Judas Priest covered her top-40 hit "Diamonds & Rust." "It's so rare that anyone covers anything of mine," she says. "I met (lead singer) Rob Halford of Judas Priest. I gave him a hug, and he said, 'you do know that we...?' He was nervous I wouldn't like it. I said it's great, my son told me about it."

Over the course of an extraordinary life promoting social justice, civil rights, and pacifism, this legendary artist feels especially grateful for helping inspire future Czech president Vaclav Havel. Invited to play a music festival in communist Czechoslovakia in 1989, she helped him avoid arrest.

When her microphone was silenced because she sang an anti-Communist song, she proceeded to sing a cappella for the 4,000 strong audience. She spoke in Slovak at the concert praising Havel and the attending human-rights supporters. Havel later cited her as a great inspiration and influence in his country's Velvet Revolution overthrow of Communism.

"It's one of the incidents where I did make a difference," she says. "It was very gratifying to see that in print when he wrote about it."

While there are many courageous moments in her life, she points out: "The most courageous thing I did for years was walk out on stage because I had such stage fright. It paled any political stuff I might have been doing."

As for the turbulent times we live in, Baez feels somewhat hopeful. "We've been waiting for years for people to have the feeling we had way back then, that brought us together, a feeling that the other one is there with you," she says. "It was missing. People would say, I want to do something, but I don't know what. And there was nowhere to go with that. Just about anywhere you turn now, there's something you can be a part of."

Asked about any special secret to her successful longevity, she offers a joke. "An old guy who won a record for being old was asked to what do you attribute your longevity and he says, 'sheer bad luck.' I wouldn't attribute that to myself, but it comes to mind. I didn't do drugs, I didn't do alcohol, and I did political action instead. That was probably healthier than if I had gotten into drugs and sex and rock 'n' roll. And I have reasons to be alive. I think we need to do what needs to be done. I can't tell anybody what to do, but I can say it's what has made my life rich."

"BURY MY HEART AT WOUNDED KNEE"

Buffy Sainte-Marie

"Johnson felt my music should be suppressed because it was subversive."

A dedicated activist since the early 1960s, when she released the iconic anti-war anthem "Universal Soldier," Canadian First Nations musician Buffy Sainte-Marie has helped enlighten many to injustice in the world, particularly with regard to Native American rights and environmental issues.

Born into a Cree family on a reservation in Canada's Saskatchewan province in 1941, she was raised by adoptive American parents. Her dedication to Native rights led Buffy to raise awareness through impassioned songs such as "Soldier Blue," about the 1864 Sand Creek Massacre, and "My Country 'Tis of Thy People You're Dying's" profound denouncement of North America's colonization. Her chilling song "Now That the Buffalo's Gone" was sparked by the government forcibly removing Seneca Nation tribespeople off their land in the 1960s, breaking a 1794 treaty authorized by George Washington.

The inventor of "Powwow Rock," on her remarkable 1992 album *Coincidence and Likely Stories*, Buffy drew attention to the ongoing mistreatment of Native peoples, especially on the harrowing tale "Bury My Heart at Wounded Knee." It detailed a litany of crimes, including the brutal murder of Mi'kmaq tribe activist Anna Mae Aquash and the incarceration of Leonard Peltier, whose case was championed by the Dalai Lama.

"All it is really is through the heart of a poet a list of the things that have already been reported but have never been put together that way," she explains on Maui for a whale symposium. "Our situation is the same the world over; whether it's the gold rush, the uranium rush, or the land or water rush, there's somebody who doesn't want you to interfere with their complete control of natural resources. Obviously, this is not the kind of song that's going to be widely heard. Songs like this can represent the truth, but in themselves, they're not going to do that much. They're only one brick."

Other songs such as "The Priests Of The Golden Bull" referenced the radiation poisoning of Navaho uranium miners, while the ferocious "Bad End" painted a chilling picture of domestic abuse.

Coincidence and Likely Stories continued her exploration of electronic music, which she had first developed on *Illuminations* in 1968, and the tribal themes covered on *Sweet America*. A reviewer described the provocative work as "the most compelling political pop music from America since Public Enemy's *It Takes a Nation of Millions to Hold Us Back*."

Technically revolutionary, she created most of the music on a Mac computer at her Kaua'i home, crafting mesmerizing sound collages by multi-tracking layers of Indian powwow singing. "It's just me eight or ten times," she says of the potent chorus that heightens the song "Starwalker." "I sing each powwow part in a different voice, like my cousin, auntie, or uncle, so it sounds like a genuine group. People will find things (on the album) that they can't get anywhere else, and it comes from such a real place in the world that I'm lucky enough to participate in."

With her earlier album *Illuminations*, she was the first musician to release a record with vocals processed through a Buchla 100 synthesizer and the first to record using quadraphonic technology. *The Wire* magazine would later hail it as one of the albums, "That Set the World on Fire When Nobody Was Listening."

Addressing issues that some would rather ignore, Buffy has dealt with record company indifference and media exclusion, most notably when Indian activists began confronting government suppression. "I'm real naive, so I didn't know what was going on," she says. "I had been on Johnny Carson's *Tonight Show* many times, then I was asked to come on, but not sing 'Universal Soldier' or 'Now That the Buffalo's Gone,' or talk about Indian people. So I no longer performed on that show. That's when I started to play more in Asia, Australia, and Europe, and my records disappeared in the U.S.

"Ten years later, I was approached by a radio journalist in Toronto, and he wanted to apologize to me for having been one of the many, who, supported by a letter from Lyndon Johnson's White House, had suppressed my music. Johnson felt my music should be suppressed because it was subversive."

It's hard to imagine that one woman's poetry could be deemed so threatening to a nation. Author Norbert Hill suggested that had Buffy not been blacklisted, she could have had a much more visible, successful career, and the entire Indian movement would have had a positive voice.

Buffy got her first guitar as a 16-year-old teenager, but not knowing how to tune it, she twisted the tuning pegs until it resembled the sound she heard in her head. She would tune the guitar strings differently for each song she composed (ultimately inventing 32 different tunings), which inspired fellow Saskatchewan musician Joni Mitchell to develop a similar technique.

Mitchell wrote the foreword to Andrea Warner's 2018 book, *Buffy Sainte-Marie: The Authorized Biography*. Praising her as "one of folk music's unsung heroes," Mitchell wrote how she would be enthralled watching her at coffee house gigs. "Her songs were so smart, so well-crafted, and her performances were stunning."

While attending the University of Massachusetts Amherst in the early 1960s, Buffy began connecting with other Native Americans, and traveling to Oklahoma, encountered rental signs warning "No Indians." Studying Oriental Philosophy and Religion, she read the *Tao Te Ching* and the *Upanishads* and became intrigued with classical Indian music.

Moving to New York, she began singing in coffeehouses in Greenwich Village. Her debut album, *It's My Way!*, was released in 1964, leading *Billboard* to name her the best new artist of the year. *Pitchfork* later praised *It's My Way!* as "one of the most revelatory debut albums of the 1960s."

It included "Universal Soldier," which was adopted by Donovan in the U.K., where it became a Top 10 hit. In time, Janis Joplin and Courtney Love, would cover her powerful anti-drug song "Cod'ine," from the album. "Until It's Time For You to Go," from her follow-up album *Many a Mile*, became a favorite for Elvis to perform in concert.

A multi-faceted artist, Buffy would turn to country in 1968 with her Nashville album *I'm Gonna Be A Country Girl Again*. A couple of years later, she enlisted Neil Young and Crazy Horse to back her on *She Used to Wanna Be a Ballerina*, which included a cover of Young's "Helpless" and Leonard Cohen's "Bells.'

With her groundbreaking album *Illuminations*, she collaborated with electronic music composer Michael Czajkowski, employing the Buchla 100 synthesizer. "Back then, she just strummed her guitar and you would swear that the room changed color," Czajkowski reported on first meeting her. "I don't know if you would call that musicality or mysticism."

In 1983, Buffy won an Academy Award for co-composing "Up Where We Belong" for the hit movie *Officer and a Gentleman*. She recorded her own version in 1996, backed by Kaua'i musician Pat Cockett on Hawaiian slack key guitar.

At the age of 74, she released *Power in the Blood*, which was declared the Canadian album of the year at the 2015 Polaris music awards. An epic work, a *NPR* review noted: "Those who know her mostly by reputation as a standout of the early '60s folk revival will be delighted to discover an artist who's more Bjork than Baez, more Kate Bush than Laurel Canyon."

The highlights included a stunning re-working of UB40's anti-apartheid anthem "Sing Our Own Song," which she transformed into a mighty de-colonization anthem, using a powwow sample by the Northern Cree drum group. She closed *Blood* with the uplifting prayer for our planet, "Carry It On."

Singling out the title track, which fused elements of powwow, electronic dance, dub, rock, country-noir, spoken word, and vocal distortion, *CBC Music* proclaimed *Power in the Blood*, "the defining Canadian album of our time."

Whether she's singing songs of protest or love, many have been influenced by her music. "A lot of young men would come to me and say you're the reason I moved to Canada," she recalls about the impact of "Universal Soldier." "They didn't want to participate in the Vietnam

War. And teachers will come to me and say they first found out about living Indians instead of dead ones through my records."

And then she laughs about those touched by her romantic side. "I wrote a song called 'Until It's Time For You to Go,' and people would say we got married and played your song. Then I wrote 'Up Where We Belong,' and I had people again telling me that was our wedding song."

Continuing to record empowering protest music, her most recent work, *Medicine Songs*, elevated her to a rarefied position that few veteran artists have attained. She keeps banging the drum, with incendiary songs like "The War Racket" and a re-working of "You Got To Run (Spirit of the Wind)" with Inuk throat singer Tanya Tagaq.

In the album liner notes, she wrote: "What troubles people today are still the same damn issues from 30-40-50 years ago: war, oppression, inequity, violence, rank-ism of all kinds, the pecking order, bullying, racketeering, and systematic greed."

"CARRY ON"

Crosby, Stills & Nash

"I believe we have brought happiness to people."

Settling in Lahaina on Maui in the early summer of 1973, David Crosby, Stephen Stills, Graham Nash, and Neil Young began working on a projected follow-up to their seminal *Deju Vu*. Tentatively titled *Human Highway*, half a dozen songs were later recorded back on the mainland. But then, the iconic quartet abandoned the project.

The planned album cover photo was taken by Nash one sunset at Lahaina's Baby Beach, using a time exposure. Crosby calls it, "my favorite shot of us." While some tracks surfaced on later releases, *Human Highway* was profiled by *Rolling Stone* as one of "15 Legendary Unreleased Albums."

The magnificent vocal fusion that defined the group's harmony-orientated, rock sound emerged in Joni Mitchell's living room one day. "It was so amazing, we actually stopped singing and started laughing," Graham Nash recalls. "David had just been thrown out of the Byrds, Buffalo Springfield had broken up, and I was coming to the end of a bad relationship with the Hollies. To hear this brand new sound that none of the three of us had ever heard was quite amazing."

Renowned for their intricate vocal harmonies, stellar musician-ship, and timeless songs, CS&N became the voice of the Woodstock generation. "I've always loved harmony and quality of craftsmanship and song, always trying to go for the song that means something, that actually says something," says David Crosby. "If you write songs about something, they have lasting value. If you write them just to get your ya yas off, they're fun to dance to and wiggle around, but they don't have that lasting connection."

While they were perceived as the first 1970s supergroup, all three musicians had felt discontented with their previous group affiliations and desired to create a less limiting association. "We tried to explain right off the bat that we had all been in different bands called the something, and we didn't want to be the something," says Nash. "We wanted to be David Crosby and Stephen Stills and Graham Nash. Next time it might not be only the three of us, but four of us, or only two."

Before he teamed with Crosby and Stills, Nash had spent years with the Hollies, the popular British group who scored an amazing total of 21 Top 20 hits in their homeland. Nash's gift for writing bright pop tunes helped CS&N with their early chart successes like "Teach Your Children" and "Our House." "It was expected the first couple of singles would be mine," he says. "I had come from the Hollies, and we were famous for wonderful, three-minute pop songs, and I guess my writing sensibilities had fallen into that kind of thing."

A resident of Kauai for many years, Nash loved living in Hawai'i. "I'm from Manchester, and all of a sudden, I end up in paradise," he marvels. "I'm thankful for being allowed to live in such a paradise as the Hawaiian islands. I've written a dozen songs on Kauai, including "Out on the Island," "Just a Song Before I Go," and "Wasted on the Way."

As a founding member of the Byrds, Crosby helped create and popularize the highly influential folk-rock sound. Known for crafting memorable songs with interesting tunings and unusual melodies, he explains: "I listened to a lot of classical music and a lot of jazz. It made me want to play kinds of chords that were difficult, and I really couldn't figure out regular tunings, so I started retuning the guitar to get different inversions of the chords. I just really enjoy doing that."

Beginning his career with Buffalo Springfield, Stephen Stills' landmark song "For What It's Worth," about L.A.'s Sunset Strip police riots, landed the band in the Top Ten. Crosby once proclaimed Stills was "the best guitar player alive," and Jimi Hendrix once praised him as the greatest guitarist he'd ever played with. Still's debut solo album marked the last time Hendrix was heard on record and the only one in rock history on which Eric Clapton and Hendrix both played.

Stills was co-owner of the Studio 505 club in Lahaina for a while. His Maui connection included playing guitar on Hapa's best-selling debut album, featuring Barry Flanagan and Keli'i Kaneali'i.

CS&N's collective emphasis on individual expression helped them survive. "We would have killed each other had we not (had freedom)," says Nash. "We all write so much, and on any one record, there are only 10 to 12 tracks, so ideally, there are three or four songs each. We write much more than that, so what do you do? If we were in a band where we couldn't record with Neil (Young) or James Taylor, or Jackson (Browne), we would have been crazy."

Since their early days, CS&N often created meaningful music with an activist edge. From "Find the Cost of Freedom" and "Ohio" to "After the Dolphin" and "To the Last Whale," the musicians championed a variety of key political and environmental issues.

Crosby has long been known for his dedication to social activism. His interest in the power of music to foster change led to his book and documentary *Stand and Be Counted: A Revealing History of Our Times Through the Eyes of the Artists Who Helped Change Our World.* "I've had a fascination with music and activist rights from encountering the Weavers and Odetta and people like that," he says. "It went from there to civil rights, women's rights, human rights, anti-nukes, and anti-war. I've had these good examples like Pete Seeger and Woody Guthrie, and Joan Baez, people who really stood up for what they believed in and really put their lives on the line. Harry Belafonte walked with Dr. King in Selma and Montgomery with rifles in the bushes. It's very inspiring. Human beings can be incredibly inspiring. One act of exemplary humanity can do so much good in terms of leading you to do what's right."

Among the causes Crosby and Nash have championed over the years, the duo journeyed to New York City in 2011 to perform at an Occupy Wall Street rally. The *Occupy This Album* included a powerful, live version of Crosby's song "What Are Their Names." "I'm just not built to sit down and shut up," Crosby emphasizes.

Nash's newer protest songs included "Almost Gone," about whistleblower Bradley Manning, and "Don't Dig Here," about a potential nuclear waste dump site at Nevada's Yucca Mountain. And there's Nash's "Burning for the Buddha," "one of the best protest songs we've ever done in our lives," says Crosby. Highlighting Tibetan Buddhist monks who have immolated themselves as a protest against Chinese oppression, "it's a stunner," adds Crosby.

Crosby and Nash last recorded a studio work together in 2004 for a wonderful double album that included the Nash song "Penguin in a Palm Tree," which mentions hanging out in Lahaina on Maui. "It comes from me describing him that way," says Crosby laughing. "I said he was such an odd duck, like a penguin in a palm tree, being an Englishman in Hawai'i. He's an incredible human being and the best harmony singer alive."

Having sold millions of records, the power of CS&N's has not diminished over time. "We're not a glamorous rock band, so it has to be the quality of the music and the timelessness of the music," says Nash reflecting on their longevity. "When I'm on stage, and I look down into the audience and see 14-year-old kids singing the words to songs that were conceived before they were born, it's a real thrill."

Nash hopes that their music can still offer some solace and inspiration. "This planet is huge, and it has a certain momentum, so to be able to change the direction of the planet and the people is a difficult job. But I do believe we have brought happiness to people. I believe we have helped make them feel less crazy, less alone, and more loved."

"HOTEL CALIFORNIA"

Eagles

"Some people think the Eagles were this sort of intense, dark, boiling cauldron of personalities."

Drive north on Maui's west side, along Lahaina's Front Street, and you will pass a church with a neon sign announcing - "Jesus Coming Soon." Eagles' fans will recognize a reference to the sign in *Hotel California*'s epic final track, "The Last Resort," which vividly evoked the colonialist destruction of Native cultures.

The Eagles sang about sailing to Lahaina, just like the missionaries in the 19th century, who came to Hawai'i to do good, as the local joke goes, and did great financially. "We had been to Maui a few years before we wrote the 'Last Resort'," Glenn Frey explained. "Don (Henley) and I were on Maui, I think in 1974 or '75, maybe the first time we went outside of Honolulu. You gather these experiences, and sometimes they end up in songs. That song is a journey. It's quite an opus."

One of America's most popular bands, the Eagles helped define the Southern California sound of the 1970s. As *Rolling Stone* noted, they "specialized in broadly appealing, masterfully crafted tunes."

Selling more than 100 million albums, Eagles' songs like "Hotel California," "Life in the Fast Lane," "Peaceful Easy Feeling," "Desperado," and "The Long Run" are still routinely played on classic rock radio stations across the nation. *Their Greatest Hits (1971-1975)* album was the best selling record of the 20th century and still stands as the top selling album ever in the U.S.

How popular are they? Drive through Winslow, Arizona, and you'll encounter a bronze statue commemorating the guy standing on a corner in the Eagles' first hit, "Take It Easy." A life-size bronze statue of Glenn Frey was added to Winslow's Standin' on the Corner Park in 2016.

A documentary on the band, *History of the Eagles*, released in 2013, traced their evolution from formative days to mass chart success, their demise in 1980, and triumphant reformation in 1994. Frey said the musicians felt it was finally time to shed light on the checkered path of the group.

Unlike some sanitized biographies, *History* is definitely not sugar-coated, as it illuminated both the highs and lows of the band's career. "There's much speculation about the Eagles because we didn't really say a lot about what we were doing," said Frey. "We didn't explain everything. So this was an opportunity to shed some light on the band. Another thing I took away from the film was how much fun it was. Some people think the Eagles were this sort of intense, dark, boiling cauldron of personalities. It may well have been, but one thing I remember was how much fun it was."

Raised in Detroit, after moving to Los Angeles, when he was invited to tour with Linda Ronstadt, Frey suggested the addition of drummer Don Henley. "When we first met, it was Don, Glenn, and I, and we did a couple of backup gigs with Linda Ronstadt," recalls Eagles' bassist Randy Meisner, while vacationing on Maui. "It felt like a good nucleus for a band. Shortly after that, Bernie (Leadon) left the Burrito Brothers, and we latched on to him."

At the time, bands like the Flying Burrito Brothers, Poco, Buffalo Springfield, and the Byrds were important players of what was dubbed the L.A. Sound, which mixed folk, country, and rock. The Eagles would take that sound and soar higher than any predecessor.

The band's first single from their debut album, "Take it Easy," written by Frey and Jackson Browne, entered the Top Ten, and two other singles were hits, the irresistible "Peaceful Easy Feeling" and "Witchy Woman."

As a follow-up, the band devised an old Western-themed concept album *Desperado*, which, while it's now viewed as one of their masterpieces, was derided (as revealed in the documentary) by one of their record labels executives as a bunch of cowboy music.

"We were really helped by Linda Ronstadt recording 'Desperado,'" said Frey. "It was a big boost for the song again and re-stimulated the album. It

was one of the first songs that Don Henley and I wrote together. It's just a treasure in our catalog."

How do they approach songwriting together? "Don Henley is one of the most well-read people that I know, and I used to jokingly sit down with him and say Don, what's pissing you off? They (songs) usually come out of conversations. We're very comfortable talking with each other, and sometimes he will have song ideas or titles, and I will have song ideas or chords. We just start talking and stirring the pot a bit, and usually, something happens."

With the release of the Grammy-winning *Hotel California* in 1976, the Eagles conquered the world. The album was certified platinum in one week and eventually sold more than 30 million copies worldwide. The singles "New Kid in Town" and "Hotel California" hit number one, and "Life in the Fast Lane" made the Top 20.

Recalling his time with the Eagles, Meisner says, "it was fun in the beginning, but towards the end, it got hectic. After *Hotel California,* I thought it was time to leave. It wasn't that relaxed friendship we had together."

Meisner's "Take It to the Limit" is considered one of the band's greatest songs. It's his favorite composition. "With the Eagles, it was always one of the biggest ovations we would get," he notes.

Inspired by Linda Ronstadt, Frey released his last solo album, *After Hours*, in 2012. "Linda made some records with Nelson Riddle, and they were just beautiful records, immaculately assembled with not a note out of place," he explained. "When I played with Linda, she was basically a country rock singer. Once she attained some success, she went out and showed all of us that there's more to life than pop music. She put no limits on the journey she wanted to take. I was inspired by that. I wanted to make this kind of record for a long time."

On his first solo album in 20 years, he covered classic love songs including standards like "Sentimental Reasons" and "My Buddy," along with more recent tunes like the Beach Boys' "Caroline, No" and Randy Newman's "Same Girl."

Did he have any apprehension about taking on iconic material? "You feel like you're sort of a caretaker, and you don't want to mess anything up," he reported. "My approach was respect for the material and be true to the melody. It wasn't like I was going to change very much in the way the songs are. My intention was to not goof anything up."

After decades of crafting Eagles' music, Frey said he still felt pretty amazed that their music is so loved. "Every time I walk on stage, I'm reminded of that. It's just a very good feeling to know that I'm still able to go out and perform either by myself or with my friends. It feels good."

Following Frey's death in 2016, Don Henley posted: "Glenn was the one who started it all. He was the spark plug, the man with the plan."

"NICK OF TIME"

Bonnie Raitt

"We're here on the earth to give back. We're here to promote love and ease conflict."

For more than five decades, Bonnie Raitt has consistently produced spellbinding music, an infectious amalgam of blues, rootsy rock, funk, and gorgeous balladry that has earned her widespread acclaim. One of the most admired female musicians performing today, Raitt is loved for her soulful singing, captivating songwriting, and exceptional guitar playing.

Blues legend B.B. King once proclaimed her, "my favorite slide guitarist." "That was the greatest compliment I could ever get in this life," says Raitt. "If I happen to be his favorite, I'm so proud to know how happy I make him. I know he's sincere because he's told me in person for years, and then he said it public."

While female blues singers were common when she began making records in the early 1970s, female blues guitarists were rare. Her passion for slide guitar began in her teen years. "I heard it on a *Blues at Newport* album when I was 14, with John Hammond playing, and Robert Johnson's *King of the Delta Blues* record came out in my teen years as well," she recalls. "It always sounded like a human voice, like an extension of your heart and soul. It was so evocative and so unique, like an eerie kind of voice usually in the middle of these hellish grooves. I first fell in love with Delta blues, and then when I heard the electric blues of Elmore James and Muddy Waters, I just went crazy for it.

As a child, she remembers listening to her grandfather play Hawaiian lap steel guitar. "He was a Methodist minister who wrote over 500 songs," she explains. "He taught my mom to play, and we'd go over on Sundays, and he taught me how to play it. He put my hands on it and showed me how I could just move the silver bar across an open tuning. I was already familiar with that by the time I was six or seven.

"But I never made the connection with that instrument and the one I ended up playing until years later. Maybe there was something in my childhood that made me like that sound. The same reason why I love Hawaiian music is the reason I love slide and blues. It can be so mournful and joyous and sensual."

Raised in an activist Quaker household, she grew up believing in helping others and supporting causes. "My folks were really drawn to the idea that there was so much more engagement of the principles of easing suffering and being there for your fellow man," she says. "We're here on the earth to give back. We're here to promote love and ease conflict.

"The Quakers have had a tremendous history of standing up for non-violence and for conflict resolution and finding God in the other no matter how odious they seem. It's the practice of what Jesus taught and what Buddha taught and Muhammad. Whatever tradition, they all talk about respecting life and increasing love and peace between people.

"We collected money for refugees when I was a little kid, and I learned about the Hiroshima Maidens who came to a meeting and got to see the effect of the nuclear arms race was going to have. I refused to do the 'duck and cover' exercises because I was not going to give into this. I went to the March on Washington to stop the arms race and was active with civil rights groups and promoting Ban the Bomb and all that.

"When I was growing up, the civil rights movement was a big part of why I was involved with wanting to sing and emulate my heroes Joan Baez, Bob Dylan, and Pete Seeger. I picked up the guitar basically because of the Ban the Bomb movement and the civil rights movement, and really loving the tradition of the troubadour singing the conscience of the people, as well as just loving the ballads Joan Baez would sing and Motown records I'd hear on the radio, and the Beatles and the Stones. The tradition of being involved and doing benefits is something I've done since the first concert I gave."

Protesting the Dakota Access Pipeline with the Standing Rock water protectors in 2016, "was a fantastic, spiritually galvanizing experience," she says. "It was a very powerful weekend to go there and play the concert with friends (Jackson Browne) and reunite with so many great activists. We participated in ceremonies and prayer. It was one of the most moving, transformative experiences I've had in my whole life of activism. It had a power to it that was so spiritual. A lot of people there were healed personally. A lot of Native American kids were just transformed by being able to stand up like that for something. Regardless of what happens with the pipeline going forward, the coming together has set something in motion that no one will ever go back from. It was very beautiful."

Performing over the years on Maui, she donated the fee from one of her concerts to the Harold L. Lyon Arboretum, which preserves endangered native plants, and 'Ahahui 'Ōlelo Hawai'i, which works to ensure the vitality of the Hawaiian language. "I've spent a lot of time on Maui, and I like to give something back," she notes. "I feel a real connection, and it's important to support the local groups that are trying to keep traditional culture alive and keep the ecosystem protected. The development side certainly doesn't need a benefit."

Her connection to the island includes her Maui-based bassist James "Hutch" Hutchinson, who has played with Raitt since 1983. "There's nobody more versatile," she enthuses.

The Waianae Boys and Girls Club on Oahu was also a benefactor of her generosity when she donated $15,000 worth of guitars and accessories. The gift was made possible by a national program set up by Raitt and Fender guitars to provide disadvantaged kids with music instruments.

"I bought a Fender Stratocaster in 1969, and I've played it at every gig since then," she says. "Fender approached me about making a customized signature guitar. I wasn't interested in selling product, but I thought about using the profits from the guitar to help pay for free music lessons, especially for girls, but boys too. After all this time, there's not enough female lead guitar players. I'm hoping with the whole onslaught of alternative women musicians, young girls will have someone to look up to."

The broad scope of her material has long made Raitt's albums highly appealing. Reviewing her live album *Road Tested*, *Downbeat* magazine noted: "She may be the only artist who can effectively cover both Mississippi Fred McDowell and Talking Heads on the same night." And reviewing her 2022 album, *Just Like That*, *The Wall Street Journal* praised: "Along with Van Morrison, Raitt is one of the great song interpreters of the rock era."

Often mixing original compositions with covers, approaching a new recording project, she explains: "The first thing I want to do is to find more great songs to add to my show and to add to my repertoire for the fans and my band, so we get excited about playing some new music. And it's trying to find some grooves and lyrical topics that I haven't covered before. Every song that I've ever sung has to speak to me lyrically. It has to come from the deepest part of me, otherwise, it's not going to ring true."

For her 2005 album *Deep Water*, along with joyful rockers, soulful funk, and moving ballads (including the achingly beautiful "So Close"), Raitt delved into some edgy, experimental territory with the swampy groove of the title track and the starkly angular "Crooked Crown." "You don't want to just repeat yourself and reinvent 'Something To Talk About' or a blues tune over and over," she says. "I've got to find something fresh to keep it interesting. When I played 'Deep Water' for my band, they went, 'you've got to be kidding.' I said no, it's right up my alley. It's one of the coolest things.

"'Crooked Crown' is an unusual song, but the lyrics were so tailor-made for what I feel about what it's like to be in this position. I was looking for something new to say and some different grooves to say it in, and those two songs are the most unusual things I've ever recorded. I'm really proud to stretch and have it work. I don't want to be in a box. That just makes artists want to go off and do pottery."

Raitt was a member of the Women's Voices for Peace Choir in 2008, with Joan Baez, Phoebe Snow, Odetta, Holly Near, and Jane Fonda singing on Maria Muldaur's *Yes We Can!* album of protest and peace anthems. Backed by the funky Free Radicals band (including Maui's "Hutch" Hutchinson), Muldaur brilliantly recast classic songs like Dylan's "Masters of War," Edwin Starr's "War (What Is It Good For)" and Marvin Gaye's "Inner City Blues."

The album closed with the inspiring "Everyone in the World" by Indian spiritual teacher Amma. "Bonnie and I went together to see her," Muldaur recalled. "I spoke through an interpreter, and the whole time, she's hugging and blessing people because a woman saint has to be multitasking in every minute. We took her recording of 'Everyone in the World,' and I recorded myself, Joan Baez, and Holly Near over it. It was very moving."

While Raitt's political leanings are evident in her activist work, she rarely spells out her views on record. She didn't hold back on her 2016 album *Dig in the Deep,* railing against politicians' spinning facts and playing people on the hard-driving "The Comin' Round Is Going Through." "It's many years of money controlling too much of what goes on in Washington and too many Congresspeople and legislators bought," she says. "Whether it's big pharma or the environment or the press, it's all controlled by money. People are sick of business as usual. I wrote that song for everybody that is upset about how broken the system is by money controlling too much, and too many lies and too much b.s."

She closed *Dig in the Deep* with "The Ones We Couldn't Be," one of the most profound, heart-breaking ballads she has ever composed. "It's about regret and coming to terms with your own part as to why relationships were tough," she explains. "Everyone tries as hard as they can at the time, and I'm sorry for the one I couldn't be for them, and I know they were sorry for who they couldn't be for me. That song is written both about family members and a romantic history. It was hard. I only sang it one time, because like 'Wounded Heart' or 'Love Has No Pride' or 'I Can't Make You Love Me,' those songs cut as deep as they could possibly go, and that's why I picked them. This one I wrote is even more personal. I'm a Celtic red-headed girl, so I write in this style of music on the piano. The ballads I've written that cut the deepest I do on the keyboard because it's very emotional."

Sometimes feeling drawn to crafting and recording songs that reflect spiritual themes, Raitt explains, "There's a song called 'Cool, Clear Water' and elements of 'Nick of Time' and one called 'All at Once,' that are as much to do with the bigger kind of love as romantic love. There's a duel, prayerful aspect to them. 'Valley of Pain' on *Silver Lining* and 'Shadow of Doubt' on *Longing in Their Hearts* are really out and out prayers. It's a tricky thing to incorporate spirituality without sounding too corny or pedantic. Spirituality is really important to incorporate in the whole way you are in your political activism and the way you treat people and your band and the way you treat your lover and walking it like you talk in your everyday life."

During a time when she was facing the death of her father and mother and assisting her brother with brain cancer, Raitt found solace in some inspirational works like Eckhart Tolle's *The Power of Now*. "Going through my parents' illness and passing and my brother's illness that brought me tremendous heart opening and rethinking," she says. "It was very powerful to learn to be in the moment when you're dealing with an illness and people suffering. It was a great comfort. I do a lot of meditation and group sitting. It's helpful to know that most of what's negative is really not real. It's all a question of point of view. There are always good books that open doors like *I Am That* (by Sri Nisargadatta) and Ram Dass' books, and *The Power of Now*."

As for helpful prescriptions, she cautions about limiting one's diet of negative news. "You can poison your spirit by taking in too much negativity and watching the news more than getting informed," she advises. "I have to stay informed as an activist, but there's an addictive nature to just getting repeats of the same broadcast over and over between the newspaper and television news and radio. I personally don't spend a lot of time on the negative and see what I can do to bring about a shift in my personal life, seeing how many people I can help on a one-to-one level. I'm very lucky that through my singing and benefit work I'm able to raise money for causes."

"SWEET BABY JAMES"

James Taylor

"Music gives us relief from the prison of the self."

When the Woodstock Music Festival organizers began selecting the entertainment lineup, they had hoped to lure John Lennon to perform. Unfortunately, the legendary Beatle couldn't fly to America because of a drug bust, but folks at the band's Apple Records wondered if they would like James Taylor instead.

Why would the Beatles' label offer to substitute an American folk singer who was barely known at the time? They were fans.

Before Taylor shot to stardom in 1970 with his seminal recording *Sweet Baby James*, the future multi-Grammy-winning artist had traveled to London at a fortuitous moment. Inspired by the revolutionary spirit of the time, the Beatles had launched their own record company and sought to promote new talent. "I was the Beatles' fan of the world," Taylor enthuses. "I listened to everything so carefully and emulated as much as I could and sort of incorporated it."

Auditioning in front of Paul McCartney and George Harrison, Taylor became the first non-British artist signed to Apple and had the honor of having the first non-Beatles album released by the label. "I played them 'Something in the Way She Moves,' and they said, 'fine, let's go, we'll sign him.' It was amazing. At the time, the Beatles were recording the *White Album* at Trident Studios in Soho. They block-booked a two-month period to make the *White Album*.

"I was coming in between the times they were in the studio. When they would knock off and go to sleep was when I would get up and record, so I overlapped with a lot of those sessions. I was a fly on the wall, and George and Paul played on a couple of the songs on my first album, so yes, it was the mother of all big breaks. Dreams do come true."

The quintessential American singer/songwriter Taylor first came to prominence with his album *Sweet Baby James*. With an effortless,

156

acoustic-based blend of folk, R&B, and jazz influences, Taylor established a distinctive, easy-going style. Sometimes expressing feelings of alienation and restlessness, the gifted composer found a huge audience readily identifying with his sagas.

The composer of such treasures as "Fire & Rain," "Sweet Baby James," "Something in the Way She Moves," and "Carolina In My Mind" has kept his music vital by reaching inside his classics and rearranging them with a contemporary sensibility. "It just happens automatically in the process of playing and rehearsing them," he explains. "It's good to put in extra time so you can experiment with new things before going out. It's nice to change things up."

Moving people with his songs, he says: "In the beginning, I was mostly singing and playing to express myself and to just put myself in the world. The idea of people responding to it is something that comes if you're lucky enough to develop an audience. It has been an amazing constant throughout the years that people come to me and take me aside and tell me that the music has been really important to them at a particular stretch of their life, or that they associate it with certain times. That's probably the most rewarding thing about it that something that was useful to me and very fulfilling for me has also resonated with other people.

"I start with something that's compelling for me, something I feel really moved to express. Often it's very personal and what happens is that in the process of working that out myself, it's useful for other people in the case of some songs. They resonate with them too. It never was sort of a strategy. It wasn't premeditated. It just sort of happens that way. Sometimes I think it's a little too close for comfort in terms of how personal it is, but it's really the way I work. I'm a very sort of unconscious songwriter. I feel as though I am visited by things that are happening to me. Things feel like they get channeled through me. It's very mysterious and out of my control.

"I feel I don't really write the songs. I'm just the first person to hear them. There is a phase of writing a song where you get a certain amount of it for free; it just gets visited upon you. And then you have to work on it and flesh it out and make associations with other musical scraps from here and there and tie it together to make a song.

157

Sometimes you'll get a song that's like Venus on the Half-Shell. It's full-blown, it springs to mind. A song like that is a gift."

Sometimes dreams and sleepy states have spawned gems. "I once wrote a song called 'Millworker,' which I wrote about three o'clock in the morning," he recalls. "I woke up, went downstairs, picked up a pen and pencil, and it came in about 15 minutes, and I went back to bed. I felt as though it came from a dream. Often losing consciousness and coming back with something is part of writing. When I hide myself away, I like to be able to fall asleep and, often, I will come up with something if I'm stuck."

One of his most compelling songs, "Only a Dream in Rio," was composed after a dark period, coming out of rehab. It was prompted by a life-changing trip to Brazil, where he played to 300,000 at the Rock in Rio festival.

"In 1983, I had to sober up. It took me about a year. I had bottomed out. I had had it with my addiction, which had basically been running me for about 20 years. They seem like your best friend at the beginning, and you're the last person to realize it's just killing you. I was pretty much down and out, and I took this job in Rio de Janeiro. I happened to go down there at the very moment the country was electing its first popular, democratically elected leader in 20 years. The country had been under the iron fist of a military junta for 20 years, and I had been addicted for about 20 years. I got sober, and I went down there.

"I was a huge fan of Brazilian music, Jobim, Gilberto, they meant the world to me, and you can hear it in my music. It's very influenced by Brazilian bossa nova. So I go down there, and I have no idea whether there's going to be any response to my music, and 300,000 people are singing my songs back to me. It came at just the right time for me. It was such an affirming thing, such a positive slap on the back.

"After the show was over, Caetano Veloso, a phenomenal singer, he and his wife took me to the strangest nightclub you ever saw called the Flying Circus with pipe scaffolding, and people would climb into the structure of the scaffolding. So it was filled with people from top to bottom, as well as side to side. There were people there to celebrate the election and people who'd been in exile like Caetano Veloso, people who hadn't been allowed to play their music for political reasons. I'd never seen an audience in such an excited state.

"The combination of the soccer stadium with 300,000 people who knew my music and this celebration of the country coming back to life that's what the song is about. That was what sparked it. It's was one of those moments where everything comes together, like the Beatles in 1968. When I checked into the hotel, there was a guitar that Gilberto Gil had left in my room. I opened up the guitar case, and the song was in there. It started coming out of this guitar. It was great."

Beginning in 2008, he released a couple of *Covers* albums. "Some of the songs I've lived with for many years, and I've had versions of them on my guitar, and some of them I've played live with my band but never recorded," he explains. "We got those sessions with 12 players playing at once. It was a very live album, everything happening at once with really no overdubbing."

His most recent record, the Grammy-winning *American Standard*, featured reimagined versions of classics like "The Surrey With the Fringe on Top," Hoagy Carmichael's "The Nearness Of You," and Billie Holiday's "God Bless The Child," all sung in his impeccable, soulful style.

Passionate about environmental and social issues, he has supported the work of the NRDC, the Natural Resources Defense Council. "It's clear that the whole process of government is extremely dysfunctional and paralyzed, and it's very difficult to make changes after a long period of empowering the people who create the problem," he says. "I wonder if things ever change until they get desperately bad."

Reflecting on the state of the planet, he suggests we need saving from ourselves. "It seems like the main challenge for most living beings on the planet. Just surviving is something we've managed really well. The problem for us is to be able to control the degree to which we can affect our planet. I think over and over again it's going to come up as time goes by as the main issue. To me, what it really comes down to is the nature of human consciousness, individual as well as special (species). It's the conflict between our special existence, which is our connection to the planet, and the individuated consciousness, that we live in that is so important to us, our own particular lifestyle and life span. The conflict between the two is a very human dilemma."

During fractured times, we're fortunate that we have access to concerts where we can collectively celebrate in unified joy. "It's really true," he agrees. "It's only been about 75 years that recorded music has been listenable, and now it's ubiquitous. You hear it in the car. You've got it in your headphones when you're in the supermarket, in the doctor's waiting room. But it's different to go someplace where it's not in the background; it's the main thing going on. The fact that you've dedicated two or three hours to listen to this concert, to be there with other people who also like the music sort of makes a community. You see it most clearly in the Grateful Dead phenomenon where people would go to concert after concert, and I've got a few of those followers too. A community assembles itself around one type of art, and it's very compelling. There's something about being focused with 1000 other people having a common musical experience. There's nothing else that can do it, and it's very different from listening to it on your headphones.

"Those of us who were astounded by what came out of the stereo system back in the '70s or '60s, we never would've guessed that people in the new century would be listening to music over little tiny computer speakers that are not even as good as a car radio. It's a question of the fidelity of the music too. The combination of MP3s and the downloadable nature of most of the music we listen to has resulted in really low fidelity music, so a live performance is a real personal investment in the quality of the music."

One of the benefits of an immersive concert collective is that it can provide induction into a communal spiritual experience. "You escape," he says. "You get a momentary escape from the isolation of the individuated consciousness. You get to listen to this art form. It is a human language, but it also follows the rules of physics. An octave is a mathematical, physical reality; it can't be denied. So music either hits you, or it doesn't. It either connects, or it doesn't, and that makes it something that gives us relief from the prison of the self."

Taylor was inducted into the Rock & Roll Hall of Fame by Sir Paul McCartney in 2000. The former Beatle recalled their initial meeting in London. "We were just lucky to run into him, and he was lucky to run into us," McCartney said. "I love him."

"More and more, as time goes by, I realize how lucky I was," Taylor concludes. "I came from a family of academics and scientists. No one could've predicted it. It came out of the blue. This thing came along at the right time. It's been an amazing ride, and I'll continue to play music as long as people show up."

"MARGARITAVILLE"

Jimmy Buffett

*"I'm not the first person to create a career
out of escapism."*

If there was ever a perfect model for dreaming outside of the box and not taking life too seriously, it's troubadour Jimmy Buffett. A cultural phenomenon and beloved icon, Buffett has carved out a remarkably lucrative career around singing tropical-inflected songs about living the good life.

"I think escapism is something that is an essential part of survival," says Buffett during one of his frequent trips to Maui. "You've got to be able to blow off steam. I'm grateful that I've come up with a phony-baloney excuse to come to Hawai'i more often."

Fans at his shows, he continues, "can go crazy for a couple of hours, then go back to work. I've just really targeted our market. It's a lifestyle, and this music is part of their lifestyle. I tend to direct all my artistic endeavors at the people that like that lifestyle. I'm not the first person to create a career out of escapism."

Performing on Maui a bunch of times, Buffett's espoused lifestyle and the relaxed Hawai'i vibe are pretty synonymous. Stroll around Lahaina, and you will undoubtedly hear the strains of a tropical Buffett classic echoing from restaurants, and at the Goofy Foot surf school, you could meet owner Tim Sherer, who traveled the world as Buffett's private surf instructor.

Beginning his musical career in Nashville as a country artist, he perfected an appealing sound based on a chilled Key West vibe after moving to Florida. It took him around 15 minutes to come up with the lyrics for "Margaritaville" in 1976. A hit on his breakthrough album *Changes in Latitudes, Changes in Latitudes*, it allowed him to buy his first boat and eventually create a massive business empire founded on Margaritaville.

The concept of capitalizing on his laid-back image came to him one freezing day in Pittsburgh. "I went out one day, and I'm a marine supply and army and navy store freak. This guy recognized me and said, 'every time you come to town I order more Hawaiian shirts, and I sell out.' I started thinking and went back and talked to a friend of mine who was in the business. I came up with the ideas, and he said, 'let's get some graphic artist and do Jimmy Buffett song interpretations of T-shirts.'"

The days of hawking Buffett T-shirts are long passed. *Forbes* estimated annual brand sales of $1.5 billion in 2017 - from merchandising, record sales, stores and restaurants, and Margaritaville resorts, along with casinos in Tulsa, Oklahoma, and Bossier City, Louisiana. Latitude Margaritaville adult communities boasting a Margaritaville-inspired "no worries," tropical vibe lifestyle are planned, and One Particular Harbour on the Gulf of Mexico offers a private island paradise. By the way, the Cheeseburger In Paradise restaurant on Lahaina's Front Street is not owned by Buffett. He sued, and a settlement was reached.

But preaching escapism doesn't mean Buffett advocates drug or alcohol abuse. "I did all that stuff," he notes. "If I had to do it over again, I wouldn't have spent all that time drunk. I know that the good this music brings people certainly outweighs what I've been criticized for passing on the other level. I don't think it's any more dangerous than a nuclear missile, and there's a hell of a lot more of those around them me. When I get criticized for that, I just point that out. The good outweighs the bad. I'm proud of what I do."

Primarily focusing on touring and releasing live albums, Buffett says, "I knew my strongest asset was being a live performer, so I concentrated more on that and giving the best bang for the buck, and hopefully, people from that would be turned on to the records. I knew I was cultivating a loyal fan base."

Successfully marketing "destination" CDs to fans, these live soundboard recordings from assorted concert venues, include the CD/DVD *Live in Hawaii* taped at the Maui Arts & Cultural Center and the Waikiki Shell in 2004. "Our fan base is really into destination shows," he explains. "Maui and the Shell is one of our best-selling CDs."

Encountering Hawai'i's Jake Shimabukuro one day during a trip to Oahu, Buffett has championed the 'ukulele virtuoso, inviting him to tour with his band over the years, including playing in London, Dublin, and Paris in 2019, and recording "Come Monday" with the 'uke star on his acclaimed *Jake & Friends* album.

"He's been so supportive," Jake enthuses. "When I first started touring with him, he would have me open up the show playing the national anthem, and these are stadiums with 50,000 people. The first dozen shows my knees were shaking I thought I was going to collapse."

Buffett's connection with Shimabukuro continued with the 'ukulele star playing on successive albums from *Take the Weather with You* (which closed with a wonderful cover of Henry Kapono's "Dukes on Sunday") and *Bufet Hotel* to his Christmas album, *'Tis the SeaSon*, with "Mele Kalikimaka."

At his 2012 Maui concert, announcing it was the first time playing it in public, he debuted The Blue Hawaiians' "Swingin' Hula Girl," strumming a 'ukulele. The show also featured Maui-based reggae musician Mishka joining him on stage for "Volcano."

A year later, he collaborated with Mishka on his recording *Ocean Is My Potion*, which was released on Buffett's Mailboat Records label. Buffett performed on the catchy title track, which extolled the virtues of ocean life, and a new version of his classic "Trying To Reason With Hurricane Season."

Summing up his successful career, Buffett concludes: "I'm very blessed. I worked very hard for many years, but I always had a good time. You don't master a wave the first time. It takes a long time and a lot of hours of dedication to be good at anything, and I was lucky enough to be good at one thing. It's been a long and wonderful road. I'm grateful that I'm still doing it and that people are still coming to the shows. There's no better thrill than to get on stage and feel the energy of a big crowd. And I'm always looking ahead at the next proj- ect. It's the old sailing thing; I'm going towards the horizon. It's been a hell of a ride."

Asked about essential life tips, he simply offers, "don't look back."

"HIS JEWELED FLOOR"

Rickie Lee Jones

"I have been about defying convention since I began, and that is still my banner."

One of the most brilliant, insightful artists of our time, Rickie Lee Jones has continued to release profound works since her Grammy-winning debut album in 1979. A distinctly original, unconventional musician, she was once hailed by producer David Was as "a female Miles Davis." For her magnificent album *Balm in Gilead*, she adopted the title from the traditional spiritual "There Is A Balm In Gilead," which describes how a healing compound makes the wounded whole.

Among the album's balms, she offered the beautifully haunting "His Jeweled Floor," a contemporary hymn drawn from ecstatic Sufi poetry that celebrated a blissful union with God at the passage of death. "It was Kabir, one of the Sufi poets like Rumi," Jones explains. "I read both of these ecstatic poets. I feel this way about God, the glory and love of the relationship between the soul and its home. God by any name you choose. These poems are about the lover waiting for her beloved's touch, and the sensuality of the waiting, and all things describing our relationship with God in sensual terms, quite un-Catholic. And yet, in its way, the Catholic attempted to capture a sense of a visceral, otherworldly experience as well.

"I love these poems. I wrote this song after reading one, but the last verse was not finished. When my mother died, I wrote that there are no demons, only angels, and thought that I wanted to talk to my audience about the longing and need for a ritual, a secure setting in which to mourn and bury our parents and family, people we loved, a way to set their souls alight, to send them off with song and light, their souls we envision, on their way to a safe harbor, and we are able to feel good about the burial."

165

Singing about love and loss, hope and doubt, growth and death, Balm in Gilead maybe her greatest work. A U.K. Independent review noted: "When she's good, she changes the very light."

Two years earlier, Jones released *The Sermon on Exposition Boulevard*, another extraordinary work hailed by one critic as a "mystical masterpiece." Jubilantly rocking out – as if channeling Lou Reed and Van Morrison - the recording explored Jesus' teaching for our contemporary time, with songs improvised in stream of consciousness sessions.

"The first song is the first take of the first day, and there had been no plan really, and no idea," she says. "It just came. It was a holy hour. And much of the work then was done in much the same way, though I might have books open, or notebooks and books, and I glanced as I vamped, or I just went for it. It was really a loving and exciting recording."

The album's centerpiece, "Where I Like it Best," offers a unique interpretation of the Lord's Prayer. "The Lord's Prayer, much maligned by compulsory rote memorization, is a really beautiful improvisation as well," she points out. "He was asked on the fly how do we pray? What a question. He is telling them to find a new way, so they ask, how? He tells them, well, start like, father, no, our father, our father in heaven, and tell him how beautiful he is, remind yourself of the holiness of what you do, hallowed be thy name, and a nod, lead us to your kingdom. Thy kingdom come, lead us to your will. Let it be here as it is there with you. Show us the way. Your will be done, not mine. That way, I walk in your steps, and I trust you. This is so much already. Thy will be mine. He didn't say that, but let's just say he did, and let that be as it is in heaven.

"So we have asked and reminded ourselves of so much goodness we could do already. Then lead us not into temptation, because man, it's hard enough here already. Deliver us from evil. That's all one thought. Don't starve us; feed us. Lead us out of temptation and deliver us from evil. I thought, how would we say that if someone asked this question today, and while I am at it, I will make it real. So here is the guy or girl who asked the question on that day, and she says I wanted to pray, really.

"But how do you pray in a world like this, so much violence, and these false and terrible voices on TV who say they are Christians, they

seem so meaningless, so false, so specific to a sociological phenomenon, like a club, or a region, not really like God, spirit, transcending,
all-inclusive, hope, love. Where is that? It's not here. So I said, they
close their eyes and bow their heads and - all this was improvised.
And he said when you pray, and this is the part left out of the Lord's
Prayer, the first part, and in my opinion the most important part.

"He said, when you pray, pray from the deep part of your heart,
and don't say prayers in rote like the heathen, making a display of your
prayer. He said, as we know, a prayer is a private thing between you
and God. Don't go around town banging your bell and doing what
these TV evangelicals do, doing what these men walking around the
village do to show how holy they are. God hears every word you think
in private. Your prayer is private.

"And then I guess I took it into my own heart and said you, you
are where I like it best, this is the man and the Christ part, loving the
human, in love with human, and loving God, so attracted to the Sufi
idea, except really loving the God of humans, the humanness of the
God. You are where I want to be and long to be, and that's it; that's
the Lord's Prayer. At the end of the Lord's Prayer, deliver us from evil.
I guess I said; instead, you are where I like it best. So yeah, it's a deep,
deep thing for me."

So what was her hope in crafting a work about the essence of
Jesus? "I hoped people would be able to weigh his words, and feel
the spirit of them outside the realm of Christianity, especially American evangelical Christianity, which seems to be a runaway horse, a
cart without a horse, running down a hill. I wanted people who long
for community, for communing with their spirit, and maybe involvement with others in this way, to at least be able to make a fair decision
about Christ's words as well as the Buddha or any other prophet, or
idea, living under the yoke of so much minstrel show and jester kind
of treatment of the old rabbi.

"I thought it seems impossible for people to measure his great heart
if they do not seek it, and only hear these sounding brass, these goofy,
judgmental, intolerant Christians who are indeed very unlike Jesus or
his teachings. Not many teachings really, and the apostle Paul not necessarily the guy to give you the news. You listen to people talk about

the events of the day, or do you listen to the events of the day and talk about them? Are you letting others tell you what to think because that is a slippery slope? Many people have much to gain by controlling what you think. It is best to go to the source yourself. Read his words, only with no commentary, no editing. Go right to some book, or make your own book of the words.

"Here is what so and so said he said, in red, out of the Bible, not under any subject even. You must seek the truth, and the truth will set you free. And when you find yourself free, you will have no other road but to offer this forgiveness and hope to everyone you meet I think. I am sure no one gets into heaven until everyone gets into heaven. We must truly love the neighbor and love the enemy as ourselves. They *are* ourselves.

"Like the sea, we are one, made of drips of water, no meaning unless we are part of the whole. When we isolate ourselves, we lose our way, lost in ego, and filled with loneliness. Not that humans lead to happiness, but they are what we are, and we need them and need to heal them and to let them lay their loving hands on us."

Vaulted into the national spotlight with the hit song "Chuck E.'s in Love" in 1979, Jones' self-titled debut album won the Grammy for Best New Artist. Dubbed "The Duchess of Coolsville" by *Time* magazine, Jones' success continued with the release of the remarkable *Pirates* in 1981, which was hailed as a masterpiece of sophisticated songwriting and singing. Another superb work, *The Magazine,* followed in 1984. From its hauntingly beautiful title song and the sublime, symphonic "Prelude To Gravity" to the complex "Rorschachs" suite, *The Magazine* confirmed her reputation as one of the 20th century's most formidable artists.

Besides crafting compelling original material, Jones also excels as a gifted interpreter on albums like *The Devil You Know, It's Like This*, and *Kicks*. Among the highlights on *The Devil You Know*, she managed to make the Rolling Stones' "Sympathy for the Devil" more chilling than the original, and she delivered an even more sublime version of "Only Love Can Break Your Heart" than Neil Young. She had earlier covered David Bowie's "Rebel Rebel" on *Traffic From Paradise*. Before his death, Bowie reported that Jone's version was his favorite cover of his work.

Following ten years of writer's block, she released the *Other Side of Desire* in 2015, drawing inspiration from her relocation to the cultural melting pot of New Orleans. Strains of Fats Domino-style swamp-pop, honky-tonk, and Cajun waltzes wound through the album, with Jones playing acoustic and electric guitars, banjo, keyboards, and percussion. The U.K. music magazine *Uncut* praised it as "a record that crowns her career."

As a unique artist consistently creating amazing albums, one wonders if she sometimes feels frustrated that she doesn't receive the attention she deserves. "I suppose the level of work I do on stage deserves a lot more attention; the place should be full of kids," she responds. "It's music for all kinds of people. It's not nostalgic by any means. I have been about defying convention since I began, and that is still my banner. I think the perception of me from 30 years ago is a misunderstanding about me definitely. I believe I am kind, calm, passionate, and very human.

"That my work was so instantly edified, that I have been so copied, imitated, honored and dishonored, from McDonald's' commercials to Sheryl Crow, makes people knowing who I am, maybe a more difficult task. 'Chuck E's in Love' was only big and is only still remembered because it was so different from anything that had been going on in music. The song and I helped open the door to the folky singer-songwriter thing from some back alley where harder rougher stories were taking place. I was sexual, tough, wild, and these things mattered at that time because it had taken on a pretty false and elitist attitude, the Eagles and Joni, and all that California-isms.

"I believe that in the end, and hopefully before, the truth of things, the good of things, our revolutionary anchor, the part of all of us that wants to oust all oil and use solar energy, that wants to live together communally, that wants to save trees and save schools, normal stuff right that has been marginalized, so that it's like cute or something, well it's not cute, it's essential, and it's who we truly are.

"I think all this will be recognized in each other. You hear this somehow in my work. You come to see me, you say, hey, I know this and some part of our heart, your heart is lifted, and this I believe is my job. I play for people. They love, they are moved, they cry. I see their true selves. I love playing music, learning, courage, and sound. I love this. I see the world. I get paid. What's not to like."

"I am hard to categorize. It takes more time and effort, and it's emotional, smart, always a living experience. It's not like the Ed Sullivan show, or the Lilith Fair, or the this or the that. It's a living thing made by me. I do wonder when I will get some blue ribbons. I might be one of those people that people can't really see, you know, 'til they are dead. Some of us, we loom large in life, and when we die, people are able to see us without all that light in their eyes."

Bob Dylan at the MACC - "I hear you're a writer"

James Taylor at the MACC -
"Things feel like they get channeled through me"

Yoko Ono, Kapalua, Maui - "We felt society would benefit more
by tapping into the feminine energy"

Miranda Lambert, Maui Songwriters Festival -
"Playing music here with great friends is a dream"

Steven Tyler & Joe Perry, Honolulu -
"We were a tight, bad-ass band, and it just took off"

Steven Tyler - "I always had this affinity for hula dancing and palm trees"

Gene Simmons and Paul Stanley of KISS, Wailea - "There isn't anything that we can't do because we refuse to follow anybody else's rules"

Neil Young rocking with Promise of the Real at Charley's, Paia - "Neil has been our hero forever"

Doors' drummer John Densmore, Napili - "The entire body of work is important, our entire catalog, what we represent"

Grateful Dead, Oakland -
"The freedom is one of the special things about the Dead"

Earth, Wind & Fire's Verdine White at the MACC -
"What we're keeping alive is good music"

Diana Ross at the MACC - "The Supremes will live on in our hearts"

CALIFORNIA DREAMING

"EIGHT MILES HIGH"

The Byrds

"I borrowed some tricks from George. He was a fan of the Byrds, and I was a fan of the Beatles."

Released in March 1966, "Eight Miles High," along with The Yardbirds' "Shape of Things," helped launch psychedelic rock. While it was banned by some American radio stations because of supposed drug connotations, the landmark song charted in the Top 20.

"We weren't really trying to go psychedelic with it," Byrds co-founder Roger McGuinn explains. "Although we were experimenting with psychedelics at the time, our main point was to try and expose John Coltrane and Ravi Shankar, musicians we were inspired by. That was what 'Eight Miles High' was about."

There was a time when the Byrds were viewed as America's answer to the Beatles. Almost overnight, buoyed by the success of their debut hit single "Mr. Tambourine Man," they became one of the most popular bands in the world. *Time* magazine proclaimed they had invented a new musical movement called folk rock and in quick succession, the Byrds were credited with also helping create psychedelic rock and country rock.

Formed in L.A. in 1964, the Byrds won widespread acclaim for hits like "Eight Miles High," "Turn! Turn! Turn!," and their cover of Dylan's "Mr. Tambourine Man," which gonzo journalist Hunter S. Thompson once praised as "the hippie national anthem."

Famous for their tight harmonies and McGuinn's distinctive, jangly guitar sound, he was initially inspired by the Beatles. "George Harrison played a Rickenbacker 12-string in the movie *A Hard Days Night*, and I went out and got one," he recalls. "It's all I've ever played. I pick it like a banjo instead of a guitar to get the arpeggios. George and I got to know each other pretty well. I would see him on and off at different places. We both played the Rickenbacker 12-string, and I borrowed some tricks from George. He was a fan of the Byrds, and I was a fan of the Beatles. We had a lot in common."

While the Byrds were enamored with the Beatles, the Californian group also influenced the Beatles, and in particular, Harrison's song "If I Needed Someone." "Derek Taylor (Beatles' publicist) came over from London with a tape from George, and he said, 'George wants you to know his song was inspired by your guitar work on the intro of 'Bells of Rhymney.'"

In a DVD that accompanies McGuinn's album, *Roger McGuinn: Stories, Songs & Friends*, rock stars like Bruce Springsteen and Tom Petty marveled at the impact of the Byrds' founder. "Roger really invented folk rock," said Springsteen. And Petty added, "without Roger, there would be no me."

As a co-founding member of the Byrds, David Crosby helped create and popularize their influential folk-rock sound. Raised on jazz and classical music, in his formative years, Crosby sought out a wide range of music from jazz legend John Coltrane to sitar master Ravi Shankar and the vocal genius of the Bulgarian National Folk Choir. "It stretched the envelope; it gave me much wider horizons of music to listen to and to be affected by," Crosby says. "I was very lucky, my parents played me a ton of classical music when I was a kid, and then my brother turned me on to late '50s jazz – Brubeck, Mulligan, Chet Baker, and that quite naturally led to Miles and 'Trane."

Expanding his horizons, it was Crosby who turned George Harrison on to Ravi Shankar's music during a Byrds' U.K. tour in early August 1965. "I believe that's what George says," Crosby reports. "I believe that might be true." Crosby had earlier attended a Shankar recording session and composed the song "Why," the B-side of "Eight Miles High" and included on *Younger than Yesterday*, which featured a prominent raga-inspired, sitar-sounding guitar. Harrison subsequently first played a sitar with the Beatles on "Norwegian Wood" in October 1965.

As to whether Crosby was responsible for guiding the Byrds with their unique harmonies based on jazz and Indian modes, he suggests, "I didn't go, all right lads I'm going to show you, we just naturally did it. Gene (Clark) and Roger would write these Beatles-ish songs, and I just started singing harmony to them. I started singing harmony when I was about six. It's always been a part of me, and I just love it. I fell in love with the Everly Brothers because of their harmony."

In his book *Chronicles: Volume One,* Bob Dylan proclaimed Crosby "an architect of harmony."

Later Byrds' innovations included their fusion of rock and country on the seminal *Sweetheart of the Rodeo,* released in 1968, which included covers of Dylan, Woody Guthrie, and Merle Haggard songs. "The Byrds did it," reported acclaimed pedal steel guitarist Lloyd Green, who played on the album. "They brought country and rock together."

"It was a breakthrough," says McGuinn. "It hadn't been done before. It was a political risk because there was a stigma associated with country music to the rock people and a stigma associated with rock to the country people. So we were kind of bringing two worlds together that really didn't get along very well."

After the Byrds demise, McGuinn reinvented himself as a solo artist and has continued to tour through the decades. Released in 2014, *Roger McGuinn: Stories, Songs & Friends,* served as a snapshot of his solo act, where he wove Byrds' favorites with traditional folk songs, blues, and sea shanties.

McGuinn had been astonished to discover Springsteen was such a huge fan. "It was a complete surprise," he says. "I've always been a fan of his, so I was delighted to find it out. I didn't know he even knew who I was."

In the bonus DVD interview, Springsteen revealed it was the Byrds who first turned him on to Bob Dylan. "I had not heard Dylan's 'Mr. Tambourine Man' before," Springsteen said. "I was a child of Top 40 radio, and I heard it through Roger and the Byrds."

Over the years, McGuinn had an extensive connection with Dylan, including the *Rolling Thunder Revue*, and an invitation to play at Dylan's *30th Anniversary Concert Celebration* at Madison Square Garden in 1992. "It was a big thrill," he recalls. "There's a funny anecdote about that. I learned one of his songs, 'My Back Pages,' phonetically off the record. And at the concert, they had teleprompters at the foot of the stage. I was looking down at the teleprompter going, oh, that's not the way I learned it off the record. There were a couple of words I got wrong."

At a Byrds' reunion for a Roy Orbison tribute in 1990, Dylan joined the band on stage for "Tambourine Man." "He loved it," says McGuinn about the Byrd's coverage of Dylan's songs. "He said nice things about the Byrds initially. He's like an older brother to me."

When he mixed up some lyrics on Dylan's song "You Ain't Going Nowhere" on the *Sweetheart of the Rodeo* album, Dylan responded by mentioning McGuinn in a later recording of his song. "It's quite an honor to be in a Bob Dylan song," he notes.

McGuinn's connection to Dylan later led to him sing and play guitar on "Knockin' on Heaven's Door," featured on the soundtrack of the Western *Pat Garrett and Billy the Kid*. "Bob and I were neighbors at the time. He used to come over to my house, and he invited me to the movie studio. It was a big thrill."

Five decades after the formation of the Byrds, McGuinn remains a pioneer dedicated to bringing the centuries-old folk music tradition to a new generation. "I noticed back in 1995, the new folk singers were singer-songwriters and they were neglecting the traditional end, so I thought I'd do something about it," he says. "I started putting songs on the internet for free download. It's a mission. It's a labor of love. I didn't want to see it go away. My hope is that people will learn the songs and keep them alive."

Performing as a folk singer suits him better than trying to remain a rocker, he says. "I think it's very dignified to be a folk singer at my age. I just turned 73 (in 2015). I didn't feel comfortable being a rock star anymore. I was in the Byrds for nine years, and I've been doing the Folk Den (his free music site) for almost 20 years. Being a folk singer is fun."

Heading to Maui for a solo show, he recalls how decades ago actor Peter Fonda got him a membership in the Lahaina Yacht Club, "as a crew member of his boat the Tatoosh." He also mentions that his folk podcast includes the traditional sea shanty "Rolling Down to Old Maui." "It's one of the favorite sea shanties, a whaling song about a crew that was based in Maui."

I first encountered the Byrds in concert when they played London's Middle Earth underground club in 1968, with Mick Jagger and Keith Richards in the audience. "Was it any good," McGuinn wonders? Assured they were great, he continues: "We loved going to England, the home of the Beatles and the Stones. We thought there was something in the drinking water to make the music better." While in England, Jagger and Richards invited the Byrds to drive to the ancient megalithic site of Stonehenge to watch the sunrise.

So does he think the living Byrds will ever reform? McGuinn says while he kept in touch with Crosby through *Twitter*, a reunion is doubtful. "David wants to get the Byrds back together. All the problems we had back in the '60s are all gone, but I really don't. I'm very content to just be a solo artist."

In late 2019, McGuinn posted Crosby had blocked him on *Twitter*, after proselytizing about Jesus. "It's important that you call on Jesus to save your soul," McGuinn had tweeted.

"LIGHT MY FIRE"

The Doors

"The Doors were the dark underbelly of peace and love."

"The whole thing was great," recalled keyboardist Ray Manzarek about his time in the Doors. "But the great tragedy is that Jim Morrison died at 27. I only wish I had been in Paris to grab him by the scruff of the neck and say, get out of this debauched atmosphere and come on back to Los Angeles. Lie down on the beach, get some sun and get strong and healthy again, and let's get to work. But I wasn't able to do that."

One of the architects of the Doors' mesmerizing sound, Manzarek was one of rock's most influential keyboard players. His soloing, which reflected his classical and jazz background, was pivotal in the allure of such classics as "Light My Fire," "Riders on the Storm," "Spanish Caravan," "When the Music's Over," and "Roadhouse Blues."

Manzarek had first landed in Hawai'i with the Doors in the summer of 1968 to play a sold-out show at the old Honolulu International Center. While their fans were enthralled, the staid local press was not impressed. "The Doors could be called The Dulls," complained the headline in the *Honolulu Star Bulletin*. At least the *Honolulu Advertiser* was more favorable, noting "the Doors possess fire" and "raw sexuality," but bemoaned, "they are a snobbish quartet that takes needless rest breaks."

Following the show, the band flew to Maui, where they were filmed sailing off Lahaina, and Morrison rode a bicycle around the town. The Maui footage was included in the Doors' documentary *Feast of Friends*.

They attempted to play Hawaii again in 1969 but were banned by civic authorities after Morrison's Miami bust for lewdness. "I don't feel the show is in the best interests of the people of Hawaii," auditoriums director Guido Salmaggi reported in the *Honolulu Star Bulletin*. They were allowed to return to Oahu in 1970, and high on Maui Wowie, played for two hours, "in an inspired ganja trance," noted author Stephen Davis in *Jim Morrison: Life, Death, Legend.*

Ray Manzarek had met Jim Morrison at UCLA film school and connected with the other future members at a Transcendental Meditation class in 1965. "The Maharishi Mahesh Yogi was an Indian spiritual guy teaching courses in mantra yoga where you say a Sanskrit word over and over in your mind," Manzarek explained before a Maui show. "It hypnotizes the conscious mind and allows you to sink into your subconscious and explore the good and the bad of the subconscious mind. It was terrific. It was the same thing the Beatles got into later."

Doors' drummer John Densmore also remembers that remarkable meeting where he and guitarist friend Robbie Krieger met the future Doors' keyboardist. Interviewed on Maui while attending a Ram Dass retreat - "our roads from psychedelics to meditation are the same" - he recalls: "Robbie and I were fooling around then with legal psychedelics, but it was kind of rough on the nervous system. Robbie said, 'there's this Indian guy coming,' and this was two years before the Beatles got onto the Maharishi.

"It was only his second time here, and the first time was with Clint Eastwood and Paul Horn. You could feel the love vibe. So Ray was there, and he came up and said, 'I heard you're a drummer, do you want to jam?' After a while, Jim came to one of the meetings, and he said, 'I just want to see what he's got in his eyes.' After the meeting, he said, 'he's got some, but I'm not going to meditate.'"

But Morrison did dedicate the song "Take it as it Comes" from the Doors' debut album to the Maharishi. The title was taken from a line in the TM founder's book *The Science of Being and the Art of Living.* And Densmore told *Rolling Stone* in 2008, "there wouldn't be any Doors without the Maharishi."

Densmore had grown up enthralled by jazz and brought a jazz sensibility to the group. "I got a fake ID in Tijuana so I could see (John) Coltrane and I saw him many times," he says. "And Elvin Jones was my musical guru. Seeing Coltrane jungle it out with Elvin for 20 minutes in the middle of 'Chasin' the Trane' was so out, and that's where maybe I got the courage to just stop the beat in ('When the) 'Music's Over' and have a conversation with Jim."

In contrast, Manzarek "grew up on the Southside of Chicago, growing up with blues," he said. "There's a blues foundation to what the Doors were doing. They weren't just sex-crazed."

No one quite mined the shadow side like the Doors. "The Doors were the dark underbelly of peace and love," Densmore affirms, recalling how when they first played San Francisco, "they just stared at us with their mouths open." Referencing the band's stunning, 11-minute Oedipal drama "The End," he adds, "You need to be initiated away from your parents, cut that umbilical cord."

In September of 1968, the Doors and Jefferson Airplane played two all-night shows at London's Roundhouse, with many of England's rock elite attending - including Paul McCartney, George Harrison, Mick Jagger, and Keith Richards. The opening Airplane soared blissfully high, and then Jim Morrison stepped on stage, and we were collectively transfixed.

What would we encounter? The weekly *Melody Maker* had proclaimed: "Look out, England! Jim Morrison is coming to get you." There had been reports of audiences rushing the stage at some U.S. shows and smashing chairs, and that the Lizard King had been maced and arrested in New Haven for an "indecent and immoral exhibition." Alarming reviews warned about their "satanic, sensual, demented" music and how audiences were "deliberately whipped to a frenzy."

Morrison once suggested, "I want audiences to feel the same catharsis that the ancient Greeks felt at their plays." Prowling the London stage, he conjured electrifying intensity, and when "The End" began, under blood-red light, I swear horns protruded from the side of his head.

In a review in *Rave* magazine, Morrison was quoted as saying: "We enjoyed playing at the Roundhouse more than any other date for years." He told *New Musical Express*, "It was probably the most informed, receptive audience I've ever seen in my life."

Decades after Morrison's death, the Doors have amassed album sales of more than 100 million worldwide, and expanded versions of their classic records continue to be released, including a 50th-anniversary updating of *Morrison Hotel* in 2020.

Manzarek seemed surprised by the Doors' enduring legacy. "I'm very happy about it. We hadn't considered longevity one way or another. That wasn't the reason we made the music. You make the music to be in the moment. Music is a vibratory act of performing. Music is like Zen meditation. There's a moment in time that you seek to capture, and you're not thinking 40 years into the future. If you do your job properly, you lose yourself in the moment."

After the Doors' demise, Manzarek released several solo albums, including an innovative rock version of Carl Orff's masterpiece *Carmina Burana*. He also teamed with blues guitarist Roy Rogers. The duo's debut recording, *Ballads Before the Rain*, included interpretations of "Crystal Ship" and "Riders on the Storm," along with some Erik Satie and Manuel de Falla. Joking Manzarek noted, "never go out of the box, always play like the Doors. We did *Ballads Before the Rain* because we're a couple of laid-back guys. That was our homage to Hawai'i."

Densmore revisited some Doors' classics on the album *All Wood and Doors* by Cliff Eberhardt and James Lee Stanley. The intriguing project also managed to lure guitarist Robbie Krieger into participating. Imagine mellow, back porch versions of songs like "Break on Through" and "Moonlight Drive" played on acoustic guitars with vocal harmonies reminiscent of Crosby, Stills and Nash.

Densmore has fought hard to preserve the legacy and integrity of the band that was so significant in his life, resisting all attempts to commercialize their music and preventing the other surviving band members from touring as the Doors. "Tom Waits has a blurb on the back of my book (*The Doors Unhinged*)," he reports. "It says: 'John Densmore is not for sale and that's his gift to us.'"

It has galled many fans that their cherished music - songs considered almost sacred — has been co-opted to sell a range of products. The Beatles "All You Need is Love" for Luv's diapers and "Revolution" to market Nike sneakers (against Paul McCartney's wishes), and Buffalo Springfield's anti-establishment anthem "For What It's Worth" flogging Miller beer.

But when Apple wanted to pay $4 million for a Doors tune, and Cadillac once offered $15 million for the rights to "Break on Through (To *the Other Side)," Densmore nixed the proposals. "I heard that even Roger Waters went, 'oh my god, $15 million?" he reports laughing.*

Densmore was able to wield veto power because when the band was formed, while Jim Morrison conjured the lyrics and Densmore, Manzarek, and Krieger crafted the music, they agreed to share all composing rights. "Because Jim couldn't play one chord on any instrument, he said, 'let's split all the money, let's call it music by the Doors,'" Densmore explains.

And there was a precedent established by the band's iconic singer. While Morrison was vacationing in Europe, Buick had offered the band $75,000 to use "Light My Fire" to market Opel cars. The three States-side musicians agreed to the proposal, but when Morrison returned, he went ballistic and raged; if they aired the ad, he'd demolish an Opel on TV with a sledgehammer.

"I'm not against a new band trying to pay the rent, whatever it takes, but in our situation, Jim went crazy over 'Light My Fire,' and he didn't even write the song (it was primarily Krieger)," Densmore explains. "The entire body of work is important, our entire catalog, what we represent. He's dead, and I'm not, and I'm not forgetting that. He's my ancestor."

While Ray Manzarek and Robby Krieger toured with a version of the group called The Doors of the 21st Century, featuring Ian Astbury of The Cult on lead vocals, Densmore resisted any attempts to get him on board. "If Jim comes back, I'll do it," he says, "but why would I want to perform with a Jimitator?"

Densmore along with Morrison's parents successfully sued to stop his former compatriots calling themselves The Doors. With so much money involved, the court proceedings turned ugly, with attorneys brandishing an article Densmore wrote in *The Nation* as ammunition proving his mental instability.

"That was an exhibit thrown in my face," he reveals. "There was no case, so what do you do? Character assassination. They tried to paint me as a commie pinko, anti-capitalistic maniac. In *The Nation* piece, I quoted Vaclav Havel, who, when he became Czech president, said jokingly, 'we're not going to rush into this capitalism too quickly. I don't know if there's much difference between KGB and IBM.' It's a great line. They took it out of context and said, I said I was against making money. I'm an anarchist. My bandmates called me that too, some rough stuff. I've been carrying this alone for a long time. It took some time off my life, but I don't regret it."

Densmore was pleased to help promote the Grammy-winning documentary on the band, *When You're Strange*, which included historic and unseen footage and narration by Johnny Depp. Woven through the tapestry of their story are mesmerizing scenes from a previously unreleased experimental film shot in 1969, featuring a bearded Morrison driving through the Mojave Desert.

"I love it," he says. "It was on (PBS') *American Masters*, very cool. The brilliant thing is having the footage of Jim in the desert. We screened it at Sundance, and a big critic walked out. 'You cast an actor as Jim,' he told the director. A lot of people were confused. I love that."

The documentary comes to a close with idyllic scenes of the four musicians enjoying a sunset sail off Maui's west coast following their 1968 concert in Honolulu. Densmore smiles and adds, "In the last line of the movie, Johnny says, 'as of this date none of their songs has been used in a car commercial.'"

"WHITE RABBIT"

Jefferson Airplane

"Ram Dass said something that I believe in, that even though intellectually you know it's not going to do any good, you have to do what you think is right."

"Though I don't have any favorites," says Jefferson Airplane's Grace Slick, "the checks keep rolling in for 'White Rabbit.' For some reason, people keep playing it over and over. Keep sending those checks in."

The iconic singer whose blazing vocals and acerbic lyrics created some of the Airplane's greatest moments was on Maui closing a Jefferson Starship tour in 1984. She had previously gotten married and spent her honeymoon on the island in 1976. "We were married at the Royal Lahaina," she recalls. "We love the islands."

Slick's iconic "White Rabbit" was inspired by Miles Davis and Gil Evans' album *Sketches of Spain*. "The music is a bolero (Spanish) rip-off, while the lyrics were inspired by Lewis Carroll's *Alice in Wonderland*," she explained in her autobiography, *Somebody to Love?: A Rock-and-Roll Memoir*.

To help critique her new compositions, Slick reports she would typically imbibe various substances. "When I was taking drugs, I used to write a song and look at it again sober, then with marijuana, then with coke, and look at it again in the morning, and so on until I liked it no matter what frame of mind I was in. I don't do that anymore."

Looking back at the Airplane's formative San Francisco days, Marty Balin recalled, "It was very experimental. The main thing was we wanted to be original. Once in a while, we'd get a job, and they'd say, 'will you play these hits,' and we'd say yes, and play all original stuff, and after the first set, they'd fire us. Eventually, everything turned around."

The original leader of Jefferson Airplane and primary songwriter Balin first encountered Paul Kantner in the spring of 1965. Influenced by the folk-rock sound of groups like the Byrds, the duo set about assembling the group that became the Airplane.

"I was looking for a guy to start with, and he (Kantner) came into the club with a six-string guitar in one hand and a 12-string in the other, which is pretty rare in those days. He showed up and started to sing and got real shy and said, 'I can't do this,' and put his guitars away. I don't know why, but I said he's the guy I'm looking for."

The group's meteoric rise was fueled by replacing their original female lead singer with Grace Slick. It was bassist Jack Casady who suggested Slick join the group. "Grace was in the band Great Society, and when Signe Anderson left after the first album, we were looking for a new female singer. I thought Grace was the best that I saw in the city. I asked her to come to one of our rehearsals, and she liked it and stayed."

Blessed with an amazingly powerful voice and magnetic presence, Slick added her gift for songwriting to those of Balin and Kantner, delivering the group's first Top Ten hit, the psychedelic anthem "White Rabbit."

Asked about her fondest memories of that time, Slick recalls: "The first time we had a large rock and roll gathering with four or five bands at the Longshoreman's Hall, and the first time I played with the Great Society, the people all looked different. Everybody didn't have a Billy Idol hair-do. Now it's very much like that. Boy George doesn't look like Billy Idol, doesn't look like Pat Benatar. There's a great variety. The '60s and '80s are similar in that aspect. The '70s were a tad boring as far as I was concerned.

"This country with one decade it will be asleep, and the other will be vibrant. The '20s were called the roaring '20s, and the '30s were a depression. The '40s were a war, the '50s, everyone laid back with two cars and two kids. The '60s were vibrant, and the '70s were a snore."

The band's evolution from folk to acid rockers was aided by the cultural freedom San Francisco nurtured. "When I was in high school at night, I'd see people like John Coltrane, Miles Davis, and Thelonious Monk, and I'd see Lenny Bruce and (poets) Kerouac and Corso read," Balin remembered.

189

"Marty and me are sort of like Rogers and Hammerstein in our own way," reported Paul Kantner on Maui before a show. "There's a nice love/hate tension that finds its way into our best songs."

The Airplane first landed in Hawai'i in 1969, when they played a sold-out concert at Honolulu's Civic Auditorium and then gave a free show at the Waikiki Shell for 10,000 folks because so many fans were unable to get into the Civic. The *Honolulu Star-Bulletin* called it "one of the strangest happenings ever seen at the Shell." It was the first free concert ever in Hawai'i by a major rock band. Kantner was subsequently busted by cops who discovered him smoking pot in some bushes at a rented Diamond Head home. "Marijuana Charge Grounds Jefferson Airplane Crewman" read a *Star-Bulletin* headline.

Lead guitarist Jorma Kaukonen's entrée to the rock band required a major switch from the blues and roots music he loved playing. "It was a complete shift," he recalls. "I remember when I cut *Takes Off*, it was so different from anything I was comfortable doing. A finger-picking guitar player didn't go with a lot of that stuff, and I really had to think what am I going to do to make it work.

"It didn't start out as the rock 'n' roll behemoth it became. We were really a folk rock band, but it was a huge shift. I remember how demanding it was for me to figure out what to do because it was so totally outside my comfort zone, and that was exciting. Paul and Marty and Grace wrote these great songs that were so different from the kind of stuff that I wrote that it was a real challenge to figure out something to play with them."

"Jorma had gone out there and met a bunch of folk musicians in the San Francisco area," recalls bassist Jack Casady. "I had been playing in a lot of R&B bands in Washington, and Jorma said he had just joined a folk rock group. I said, what, you the purist? He said, 'we've got a manager that promises to pay us $50 a week whether we work or not. Do you want to come out?' I said you're on. So I joined the band."

"It was a big deal as my apartment was only $80 a month," says Kaukonen. "Jack was really the only experienced musician. He had played in rhythm and blues bands, but it was new for the rest of us. We were extremely blessed to be paid for on-the-job training."

"In the blink of an eye, we all became extremely successful. All of a sudden, we went from rehearsing in Marty's living room to being a bar band at the Matrix to having national success. I had a blast with the Airplane, and God bless Grace and the guys because the Airplane has allowed me to be a really successful musician most of my life."

One of rock's great bass players, Casady followed no rules except perhaps a drive to be creative and to groove. With the Airplane, he pushed the edges of rock 'n' roll. Besides years with the band and the blues spin-off Hot Tuna, his albums credits include Jimi Hendrix's *Electric Ladyland*.

"This was the days when you carried a bass guitar with you at all times and use any excuse you could to play with anybody and everybody," he explains the Hendrix connection. "We played Monterey (festival) and shared bills at the Fillmore, and we became friends. We'd rehearse next to the Fillmore, and a couple of times, we would hang out and jam with Jimi.

"When he was working on what became *Electric Ladyland*, we were in New York, and we went to see Traffic with Steve Winwood. Jimi invited us back to his studio. He was working on some songs and said, 'let's play this blues, 'Voodoo Child.' So Steve Winwood and me and Mitch Mitchell and Hendrix played the song. I got a call a month later, and Jimi asked me, 'Would you mind if we put the jam on the album.' It became part of the album, and in a sense, it became part of history."

As the literate visionary of the band, Paul Kantner was best known for his science-fiction-based imagery, penning "Crown of Creation," "Have You Seen the Saucers," and the "Blows Against the Empire" saga. "I was in Catholic military boarding school in second grade - I used to call it nuns and guns - and one day I found this whole raft of Catholic science fiction by C.S. Lewis," Kantner explained the dawn of his love for futuristic fiction. "I progressed through my teen years and into my 20s and 30s, ravenously devouring the concept of imagination beyond the beyond, and it found its way into my music. There are not too many science fiction rock stars. I have a niche of my own that I appreciate and enjoy."

Four years after opening the legendary Fillmore Auditorium, Jefferson Airplane closed the second day of Woodstock. During that span, they recorded *Surrealistic Pillow,* the psychedelic masterpiece *After Bathing at Baxter's,* and *Crown of Creation,* which helped define the popular rock music of the era.

Known for protest songs like "Volunteers" and "We Can Be Together," Slick stresses the importance of taking a firm position. "Ram Dass said something that I believe in, that even though intellectually you know it's not going to do any good, you have to do what you think is right. I think it's important to keep talking about let's not play with bombs. Not even on a moral level. It's just stupid. If you have to punch somebody in an argument, it just means you're too stupid to talk. You should keep talking. There's nothing we can do really until you change the genetic code which tells us to sock somebody when you're mad."

Marty Balin left the band in 1971, partially influenced by Janis Joplin's tragic drug overdose. "The night Janis died, we were playing the Winterland. It hit me hard, and I didn't want to go to the Winterland the following night because I didn't think the band was playing very well then. I didn't feel like playing that crazy music that cocaine makes. I was never into the coke thing, and I didn't fit in. Every band has a heart, and that was my job basically to keep everybody together and to communicate with all of them. They're more intellectual types, and I'm more the basic street kid. During the heavy drug days, my kind of idealism was frowned upon. I just said, screw it."

When the Airplane reformed in 1989, many hoped the band would soar once more, but a disappointing album led the group to separate. "The record wasn't any good because they took each of us into the studio alone and gave it to a producer," Balin reported. "The live shows were great. We were hot. I kept saying, why don't we record this, but nobody did. We came back home from the tour, and nobody talked after that."

At its peak, the Airplane's utopian vision combined with its brilliant acid-rock ventures created a vibrant force unrivaled by any other band of the time. The superb *Bless it's Pointed Little Head* and *Live at the Fillmore East* captured their potent dynamism on stage - an unrivaled amalgam of soaring vocal harmonies, inspired jamming, complicated rhythms, melodic songs, and wailing guitars.

"I'm very proud of it," Casady says about *Pointed Little Head*. "I thought it really captured a particular time. It captured an incredible amount of energy and song development that was quite amazing. Every year the band changed radically. Spencer Dryden was our best drummer. He had a jazz sensibility, and that freed up a lot of stuff I could do on the bass as well as Jorma on guitar."

Inducted into the Rock Hall in 1996, along with Stevie Wonder and Pink Floyd, the Airplane got the only standing ovation of the night. The Dead's Mickey Hart proclaimed them "the best in the world on many a night."

Before playing in Lahaina, in a 1993 interview, the Airplane/ Starship's archetypal psychedelic revolutionary talked about the nation's lack of wise leadership and the coming changes. He could have been discussing the turbulent days of this time. "They're (politicians) all stuck in this mold that doesn't work anymore," Kantner declared. "It's going to take something drastic to make it change. Chaos is here, and it's going to get worse before it gets better. Even in the Hawaiian islands, you will see chaos swirling. Being from San Francisco, we're constantly expecting cataclysm, so it won't be too much of a problem. But I feel sorry for people who rely on stability for the peace in their lives.

"Be prepared to deal with the unexpected," he suggested. "Don't expect the expected because it doesn't work anymore. I feel like Cassandra at the gates of Troy saying something's coming.

"The Greeks had a good translation of the word chaos long ago. Chaos was a double-edged equation, one side was normal anarchy, and the other translated as great opportunities at your feet. The Chinese have a double-faced ideogram that does the same thing. So a lot of possibilities open up when you have chaos. Something is going to come out of it, and what you do to prepare for it is sort of what we sing about."

While Kantner painted a vivid portrait of the future, he dismissed adopting any kind of leadership role. "I think of ourselves as more as news reporters in the old English tradition of broadside ballads," he said. "I like to point out nice little things and shine the light of day on interesting stuff."

Paul Kantner died in 2016, and Marty Balin in 2018. Remembering Kantner, Jorma Kaukonen wrote on his *Cracks in the Finish* website, "He held our feet to the flame. He could be argumentative and contentious…he could be loving and kind…his dedication to the Airplane's destiny as he saw it was undeniable."

And paying tribute to Balin, Kaukonen wrote, "He and Paul Kantner came together and like plutonium halves in a reactor started a chain reaction that still affects many of us today. It was a moment of powerful synchronicity."

"SUGAR MAGNOLIA"

Grateful Dead

"What we do is based on trust and that comes from being spiritually involved in what you are doing. You have to surrender to the music."

"We made something of a career by trying to break out of formulas," explains the Grateful Dead's Bob Weir on Maui in late 1989. "We're renowned for being atypical about anything in the music business. Hard knocks teaches that you have to give people what they want. We've never really learned that lesson."

Weir's most memorable songs with the Dead include "Sugar Magnolia," "I Need a Miracle," and "Estimated Prophet." On his *Ace* debut solo album, highlights included "Playing in the Band," "One More Saturday Night," and "Cassidy," which became Dead concert staples.

On the band's final studio album, *Built to Last*, Weir contributed "Victim or the Crime" and "Picasso Moon." "Victim or the Crime" aroused some controversy within the band and with fans because it peered into the dark side of the human psyche. The U.K.'s *Melody Maker* praised the song as "indisputably the Dead's finest achievement in 15 years."

"There was something of a controversy over the song because I was finally starting to pen stuff about the dark side," he says. "There was always that aspect of my personality, but I was never aware when I was young that it was something one could write about. Everybody has their darkness and their lightness. It's absurd to just write about the light stuff all your life and deny half of human nature. I'm not concentrating on the dark side, but I'm no longer going to paint everything rosy."

Formed in the San Francisco Bay Area in 1965, during the emergence of the psychedelic counterculture, the Dead relied on Robert

Hunter for lyrics. His poetic imagery was heard in everything from early Dead classics like "Dark Star" and "China Cat Sunflower" through "Uncle John's Band" and "Fire on the Mountain."

Years before the Grateful Dead unleashed their psychedelic might, Hunter played folk music with Jerry Garcia. "We were friends in our late teens, and we had a folk duo," he recalled. "Then we went country and formed a bluegrass band. Then that moved on to a jug band which I dropped out of. That was the band that became The Warlocks, which became the Grateful Dead. I always play better pencil than guitar."

For "Alligator," his first song recorded by the band, Hunter was rewarded with a sum of money which seemed vast at the time. "They said, 'how much was in the pot and how much did I want from it?' I said, would $250 be too much? So I was given that, and I brought myself a second-hand Studebaker. It felt like a lot."

Teaming with the Dead's venerable guitarist for more than a quarter of a century, Hunter's partnership with Garcia evolved to where "he plays some chords, and I come up with a line that might work. He develops the structure, and I sit and write away. I throw some lines at him, and he says, 'that's too many syllables,' so it's how about this? All of a sudden, a line comes out, which is just pure magic. It's a true collaboration as opposed to me handing somebody a bunch of lyrics and they set it or them handing me a musical setting."

Rather than suggest any thematic focus Garcia, "prefers things that are coming way from left field," said Hunter. "That's just where I come from. So many songs are written to pat ideas. It can be good, but it won't last a long time. It's the oddities that seem to hang on."

Rarely giving interviews, Hunter spent some time on Maui in 1993, conjuring up some new Dead magic for a projected studio album. "Jerry, Phil, and I are over here working on new Grateful Dead material," he reported.

"He loved it here," Bill Kreutzmann said about Garcia's affection for Hawai'i in a Hana Hou! magazine interview. "We were standing on the back of a dive boat in Kona and said, 'God, let's move here!' We both agreed and said, when the band ends, we'll move to Hawaii."

The songs for the projected studio album never saw the light of day on record until some rehearsals were released on *So Many Roads* in

1999, and concert versions on *Ready or Not* in 2019, which included a version of possibly the last Hunter/Garcia collaboration, an epic 13-minute ballad, "Days Between." Other songs composed in Hawai'i included "Liberty" and "Lazy River Road."

Spinning intriguing musical stories provided far greater satisfaction for this lyricist than manufacturing hits. "I think I'm controversial in continuing to use very unlikely imagery," Hunter stressed. "It's easy enough to write what people will grasp immediately. Why don't I write hits? No. The Grateful Dead has been controversial that way. I can write hits as easily as anyone else. I just don't try. Then we'd be a hit band, five good years and out of here."

Hunter, who died in September 2019, wrote evocative lyrics which sometimes mystified fans. "I prefer a statement that can be taken a number of ways," he suggested. "There might be shades of ambiguity. I'm mostly interested in getting the sound correct, the verbal construction, resonant imagery, and a sort of multifaceted possible connectedness. In short, I'm interested in songs that will live forever if possible."

Crafting unconventional songs unlike anything else heard on the radio, the Dead didn't use setlists, changed repertoire nightly, and rarely played a song the same way. "What we do is based on trust, and that comes from being spiritually involved in what you are doing," says drummer Mickey Hart in 1982. "You have to surrender to the music, or else you're just playing lyrics. Everything comes from there, and that's what that is built on. That's where the magic comes from. We call it the Wolf. That's when the Wolf comes out."

Asked about the Dead's early albums, the groundbreaking *Anthem of the Sun*, and *Aoxomoxoa*, Hart reported, "they're my favorite records. *Anthem* was totally inspired, a mix of live and studio. Originally we were just a bunch of kids. It was like Grateful Dead punk music. I listened to the first album the other day, and I couldn't believe how fast it was. It was three times faster than anything we do now."

Mickey was on Maui working on his own music. We had arranged to meet for an interview when a nasty car accident landed me in hospital. Graciously he came to the hospital, and we talked while I was propped up in bed.

Was it true that their label, Warner Bros. Records, thought *Workingman's Dead* was their first marketable album? "That's right, 'Ripple' and 'Casey Jones,' mellow stuff which could sell. People could listen to it. You couldn't listen to 'Alligator' for hours. *Workingman's Dead* and *American Beauty* was the next step in our evolution because we had to learn how to play music."

Marveling about the Dead's concert popularity, he notes: "The Dead doesn't work directly with the music business. We skirt it and use it when we need to. Most groups live on singles and records in general. Ours comes from live performances; that's our strength. So that when we don't make a good record, it doesn't affect us at all; we just go on, while another group could be destroyed if their record doesn't sell. We make our money with live shows, and we outsell Fleetwood Mac and all those people."

The enormous success of the Dead brought problems for the band. They became almost too big. "It would be nice to have another successful record, but it only makes us bigger and bigger," says Hart in a 1989 interview. "I think it would be better for us to get a little smaller. Bigger isn't better. Some of the better places we've played don't want us back because too many people show up, like Alpine, Denver, Rochester, Syracuse. The impact on the communities is so incredible. There will be 40,000 people inside and 40,000 people outside. Now they come with bolt cutters. It's sort of the militant Deadhead."

In 1978, the Dead traveled to Egypt to perform in front of the Great Pyramid of Giza. Legendary promoter Bill Graham recalled the shows as "one of the great experiences of my life." The epic event was captured on *Rocking The Cradle: Egypt 1978*.

"I loved being there," drummer Bill Kreutzmann recalls on the phone from his Kaua'i home. "They closed the pyramid down to other tourists. Our group went in by ourselves for a couple of hours. It was really far out."

"We recorded there on The Who's equipment with speakers lined up pointing out to the desert so you could hear for 50 miles out there," says Hart. "That brought the (Bedouin) camel caravans in to watch us. The first night they stood by the camels, then by the third night, they were in front of the stage dancing. It was the first band they'd ever seen, and we got 30,000 watts of power going out. We even miked the King's Chamber and used it as a reverberation unit. It was a full lunar eclipse. There were Deadheads from all over the world. It was an electrifying experience."

Following the group's concert in Cairo, Hart traveled down the Nile for a month, recording Egyptian folk music, later released as *The Music of Upper and Lower Egypt*. "You can't just walk in and get this kind of music," he explains. "You have to seek it out. You have to hang out, drink beer and smoke some hash. Playing with them was one of the high points of my remote recording career.

"Most of the music I deal with is transformative in nature," he continues. "That's what I look for in music, the spirit side. It moves you into other states. That's what music is supposed to do - to ease the pain and show you where it is, where it was. It's a guidepost, and it's medicine. It's got an enormous power in the right hands."

Hart's love affair with world music led him to mythology expert Joseph Campbell. The two became close friends. "He was one of the few people in the world that I could get together with, and we could sit up all night and talk about the shamanic uses stalactites in 20,000 B.C.," he enthuses. "That's where our interest was, the use of percussion and drums and the transformative power of it."

Collaborating with Indian tabla virtuoso Zakir Hussain in the Diga Rhythm Band, Hart released "my attempt at 20th Century Javanese gamelan music. This transmitted into the Rhythm Devils, which was me and Bill Kreutzmann playing percussion in the middle of Dead sets. So we go crazy for 30 minutes.

"Francis Coppola came to see us and wanted this music for the movie *Apocalypse Now*. We worked for three months on it. I played with Airto and Flora Purim and all the great drummers in the world and went up the river with it. I learned the rhythm of the war, and it obviously worked because we won an Oscar for the soundtrack. Though I almost went crazy. The moral implication of it was so strong. It made my life miserable."

The Grateful Dead came to an end in 1995, following the death of Jerry Garcia. Various configurations followed, including The Other Ones, Phil Lesh & Friends, Ratdog, and Dead & Company.

"You can rock and roll till you die," Hart concludes. "Rock is a state of mind. Not only do you have to be physically and mentally prepared, you have to be spiritually too. You have to really get it together to rock hard for a long time. I believe you have to rock for 30 or 40 years to really learn it. Great violinists work at it for 40 and 50 years to become maestros. As long as we stay healthy and we like each other enough and appreciate all our work, we'll last."

"FLY LIKE AN EAGLE"

Steve Miller

"When I got done with the tour, it was number one, and there was a check in the mailbox, and I was no longer poor."

Decrying the social injustice of poverty, hunger, and homelessness while offering an inspiring affirmation, Steve Miller's classic song "Fly Like an Eagle" was seeded by this legendary musician's early days of student activism. "When I was in college, I was a Freedom Rider," Miller explains. "I got on the bus and headed to Selma, Alabama. I was a member of the Student Nonviolent Coordinating Committee, and I went to a very radical university where there was a lot of social awareness.

"That always stuck with me. I wanted my music to mean something more than just pop music. That song was developed over a long period of time, years of touring. It was a big jam tune where you dimmed the lights, turned on the mirror ball, and played for 30 minutes. I'm very pleased with that song. It was a pinnacle of music and political thought, and social conscience. A really good hit has a lot of levels in it. That one has layers."

While he has never won a Grammy and was only inducted into the Rock and Roll Hall of Fame in 2016, Miller achieved phenomenal commercial success with a series of hit singles and albums beginning with *The Joker*. Combining the lyrical finesse of a literature major with deep-rooted musical smarts, he became one of the most popular artists of the classic rock era.

Early in his career, a move to Chicago led to Miller jamming with some blues greats. "T-Bone Walker taught me how to play guitar when I was nine years old," he recalls. "When I got to Chicago, the original Butterfield Band was just amazing. I saw them and thought I want some of this. Seeing Butterfield, the light bulb went off. Maybe I could get a record contract too.

Miller had grown up in Dallas, Texas, where he had become friends with future Miller Band musician Boz Scaggs. "We played in high school together, and I was in university with him for about a year," Scaggs recalls. "We were very close friends and then went our own way. Three or four years later, he was somewhat established with the Steve Miller Blues Band in San Francisco in the mid-'60s. One of the musicians in the band took off, and Steve called me and asked if I would care to join. I was living in Sweden at the time, and he sent me a ticket, and I ended up staying for a year."

"When I got out to San Francisco, it was more a social phenomenon," says Miller. "It took me a while to figure it out. The Grateful Dead could hardly tune their instruments, and they were all stoned on acid, and they took 10 minutes between songs. I showed up with a tight little band. It was a good spot for us. The Dead and Jefferson Airplane were all folkies when they started. Chuck Berry's coming to town. Oh my God, whose going to back him? Let's call Steve. When we went to London in '67 to record *Children of the Future*, we were kind of ahead of the curve with blues."

For their debut album, the musicians flew to England to record with acclaimed producer Glyn Johns, who had worked with the Beatles, The Who, and the Rolling Stones. "At the studio we were working, Joe Cocker was making his first album, and Jimi Hendrix was working upstairs, and the Stones would come in and do overdubs," Scaggs remembers. "It was a time and a place that was indescribably amazing, a key time for British music. We were right in the middle of it."

Before he joined the Miller Band, he had spent time on the streets of Europe as a busker. "You stand in front of the metro or cinema and break out the guitar and wail away and pass the hat, and then the cops would come, and you'd runoff," he says. "It wasn't a full-time occupation. It got me from point A to B."

Scaggs played with Miller on the landmark recordings, *Children of the Future* and *Sailor*, and then he left for a solo career. "It was mutually agreed upon," he says. "Steve had his ideas of where he was going, and I had different ideas. The experience was a great one for those two albums for both of us. It was the first songs that I had written. Our styles were going in different directions. He went off with his ideas, and I got my first recording contract with Atlantic."

The Steve Miller Band's third album, *Brave New World*, included a certain Paul Ramon (Paul McCartney) playing on "My Dark Hour." "I was scheduled to go to England to mix *Brave New World* with Glyn Johns, and he was working with the Beatles at the time," Miller says. "I arrived, and Glyn said, 'let's go to George's house.' I met George, and he made me feel so good. He said he loved what I was doing. Are you kidding? So I went to a session, it was 'Get Back.'

"The next day, they were going to cut some tracks, and Ringo and John didn't show up. So we jammed for a bit, and then George took off, and Paul and I really hit it off. He got on drums, and I got on guitar, and Glenn said, 'let's record it.' I had this little tune, and then Paul played bass, and Paul and I sang background. I went back to the States thinking I just did a song with one of the Beatles. It started a friendship, and we've done a lot of stuff since then."

The release of *The Joker* in 1973 heralded a major shift in Miller's career, which saw him gravitate from playing theaters to stadiums. "We were really struggling for seven years trying to get somewhere," he reports. "We were kings of the underground and bigger in England than the States, but we couldn't get on television, and AM radio wouldn't touch us.

"I was pretty much at the end of the line. I remember finishing the album, and some kid at the record company said, 'I think 'The Joker' is really a hit.' I didn't have any idea, and I was mad at the company because they weren't giving me any support. I just said, please have the record in stores in the cities I'm playing in. When I got done with the tour, it was number one, and there was a check in the mailbox, and I was no longer poor. So I called up my agent and said, I'm not going to tour next year. I'm going to work on a new album. I ended up working for 18 months and made *Fly Like an Eagle* and *Book Of Dreams*. And in that time, we became kings of AM radio, and everything changed. But it was a very long, slow, hard slog."

In concert, you can sometimes hear Miller perform an acoustic version of "The Joker." He has wondered about releasing an acoustic collection of his hits. "But the question is, how are we going to sell records now. You think you could walk into Capitol Records, and hey, this is a good idea. But they're just about out of business. They sold the tower for condos. EMI was bought by a company that specializes in waste management, hotels, and gas stations.

"Basically, I'm finding the people interested in manufacturing and putting out records are not even music people, like somebody at Walmart or Best Buy. They just want to see the Steve Miller logo. They don't care what's in the record."

Miller returned to his rocking blues roots with his most recent studio album, *Let Your Hair Down*, which featured vocalist Sonny Charles, the former lead singer of the Checkmates soul band. "With Sonny Charles in the band, it's like Otis Redding joined. It's kind of a miracle at this stage of a career to have somebody of that quality join the band. I went to Vegas to see Elton John, and we had dinner. I played him the album, and he was knocked out. That was a good sign. He liked all the vocal harmonies."

In recent years, he contributed to the tribute album *Art of McCartney*, had his music covered by Rickie Lee Jones, Seal, and Kenny Chesney, and was sampled by the likes of Shaggy, Fatboy Slim, and Public Enemy.

Like many classic rock artists, over the years, Miller has found his music appealing across generations. "It's the songs, they're fun to sing, and they sound good," he says. "It's pretty hard not to sing the chorus of 'The Joker.' In the '90s, it was shocking that 85 percent (of his audiences) were between the ages of 10 and 20. Our shows are kind of more than a headbangers ball, it's a rock show, and they learn about blues and jazz. In the last five years, the audience is more mature. It goes from about 1968 to now."

"WOODSTOCK"

Wavy Gravy

*"Good morning, what we have in mind
is breakfast in bed for 400,000."*

"When we played Woodstock, it was a transcendent moment," recalls Edgar Winter about performing with his brother at the historic festival in 1969. "Looking out over this endless sea of humanity and seeing them united in a unique way, I realized music is a positive energy that can bring people together and transcend boundaries. Woodstock was like a spiritual awakening."

"It became a touchstone for the generation," suggests Country Joe McDonald. "It was a symbol of the peace and love era. It was very large, and in many ways, the opposite of what was happening at the time in the country. There was the war, campus unrest, the generation gap, and racial strife."

Heading Country Joe and the Fish, McDonald provided one of the early crowning moments of the festival, leading close to half a million in his famous "Fish Cheer."

"It was a mistake," he says of his solo inclusion in the program. "It was Friday, and no one else could go on, so they pushed me on stage. I was supposed to play with the band on Sunday, so I didn't really want to do it. I was quite shocked that everyone was singing and clapping along. They weren't paying much attention to anything I did before that. I'm sure it's the first time that anyone got half a million people to yell fuck. It seemed an adequate epithet for complaining about the (Vietnam) war."

Richie Haven's electrifying performance opening the festival catapulted him to fame. His jubilant "Freedom" was immortalized in the Oscar-winning *Woodstock* documentary and became an anthem of the time and a staple of his career. "I sang every song I knew, and when they asked me to go back on one more time, I didn't know what to sing, so I improvised 'Freedom,'" he recalled in a 1988 interview.

"The music was just a vehicle to say what people felt," he suggested about the impact of Woodstock. "Rock and roll is the vehicle, and it's never going to die."

Also taking the stage solo at the festival, John Sebastian of Lovin' Spoonful fame. "I went there simply to be a part of what I heard was going to be a wonderful several days of music, not as a performer, but simply to be in the audience," he explains. "On the second day, it had been raining, and it was muddy, and at one point, I was standing on stage with the promoters. Chip Monk said, 'we need somebody to hold the crowd just with an acoustic guitar so we can sweep the water off the stage.' I'm looking out at the audience, and they are both looking at me. I say I didn't even bring a guitar. They said, 'you have five minutes to find one,' so I borrowed a guitar and went on. It was amazing."

For Carlos Santana, Woodstock served as the pivotal entry to the world of his transcendent Latin rock music. "Woodstock was about collective consciousness, unity, and celebrating," he says. "Woodstock was multi-layered, Ravi Shankar and Jimi Hendrix, all the colors were there." He declined to play the 25th-anniversary concert - "this one's only vanilla, and I wasn't interested in duplicating grunge white music."

For the Grateful Dead's Bob Weir the festival was basically a wonderful party. "There were a few politicos running around raving about the political significance and consequence," he says, laughing. "Everybody I knew was looking at them like they were completely crazy and missing the whole deal. We were having a great party, and they were talking politics. Nobody else saw it that way."

Ask Wavy Gravy how he got to stand on stage in front of half a million rock fans as an emcee at the festival, and the iconic hippie prankster launches into an amusing, convoluted narrative that begins with his formative days as a beat poet in New York's Greenwich Village.

"We have to go back to the late '50s when I studied at Boston University," Wavy explains. "I was a teenage beatnik and studied jazz and poetry. I was at the best place called the Gaslight (Café), and I eventually talked the owner into allowing folk musicians to play in between the poems. As I got tired of reading my poems, I started talking about the weird stuff that happened during the day. The next thing you know, I'm opening for Peter, Paul and Mary, and Thelonious Monk, and John Coltrane, doing this stand-up philosophy. When Woodstock time rolled along Chip Monk, who built the stage at Woodstock and used to do lights at The Village Gate where I performed with Monk, he knew I could get on a microphone."

To keep things mellow at the fest Wavy and Hog Farm commune members were hired to organize the "Please Force." "What I did was life support announcements and come on between bands and told people where the medical stuff was, that the acid wasn't going to kill them, and I had some great lines in the film. The one that was picked by *Entertainment Weekly* as one of the top entertainment lines of the 20th century was – 'Good morning, what we have in mind is breakfast in bed for 400,000' – which was when we introduced hippies to granola."

Wavy became part of a group known as the Merry Pranksters that traveled across the country in a psychedelic painted school bus, chronicled by Tom Wolfe in *The Electric Kool-Aid Acid Test*. Metamorphosing from beat poet to psychedelic jester, he began devoting his life to helping others, in time adopting a clown persona partly because "the police did not want to hit me anymore."

So the story goes, blues legend B.B. King provided his name change at the Texas Pop Festival in 1969, two weeks after Woodstock. "I was lying on stage," he recalls. "It was before one of my multiple back surgeries. I started to get up, and I felt this hand on my shoulder, and it was B.B. King. He said, 'you Wavy Gravy?' Yes sir. 'Well, Wavy Gravy, I can work around you.' He picked up Lucille and played until sunrise."

SUNDOWN IN NASHVILLE

"KISS AN ANGEL GOOD MORNIN'"

Charley Pride

"Our country grew up with a segregation policy, a them and us syndrome. It has infested all walks of life, including music."

"I am the whole ball of wax: Elvis Presley, Ernest Tubb, B.B. King, Bob Dylan, Nat King Cole, and Frank Sinatra all combined into one." That's the late country star Charley Pride talking to *People* magazine in 1980.

Such an audacious pronouncement was not undeserved. With 36 number one hits, 52 top-10 songs, and more than 70 million albums and singles sold, Pride became one of country's greatest legends. RCA Records' second bestselling artist after Elvis Presley, he was the first Black artist to have a number one country record and the first artist to win the Country Music Association's male vocalist award two years in a row.

"Whatever I have done, I've always tried to do a good job," he said interviewed on Maui in 1984. "When I was a cotton picker, I was pretty good. I put an emphasis on doing a good job. I don't have any gimmicks. I'm an actual person who goes out and sings. I'm just myself, and this permeates to my audience. Every time I go out on stage, I want to do the best show I can."

Born in rural Mississippi in 1934, in a family of 11 brothers and sisters, Pride labored long hours as a child in the cotton fields, earning three dollars for every 100 pounds he picked. Mississippi at the time resembled a feudal society where conditions for many black plantation workers weren't far removed from slavery.

"As a child, I listened to country," he recalled. "My dad was very traditional and controlled everything. We had an old battery radio, and he controlled the knobs, and so we grew up listening to the Grand Ole Opry." Living a relatively sheltered life, he was surprised to discover that not everyone was gifted with a good voice. "We all could sing as kids, and living in Mississippi, I wasn't around too many people, and so I thought everyone could sing."

Before singing professionally, Pride was attracted to baseball and played in the Negro American League in Detroit and with the Memphis Red Sox in the 1950s. After some military service, his baseball career continued with the Los Angeles Angels and the New York Mets. During intermission at games, he would often pick up a guitar and sing a song over the PA system, amazing audiences with his rich baritone vocals.

Part Black and part Choctaw Indian, Pride's ethnicity in a predominately white musical market was initially a matter of concern. His first manager didn't dare mail out any PR photos until his first release, "The Snakes Crawl at Night," became a big hit.

Initially billed as Country Charley Pride (his manager had initially suggested George Washington III), audiences were surprised when he would walk out on stage, often to complete silence. He would disarm them by joking about his permanent tan.

Some radio stations boycotted his music for a while, but by 1967 he became the first Black singer to appear at the Grand Ole Opry. Facing racism at a CMA show, Loretta Lynn was warned not to hug Pride onstage if he won. Lynn not only hugged him, she kissed him. It echoed a time when Willie Nelson championed Pride at a Texas club by kissing him on stage. "Charley's been treated unfairly," Willie told *Parade* magazine. "The owner of the club, who's a real good friend of mine, was a solid redneck, and he didn't want him there. So I kissed Charley on the mouth."

Pride is philosophical about traditional country music's appeal to white audiences. "Our country grew up with a segregation policy, a them and us syndrome," he said. "It has infested all walks of life, including music. It's a historical thing from generation to generation until we can get to one country where we're all just Americans."

Over time he would perform with many country greats including Willie Nelson, Dolly Parton, and Johnny Cash. It was Cash who persuaded Pride to pursue a country career.

A big fan of astrology, he began studying planetary influences after reading Linda Goodman's *Sun Signs*. He wrote in his autobiography *Pride: The Charley Pride Story*, "I believe it is possible to tell what sign people were born under by watching their eyes, watching how they walk, how they talk."

Pride released his most recent album, *Music in My Heart*, in 2017. *My Kind of Country* praised it as "Charley's best album in over twenty years." He was honored with the Willie Nelson Lifetime Achievement Award at the Country Music Association awards in November 2020, where he performed "Kiss an Angel Good Mornin.'"

He died a month later of Covid complications at the age of 86. Trisha Yearwood posted: "Charley Pride was a hero, and a trailblazer in country music. Everyone who had the pleasure of knowing Charley loved him." And Dolly Parton posted: "I'm so heartbroken that one of my dearest and oldest friends, Charley Pride, has passed away."

"DON'T IT MAKE MY BROWN EYES BLUE"

Crystal Gayle

"I've always thought I was probably a cabaret singer in another life."

O ne of country's legendary female artists, Crystal Gayle has often stepped beyond her roots to explore musical avenues that may surprise those only familiar with her hits. Spend time with this charming entertainer, and you'll hear about her love for Celtic and New Age music, how she'd slip a Billie Holiday standard into her earlier recordings, about her desire to release a Native American album, and a feeling that maybe she was really destined for the Broadway stage.

Perhaps Gayle's most adventurous recording is her 1999 tribute to Hoagy Carmichael, a critically acclaimed project that she had dreamt about since meeting the legendary composer. "I got to work with him in the summer of 1981, and he died in December, and from that moment I wanted to do this album," she says. "It just took me a lot longer than I wanted. It was so hard to pick a few songs.

Crystal Gayle Sings the Heart & Soul of Hoagy Carmichael featured 15 classics from *Stardust* to *Georgia on My Mind*. Showered with laudatory reviews, she was hailed as one of America's truly great singers. "I love singing really good songs, and for me, this was a tribute to Hoagy as well as an opportunity to put them in my style," she continues. "I've always thought I was probably a cabaret singer in another life. I actually should have been on Broadway doing show tunes. I love the style of music of the '30s and '40s."

The younger sister of country legend Loretta Lynn, Gayle was born in the Appalachian coal-mining town of Paintsville, Kentucky, and raised in Indiana from a young age. While growing up, she traveled and sang country music with her famous sister for a few weeks each summer, absorbing a wide range of musical influences. "My roots are definitely country," she states. "I grew up in the business of singing with my brother's bands on weekends and of course having a sister as famous as Loretta growing up, you are country.

"I love it, but I also grew up with a great music teacher in high school and sang in all the choral groups, and we sang everything from swing to blues. With this background, when I graduated, I didn't think I'd have to just sing and record country. I'm a singer. If you look back through my albums, I've thrown in a Billie Holiday song here and there. I got away with it. I've been lucky that through the years, my fans expect a little of everything."

It was her famous sister who suggested Gayle creatively spread her wings. "Being the sister of Loretta Lynn didn't hurt at all in the sense that her little sister could do anything if she agreed. When I started recording, my sister was the one who told me to not sing real country. She said, 'we already have a Loretta Lynn, we don't need another one, and you'll only be compared to me.' I grew up singing all of her songs, and she said, 'quit singing them, I don't want you singing my songs anymore.' I would probably have never had the success that I've had if I had just done the type of material my sister did. It would not have worked."

Having a popular country star as her sister proved both a boon and challenge, she reports. "It closed lots of doors as well as opened them. It didn't bother me that when I first started out, I was billed as Loretta Lynn's little sister. Of course, I have a whole different perspective than someone else who might not have made it that's been related. I realized I had to do it on my own."

Signing her first recording contract while still in school, Gayle's debut single, *I've Cried (The Blue Right Out of My Eyes)*, composed by Lynn, reached the Top 25 on the national country music charts. Emerging from her sister's shadow, she soon established her own iden-tity earning a string of hits, including *Wrong Road Again, Beyond You, Somebody Loves You,* and *Never Miss a Real Good Thing*. With her fourth album, *We Must Believe in Magic*, Gayle became the first female country artist to achieve platinum sales status.

That album included the international country and pop smash, *Don't It Make My Brown Eyes Blue*. The jazzy, Grammy-winning song became her signature. It was recognized in 1999 as one of the ten most-performed songs of the 20th century.

Breaking the Nashville mold and record company suggestions, she produced huge hits around the world with ballads. "'When I Dream,' 'Talking in Your Sleep,' as well as 'Brown Eyes' were big ballad songs," she notes. "Record companies would say, 'you can't release a ballad.' They're harder to get played because radio stations like the up-tempo, happy songs. But we did good with them."

Viewing the state of country music in the late 20th century, Gayle observed a profit-obsessed business, "where cycles (of success) are a lot shorter. Someone can have a million-selling album and be off the label in two years. It's sad. Nashville has changed. Companies have brought in the pop mentality, which I didn't have to contend with until the latter part of my career. It was more they really wanted to help an artist and be there for an artist. Now it's give me a hit song, or you're gone."

In her formative days as a country artist, "you could build a career. I worked for quite a few years without a band. I just picked up bands that played in clubs I worked. Then I worked with some artists that had their own band, and I'd use them. That was what country was."

So how does she view her place in country today? "I've been lucky to have a career that's not just based on hit records," she says. "But I have had over 18 number ones, and *Brown Eyes* was one of the top ten most-played country songs of the 20th century. I still have a good time performing, and I love singing."

She has talked about recording a work that honors her Native American heritage. "I'm Cherokee, and my sisters and I love our heritage," she says. "We grew up with a love for nature and the land, and I definitely need to do a Native album. My sister Peggy has written a couple of wonderful songs that are about being Native American that I want on it."

In 2019, she released *You Don't Know Me*, which featured a collaboration with sisters Loretta and Peggy. It marked the first time the siblings recorded together. A return to classic country, the album included covers of songs originally recorded by artists such as Patsy Cline, George Jones, and Willie Nelson.

Before closing, one more question arises - about her fondness for long hair. Besides her gorgeous voice, Gayle is known for her amazing tresses, which reach to the floor. "When I was very young, it was always kept very short, as short as a boys," she explains. "My mother worked the night shift as a nurse, and I would meet her as I was leaving for school. She would be trying to fix my hair and wash the dirt off my face, so she found it was easier if I had real short hair. I think it stemmed from me wanting to have hair long enough to put into a ponytail, and I just took it to the extreme."

"GUNPOWDER AND LEAD"

Miranda Lambert

"My defining moment in my career was singing with Willie
and Kris Kristofferson for Merle Haggard
at the Kennedy Center Honors."

I n late July 2020, when Miranda Lambert's song, "Bluebird," hit No. 1, the country superstar announced on *Twitter*, "I'm celebrating happiness and artistic freedom in a time where we all feel a little caged. I have spent my life doing what I love and I feel more blessed and humbled than ever to have this song of hope resonate with you all."

One of the highlights of her Grammy-nominated album *Wildcard*, she says the inspiring track is one of her favorites. Singing about nurturing her heart, and illuminating her soul, it was co-written by Luke Dick and Natalie Hemby. "Luke Dick had sent me some lyrics, and he had read somewhere about keeping a bluebird in your heart, and it really moved him, so we wrote off that emotion," she explains before a Maui concert. "I love that song. It's got darkness and hopefulness."

Headlining the 2019 Maui Songwriters Festival, Lambert was thrilled to be back in Hawai'i. "Maui is a magical place. Playing music here with great friends is a dream. You get to be in the most beautiful place singing country music. I don't know what's better than that."

A trailblazer of modern country, Lambert has sold millions of albums, won numerous awards, including two Grammys, and topped the country charts with memorable hits like "The House That Built Me," "Gunpowder and Lead," and "Mamas Broken Heart."

Influenced by country greats like Loretta Lynn and Merle Haggard, she is known for adopting feisty, rebellious personas in her songs. She starkly warned an abusive ex on "Gunpowder and Lead," was enraged about a woman who stole her man on the rocking "Crazy Ex-Girlfriend," and was slyly insulting on "Only Prettier."

Forming her first band, Texas Pride, while still in high school, Lambert competed in the Nashville Star talent show, which led to an Epic Records contract. From her earliest days, she dreamed of becoming a country musician. "I never wanted to be anything else," she recalls. "By the age of 17, I made up my mind I didn't want to go to college. I just wanted to be in a band and chase this dream."

And she was determined to follow her own muse. "I was so hungry and ready to get where I wanted to go that I always went with my gut, no matter whether it was the right business decision. I chased it with my gut and my heart."

Success came quickly, with her first album debuting at No. 1 on Billboard's Top Country chart in 2005. She would go on to become the first country artist to see her next five albums debut at the top of the Billboard charts.

By 2011, she had teamed with Ashley Monroe and Angaleena Presley to launch the female country supergroup, the Pistol Annies. Their Grammy-nominated *Interstate Gospel*, was proclaimed a masterpiece and 2018's best country album. Lambert's winning streak continued with the platinum-selling *The Weight of These Wings* hailed as "Unflinchingly honest, emotionally resonant and deeply personal" by *PopMatters*.

Released in 2016, after her divorce from country star Blake Shelton, it ranged in tone from the rockabilly flavored "Ugly Nights" to the stunning lament "Vice," which exposed her heartbreak. Then came *Wildcard*, her latest "country rock masterpiece," praised *Rolling Stone*. "I'm excited about my new record," she says. "I'm newly married and happy, so I'm just living the dream."

Over the years, Lambert has recorded with a number of legendary artists, including Dolly Parton on a remake of "Dumb Blonde" with the country icon in 2018. "Dolly was my last bucket list that I hadn't met," she enthuses. "When I got to meet her and record with her, it was like...she just sprinkles magic wherever she goes. Being in her presence, you feel like you are learning so much by just talking to her."

Teaming with John Fogerty on his classic "Wrote a Song for Everyone" was another highlight. "Oh my God, I'm such a fan, and he's such a sweetheart," she says. "I've got to sing with him a few times, and I've got to sing with Kris (Kristofferson) too, and those are the moments that you don't forget. You can't believe it's happening."

And there's Willie Nelson. She sang with Willie on his hit album *To All the Girls*. "My defining moment in my career was singing with Willie and Kris Kristofferson for Merle Haggard at the Kennedy Centre Honors," she says. "When people ask what was your biggest highlight, I have to say that. If you're from Texas, that makes sense."

Among her other collaborations, she recorded a rousing version of Elvin Bishop's rock classic "Fooled Around and Fell in Love" with Maren Morris and the female artists from her 2019 *Roadside Bars & Pink Guitars* fall tour. "There were six different artists plus the Pistol Annies," she explains. "I was trying to think of what song would be right. I'm a huge fan of Rod Stewart's version of the song, and I thought that's the one."

She felt inspired after hearing Stewarts' cover played on Nashville's Hippie Radio station. "If I have the radio on, that's mostly what's it on," she says. "It's great."

Lambert released the critically acclaimed *The Marfa Tapes* in May 2021, teamed with Texas musicians Jon Randall and Jack Ingram. It was recorded live in the West Texas desert with just three microphones, three voices, and one guitar. Her 2021 Christmas recording with the Pistol Annies was also widely lauded. "With *Hell of a Holiday*, Pistol Annies once again live up to their billing as an all-star trio," noted *Country Standard Time*.

Winner of the 2022 Entertainer of the Year at the Academy of Country Music Awards, Lambert subsequently released *Palomino*, which included new collaborations with the Highwomen's Natalie Hemby.

Along with Morris and the Highwomen supergroup, Lambert has helped shift the face of country, empowering women as members of all-female ensembles. "I'm a huge fan of Maren," she says. "We're kindred spirits, and there's a kinship. Both of us go with our gut and heart. It's nice to be supportive and be supported. I think we've been loud enough that people are paying attention."

"NO PLACE THAT FAR"

Sara Evans

"I'm a big fan of great lyrics and always try to record songs that I think will stand the test of time."

"I've been performing on stage singing country music since I was four or five years old," recalls Sara Evans. "It's all I've ever known. It's in my blood."

Loved for top hits like "Suds in the Bucket," "A Real Fine Place to Start," and "A Little Bit Stronger," Evans, "grew up listening to country music from a very young age. But as I grew older, I branched out and started listening to pop and rock. Country music is my home, and I love great country songs. I definitely view myself as a country artist, but with so many additional dimensions."

One of country's top female performers, her debut album, *Three Chords and the Truth*, was hailed by some critics as one of the best albums of the year. She followed up with *No Place That Far*, which sold gold, and by 2000, her album *Born to Fly* sold double-platinum.

After releasing *Stronger* in 2011, which topped Billboard's country album chart, she next produced *Slow Me Down*. Packed with memorable songs, many with a pop flavor, its appeal was broad. *AllMusic* praised: "This is an adult contemporary pop album, the kind of music made for the crossover diva Evans now is."

"I definitely did skew a little more pop overall with the *Slow Me Down* album, which was a conscious decision to stretch and try something a little different," she explains. "I've always had a balance in my music between pop and country that seems to fit my voice well and who I am as an artist. I like to have variety and show the versatility in my voice. My musical tastes have always been pretty varied."

When some of Nashville's brightest stars teamed with rockers, the Doobie Brothers, for the country-infused album *Southbound*, one of the highlights featured Evans teaming with Michael McDonald on "What a Fool Believes." "She killed it," Doobie's Pat Simmons reported. "That was one of the best cuts. For me, it almost makes more sense having a woman singing it."

"I was thrilled when I got the call to sing with Michael," she says. "I grew up listening to the Doobie Brothers. I have always been a huge fan. Every time I hear his vocals, I'm just blown away."

With male stars like Blake Shelton, Brad Paisley, and Toby Keith featured on *Southbound*, the album easily fit country radio formats at a time when many leading female country artists struggle for airplay.

"Country music right now prizes male youth and aggression over female experience and assertiveness," noted a NPR review of Evans' Slow Me Down.

"Country radio is in a very interesting phase right now as they aren't playing hardly any female artists," Evans reports. "I was one of a handful of females that country radio did play last year (2014), and I am so blessed and grateful for that. I hope that we soon get back to more balance though."

A study by University of Ottawa professor Dr. Jada E. Watson about gender representation on country radio between 2000 and 2018 found that, on average, male artists were five times more likely to be heard than female artists, and the disparity rose to close to ten times more in 2018.

Watson wrote: "By playing mostly men, radio is training listeners to appreciate just one type of voice, one type of sound, one type of narrative subject position or story. As a result, women's voices have been marginalized, their achievements have been minimized, and their narrative voice limited."

"When I first started in the business, it was fairly balanced, if not slightly leaning heavy on female airplay," says Evans. "I'm very thankful that I did hit the scene when I did."

Dazzling across genres, Evans shined in 2020 on her acclaimed covers album, *Copy That*. With songs ranging from The Knack's "My Sharona" and Hank Williams' classic "I'm So Lonesome I Could Cry" to Carol King's "It's Too Late," *Nashville Lifestyles* praised, "Visiting six different decades, she delightfully coaxes disco, Brit-pop, new wave rock, and more into the 21st century."

Acclaimed as an artist who sings with power, grace, and dignity, Evans says she hopes her music "touches people and makes them feel something. Whether it's joy or sadness, as long as it moves someone, I'm happy. I'm a big fan of great lyrics and always try to record songs that I think will stand the test of time either now or 20 years from now."

MELE O HAWAI‘I

"E KU‘U MORNING DEW"

Eddie Kamae

"We have a collective responsibility to safeguard Hawai‘i's fragile heritage."

Revered musician/filmmaker Eddie Kamae spent many years helping perpetuate Hawaiian culture through leading the Sons of Hawaii and directing his award-winning *Legacy* documentaries. "I've seen some of the most beautiful things happen where everything was aloha," Eddie once said. "You can't sell aloha. That's what's missing. My teachers always said to share with your heart. They knew the Hawai‘i of old wouldn't be around long. That's what keeps me going."

Hailed as a living treasure, as a filmmaker, he patiently documented Hawai‘i's rich cultural legacy beginning in the mid-1980s with his *The Hawaiian Legacy Series*. Premiering his first documentary *Li‘a: The Legacy of a Hawaiian Man,* in 1988, subsequent films included *Listen to the Forest; Words, Earth & Aloha; Ki Ho‘alu: Slack Key; The Hawaiian Way;* and *Lahaina: Waves of Change.* His last film, *Those Who Came Before: The Musical Journey of Eddie Kamae*, was released in 2009.

"My main focus is the children because they need to know this," Eddie explained his mission. "Everybody used to share and love one another. When I was a little kid on Maui, I experienced the time when everybody shared; everybody waved good morning. Everybody was happy. People today say I'm Hawaiian; you're not. That's baloney as far as I'm concerned. I'm tired of this nonsense. If you're born and raised here, you are Hawaiian. Hopefully, the young ones will hear this and continue.

"The elders have so much to offer. You need to go there and inspire them to express their opinions and thoughts about what life is all about. That's what I want to capture, so the little ones can understand what was life in the old days. How did they survive the hardships? Togetherness, respect, and kindness were important in the old days. It's what's missing today. Love was the most important ingredient in Hawai'i. Hawaiians really had this aloha and feeling. I want to bring that back. We have a collective responsibility to safeguard Hawai'i's fragile heritage."

While he was diligently archiving the essential traditions and voices of Hawai'i's kupuna for future generations, there were moments when Eddie missed the joyous times of playing with his old compatriots. Supported by a new group of musicians, at age 80, he returned to the recording studio and released his first new music in 25 years. *Yesterday & Today* seamlessly combined the old and new, dipping into the Sons of Hawaii's rich treasury with songs recorded by Joe Marshall, David "Feet" Rogers, Moe Keale, and Dennis Kamakahi, interwoven with material recorded by the new Sons featuring Mike Ka'awa, Ocean Kaowili, Paul Kim, and Analu Aina.

"When the boys passed away, the old group, there was just a few left, Dennis Kamakahi and George Kuo," Eddie explained over lunch at Wailuku's Tasty Crust. "I thought that was the end. Time went by, and I met new musicians. I found the right musicians, the steel sound, the rhythm, slack key guitar and bass, and the voices. It was a sound similar to what I did before."

"Eddie was always saying, 'I'm not going to be playing live music anymore, I'm too busy doing films,'" added his wife, Myrna Kamae. "But all this time, he was missing the steel guitar of Feet Rogers and the rhythm pattern from Gabby, and he found that."

Among the new recordings on *Yesterday & Today* was a version of his classic "E Ku'u Morning Dew," marking the first time he had sung the lead vocal on the song he composed, and the moving "Maka Ua," ("Little Raindrops") composed by Eddie and Myrna.

"It was the first song we ever wrote together," said Myrna. "We wrote it years ago, about 1966, but never recorded it, and he's never really played it live either. It was a rainy afternoon and we were talking and made up this song. So we dusted it off."

Throughout the years, Eddie kept some sage advice in mind, heard from his teacher Sam Li'a, who composed the classic "Hi'ilawe" – "Play it sweet and keep it simple, that's Hawaiian music," Li'a pronounced. "And he always told me, 'play it for the children Eddie.' All his life, he played for children."

Eddie's mother was born in Lahaina, and he grew up between Honolulu and the West Maui town. He met Myrna in Lahaina in 1965. A self-taught musician, he was 15 when his brother brought home a 'ukulele he had found on a Honolulu city bus. Though he knew no chords and had no idea how to play, he loved the sound. Within a short time, he became one of Hawai'i's greatest players.

Resisting Hawaiian music, at first, he applied his talent to Latin, pop, and jazz, and earned a reputation as a master of his instrument. "My father asked me if I would consider playing Hawaiian music, but I told him I thought it was too simple," he recalled. "In later years, I found out it wasn't simple at all."

It was not until he met Gabby "Pops" Pahinui that he experienced the joy of playing Hawaiian music. "When I heard Gabby play the first time, I said now I know why my father asked me to play Hawaiian music. Gabby played the same rhythm that I liked in Spanish music. Old folks would shed tears with his voice and songs and his style of playing slack key. It was the sweetest slack key."

A key figure in the Hawaiian cultural renaissance, the Sons of Hawaii enchanted audiences for close to thirty years. Formed in 1960, they were an immediate hit, helping spawn a revival of interest in traditional music. Hired to play at The Sandbox in Honolulu, word of their magical music rapidly spread, and they soon became the highest-paid Hawaiian music group in the state.

"I didn't know how far we'd get with Hawaiian music," Eddie said. "I knew I was heading in the direction of Hawaiian music because there was nothing but people, crowds of people all the nights we were there." He remembered being surprised by the diversity of their audience - wealthy residents in tuxedos, curious tourists, school kids from Punahou, all wanting to hear this new distinctive Hawaiian sound. "That's when I knew there was a place for Hawaiian music, and a Hawaiian could make a living from it."

To help enhance his understanding of the music, Eddie embarked on years of research, uncovering a wealth of old songs. "I went to the museum and every place you could think of, and I finally realized it might be out there in the islands, down in the gullies and valleys. That's where I found a lot of them. It was with the older people. They were protective of their family 'jewels.' I was able to talk to them and tell them that I was concerned about Hawaiian music, and they were kind enough to share."

This important work was honored in 1979 when he was designated a Living Treasure of Hawai'i. "When I play a song, I think about the person who wrote the song, the place, the way the verses are written, what is felt," he explained. "You have to find the right rhythm and technique which sells it. Dressing up a Hawaiian song is much harder to do than any other music because it's so simple. Sometimes it takes me a week, even more, to really feel a song. You can just play it, but then you're just doing it for people to hear. Finally, when you present it, people love it, and it draws tears to your eyes."

For most of his life, Eddie felt divinely guided. Doors opened, events unfolded, and pertinent people showed up just at the right time. "I always ask my spirit friend," he said. "My mother always told me, 'you ask, and you thank.' When I did my first film, it was amazing how things happened. We were at Waipi'o Valley, and I was walking with my 'ukulele, looking for my teacher (Sam Li'a), and it was hot and humid, no wind. My cameraman was filming me, and I said when I get passed a tree, call. He didn't call because what he saw in the camera shook him up. The leaves of the tree and the bushes on both sides were rustling and nowhere else. And there was no wind.

"Myrna was having breakfast with a Hawaiian woman, and she asked, 'where's Eddie?' Myrna says, 'he's filming in Waipi'o Valley.' The woman turns and says, 'he's already successful.' When Myrna told me that, I said, call her up, let's have breakfast. I said I've just started, and you said I'm already successful. She smiled and told me, 'Sam Li'a told me.'

"I asked her about the incident with no wind and the leaves rustling, and she said, 'Oh Eddie, the spirits there love you.' That's what it's all about. I know my spirit friend is there. All you have to do is ask."

"HAWAI'I '78"

Israel "Iz" Kamakawiwao'ole

"Part of my life mission is to help increase peace between people, and we have to start with the children."

"What the world needs right now is aloha, and that's our job," announced Israel "Iz" Kamakawiwao'ole in a 1987 interview. "That's what we are projecting wherever we go and play." The leader of the Makaha Sons of Ni'ihau at the time, he added, "If the world had aloha, everybody would be all right."

A revered icon in Hawai'i, Bruddah Iz, as he was affectionately known, became world-renowned through his memorable recording of the *Wizard of Oz* classic "Over the Rainbow," blended with Louis Armstrong's "What a Wonderful World." The moving medley - unplugged simplicity, just his angelic voice, and rhythmic 'ukulele strumming - was captured live in one take.

Initially released on his *Facing Future* album, it went on to sell more than four million copies, remain on *Billboard*'s World Digital Song Sales chart for more than 500 weeks, and was prominently featured in many TV shows and movies.

Iz had dedicated the medley to one of his musical heroes, Gabby Pahinui. "It was something that if Gabby was here, he'd dig that song to the max," he enthused in a 1994 interview.

Mountain Apple Company president Jon de Mello remembers: "We were always ready when he was in record mode. A lot of times, it would be in the middle of the night, and sometimes the first takes were the best. After the third or fourth take, he'd start getting train wrecks."

Iz recorded another version of "Over the Rainbow," without the addition of "What a Wonderful World," which was included on the posthumously released album *Alone In IZ World*. "It was a favorite song he liked, and he was feeling good that night," says de Mello, who played a pivotal role in Iz's life as producer and manager. "The

227

recording was spectacular in my eyes because of the way Israel felt. He had such enormously intuitive ideas. He knew what the people wanted to hear."

Formed in 1976, the Makaha Sons of Ni'ihau, as they were initially known, began modeling idols at the time, such as Gabby Pahinui, Sunday Manoa, and the Sons of Hawaii, proudly continuing a tradition of grassroots Hawaiian music. The group name reflected that Iz and his brother Skippy Kamakawiwao'ole's mother and father were both born on the remote island of Ni'ihau.

As children, Iz and Skippy grew up in an influential musical environment. "Skippy played music all his life, he was self-taught," Iz recalled. "I picked up music from my mom, my dad, and my uncle (Moe Keale). I started 'ukulele in 1963, in third grade."

As an 11-year-old, Iz played on a boat with his brother Skippy's band. "It was boat music, hapa-haole with some calypso," he said. As a teenager, he embraced Hawaiian studies and also found time to enjoy rock. "Through all of this, I was listening to rock 'n' roll, Jimi Hendrix, Steppenwolf, and all those guys. But at home, it was all Hawaiian music." Witnessing Bob Marley at his historic Waikiki Shell show also inspired him, and he suggested the Sons adopt the occasional reggae influence.

At the time of the Sons' first album, *No Kristo*, in 1976, their ages ranged from 15 to 21, making them one of the youngest groups in the state. Iz remembers the excitement of first hearing their music on the radio. "I wanted to jump out of the car and tell the person in the next car, listen to the radio," he said. "Listen to KCCN. We're on the radio."

One of the group's most requested songs, "Pakalolo," was written by Iz while he was in school. "Playing music (professionally) in high school, 10th grade, I would work evenings from nine to one. By the time we get home to Makaha and I hit the deck, it's about two in the morning. So I get up at about ten to go to school, fall asleep and I have to go home 'cuz I was so tired. Pretty soon, I started having deficiency notes that Israel's falling behind on his work."

His counselor suggested his teachers create a special project for him so he could graduate. "Pakalolo" was one of the assignments. "They wanted me to evaluate against. They wanted me to write a song for

English and social studies. 'Pakalolo' was the song I'd written for credit to graduate from high school."

In the late 1970s, the band made important statements about Hawai'i's changing landscape. With the song "Hawai'i '78," Skippy narrated how the ali'i would sadly react to contemporary Hawai'i.

It was a time for action, Iz remembered. "At that time - Kaho'olawe, the movement - we felt there was an obligation for us to have people aware of what's happening. As you get older, you grow, you mellow out. And then, as the years go by, you learn all this world needs is aloha. It's simple but effective."

The group experienced a major upheaval in 1982, with the death of Skippy from a heart attack at the age of 28. "I was sure we could carry on," Iz says about those hard days. "All I needed was the support for my other brothers."

The tragedy inspired Iz to change his lifestyle. "I was the party animal," he revealed in 1987. "I learned the lesson about health. I'm still working on the weight. I learned about respect for other people and my own well-being. It's to make the best out of what we've got. There are three things you got to have in this life. One is faith, the other is hope, and we're still hoping, and charity, something you can't find any place," he said laughing. "It keeps you humble, it pays to be humble, and we're humble people. So we just project good feeling." But, he hastened to add, "it doesn't mean we're not educated."

Over time, Iz became identified as the figurehead of the Makaha Sons. Positioned at center stage in concert, his large size and lead vocal prominence dominated the group. "It's up to us to keep the standard," he said in 1992. "I wouldn't say it's an easy job," he continued, laughing. "It's just somebody has to do it. Our native Hawaiian culture is taking a back seat to the Americanized nation all these years. We're really getting the second-best of everything, and a lot of stuff is almost gone. Our music and culture is the last to hold on to. We hold on to culture so kids can enjoy it. We've got to guide our kids whatever way we can. Learn your culture and know what Hawaiian is all about. Respect your kupuna, and Hawaiian music is going to live forever."

When he left the Makaha Sons in May 1993, some wondered whether the group would continue. "For about a year before he left, people would ask 'how's Israel, I hear he's leaving the group,' says the

Sons' Jerome Koko. "Then he did an interview with *MidWeek* (the Oahu paper), and that blew everything out of proportion. No one had the dignity to come to us three guys and try to see what our side of the story was. They took 100 percent from Israel that everything he said was true. It caught us by surprise.

"Because of Israel's size, music was his whole job. That was his only source of income. So we built the show around him, which may be, in the long run, was a mistake, to give him the burden of everything. We made him the P.R. man. We gave him the title role of running the show. Me, Moon (Louis "Moon" Kauakahi), and John (Koko) just colored what he did, building everything around him. So when people heard the Makaha Sons of Ni'ihau they just saw this picture of this big guy sitting there.

"When we were together, the thing we had was great, but we just went to other islands. Israel didn't want to travel, just stay home and do island stuff. In the 18 years we were together, we did three or four mainland gigs. When the breakup came, people didn't see the talent that we had. We suffered for a year and a half. We had jobs, but it wasn't as busy as when we were all together. We restructured everything, and it took about a year and a half to set an identity as the Makaha Sons without Israel. We always had to prove ourselves. I think it came out best for him and for us."

Out on his own, *Facing Future,* released in 1993, became the best-selling album of all time by a Hawaiian artist. Expressing a sense of revitalization he felt at the time Iz opened *Facing Future* with a monologue intro to a re-recording of the classic "Hawai'i '78." "I feel free now," he stated. "I was just confined."

With feelings intensified around the sovereignty issue, he felt it was time to revisit the Makaha Sons' powerful indictment of overdevelopment in the islands. "There's all this awareness of sovereignty," he explained. "I thought it was time to do it again." Reflecting on the changes that had taken place since the debut of "Hawai'i '78," Iz suggested, "everybody is so aware of the illegal occupation of the state. Now it's a whole different ballgame. I know so much now about the illegal overthrow and Hawaiian ceded lands. There's a lot of retribution that needs to be done."

While some songs benefited from a lush production, a few were distinguished by sparse arrangements that focused on his voice and 'ukulele. "I was getting back to basics, keeping things real simple," he said. "Simplicity is the key to a lot of Hawaiian music. Sometimes it gets too overly produced."

No longer relying on his Makaha Sons' bandmates for support proved initially challenging as a solo performer. "Let me tell you, the first time I hit the stage, I was cracking," he said. "I was nervous to the max. I was so used to performing with the other three guys. Basically, we'd been together for 17 years, and all of a sudden stage lights come on, and I turn to the side, and they ain't there. I'm getting used to it. Facing future is sometimes difficult. Some people take chances, and some people don't. I'm taking chances, andI'm growing in more ways than one," he laughed.

Iz's final album before his passing in June 1997, *N Dis Life*, ranged from a sublime version of the classic "Hi'ilawe" to a stirring version of the sovereignty anthem "Living in a Sovereign Land." On a Jawaiian take of Mel & Tim's 1972 hit "Starting All Over Again," he counseled folks to face hardships and keep moving forward.

"It's basically for everybody as far as sovereignty and all that, starting all over again," he explained in an April 1997 interview. "I do songs that people can reflect on. It's kind of like therapy. A lot of times, I hear people asking, 'how are you doing?' They think I'm in therapy, but everybody who purchases the CD, they're getting therapy," he said laughing.

Concerned about teen drug use in Hawai'i, Iz included Del Beazley's song "Johnny Mahoe" on the album. "Part of my life mission is to help increase peace between people, and we have to start with the children," he said. "So I talk to a lot of kids and share the manao, get the positive juices flowing, so hopefully they can make the right choices. I have an obligation to do what I'm doing and speak out about things that are not right."

Knowing that fans worried about his increasing weight, he reported: "Last week someone told me, 'eh cuz I heard you passed away.' I said, wow, stop the rumors cuz."

A sold-out performance at the MACC's Castle Theater brought him much joy. One of the last shows he ever played, Iz reported how he loved performing in such a grand setting.

After he passed from complications stemming from his weight, Gov. Ben Cayetano decreed that his body would lie in state at the Capitol. An estimated 10,000 fans showed up to pay their respects. He was cremated, along with his vintage Martin ʻukulele, which he had used to record "Over the Rainbow," and his ashes were carried on a traditional Hawaiian voyaging canoe.

Released close to a year after his death, *IZ in Concert*, captured the magic, lively spirit, and towering presence of one of Hawaiʻi's most beloved musicians. In the liner notes, his wife Marlene summed up his mission: "Israel left the earth with a message - to share, to love everyone unconditionally, whether that person, no matter what color, was good, bad, right, or wrong."

Then in 2001, *Alone In IZ World,* compiled previously unreleased songs, moving unplugged moments, and never before heard arrangements of some of his most popular songs. Alone in the studio, often working late into the night, producer Jon de Mello poured over hundreds of hours of tapes reliving fond memories and sometimes feeling an overwhelming loss.

"I found myself many times late at night just sitting sobbing, it was very emotional," de Mello reveals. "He and I had talked about it, that someday there was a possibility that I would have to do this. He knew he had broken all odds. He had lived ten years past the average of anybody of that size, and he had watched his whole family die except for one sister."

Over the months, de Mello would often sense the calming presence of the Hawaiian superstar hovering close, somehow assisting the project. "It was a very interesting creative process, him moving through me somehow," de Mello continues. "It was so interesting building it, him on another plane of existence, and yet so close. There were a couple of times when I stopped the tape recorder, and I heard words, and I would turn around thinking he was behind me. It was very spiritual and spooky. I can't explain it, but he felt like he was right in front of me all the time. It was like Israel was working through me."

In the unplugged moments, we heard Iz unadorned, singing and strumming his ʻukulele on songs such as "Henehene Kou ʻAka," "Panini Pua Kea," and "Over the Rainbow." To capture those moments, de Mello employed a novel technique. He would sit right in front of Iz.

"I'd sit just two feet away, square in front of him. It was just to get more personal and get more things out of him because I would stop him in the middle of a song and say, try again or pick it up from a verse. It was a lot easier doing that right in front of him. He'd close his eyes and start playing and singing, and inevitably, almost at the end of every song, he'd crack open his eyes and look down at me and say, 'is that all OK, is that all right?'

"I'd try and calm him down too because sometimes he would get amped up, real excited about what he was doing. My thing with him would be to breathe deep. Now we're going to record this song, so breathe deep for 30 seconds and relax and play just like you're in the backyard. The breathing on the tracks at the opening of 'Starting All Over Again' and another song is his deep breathing when everyone was waiting for him to do the count off."

Five days before Iz died, he called de Mello from the hospital. "He wasn't doing too well and said, 'can you come and see me.' I went over and saw him, and he ushered everybody out of the room. He just wanted to talk with me, and he looked me right in the eyes and said, 'do you remember what you promised me.' I said, 'yes, of course I do.' He said, 'can you do it?' I said, 'I can do it.'"

When Iz ventured out on a solo career leaving the Makaha Sons, he signed a recording contract with the Mountain Apple Company, mindful of one primary goal. "He asked if I could promise one thing," de Mello recalls. "He said, 'all I want out of this Jon is my family to be taken care of.' Through the seven and half years of recording, he never changed that focus."

Alone In IZ World included a new version of "Starting All Over Again." It opened with Iz talking about facing death: "I'm not scared for myself for dying, because I believe all these places are all temporary, this is just one shell. Because we Hawaiians, we live in both worlds, we live on both sides. So if I went now, that's alright."

Love and appreciation for Iz's music have continued to blossom over the years. The official video of "Rainbow" has amassed more than one billion views on *YouTube*, with many posting how it provided solace during the 2020 Covid pandemic.

"HOME IN THE ISLANDS"

Henry Kapono

*"Hawaiian music is so beautiful and flowing and graceful
that if I was going to do something different, then I
needed to go all the way."*

An invitation to open a Honolulu concert for Frank Zappa in 1973 helped popularize Hawai'i's legendary Cecilio and Kapono. The duo had been playing in relative obscurity at Waikiki's Rainbow Villa club when they were offered the opportunity to open for the rock star.

"We were two guys with music in our hearts, and we played to a packed house for 15 minutes," Henry Ka'aihue Kapono recalls. "We got off stage, and the crowd was cheering and screaming hana hou, and we were walking out when Frank goes, 'hey, where are you guys going?' He goes, 'get up there. They want you guys back.' So we went back up and did 'Suite Judy Blue Eyes,' and it brought the house down.

"We went back to the club, and there was a line out the door. The first three months of our career, it had been empty there. A lot of people had come straight from Frank Zappa. Our life changed after that. For eight straight months, six days a week, there were lines outside. It was amazing."

From humble beginnings, Cecilio and Kapono soon captivated the islands with their trademark sunny sound heard on favorites like "Friends," "Lifetime Party," "Sailin,'" and "Highway in the Sun." *The New York Times* once proclaimed: "Cecilio and Kapono were Hawaii's answer to Simon and Garfunkel."

Once signed to Columbia Records (the first group from Hawai'i with a national recording contract), their popularity soared, culminating in headlining shows at Aloha Stadium playing for 30,000. "It all went by so fast," Kapono says. "We rode it and enjoyed it and had fun. We were doing what we loved doing."

By 1981, the fun was over, and Kapono decided to pursue a solo career. "C&K was embedded in the hearts of so many people, separating like that broke everyone's hearts, but we had to start thinking about ourselves," he explains. "We weren't making the kind of money we thought we should have been making. We had to go our separate ways. But C&K was so strong in people's minds and hearts that they didn't want to hear my own stuff. I got to the point where I had to find some kind of bridge and find a place for me. So I started building a new audience and not playing at places where a lot of people knew who C&K was. It was a whole learning process."

For more than four decades, Kapono has been one of Hawai'i's most popular, successful, and consistently creative artists. One of the first local entertainers to write a song fusing reggae and Hawaiian influences on his debut solo album *Stand in the Light*, he foreshadowed the influential Jawaiian movement.

It was Kapono who created the term for the new fusion of Jamaican reggae and contemporary Hawaiian music. "Back in the '70s, I was turned onto the movie *The Harder They Come*, and from that point on, I was hooked (on reggae)," he reports. "I wanted to see if it was something I could make my own. It turned out to be a great song for me. I was talking with (Brother) Noland about listening to reggae and trying to incorporate it into Hawai'i, and I said I came up with a thing called Jawaiian."

Pursuing an innovative solo path, over the years, he's sung everything from Hawaiian classics to rock 'n' roll, acted in a major Hollywood movie, produced a TV documentary on Hawaiian sovereignty, wrote a popular children's book, *A Beautiful Hawaiian Day*, about aloha and taking care of the land, and composed many songs that remain island favorites.

In support of Hawaiian rights and sovereignty, he recorded the protest song "Broken Promise" after reading an expose in *The Wall Street Journal* about the Hawaiian Homes program. Opening with a statement about the illegal overthrow of Queen Lili'uokalani by a group of American businessmen in 1893, he was joined by fellow Hawai'i legends Roland Cazimero, Israel Kamakawiwao'ole, and Cyril Pahinui.

The powerful song won "Song of the Year" and "Single of the Year" at the 1992 Hōkū Awards.

He followed up with *Kapono*, a collection of songs about the Hawaiian sovereignty movement, which seeks a form of sovereignty for the state. It included an updating of Liko Martin's famous protest song "Nanakuli Blues" (also known as "Waimanalo Blues"), a reflective solo take on Buffalo Springfield's "For What It's Worth," the Eagle's "Last Resort" about destructive colonialism, and the slack key instrumental "Song for Liliu (Queen Lili'uokalani)."

In 1997, he opened his *Home in the Islands* album with the song made famous by the Brothers Cazimero, which he had composed, but never recorded before. "I was driving in Colorado heading to North Dakota, and I was really missing home," he explains the song's inspiration. "We were doing a lot of traveling, out on the road for six months, but I still felt that strong connection to Hawai'i. I wrote it for the Island Band, then Robert Cazimero heard it and wanted to do it, and so history was made. They made it their song, and then finally I decided to do my own version."

A Native Hawaiian musician, he released his first album sung entirely in Hawaiian, *The Wild Hawaiian* in 2006. Bearing little resemblance to anything he had previously recorded or what anyone in the islands had created before, it was a landmark project, the boldest, and the most radical and innovative album of his career.

Completely shifting musical direction at the age of 57, he interpreted a handful of Hawaiian classics as contemporary rock songs and composed a couple of new rocking Hawaiian language compositions that paid tribute to his culture. "At times, its sound suggests Jimi Hendrix or Carlos Santana," *The New York Times* praised.

As if channeling the ferocious power of the Red Hot Chili Peppers and the scorching guitar of Hendrix, Kapono opened *The Wild Hawaiian* with a stunning version of Kui Lee's "Na Ali'i," rendered as a slamming, hip-hop flavored rocker. "The lyrics speak about paying respect to our ancestors, the kings, and queens, and they talk about King Kamehameha's battles," he explains. "For many years people have been asking me why I haven't done a Hawaiian album. I've wanted to do something Hawaiian but until now, I haven't felt it was the right time. I'm always trying to do something different, and the ultimate challenge for me is to try and create Hawaiian music with a universal appeal.

"Once I got the arrangements for 'Na Ali'i,' that solidified the direction I was going. 'Na Ali'i' really rocks; it's really hard rock. I wanted to keep that energy and be diversified, to expand the target to not only older folks but younger kids as well. I really wanted to do something different, adding an edge and power to Hawaiian music. Hawaiian music is so beautiful and flowing and graceful that if I was going to do something different, then I needed to go all the way."

Primarily known as an acoustic guitarist, the Grammy-nominated album highlighted his growth as a gifted electric guitarist. His playing on "He'eia," a radical revision of an old chant that honors King Kalakaua, was particularly striking. "I was afraid of it when I first started because the acoustic guitar is so friendly," he reveals. "The electric guitar can be scary. I always listened to Jimi Hendrix and Stevie Ray Vaughan, and I picked up stuff and became more confident."

Respecting the essence of the traditional material he interpreted, Kapono closed the album with two Hawaiian classics – a stately version of Sam Li'a's "Hi'ilawe," and Queen Liliu'okalani's "Ke Aloha O Ka Haku" (The "Queen's Prayer").

With so many versions released of "Hi'ilawe," Kapono wondered what he could bring to it. "Gabby is the king of 'Hi'ilawe,' what do you do next? I thought I'd have to do it in a way that pays respect to Gabby. Musically it gets bigger and more powerful, and the keyboard (played by Pearl Jam's Boom Gaspar) gives it more space. To me, it has a U2 vibe."

Treating Queen Liliu'okalani's signature song as a plaintive ballad, he opened acoustically, and gradually built tension to a rousing electric guitar finale. With its powerful message emphasizing compassion and forgiveness, it triumphantly closed a brilliant record. "She's one of my favorite songwriters and such a courageous leader," he notes. "In the song she was saying, though things happened and it might not have been right, we've got to forgive. If we don't do that, we'll never be able to perpetuate our culture. In some ways, it was saying to me if we can do this, we can free her. Our images are of her in prison, and we can let go of that and set her free, and the only way we can do that is as her people setting ourselves free. The universal truth is that if we don't forgive people, we never move on."

Growing up in Kapahulu, outside of Waikiki, like many of his generation, Kapono was discouraged from learning Hawaiian. His parents, who were fluent in Hawaiian, had been raised in a time when children were punished in school for speaking just one word of Hawaiʻi's ancient language.

Shortly after the overthrow of Hawaiʻi's monarchy, a law was passed that only English could be used in schools. It was only in 1978 that Hawaiian was recognized as the official language of the statei, and the ban was officially lifted in 1986.

"My parents were afraid we'd get lickings (hit) in school because that's how they grew up," he recalls. "If I walked in on a conversation when they were talking Hawaiian with friends, they'd all stop. It was really weird. I never understood why until recently. These little things start to mount up. I've been watching the sovereignty movement carefully, and I have my own opinions. I do think Hawaiʻi really needs leadership, and Hawaiians really need good leadership."

First taking ʻukulele lessons from his father, Kapono taught himself guitar listening to records and songs on the radio. A Punahou School graduate, before forming C&K, he spent time in Vietnam during the war playing at army bases.

He revisited the glory days of Cecilio and Kapono in 2018, gathering a group of acclaimed, young artists to add their distinctive accent to timeless classics on *The Songs of C&K*. The collection included Maui's Grammy-winning Kalani Peʻa with a memorable version of Stevie Wonder's "All In Love Is Fair" (originally featured on the *Cecilio & Kapono* album). Jazz singer Starr Kalahiki transformed "You and Me" into a passionate torch ballad, while Paula Fuga dramatically closed the album with a stunning version of "Song for Someone."

Kapono's recent album, *Welcome 2 My Paradise*, spotlighted his talent across genres from the island reggae of "Everything" and the Caribbean lilt of "Forever Man" to the sweet ballad "Love You Forever" and the catchy rocker "Long Train." On the closing "Celebrate," he expressed gratitude for the wonder of life. "It's about being thankful for all the things that we take for granted like the earth, the sky, and the ocean, celebrating it every day," he says. "We live in paradise."

To keep spirits up during the pandemic, Kapono began posting daily virtue words online (like dignity, enthusiasm, and hope) along with uplifting "Positive World" videos. "It's putting positive energy out into the world," he explains. Also releasing the inspirational, six-song EP *Sunny Town*, he followed up with *Searchin'* and combined both EPs into *Henry's House*, which won a Hōkū for Contemporay Album of the Year in 2021. "It's all positive, happy stuff," he says. "During these times everybody needs a little joy in their life."

"THE BEAUTY OF MAUNA KEA"

Keola Beamer

"We have to try to keep the aloha alive. It truly is Hawai'i's greatest gift to the world."

The inscription "Malama ko aloha," on the gravestone of revered Hawaiian treasure Winona Kapuailohiamanonokalani Beamer, is a potent reminder of the importance of cherishing the essence of aloha in our hearts.

When Keola Beamer was growing up, his mother, Aunty Nona Beamer, would often remind him to malama ko aloha (keep your love). "For my brother and myself, aloha became a way of being in the world," he explains.

"The idea of malama ko aloha was passed down from my mom to me. It came from one of our ancestors, Princess Manono, who with her husband, the high chief Kekuaokalani, was killed in the battle of Kuamo'o in Kona. This was during the reign of Kamehameha II. They were part of the Hawaiian nobility that was opposed to changes that other royal factions were adopting, like the abolishment of the Hawaiian religious system.

"Both Manono and her husband were killed by musket fire. First, he fell in battle, and then she picked up his spear and with the words 'malama ko aloha,' keep your love, she continued in the battle and was killed. This was passed down through the generations of my family, and it had a wider context. It became cherish the aloha within you. As Hawai'i becomes more westernized, you can feel aloha dissipating. People become ruder and less kind to each other. In terms of quality of life and quality of being, we have to try to keep the aloha alive. It truly is Hawai'i's greatest gift to the world."

When Keola released his groundbreaking solo album *Hawaiian Slack Key Guitar in the Real Old Style* in 1972, it introduced the sweet beauty of the Hawaiian slack key guitar to a new generation at a time

240

when this unique art form was dying. It also provided many with their first encounter with the ethereal sound of the ancient Hawaiian 'ohe hano ihu, bamboo nose flute.

"Not too many people understand the nose flute," Keola explained in a 2004 interview. "It's a wonderful instrument with a very evocative sound. When I really think about what Hawaiian music is, I always end up going back to the nose flute. It's not the guitar because that's pretty new in the overall scheme of things. The guitar came in 1830, but the nose flute way predated western contact."

Responsible for introducing the 'ohe hano ihu to contemporary recordings, Keola learned how to play it at Kamehameha Schools. "A lot was my family influence as strong keepers of the culture," he continues. "Nobody ever really recorded it before with any intent. They are very difficult to tune, and each has a different personality. So it began with that album in 1972, and then my brother and I began doing some stuff together wrapping it more into the music."

Besides Hawai'i, this fascinating instrument was played by native cultures in Madagascar and the Philippines. "In our culture, it came from the thought that a man could lie with his mouth, but you can't do that with your nose," he explains why Hawaiians played the flute with their nose.

Tracing a rich lineage back to the 15th century, Keola is recognized worldwide as a master of the Hawaiian slack key guitar. Steeped in tradition, his great grandmother was the legendary composer and hula master Helen Desha Beamer, his grandmother Louise Beamer was an acclaimed teacher, and his mother refined the term Hawaiiana.

"I want to make my ancestors proud and my immediate family proud of what I do, and that's a tall order considering some of the folks we've been blessed within our family," he notes. "I think one of the things I'm most proud of is the 'ohe (flute) sound that I get in my recordings, and native instruments like the kā'eke'eke, the bamboo pipe, and pū'ili, the split bamboo. I find in a strange way they transport me in time. When I hold the instruments in my hands, and I make that first connection or sound, I find myself moving backward in time."

One of Hawai'i's 'most gifted guitarists, over the years, Keola has refined his unique style to create exceptionally beautiful music imbued with grace and serenity. Many listeners feel so moved by his music that they send him letters of appreciation.

"I get some beautiful letters from people who swear by this coming into their lives and helping them," he reports. "There's a healing aspect to it. There was one that just brought me to tears. I showed it to my wife, and we both started crying."

Such poignant moments remind Keola of the time when he first felt moved by the beauty of music. "I came to love music when I was a boy about nine years old," he recalls. "My mother had taken me to a Hawaiian luau in Nu'uanu, and for some reason, I wandered into the backyard away from the party. I heard the most beautiful music I had ever heard in my life. It was like silk in the air. So I followed it into the next yard and found a Hawaiian man sitting playing slack key guitar. I had never really heard it before. The way he was playing it was so beautiful.

"The strange thing was when I got to him and sat down at his feet, he looked at my face and realized I was not a member of his family, and he turned his back and stopped playing. That was Hawaiian slack key guitar in those days, no access. You can understand it from a cultural perspective because Hawaiians had lost so much, their culture, their language, their religion, everything falling apart around them. So what good was this sharing? It was destroying everything.

"So the special art forms, the chant, and hula just naturally dove way underground. My great-grandmother had to teach secretly. Those special things became hidden, and the problem was that it began to die. Then somewhere around the time when Gabby Pahinui began recording, the whole paradigm began to shift, and all the players realized you've got to hold this stuff with an open hand and let it breathe, and the whole thing turned around."

Long a pioneering innovator, he has continued to seek new avenues of expression while retaining a firm link to the past. "I really respect our traditions and where they came from, and I believe you have to breath new life into art," he says. "I think that helps it grow and bring new people in. We came so close to losing it all, we understand what the darkness is all about, so if you have any love or interest in Hawaiian slack key guitar, we are there for you as best we can."

Celebrating the essence of the islands, a reverential connection to the past whispers through his songs. "A lot of musicians will say songs came through them," he notes. "I feel there's something greater than us, and Hawaiians believe in the aumakua (family gods) level of existence, and in this atmosphere above us is this beautiful flow of creative energy, and that's our ancestors and protective spirits. If you stay open to the universe and let these things reach you, it takes you to some wonderful places."

A classical sensibility and a depth of understanding of the importance of space in music help make Keola's slack key guitar playing unique and especially moving. "The spaces between the notes are important, the air, that's the kolonahe (gentle, peaceful) part," he says. "Sometimes you find a pianist who has beautiful technique, but such a cluttered style, there's no room for you. With the nahenahe (soft, sweet) slack key, there's a space to bring yourself in. I think the spaces are as important as the notes."

Praise for his playing includes *The New York Times*, which hailed him as "the quintessential Hawaiian slack key master," country legend Willie Nelson, who proclaimed: "Keola Beamer's style is the best there is on the planet," and Paul Simon, who applauded him as "an exceptional musician."

In 2006, Keola released the marvelous album *Ka Hikina O Ka Hau – The Coming of the Snow*, where he interpreted compositions by classical composers such as Eric Satie and Maurice Ravel. It was the culmination of a five-year-long journey to discover how slack key's unique palette could enhance the music of some classical greats. "The music of the classical masters has always been inspiring to me," he says. "The more I progressed in my own studies with Hawaiian slack key guitar, after about 30 years of playing, a path began to come together for me. I was fascinated by the beautiful colorations of the Hawaiian slack key guitar. When you get into it very deeply, each tuning is like a tonal palette. Each tuning has a beautiful coloration. It's like painting with tones. You can go places with Hawaiian slack key that you would not be able to go with a regular classical guitar. I thought it would be a wonderful new approach to classical music taking these modal tunings from ki ho'alu."

Later teaming with Moloka'i's falsetto star Raiatea Helm for the wonderful album *Keola Beamer & Raiatea*, he recorded a unique version of John Lennon's "Imagine," adding Hawaiian lyrics. "After 40 years, it still spoke to me, and the way the world is going, it feels like it's even more relevant now," he says. "It's a very powerful compelling piece, and to honor it in our own 'Ōlelo Hawai'i gives it a new context. To me, that song goes right to the human heart."

This new "Inā/Imagine" also featured the unique sound of the ancient 'ūkēkē, a small stringed instrument played with the mouth, that had been resurrected for contemporary times by Aunty Nona Beamer. "It's probably one of the few records on the planet that opens with the sound of the 'ūkēkē," he says, laughing.

Keola's music had been heard on various soundtracks, including the Oscar-winning movie *The Descendants*, which featured four of his songs. Along with Maui-born slack key guitarist Jeff Peterson, they were the only two artists invited by the film's director to record specifically for the Grammy-nominated soundtrack. "I'm pretty sensitive about doing stuff that is culturally correct," he emphasizes. "Over the years, I've had quite a few tenders to do music for stuff, and after I've had a general idea of the movie, I've declined because they were embarrassing in a cultural sense. I'm not going to add my name or talent to some boobs on the beach thing."

In recent years Keola and his wife, Kumu Hula Moanalani Beamer, began touring the world as cultural ambassadors sponsored by the U.S. State Department. Traveling to Brazil, Columbia, Venezuela, South Africa, and Zimbabwe provided opportunities to share the beauty of aloha. "To share love and compassion is huge," he says. "What a great opportunity to help spread the beautiful philosophy of aloha around the world."

Most recently, Keola was heard on the enchanting CD *Himalayan Sessions*, recorded in Nepal, Tibet, and Bhutan, which compiled contemplative compositions by the guitarist, the late world-renowned flutist Paul Horn, and Grammy-nominated musician Christopher Hedge. Including selected inspirational quotes by His Holiness the

14th Dalai Lama, the unique recording benefited the Aloha Music Camp, which provides 'ukuleles to children in third world countries.

"I remembered when my brother and I were children we didn't have any money," he says, "but my mom bought 'ukuleles and the 'ukulele brought joy into our lives, so much so that we didn't even realize we were poor. Small fingers are happy on the 'ukulele. It made us happy and kept us out of trouble."

Reflecting on his storied career, Keola concludes: "I almost feel like I'm still a kid struggling to bring something out or try something new, though I'm perceived as someone who has done a lot and gained a lot of respect. I guess I'm still looking for that old guy with the guitar. Picasso once said, 'that the act of creation is an act of destruction,' but I've never really felt that. The old good, great, wonderful stuff is still there. I didn't make it disappear when I tried something new. I just found another path under the trees."

"KAUANOEANUHEA"

Keali'i Reichel

"Everything I've done is ultimately based on the work I've done in hālau, whether it's chant, composition, choreography, or teaching philosophy."

When Native Hawaiian activists flocked to Maunakea on Hawai'i Island in the summer of 2019, protesting plans to construct a new telescope on the sacred mountain, Maui Kumu Hula Keali'i Reichel joined with Hawaiian elders on the summit.

"As practitioners, it behooves us to take a stand," Keali'i explains. "That mountain is our tutu, our grandmother. The deities that reside there, for my family especially, we connect to the snow goddess Poli'ahu. The re-connectivity for me was quite powerful up there."

Heartened to see the current flourishing of Native awareness, he continues: "We've moved into an amazing phase of cultural and political awareness. Maunakea is important to us to keep the re-connectivity to the elements alive and make sure to keep unnecessary development. There's enough up there. We don't need any more. The majority of practitioners are at the front lines of the cultural and political renaissance.

"I've been around a long time. I've been through the Honokahua burials (at Kapalua on Maui) and the bombing of (the island) Kaho'olawe, all those pivot points in modern history. They were important to us and helped create this new generation of forward thinkers within the Hawaiian community, and never have I seen such unification. It's been very unifying like nothing else ever before. It's remarkable."

Keali'i first captured the islands in the mid-1990s, with an innovative artistic vision weaving elements of traditional Hawaiian music and romantic pop into delicately textured works of beauty. His debut album *Kawaipunahele*, set the stage for the meteoric rise of this revered entertainer, who produced two of the most popular albums in the history of Hawaiian music in just a couple of years.

"It took us by surprise," he says about the early success. "Almost overnight, it kind of changed our lives, my partner, and the hālau and my family. I had no intention to pursue this as a career. It was just to put out new music and to express myself. We came to a pivot point where we could continue focusing on what we were doing or take this new path, and it came very close to not taking the new path. The rest is history."

Beginning with the multi-Nā Hōkū Award-winning *Kawaipunahele* (released in 1994), through the follow-up *Lei Hali'a,* and later *E O Mai,* he amassed some astounding sales figures. Early in his career, combined sales of all three albums passed the 750,000 mark - an achievement never previously attained by a local artist. Record-breaking sales landed him in *Billboard* magazine's world music chart. "That was the first time ever for a Hawaiian artist," he explains. That prompted a handful of major record labels to court him with a contract.

And all this for a Maui-born musician who once doubted anyone would want to hear him sing. "I find my voice irritating," he once revealed. "But I do it because people like it, and if what I do has made your life better, then it's my obligation to do it. I love bringing joy to people who enjoy it. But I find no comfort and solace in my own work, and I find that extremely ironic."

Born Carlton Lewis Keali'inaniaimokuokalani (the handsome chief who rules over the heavenly lands) Reichel, this gifted singer, composer, chanter, educator, and Kumu Hula grew up in Lahaina but spent many weekends with his maternal grandmother in Paia absorbing the old ways.

Studying hula in the late 1970s with Peter Pekelo Day, Keali'i met future Kumu Hula Uluwehi Guerrero. "We answered an ad in *The Maui News* that was seeking men and women who are interested in doing the ancient dances of Hawai'i," Uluwehi recalls. "With the renaissance of Hawaiian music, hula, and language in the late '70s, there was a lot of movement going on as far as people wanting to find their identity. What it is to be Hawaiian, what do I do to make me feel Hawaiian?"

Establishing a hālau together, they also formed the music trio Maui O Kama. "We met Onuffre (Eleccion) through Auntie Iola Balubar," Uluwehi continues. "We didn't use our Hawaiian names at that time. Keali'i was Carlton, I was Rodney, and Onuffre, a pure Filipino, was Kimo. We got our first gig out at the Kapalua Bay Hotel for a Hawaiian afternoon."

Keali'i's phenomenal commercial and critical winning streak continued with *E Ō Mai*, which blended beautiful Hawaiian ballads with some engaging contemporary pop and two stunning covers of Sweet Honey in the Rock songs. A stunning adaptation of the a capella group's moving lament "Ballad of The Broken Word," it included an 18th-century prophecy by Hawai'i Island kahuna Kapihe.

"The chant in the song is a prophecy that says everything that's built up now will crash," he explains. "It's part of ceremonial protocol we do when we protest, we chant it over and over. The power of the word is all-encompassing, and the more you do it, the truer it becomes. Every time the song plays, it creates that power, that mana."

Twenty years after his groundbreaking debut, he released the magnificent *Kawaiokalena*, which he hinted would be his last album. It immediately shot to number one on iTunes' top 100 world music albums chart, and earned eight Nā Hōkū Awards in 2015, including Male Vocalist, Hawaiian Music Album, and Song and Album of the Year.

Including chants, traditional Hawaiian songs in the hula tradition, new Hawaiian language compositions, and a couple of contemporary covers delivered in Reichel's unique style, the album was a loving homage to his upland Maui home and its transcendent surroundings.

"All of my previous albums were Wailuku-centric because that was where I was based, and I moved up here and had to relearn the geography, the cultural topography, and the elementals up here because it's a different universe, especially up at Pi'iholo," he explains. "I wanted to bring to light some of the traditional names of the winds and rains and bring some of that imagery into today's consciousness. I didn't reinvent the wheel because there are chants of Pi'iholo that have the same kind of imagery."

As to whether it was his last album, he says, "It's meant to be a bookend to Kawaipunahele. I'm not going to disappear, but as far as a full-fledged project, I think this is it. I might do a single here or there and be a guest artist on somebody else's album. So this is a good bookend. What a ride. I'm a lucky man."

His primary focus shifted to creating a new permanent home for Hālau Keʻalaokamaile on donated land in Olinda. With grants from the Office of Hawaiian Affairs (OHA), a USDA Beginning Farmers and Ranchers grant, and one from the Administration for Native Americans, he explains: "The OHA grant was to reforest six acres, and we brought in community groups to learn protocols and sense of place and reconnectivity to the elements utilizing chants to incite growth in the plants and in the land. That's what they are accustomed to. That's what they used to hear.

"The harmonics of chant can be quite exciting to the land. It works. We did experiments where we chanted after planting a field and then one field we didn't, and that field kind of fell off, and we had to redo it. The field next to it grew and was happy and thick and lush. That kind of environmental kinship through hands-on work, through harmonics, through chanting, through reconnectivity to the elements, that's a deeper level of aloha ʻāina. It's quite powerful.

"The hālau is such a big foundation in my life," he concludes. "The older I get, I gravitate even more to the hālau. It's what I've always done, and everything I've done is ultimately based on the work I've done in hālau, whether it's chant composition, choreography, or teaching philosophy. It all points back to that. No matter what happens, I hope it will always be there."

"HOWLING AT THE MOON"

Willie K

"I remember the first time I heard 'The Thrill is Gone' as a kid. I thought this is cool stuff. When Stevie Ray Vaughan came into the picture, that was it."

A mighty presence in Hawai'i, there was no one like Willie K - in the islands, in America, even in the world. Wherever he played, audiences were amazed. Performing solo in Berlin, opening for the UK pop/soul band Simply Red, Willie recalled: "They had never seen an opening act get two standing ovations at a stadium in Berlin."

"Still to this day, I have never seen anyone control a crowd the way he did opening for Simply Red all on his own," marveled producer Hanan Rubinstein.

Then there was a memorable private gig in Venice, Italy, for a birthday group of mostly older Hasidic Jews. "He starts singing in Hebrew, and I looked at him, thinking, oh no, he's finally done it, he's faking it," recalls Maui musician Eric Gilliom. "But within a matter of minutes, the whole front row of these Hasidic Jewish men stood up and started dancing like *Fiddler on the Roof*." "They couldn't believe a guy from Hawai'i knew this popular music from Israel," added Willie.

Leading musicians would often praise him, including Prince, who anointed him a "funky motherfucker." On stage at his 2003 Maui concert, he announced: "We've been looking around this island for some funky music. Willie K, he's funky."

Mick Fleetwood lauded him as "a gladiator, talented above all imagination." Fleetwood Mac's legendary drummer recalls hearing about Willie's prodigious talent from musician friends ("it might have been Paul McCartney") before moving to Maui. "Have you heard about this guy, this player, this singer? It was like when people back in the day in England would say, 'you've got to go and hear Jeff Beck. He's fucking unbelievable.' It was that sort of a vibe. He was a truly amazing talent with the voice of an angel."

Born William Awihilima Kahaiali'i, he died peacefully at the age of 59 in 2020, after enduring a lengthy battle with lung cancer. Through the course of his illness, experiencing great pain, Willie demonstrated remarkable resilience, continuing to perform and post inspiring *Facebook* videos. "I'm a lucky guy," he posted. "The whole state of Hawaii is amazing. I'm really blessed. God bless you all."

After his passing, rock legend Alice Cooper posted a tribute. "What a unique privilege to have known the late great Willie K. God gave him the hands of Eric Clapton, the voice of Andrea Bocelli, and the heart and soul of the Hawaiian Islands. He was truly one of a kind."

Dazzling audiences for years with his extraordinary talent and versatility, he could embrace the incendiary spirit of Jimi Hendrix, the passionate blues of Stevie Ray Vaughan, and the Hawaiian soul of Gabby Pahinui. One day at a benefit for the Maui Dharma Center, he stood next to Willie Nelson invoking Patsy Cline on stage dueting with the country legend on the classic "Crazy."

The pivotal encounter led to Nelson taking Willie K on the road with him, including performing at a July 4th picnic in Texas. "It was awesome," Willie recalled. "I've never seen so many white people in one place at one time," he added, roaring with laughter. "There were thousands of them. My tribute to Stevie Ray Vaughan really kicked it off. Everybody really liked that."

George Benson was also an admirer. A memorable night at the old Hapa's in Kihei saw Willie crowning a club run with a jaw-dropping jam with the Benson, soaring on a 20-minute version of "On Broadway," that spanned the worlds of jazz, blues, and rock.

Born in Lahaina to a musical family, Willie played bass with his father, Manu Kahaiali'i, starting at the Sheraton's Black Rock Terrace. Anyone who saw him play in the early 1980s might have imagined Jimi Hendrix had reincarnated on Maui. The rock guitar god was an obvious influence in technique and even stage presence, and like Hendrix, Willie would pick an electric guitar with his teeth. "Some people thought that I wanted to play like Jimi Hendrix, mainly heavy rock," he recalled in his formative days. "I like versatility on the guitar, the weirder the sound, the better."

Known for his extraordinary impersonations, Willie could perfectly imitate the cast of stars on the "We Are the World" benefit song. "Because I was doing impersonations of Willie Nelson, that's how I ended up on the road with Willie Nelson," he recalled. "After how many years of impersonating him on stage, now I'm actually singing with the guy. It's really bizarre."

Years later he recorded a brilliant duet with the country star on his *Willie Kalikimaka* album, with the two Willies combining talents on a transcendent, country bluesy style rendition of "Away in a Manger."

Releasing *Willie Kalikimaka* simultaneously with *Nostalgia*, his third album with Amy Hanaiali'i, Willie had avoided producing his own music because of disgruntlement with the music business. "I had never been allowed to say even anything in the recording studio when I did my last four albums," he revealed at the time. "It was everyone else's ideas. They weren't mine. I could throw in ideas, but I had no control. That was one of the reasons why I didn't record for a long time. I didn't think I would be able to handle it again with someone else controlling the album."

Willie earned a pile of Nā Hōkū Hanohano Awards for his first three albums in the early 1990s, and then began collaborating with Amy Hanaiali'i, beginning as a producer, then as a duo, they released two hit albums which earned them four Hōkū Awards, including Hawaiian Album of the Year and Song of the Year. A recording of their 2003 concert tour, *Amy & Willie Live*, was nominated for a Grammy Award. "I wouldn't have made it without him," Amy noted. "Willie molded me as an entertainer."

Willie provided Amy with a key to success blending contemporary arrangements with her classic style of falsetto singing, while she provided a vehicle to nurture his Hawaiian roots. "Mountain Apple asked me to produce her first album, and I was scared," he recalled. "But becoming a producer was a blessing, actually. I'd been asked to do Hawaiian music, and I don't know if I really want to do a Hawaiian album. There's a difference between hearing it on a CD and seeing it performed live. I prefer playing Hawaiian music live. It's totally different. Keali'i Reichel does a wonderful job with his music. You can always recognize it, and it's exactly what he should be doing. He has an identity.

"It's hard to find my identity around Hawaiian music because it's basically all around the Sons of Hawaii, Hui Ohana, and Gabby Pahinui. If I put it out on an album, everybody would say he's doing something like Gabby did 20 years ago. But if you see it live on stage, you end up missing music like that. So that's why I hold back on recording Hawaiian music. But the blessing was I got to put it behind someone else. It was very comfortable because it wasn't featuring me."

A radical follow-up to her Nā Hōkū-winning album *Hanaiali'i*, Amy's *Nostalgia* reinvented classic hapa haole songs, re-framing them in Hawaiian with novel arrangements that embraced blues, swing, '50s rock, and breezy Brazilian music. "It goes way East," Willie explained, laughing. "'Beyond the Reef' is like a full-on opening riff of B. B. King. Amy sings Hawaiian, but it's all done in blues. 'Hukilau' is like a bebop blues swing with a Les Paul-Mary Ford-type rhythm. 'Rock-a-Hula Baby' is like an Eddie Cochran thing. I just went all out on this one. The Hawaiian community might get mad about this one. There goes Willie again."

Among famous musicians attracted to playing with him, Mick Fleetwood invited Willie to be part of the Island Rumours Band he formed on Maui. Initially skeptical of fusing classic Fleetwood Mac songs with Hawaiian music, he recalled at the time: "I raised an eyebrow at that, but that's what I've been doing for 30 years, rocking and Hawaiian."

"Through the years, we played a lot," says Mick Fleetwood. "He was unique, just him and his guitar. It would make your mouth fall open. No one else in my life that I've admired ever had that."

This amazing artist could sing and play virtually anything. No other musician in Hawai'i could come close to his vast stylistic range. "It gets boring," he reported. "You've got to entertain yourself all the time." His former partner in the Barefoot Natives duo, Eric Gilliom, suggested in 2006: "He comes from some other world that's not known to mankind. He's the greatest entertainer of Hawai'i."

Some of his best-loved songs include "Katchi Katchi Music Makawao," "Rains of Ko'olau," "My Moloka'i Woman," and "You

Ku'uipo." And his love for opera could bring audiences to tears with a jaw-dropping take on "Nessun Dorma."

"I've always been a fan," Willie said about opera. "It's just that it's been tucked away in a closet in my head for years. Mario Lanza did a movie about Caruso, and I remember watching it when I was about nine. Ever since then, I've loved (the aria) 'Vesti la giubba.'"

In his later years, Willie most came alive fronting his Warehouse Blues Band. "I love playing the blues, and I don't think that's ever going to change," he reported. "Blues is so special to me because it's the only type of music where both vocals and guitar can become emotional at one time. I remember singing the blues when I was like six or seven, singing old standards that my father used to sing. I remember the first time I heard 'The Thrill is Gone' as a kid. I thought this is cool stuff. When Stevie Ray Vaughan came into the picture, that was it. I was lost after that."

In 2012, he released *Warehouse Blues*, a brilliant album of original material that paid tribute to some of the musicians he admired, from John Lee Hooker and Muddy Waters to Stevie Ray Vaughan and Carlos Santana. Standouts included the ZZ Top flavored "Howling at the Moon" and the searing Peter Green/Fleetwood Mac influenced "Heart Aching Blues." "That was because of Mick," he said. "I'm just rocking out 'til I check out."

Willie's last recording, *Tropical Plantation Blues*, paid tribute to Maui's plantation days with catchy songs like "Rooster Crowing," "Cane Truck Hauling," and "Amber Sky Blue." He had been inspired by the PBS *American Epic* series that explored the roots of modern American music, including Delta blues pioneer Charley Patton.

"Blues guys like Charley Patton would take the train and stop off at every plantation and play for all the workers," he explained. "It brought back memories of being a teenager in Lahaina. I wrote songs about working in the sugar cane and hard life in the plantation. It's probably one of my best works yet."

After he passed, having sung with Willie on stage at his annual blues festivals, Fleetwood's on Front St., and New Year's Eve benefits on Maui, Aerosmith's Steven Tyler posted a memoriam: "Thank you for your sharing genius and heart! We will all miss you. Rest in aloha, uncle Willie."

"KALAWAIʻANUI"

Amy Hanaialiʻi

"It's always good to pay respect to the old divas of Hawaiʻi and do my best to try and carry on the tradition."

In a striking video for the title song for her 2019 album *Kalawaiʻanui*, Amy Hanaialiʻi stood on the deck of the Moʻokiha o Piʻilani ocean voyaging canoe, accompanied on pahu drum by her cousin, Kumu Hula Micah Kamohoaliʻi, as it sailed the Kealaikahiki Channel between the islands of Lānaʻi and Kahoʻolawe. "Micah was chanting priest names, and my brother was captaining the canoe, and I'm singing," Amy explains. "It was epic."

The Aloha State's top-selling female artist, Amy's marvelous *Kalawaiʻanui* album, earned the Hawaiian music star a Grammy nomination. Singing primarily in Hawaiian, with five songs co-composed with Kumu Kamohoaliʻi, the album included the mesmerizing tribute "Mauna Kea Kuʻu Iwi Hilo." "I wrote some deep things about Mauna Kea and the struggle we're having," she says.

Closing the album on a triumphant note, Amy premiered the "Queen's Anthem," a remarkable song that addressed Queen Liliʻuokalani's shameful imprisonment after a U.S. military-backed coup.

One of Hawaiʻi's most versatile singers, Amy can effortlessly cover a range of genres from Hawaiian, pop, and jazz to blues, standards, and show tunes. Earning 18 Nā Hōkū Hanohano Awards and six Grammy nominations over the years, she has routinely topped Billboard's world music chart, and her notable performances include singing for the Dalai Lama and for President Barack Obama at two inaugural balls in Washington, D.C.

Born and raised on Maui, Amy was encouraged to sing Hawaiian music by her grandmother, Jennie Napua Hanaialiʻi Woodd. One of the original Royal Hawaiian dancers, she performed at New York's

Lexington Hotel and taught hula in New York and Hollywood for 40 years.

A gifted interpreter of female falsetto singing, Amy first struck gold with her recording *Hawaiian Tradition*, earning Hōkū Awards for Album of the Year, Hawaiian Album of the Year, and Female Vocalist. It was the first album sung entirely in Hawaiian to make it on Billboard's world music chart.

Widely praised for breathing new life into a Hawaiian vocal tradition, her second album with Willie K, *Hanaialiʻi*, won the duo Hawaiian Album and Group of the Year honors. Their adventurous follow-up, *Nostalgia*, won the Female Vocalist of the Year award, as did her subsequent solo work *Puʻuhonua*.

Her pride in helping perpetuate the haʻi falsetto tradition bore full fruit in tributes she paid on *Puʻuhonua* to mentors such as Aunty Genoa Keawe, Leinaʻala Haili, and Myra English. "It's always good to pay respect to the old divas of Hawaiʻi and do my best to try and carry on the tradition," she notes. "It's a heavy responsibility to do it and to do it correctly. When my grandmother asked me to sing Hawaiian music, it was very important for me to do it the right way. I learned from a very young age that you always pay respect to the kupunas of music."

She showcased more facets of her talent on *Friends & Family of Hawaiʻi*, collaborating with a remarkable collection of leading male artists. Blending Hawaiian standards and original compositions with familiar pop tunes, she recorded duets with musicians ranging from Kealiʻi Reichel, Robert Cazimero, and Henry Kapono to John Cruz, Dennis Kamakahi, and Palani Vaughn. "We have such amazing male talent in Hawaiʻi, and I thought it would be a chance to spread my wings a bit and crossover into genres that people are not used to hearing me sing," she says.

One of the highlights featured a duet with country legend Willie Nelson on a remake of Van Morrison's classic ballad "Have I Told You Lately." "We were trying to find a song that Willie hadn't recorded that would pay respect to his voice and would make a great duet," says Amy. "He fell in love with it. It was really an amazing experience. He takes his headphones off and says, 'well, you sound fine darling.'"

Fifteen years after their last studio album together, Amy returned to collaborating with Willie K on *Reunion* in 2014. Opening with the rocking "Hawaiian Man," which she composed for Willie, it ranged from timeless sounding hula songs that could have been recorded in the 1950s to the moving country/gospel ballad "Down By the River." It closed with the extraordinary "Who's Got the Water," which recalled Hawaiian Native rights' classics like the Makaha Sons' "Hawaii '78" and Brother Noland's "Waikiki (Look What They've Done)."

"It's a phenomenal song," Amy emphasizes. *"Every indigenous people deal with who has got the water. Willie expanded it, and it became a masterpiece."*

After *Reunion*, Amy spread her creative wings with 2016's *Chardonnay*, focusing on smooth R&B ballads. Collaborating with acclaimed producer Michael Ruff, she shined on "Meaning of Love's" dreamy paean to devotion and the seductive Ruff original "Leave the Light On," featuring a sensual rap by Fiji. Known for imaginatively revamping familiar material, she transformed Bob Marley's "Waiting in Vain" into a sultry, neo-soul ballad.

When she's not recording or touring, Amy enjoys connecting with her roots by spending time on Moloka'i and heading to a remote valley, where her grandmother was raised. "Now I understand why my grandma would go from Hollywood to Moloka'i," she says. "It's to get that grounding. I feel very fortunate that I have that. So many entertainers are out there with no focus or grounding. It keeps me humble too. I think being on Moloka'i has helped the most."

"KAU KA PEʻA"

Kalani Peʻa

"I am so into being a modern Hawaiian."

Resplendent in a dazzling, multi-colored jacket, Mauiʻs Kalani Peʻa was among the artists kicking off the Grammy Awards Premiere Ceremony in Las Vegas on April 3, 2022. The rousing opening number featured a special multi-nominee performance including folk singer Madison Cunningham, Indian artist Falu, jazz vocalist Nnenna Freelon, John Popper, bluegrass gospel group The Isaacs, and Peʻa, performing Sly & the Family Stoneʻs "Dance to the Music."

Kalani stepped out on stage singing in Hawaiian before joining the collective ensemble on "Danceʻs" English chorus. "This is a great exhibition of regional music, with Kalani Peʻa showing off Hawaiian heritage and Falu her Indian roots," reported *Riff Magazine*.

"I think I brought more delight to the stage with ʻŌlelo Hawaiʻi, and with my contemporary take on it," says Kalani. "It was an honor to feature ʻŌlelo Hawaiʻi. Out of 80 plus nominees they could have chosen anyone, from classical to folk to country and bluegrass and they said ʻwe want Hawaiian language.ʻ"

Winning his third Regional Roots Grammy at the ceremony for *Kau Ka Peʻa*, he announced, "Iʻm proud to be Hawaiian." With a speech that included dedicating his win to King David Kalākaua, who revitalized hula, "which was banned in our culture," he concluded, "This pandemic didnʻt stop us from creating music for the world to heal."

"It was astonishing," he says about his third Grammy win. "The Academy respects me and Hawaiian music."

One of Hawaiʻiʻs rising stars, Kalaniʻs latest recording was compiled and recorded during the 2020 pandemic. It paid homage to loved places and people, especially Hawaiʻiʻs monarchs. "Kūhiō Makamae" paid tribute to Prince Jonah Kūhiō Kalanianaʻole and his resistance to the overthrow of the Hawaiian Kingdom and illegal annexation of Hawai'i, while "'A'ahu Poli'ahu" was a beautiful tribute to Poli'ahu and Lilinoe, the snow and mist goddesses of Mauna Kea.

Gifted with a gorgeous voice and a flair for composing resonant Hawaiian songs, this contemporary Hawaiian musician released his first album, *E Walea*, at the age of 33 in 2016. Fluent in Hawaiian and passionate about perpetuating the culture, he explains, "Coming from a Hawaiian language background, I perpetuate Hawaiian language, and find a way to tell my stories through music, and it's not totally traditional."

He became the first Hawaiian music recording artist to win the Roots Grammy category in 2017, for *E Walea*. He also earned a Contemporary Album of the Year Nā Hōkū Hanohano award, making him the first solo artist to win both a Grammy and Hōkū for the same album.

"Maui-based singer Kalani Pe'a took home the prize this year, and though he comes from traditional roots, he may not look or sound like the usual vision mainlanders have of Hawaiian musicians," noted a *Paste* magazine article. "He's most comfortable in Versace glasses and his trademark bowtie."

It marked the first time a Hawaiian artist had won since the Roots category was created in 2012 (after the Recording Academy abolished the award for Best Hawaiian Music Album). Regional Roots nominees have included Maui musicians Keali'i Reichel, George Kahumoku, Jr., Josh Tatofi, Kamaka Kukona, and Na Wai 'Eha.

Singing from a young age, music became a form of therapy for him. Raised on Hawai'i Island, at age four he was diagnosed with a speech impediment. Conventional speech therapy didn't seem to work for him, so his mother suggested he start singing to help him pronounce words.

There is evidence that the brain functions differently for singing than it does for talking. Famous musicians like Carly Simon, B.B. King, and Bill Withers all had issues with stuttering. A 1982 study by researchers at the University of New South Wales saw a 90% reduction in stuttering following 10 minutes of singing.

"I stammered and stuttered so much," he recalls. "I remember sitting with a strict speech therapist and she wanted me to say words in an abrupt way. I stuttered so much that my mom said, this is not working out. So she decided to sing me children's melodies and she read me books like *The Giving Tree*, and she would sing the words to me. My mom put me in chorus and vocal training. One of my first songs was The Temptations' 'Just My Imagination.' I love the oldies, R&B music, and big band music. I grew up with all kinds of music. You have a melting pot in Hawai'i of cultural diversity."

Kalani views himself as a modern Kānaka Maoli who can cite Genoa Keawe, Helen Desha Beamer, and Kekuhi Kanahele as inspirations while idolizing Luther Vandross and Luciano Pavarotti.

Very stylish in his attire, he emphasizes, "I've always been into innovation. Perpetuating traditional practices of our kupuna is very important, but I'm not going to put a malo and aloha T-shirt on my cover. I'm a guy who wears a blazer and loves bowties with flowers on it. I love to dress up. I am so into being a modern Hawaiian. This is who I am."

Shining also as a soul/pop singer, his debut album featured two English language songs, the lovely ballads "You Are So Beautiful" and "Always and Forever," which were updated with the addition of Hawaiian lyrics. "They're my all-time favorites," he enthuses. "I have an R&B style. This album describes me as an R&B, Hawaiian contemporary singer."

He raised the bar again with his impressive second album, *No 'Ane'i* (*We Belong Here*). Special guests on the recording included Amy Hanaiali'i and Willie K on "Hilo March," and Ho'okena and the Makaha Sons' Moon Kauakahi on the upbeat original "'Elala He Inoa."

"As I was doing my second album I wanted to feature idols and great entertainers who played an important role in my life as a child," he explains. "Uncle Willie shared his 'ukulele talent and Amy flew with me to Oahu. I've been following their music over the years. It was a great start to feature those who have paved the path and held a torch for young artists like myself. And I wanted to feature my idols Ho'okena and Moon Kauakahi. I'm so happy they all approved to help this big boy out."

As for the significance of his most recent Grammy-winning album, he says, "I needed to create this album with a new theme song to instill the value of where we come from, having a sense of place, self-reflection and identity. We all have to chart our own journey."

"SEA OF LOVE"

Raiatea Helm

"I do it for the kupunas because they don't get this kind of music much. Many of the singers have passed on, and it's up to me to carry it on."

Few entertainers in Hawai'i have made such an impact with their debut album as Moloka'i's falsetto star Raiatea Helm. Only 17 years old at the time, she easily won the Nā Hōkū Hanohano Award for Female Vocalist of the Year for *Far Away Heaven*.

Many folks were amazed that such a young talent could interpret classic Hawaiian standards with such soulfulness and depth. The niece of legendary Hawaiian activist/singer George Helm, she sounded even more assured on her *Sweet and Lovely* follow-up. Assisted by guest artists including Keali'i Reichel and falsetto legend Aunty Genoa Keawe, she delivered a superb collection of Hawaiian and hapa-haole standards.

Besides gorgeous renditions of classics like "Alika" and "Kalama'ula," and a sweet duet with Reichel on "Haole Hula," Raiatea demonstrated her gift as a pop singer closing the album with a marvelous version of Etta James' classic "At Last."

She felt blessed to have Aunty Genoa's help. "To have her involved was really special," Raiatea recalled. "When I grow up, I can say to my kids and grandchildren when I was a girl, I recorded with this lady who was a legend." As for the Etta James cover, she explained: "The album was a family project, and it was good to get input from my mom and dad. They chose songs for me because they know my voice and what suits my range. With 'At Last,' I didn't think I was going to pull it off. At the time, I thought I was in love and had a boyfriend. I thank him because I could feel the song."

Once again winning the Female Vocalist of the Year award, she also had the distinction of being the first solo female vocalist from Hawai'i to receive a Grammy nomination.

She earned another Grammy nomination for her third album, *Hawaiian Blossom*. Accompanied by legends like Robert Cazimero, Ledward Kaapana, and the Makaha Sons' Moon Kauakahi, *Hawaiian Blossom* featured several gems, including "Manawaiopuna," recorded by her late uncle George Helm, with Robert Cazimero on backing vocals, and the lovely "E Ku'u Sweet Lei Poina 'Ole" with Led Ka'apana on slack key. It also included a string-embellished version of "Pua Tubarose," the classic song which initially inspired her to begin singing Hawaiian music.

Hearing her sing classic songs so perfectly, it sometimes felt like she had stepped in from the past, like an old soul inhabiting a young body. "A lot of people say that," she noted. "I've thought about it. It's interesting."

Some folks were surprised when she expanded her artistic horizons, delving into the world of rock 'n' roll as an initial member of the Island Rumours Band founded by Mick Fleetwood. Besides singing Hawaiian songs like "Lei Lokelani," she immersed herself in the repertoire of Fleetwood Mac, totally nailing Stevie Nick's "Rhiannon."

"It was a total surprise, totally different from what I do," she enthused at the time. "I've had a desire to find something other than Hawaiian music, like jazz, but rock 'n' roll came out of the blue. I'm a big Stevie Nicks fan, but I don't know if that's really my gig because I've got other plans for my music."

Fleetwood was inspired to ask her to join his new band after catching her in concert. "I saw Raiatea at the Maui Arts Center with her father and fell in love with her," he recalled. "She's a really talented singer with such presence."

Attending a rehearsal at Fleetwood's Upcountry home, I was mesmerized as the Rumours Band tore into the Mac classic "World Turning." As the musicians rocked collectively in a circle, Raiatea beamed and danced to the driving beat. With the energy rising, you could feel joy in the air as the musicians focused on Fleetwood, anchoring the colossal sound.

The accelerated success of Raiatea's early career took her family by surprise. Having spent time dancing with Moana's Hula Hālau and with her father at The Lodge at Molokai Ranch, she was asked to sing for her mother's birthday in 1999. "We didn't know she had talent," explained her father, Zachary Helm. "Everybody was shocked. Family members cried they were so moved."

"They didn't know I could sing because I was such a shy person growing up," Raiatea recalls. "I was a very kolohe girl. I danced hula, but I have to admit I didn't really enjoy it because I was a tomboy. I preferred basketball to a hula skirt. For some reason, Hawaiian music came out of the blue."

She had been inspired hearing Nina Keali'iwahamana sing "Pua Tubarose," at a televised Kamehameha Schools contest. "I never knew this music existed or who this lady was until I saw her on TV," she explains. "I watched the Song Contest in 1999, and they put on a big show at the intermission. I was 15 years old, and I had to find Hawaiian music myself. If I hadn't watched that program I wouldn't be singing now."

Holed up in her bedroom, she practiced daily. "I learned by myself just listening to other people," she says. "It was funny because I hadn't heard these people when I was young. I never knew who Genoa Keawe was and Nina Keali'iwahamana. I wasn't so into Hawaiian music when I was young. It just came to me and hit me real hard, and I was so into it."

Fueled by a love for traditional Hawaiian music, she reports she feels very emotional when she sings falsetto. "It's real soothing. The feeling is awesome. It's like I live the music, and I put my all into what I do. I love what I do, and it makes me happy to see how happy people are when they listen to me. I do it for the kupunas because they don't get this kind of music much. Many of the singers have passed on, and it's up to me to carry it on. I want to encourage other young people to do the same. Nowadays, they have all this island music and reggae. It's OK, but how are you going to carry on the culture with this music. It's not Hawaiian."

In 2010, an inspired teaming on the album *Keola Beamer & Raiatea* provided a perfect vehicle for both artists to soar creatively. It encompassed original songs, a cover of "Who Knows Where the Time Goes" by British singer Sandy Denny, and a Hawaiian adaptation of "When I Look in Your Eyes" from the musical film *Doctor Dolittle* that showcased Raiatea's stunning vocals.

"All of a sudden, I had this new tonal palette to play with in her voice," says Keola. "Through that, I kind of fell in love with my craft again."

Raiatea revealed the project also helped inspire her. "I had been in the process of doing my own solo album and was meeting with composers. I was all ready to go, but something inside said, maybe this is not the right path for you. All of a sudden, I felt kind of lost. I think a lot of artists come to that point in life after you do your first and second, and third CD. Are you going to do something different? That's when I thought about maybe doing a duet CD with Keola, and I didn't realize he was thinking the same thing."

Following her brilliant collaboration with Keola Beamer, she set her sights on a bygone era with *Sea of Love*, evoking the romance and magic of a simpler time. From its alluring, retro cover to the last strains of steel guitar on the closing song, Raiatea's album embraced listeners in a sea of nostalgia.

"At the beginning of my musical journey when I was 15, my dad had given me two CDs, one by Lena Machado and by Leina'ala Heine," she explains. "I fell in love with Leina'ala's sound because she had these cool arrangements with the (percussive) brushes and vibes and piano, and cool jazz guitar. She had one song, 'Namolokama,' and I fell in love with it. So from then on it was all about planning and preparing and being able to do justice to that sound."

Surrounded by a stellar group including Bobby Ingano on steel guitar and Jeff Peterson on guitar, Raiatea eloquently re-imagined the "Hawaiian Club" music of the '50s and '60s Waikiki. "This particular period was called club music, and it was performed in Waikiki," she explains. "I've always wanted to do an album like this. It's definitely my favorite album because this is all me. I love to sing old Hawaiian songs. It makes people happy."

Mixing classic Hawaiian, hapa-haole, and pop songs, she wove her vocal magic on a classy collection of compositions, including a jazzy take on the classic "The Cockeyed Mayor of Kaunakakai" and singing in Hawaiian and English on the *Sea of Love* title track.

To close the album, she reached back to the 1930s and a celluloid vision of tropical romance with "Moonlight and Shadows," originally recorded by Dorothy Lamour for *The Jungle Princess*. "I really admire the romance side of old Waikiki," she says. "I love looking at old pictures of Hawai'i. The music was more vivid than today. You could see and feel the water and sand and palm trees. They were so classy and dressed nice. And all of a sudden, it went away."

Since releasing *Sea of Love,* she contributed to the Mana Maoli Collective's powerful remake of "Hawai'i '78," and completed a bachelor's degree in Hawaiian music.

"I really want to master my craft," she concludes. "I want to perfect my understanding of the gift that I have. My gift to people is to make them happy. I love to sing and see people happy listening to my music."

"WHILE MY GUITAR GENTLY WEEPS"

Jake Shimabukuro

"I think the 'ukulele is the only instrument in the world where you can just say the name, and it will make you smile."

Impressing Hawai'i audiences in his younger days with his remarkable talent, Jake Shimabukuro's impromptu performance of George Harrison's "While My Guitar Gently Weeps" transformed him into a global sensation. Filmed at John Lennon's Strawberry Fields memorial in New York City's Central Park, a YouTube video went viral, and amassed more than 17 million views.

"The video changed my life," he marvels. "I was in the right place at the right time. George was one of my heroes growing up, and he was a 'ukulele player."

Jake was even praised by Harrison's wife, Olivia. "She sent me a nice email about how she felt about my playing and recording her husband's tune."

"We should all be grateful that a new generation of players, such as Jake Shimabukuro, have emerged with renewed enthusiasm and virtuosity," Olivia Harrison wrote in the liner notes of *Walking Down Rainhill.*. "I especially love Jake's versions of George's songs."

When it comes to the 'ukulele, Jake is widely acclaimed for his astonishing versatility. Sometimes billed as "the Jimi Hendrix of the ukulele," he seamlessly fuses a spectrum of influences from jazz, blues, rock, funk, Hawaiian, classical, Latin, and bluegrass into his repertoire. Famous fans include Pearl Jam's Eddie Vedder, who praised: "Jake is taking the instrument to a place that I can't see anybody else catching up with."

Having experienced many memorable moments during his celebrated career, an opportunity to play at Liverpool's legendary Cavern Club, where the Beatles started, almost left him speechless. "It was awesome," he enthuses. "I couldn't believe it. I flew from Honolulu and got there at noon and by three p.m. I was on the Beatles' *Magical Mystery Tour*. That's how excited I was. I got to touch the front door of George Harrison's house where he grew up, and I went to Strawberry Fields and Penny Lane, and we ended up at the Cavern.

"There was a Beatles' cover band playing, and I got up there and played 'In My Life,' 'Something,' and 'Why My Guitar Weeps'," he continues. "It was crazy because the Cavern is a loud bar, and it's like playing in a cave, but when I started playing, it was unbelievable. You could hear a pin drop. The manager said, 'I've never heard this place like it.' It was incredible."

Jake had previously briefly visited the U.K., when he was invited to play for Queen Elizabeth II at a charity show, performing "In My Life" with Bette Midler. "I did get to meet the Queen," he notes. "It was the most nervous I've ever been meeting someone, shaking hands with royalty, and meeting the Queen. She looked at me and said, 'you play such a beautiful instrument.' I said thank you very much, and I kept bowing the whole time."

Jake loves uplifting folks with his playing. "I think the 'ukulele is the only instrument in the world where you can just say the name, and it will make you smile," he says. "When I travel to different places, and I'm at the airport or in a restaurant with my 'ukulele case, people always ask, what's in the case? They're expecting me to say a violin, but when I say it's a 'ukulele, they immediately smile and share a story about how they were in Hawai'i. It's an instrument that promotes conversation. It encourages people to let their guard down. It's so friendly and inviting."

Taught by his mother, Jake began strumming an 'ukulele at the age of four, discovering a natural affinity for the instrument. "It's where my special passion lies," he says. "Every morning, she would sit down for a few hours and teach me basic chords, and we'd sing songs and had a great time. As I got older, the 'ukulele became a representation of that time I spent with my mom. I would religiously practice. My parents, sometimes late at night, would have to scold me and take it away from me. That's how I learned to play with so much dynamics. I can play soft parts very softly and still get the articulation. That came from all those years practicing in my bedroom late at night playing softly so my parents wouldn't hear me."

As he progressed, he felt it was essential to define his own voice with the instrument. "I had to do my own thing," he continues. "I had to find something I could do. That was the chance to try and be innovative and create a sound and style that represented me. It was a matter of learning to express what was inside of me to bring out emotions I had inside through the 'ukulele."

Admired for his remarkable ability to take the 'ukulele into uncharted territory, he feels like he has been on a mission to make the instrument cool. "It's always been my mission to show the 'ukulele is capable of playing jazz, rock, pop, and classical music. To show that it is a very serious instrument that requires a lot of dedication and commitment. It's not a stepping stone to a guitar. It's its own instrument with its own character and essence."

A gifted interpreter, his recordings have featured a range of inspired covers from New Order's "Bizarre Love Triangle" and Sting's "Fields of Gold" to Chick Corea's fusion instrumental "Spain," Schubert's "Ave Marie," and Paganini's famous violin work "Caprice No. 24." Particularly proud of the Paganini interpretation, he reports, "that was the most challenging piece I've ever tackled. It was not just learning how to play it, but trying to be creative and innovative with the arrangement. The 'ukulele only has two octaves, and that piece requires three octaves or more. So I had to use a lot of artificial harmonics and create different techniques with my right hand to mimic the slurs of a violin. I rented a hotel room for a few nights, and I didn't leave the room. All I did was eat and play."

On his 2011 album, *Peace Love Ukulele*, which topped *Billboard's* World Music chart, Jake took on the challenge of adapting one of the greatest rock songs of all time – Queen's epic "Bohemian Rhapsody." "Often in interviews, I'm asked if I think any song is possible on 'ukulele, and I always say, you can make any song work," Jake explains. "I've been asked many times, 'can you play Queen's 'Bohemian Rhapsody?' People don't expect to hear a song like that on the 'ukulele."

The vocals alone on Queen's magnum opus required 180 separate overdubs, so Jake knew he faced a formidable task. "It was a huge undertaking," he continues. "There were so many moments I wanted to throw in the towel. The hardest thing was the transitions from almost being like a whisper and then coming out aggressively with a head-banging piece and then an almost operatic, playful feeling. A solo 'ukulele arrangement is the complete opposite approach to the classic 'Bohemian Rhapsody' that we all know and love."

Jake's astonishing interpretation of "Bohemian Rhapsody" was praised by Queen guitarist Brian May, who said, "it really is exquisite."

A few years later, on *The Greatest Day*, the "Hendrix of the 'ukulele" finally interpreted a song by the guitar icon, "If 6 Was 9," from *Axis: Bold as Love*. "I always shied away from doing it because it's Jimi Hendrix," he says. "But I thought what's the best way to cover a Jimi Hendrix tune, well you get the world's greatest dobro player, Jerry Douglas, to play on it, then no one can say anything. It's one of my favorite Jimi Hendrix songs."

Attracting the attention of leading musicians over the years, he's toured with Jimmy Buffett and Bela Fleck and the Flecktones. His guest recording spots include playing with jazz guitarist Earl Klugh, teaming with reggae star Ziggy Marley on "Beach in Hawaii," and performing with legendary cellist Yo-Yo Ma on his Grammy-winning CD *Songs of Joy and Peace*, for an instrumental version of John Lennon's "Happy Xmas (War is Over)."

In late 2021 Jake released the brilliant *Jake & Friends*, a mostly duets album guaranteed to expand his popularity. It featured an impressive array of musicians collaborating with the 'ukulele player, including Willie Nelson, Bette Midler, Ziggy Marley, Michael McDonald, Jon Anderson, Vince Gill and Amy Grant, Allman Brothers' guitarist Warren Haynes, Jack Johnson with Paula Fuga, and Lukas Nelson.

Covering songs associated with the artists and some Beatles tunes, it included "On the Road to Freedom," a "13-minute killer song" with Haynes, that recalled some of the Allman Brothers' fiery jamming.

"I've been working on it for a couple of years," he says. "A lot of them are duets, just the 'ukulele and them singing or strumming a guitar. Everyone sounds amazing. It's such an honor. To hear Willie Nelson singing 'Stardust' with just the 'ukulele or hear Bette Midler singing 'The Rose' with the 'ukulele it blows my mind. Vince Gill and

Amy Grant did a duet of 'Something.' I would want to get married again to my wife just so I could dance to that."

With Michael McDonald, they covered the old Moody Blues tune "Go Now," with Jake playing tenor 'ukulele and McDonald playing a baritone. And Jon Anderson teamed with him for the Beatles' epic "A Day in the Life."

Showcasing the 'ukulele's versatility, this virtuoso reports he never stops learning. "I'm still trying to figure out more things. Almost every night, I'm discovering something new on the instrument. I'm constantly switching out gear trying different things. It's all part of the growing process. I love it. As long as I feel I'm growing and learning, that's what fulfills me."

"RAIN ON SUNDAY"

Paula Fuga

"I knew that one day I would travel all over the world sharing my music with people and that music would be the vehicle."

P aula Fuga's album *Rain on Sunday* marked her first full-length studio recording since her award-winning *Lilikoi* debut. With songs about connecting with nature, overcoming adversity, and the importance of focusing on love, she says: "I hope this album inspires people to open up. I hope they feel the love that every single musician put into these songs, and I hope it heals whatever's inside them that needs to be healed."

Released on Jack Johnson's Brushfire Records label in the summer of 2021, it featured primarily original songs, including a catchy reggae-flavored cover of Sade's "Lovers Rock" and George "Boogie" Kalama's "Hōkūleʻa Star of Gladness" tribute to the pioneering, double-hulled ocean voyaging canoe which has sailed around the world.

For the first single from her album, Paula teamed with long-time friend Jack Johnson for a duet on the moving "If Ever," joined by Ben Harper on lap-steel guitar. The song addressed the loss of both musician's fathers.

After hearing rough mixes of the album, Johnson suggested she release it on his own label. "It was such a relief to have Jack's support and have him jump on the album with a brand new song that we wrote together," she says. "My life is so full of magic. The stars always align for me.

"Before this, I was just cruising, the last 15 years," she adds, laughing. "Hardly a care in the world. I would take whatever gig came my way if I'm into it. If not, I pass it by. I wasn't hustling. Now I've been elevated to another level in my career. It requires more focus and intention. For this album, I was relying on my 2020 income to pay for it all, and all my gigs were canceled. It was a huge loss. I felt helpless."

"Paula's voice is powerful and yet soothing at the same time," Johnson reported. "When we bring Paula out to somewhere like Colorado, and I invite her on stage, any song she starts, we have to stall for a moment because the crowd goes wild. The whole crowd puts their hands in the air and starts cheering. It's like a spiritual moment."

Born in Louisiana in 1978 (her dad was in the Army), Paula moved at an early age to Oahu. "I always believed the reason why I love soulful music, especially blues and Motown, is because I was born in Louisiana," she says.

As a child, she spent time homeless and saw how drugs could destroy families. "My life is a miracle," she emphasizes. "I was homeless on the beach by the time I was five years old. I lived in a car, in all kinds of weird, crazy situations. But I truly believed that good things would happen to me if I just kept being a good person. Drugs were all around when I was a kid, and I could have taken the wrong path. I look at my life, kind of like Cinderella's life. I know how miraculous it is for me to be where I am. I knew that one day I would travel all over the world sharing my music with people and that music would be the vehicle."

Shaped early on by gospel, blues, classic soul, the infectious rhythms of reggae, and sweet Hawaiian music, Fuga began playing 'ukulele in high school, studying under master teacher Roy Sakuma. By her junior year, she was writing songs and poems and felt the calling to immerse herself in Hawaiiana.

Enjoying empowering and elevating, Paula routinely entrances audiences. Singing primarily in English, her strongest material, such as "Lilikoi," the title cut of her Hōkū-winning debut album, blends English lyrics with 'Ōlelo Hawai'i. Once categorizing her music as "oregano blue," she has described it as "original music influenced by reggae and rhythm and blues."

Some mainland reviewers have proclaimed her a Hawaiian soul queen. "It makes me feel like they recognize who I am," she says, laughing. "When I think of soul queens, I think of Aretha Franklin and Chaka Khan, the amazing voices I grew up listening to. I'm very aware I'm a soulful singer."

In 2010, she released a five-song EP featuring collaborations with Jack Johnson and Ziggy Marley. The hit-packed *Misery's End* featured a newly recorded version of her memorable song "Country Road"

- originally released on a Mana Maoli Hawaiian immersion school benefit album - which became a popular duet with Johnson on his tours.

"I wrote it and thought of him when I was writing it, but I had never met him yet," she reveals. "I was on the road and had my 'ukulele with me and was all irritated because there was an accident and I wanted to get to work. I was sitting there worrying about the time and thought how selfish of me. Here you are complaining, and you're in perfect condition while somebody else had a terrible accident. So I just started writing a song then and there. Jack loved it, and we recorded it. A few months after, I went past the spot where I wrote it, and the road there is called Johnson Road. What a trip."

Helping Native Hawaiian causes in July 2019, Paula and Johnson traveled to the top of Mauna Kea on Hawai'i Island, paying respect to the mauna protectors halting telescope construction, singing "Better Together" and "Constellations."

Besides captivating people with her music, Paula enjoys inspiring youth with her miraculous life story about overcoming adversity. "Since my career began, I haven't stopped being an inspirational speaker for various foster youth groups throughout the state," she says. "It's something I'm very passionate about. When you go through a traumatic experience, and you come out victorious, it's your kuleana, your responsibility to help those who are in that same situation. I don't feel obliged to speak to these kids. I feel it's my responsibility. It's my calling in life, what I'm meant to do. To show them that they can a have a big dream, no matter where you start, you can achieve your dream."

After playing at a convention at the Grand Wailea on Maui in 2020, British superstar Ed Sheeran hopped on a plane to Oahu and headed to Jack Johnson's north shore house to hang out and jam with him and Paula. "When you meet him, he's genuinely interested in you," says Paula. "He shared some of his new songs, and I shared some songs. Ed flew to Honolulu from Maui just to hang out with Jack."

Paula discovered Sheeran especially loved seeing that fans were enjoying his show on the beach in front of the Wailea resort. "That was the best part of it he said, because they were there to watch him, all those Maui fans. He really appreciated that. I forgot to tell him out of all the islands, Maui's the most supportive of live music."

Israel "Iz" Kamakawiwaoʻole & the Makaha Sons, Maui -
"What the world needs is aloha, and that's our job"

Raiatea Helm & Keola Beamer - "If you stay open to the universe and let things reach you, it takes you to some wonderful places."

Willie K & ZZ Top's Billy Gibbons, Kahului Airport -
"I like versatility on the guitar, the weirder the sound, the better"

Smokey Robinson with Eric Gilliom, Amy Hanaiali'i & Richard T. Bissen, Jr. at the MACC, photo by Teresa Skinner - "I've been very blessed to be in show business this long"

Herbie Hancock, Oahu - "It took several years for people to realize I was going to do acoustic jazz and electric pop music."

Chick Corea, Oahu - "Every time I play and make music, it's a celebration"

Paul Horn, Kula, Maui - "The power of music
is much more than entertainment"

Jimmy Cliff, Maui - "My mission is to innovate
and clear the way and set things straight"

Toots & the Maytals - "We put the music where it was supposed to be"

Ziggy Marley - "We haven't had that spiritual revolution that we need"

TAKE ME TO THE RIVER

"THE TRACKS OF MY TEARS"

Smokey Robinson

"I've been very blessed"

Acclaimed as the "poet laureate of soul," Smokey Robinson composed his first song at five and scored his first million-selling single with The Miracles at 21. "Shop Around" was also Motown Records' first million-seller.

With timeless songs including "The Tracks of My Tears," "Ooo Baby Baby," "I Second That Emotion," and "The Tears of a Clown," few have matched this living legend's gift for crafting lyrics that speak to the heart and soul. Motown's founder, Berry Gordy, has called him "the soul of Motown."

Robinson made his Maui concert debut in April 2022. And at the age of 82, he still sounds amazing, crediting his health to taking care of his body and mind. "I've been very blessed to be in show business this long," he says before the show. "Your voice is your instrument, so if you keep yourself in shape your instrument is going to be there when you need it."

This health regimen includes yoga and watching his diet. "I've been doing yoga for almost 40 years," he explains. "I'm very passionate about it. It's one of the best things I've ever done for my life. It helps to keep your body stretched out and you keep the blood flowing through. And I don't eat red meat. Up until February of 2020, I was a vegan for about five years. I haven't had any red meat for 40 years."

Born and raised in Detroit, he grew up hearing records by legendary female singers like Sarah Vaughan, Ella Fitzgerald, and Billie Holiday played in his house. As far as jazz he heard Charlie Parker, Dizzy Gillespie, Thelonious Monk, and Miles Davis.

Forming The Miracles while he was still in high school, they were the first vocal group signed by Motown. On the ground floor of Motown, he helped steer the label to become a global phenomenon. "That's one of my proudest achievements," he says. "I was there on the first day. I grew up at Motown. It was a great place to grow up, especially as a songwriter."

With The Miracles, he toured the South on Motortown Revues when racism was rampant. At a Mississippi gas station, one of the Miracles was threatened with a gun. "There were times when we were lucky to come out alive," Robinson told *The New York Times*. At one concert The Temptations and the Four Tops took turns standing at the side of a stage armed with baseball bats in case there was trouble.

President Barack Obama referenced that volatile time, when Robinson performed at "The Motown Sound" tribute at the White House in 2011. "At concerts in the South, Motown groups literally brought people together - insisting that the ropes traditionally used to separate black and white audience members be taken down," Obama announced.

An early influence on the Beatles, they recorded his song "You Really Got a Hold On Me" on *With the Beatles*, and Paul McCartney once commented, "Smokey Robinson was like God in our eyes." George Harrison would later record his own tribute, "Pure Smokey." "I'm a big fan of Smokey Robison, because musically he's so sweet he makes you feel nice, he makes me feel good," Harrison reported.

When Bob Dylan was asked at a KQED press conference in San Francisco in December of 1965, "What poets do you dig?," he responded with a list that included Rimbaud, Allen Ginsberg, and Smokey Robinson.

While some Motown musicians like The Temptations and Marvin Gaye embraced social issues in their songs, Robinson stayed with his winning formula until his debut solo album *Smokey*. Featuring a member of the Native American rock band XIT delivering a Sioux medicine man chant, "Just My Soul Responding" referenced the impact of the Vietnam War and life in the ghetto.

A champion of Gaye's masterpiece *What's Going On*, he had persuaded Berry Gordy to release it. "He was one of the greatest singers ever," says Robinson. "Marvin was one of the most fantastic singers to ever live."

Having impacted so many over the decades with his songs, recent *YouTube* comments on "The Tracks of My Tears," include - "being in Vietnam this music kept me going," and a 19-year-old who posted, "the lyrics made me feel less lonelier since I was 15."

In recent years he released the Grammy-nominated *Timeless Love*, covering standards like "Fly Me to the Moon," and "Night and Day." *Smokey & Friends* in 2014 featured famous artists like Elton John joining him on "The Tracks of My Tears," Steven Tyler on "You Really Got a Hold On Me," and James Taylor on "Ain't That Peculiar."

Some years earlier he produced the inspirational album *Food for the Spirit*, "to feed people's spirits," he explained to *The Oakland Press*. The album referenced his former descent into darkness with the funky track "Gang Bangin,'" which addressed drug-addicted lost souls. He had become a cocaine addict after leaving his wife and Motown.

In his autobiography, *Smokey: Inside My Life*, he described a miraculous prayer healing by L.A. pastor Jean Perez, who somehow knew that he was close to death. She laid hands on him and passed out, twice.

"It was God's will that I go there and have this woman pray over me because I had damaged myself so terribly with smoking cocaine and weed," he explains about that pivotal moment. "I went there and everything that was happening to me I wasn't telling anyone because I didn't want anyone to know. I didn't want my public to know. I didn't want my fans to know all the things that I was going through physically, emotionally, and mentally. I went there and this woman told me every last thing. She said God had told her and God had sent me there to be healed. That night I was healed. That was May 1986. That night I went in that church and I was a junkie, a cocaine-weed junkie. I came out and I was free. I tell people that story because once you give it to God, that's it."

"WHERE DID OUR LOVE GO"

The Supremes

*"In our minds, we were already stars.
It's just the world didn't know about it."*

"They didn't want to take us," Supremes' co-founder Mary Wilson recalled about Motown Records initial refusal to sign the group. "I think we were too young. We were 16, but we had been singing for a couple of years. We stayed there every day until we became part of the family, and then they started using us."

Diana Ross, Florence Ballard, and Mary Wilson grew up together in Detroit's Brewster housing project. As teenagers Wilson and Ballard made a pact to form a group. "Two of the Temptations, Eddie Kendricks and Paul Williams, were part of another group at the time, and they really formed the group," Wilson explained. "They got Florence, and she brought me in, and one of the other members brought Diane in."

It was 1960 when the Shirelles and the Chantels were big, and the Andrews Sisters were still making waves. These were the female acts the Supremes had grown up listening to.

Before their star ascended, they headed down South as a support act with the Motortown Revue, where they dealt with restaurants refusing service, locked doors on "white" gas station bathrooms, and their bus being shot at in Georgia. At some theaters on the tour, black fans were relegated to balconies, with only whites allowed on the floor. "If it was one floor, the blacks would be on one side, the whites would be on another side," said Wilson.

After they were signed, it would take five years before they topped the charts with their first hit, "Where Did Our Love Go," and were no longer known at Motown as the "no-hit Supremes."

From the beginning, their course was strictly controlled. "We were very happy that Motown recorded us, and let's face it, in those days, there weren't many companies giving out record deals, so we were very thrilled," she said. "We wanted the input. We were basically told what to do, and it was okay because we were working with very creative people. After we became very popular, we said, now wait just a minute, we're 21, we don't need chaperones and this and that. We were growing up. It's like being with a parent where you say; I'm out of school now. I want to do what I want to do. They didn't want to give us that freedom."

The Supremes became Motown's most commercially successful group. After "Where Did Our Love Go" hit number one in 1964, within six years they had chalked up 12 top hits with classics songs like "You Keep Me Hanging On" and "Love Child."

Wilson said the group really wasn't surprised by the extent of their success. "We were ready for it because by the time we had our first hit in 1964, we had been singing since 1959. In our minds, we were already stars. It's just the world didn't know about it."

She recalled many wonderful times with the Supremes. A highlight was their first trip to London, where audiences responded, "like people treated the Beatles." Appearing on Ed Sullivan's TV show was also a thrill. "All the Ed Sullivan shows were wonderful. We were on television every other Sunday, and for Black artists, that was rare."

The first African-Americans featured on the cover of a TV magazine, both Oprah Winfrey and Whoopi Goldberg later told Wilson that the Supremes' appearances on *Sullivan* had a major impact on them, demonstrating that Black people could succeed. "These were brown women as they had never, ever been seen before on national television," Goldberg wrote in the foreword to Wilson's book, *Supreme Glamour.*

Included on the cover of *Time* magazine in 1965, along with the Beach Boys and Herman's Hermits, an article on "Rock 'n' Roll: The Sound of the Sixties" declared: "The best brown sound is, of course, that sung by Negroes," and the Supremes were "the prize fillies in Gordy's stable. They are the reigning female rock 'n' roll group."

As to why they became the most popular female group in history, Wilson said she was not sure. "I really don't know. We wanted it so much, and we worked hard at it. The proof of it is Diane's success and of her going on after the Supremes. That's why I continued on. Unfortunately, Florence couldn't do it."

Alcohol problems and friction with Motown president Berry Gordy, Jr. caused Florence Ballard to be fired from the group in 1967. Marvin Gaye once described her as "a hell of a singer, probably the strongest of the three girls." After an unsuccessful solo career, she died living on welfare at the age of 32.

Wilson was deeply affected by the tragedy. "Most people who aspire to be great do it out of some sort of vulnerability or insecurity," she suggested, "and when the public takes you in and takes you so high, then when you no longer can give them what they want, they can really take you down. If you don't try to aspire to more and just give up, it's very tragic."

Ballard attempted to sue for $8.7 million in 1971, claiming that Gordy and Diana Ross, and others conspired to push her out of a fortune in royalties. The case was dismissed without a trial.

At the peak of their popularity in 1967, Motown raised the Supremes' individual weekly allowance from $50 to $225 a week. "All the money we made would go to Motown except for the allowance we were getting," Ballard reported to journalist Peter Benjaminson in *The Lost Supreme: The Life of Dreamgirl Florence Ballard.* She told *Jet,* "All the money we made off concert dates went back to Motown."

In *Detroit 67: The Year That Changed Soul,* author Stuart Cosgrove noted that Motown reported that "Where Did Our Love Go" sold more than one million copies resulting in each Supreme receiving only $7,237, from which development and studio costs were then deducted.

Benjaminson revealed in *The Lost Supreme,* if one of their records sold a million copies, each Supreme would end up only receiving $5,000, from which was subtracted her share of the cost of all preceding unreleased records by the group as well as her share of all the costs of the record for which she was receiving royalties.

With Ballard replaced by Cindy Birdsong, they were subsequently billed as Diana Ross & the Supremes. Two years later, Ross announced she was quitting for a solo career. Wilson said she felt a change was coming. "We were aware probably after the fact. After we knew what was happening, it was almost too late to change our course."

The Supremes continued without Ross, adding Jean Terrell and shifting to a more soulful sound reflecting the times, delivering a funky take on the Beatles' "Come Together," along with releasing hipper songs like "Stoned Love's" plea for peace and the anti-Vietnam war song "Bill, When Are You Coming Back?" Collaborating with the Four Tops for three albums, highlights included covers of Sly Stone's "Everyday People," Stephen Stills' "Love the One You're With," and Laura Nyro's "Stoned Soul Picnic."

One of their biggest post-Ross hits, "Stoned Love," with Terrell on lead vocals, was almost not released because Berry Gordy thought it condoned drugs. It was about love and peace.

Having never performed in Hawai'i before, Diana Ross made her Maui debut in 2015, with a phenomenal show at the MACC. At the age of 71, this legendary icon sounded as compelling as when she fronted the famous trio in the '60s. Dazzling her sold-out audience with numerous glamorous costume changes, she thrilled with hit after hit from "Baby Love" and "Love Child" to the anthemic "Ain't No Mountain High Enough" and Gloria Gaynor's "I Will Survive." Some days later, she sang at the wedding of her youngest daughter Chudney, in Kapalua, Maui.

In recent years Wilson became a musical activist as part of the Truth in Music bill, which prevents impostor groups from performing under the names of the '50s and '60s rock and roll groups, including Motown acts like the Supremes and The Marvelettes. She published four books on the legendary group, including the latest, *Supreme Glamour.*

Mary Wilson died in February 2021, at the age of 76. "I have so many wonderful memories of our time together," Diana Ross posted in tribute. "The Supremes will live on in our hearts."

Released posthumously, *Mary Wilson - The Motown Anthology*, compiled two discs of her Supremes' and solo work, including the unreleased track, "Why Can't We All Get Along," about the group's strained relationship. An accompanying booklet included tributes by Dionne Warwick, the Temptation's Otis Williams, Martha Reeves, and Paul McCartney. *Uncut* praised the collection as a, "long overdue celebration of a supreme talent."

"WALK ON BY"

Dionne Warwick

"Bacharach and David were my tailors, and I was the one who wore the garments."

"I don't think I would refer to myself as a great singer," says Dionne Warwick, one of the top-charted female vocalists of all time. "I would say I come from a wonderful family of singers, and it's almost preordained that I would sing. Everybody in my family sings, so I guess I'm just blessed. I consider it an enormous gift with an enormous responsibility."

A five-time Grammy winner, this pop and soul icon has sold more than 100 million records. Collaborating with the duo of Burt Bacharach and Hal David, masterminds for all of her hits from 1962 to 1971, Warwick racked up 30 hit singles and close to 20 best-selling albums during her first decade.

Many of her songs are classic show-stoppers, including "Walk On By," "Do You Know the Way to San Jose," and "I'll Never Fall in Love Again," "What the World Needs Now," and "Then Came You," her million-selling duet with The Spinners.

Her velvety voice combined with the sophisticated pop compositions of Bacharach and David has been portrayed as a match made in heaven. "I still describe it the way the industry chose to describe it ages ago, as the triangle marriage that worked," she says. "It was such a joy to sing some of the most meaningful words of our time by Hal David, and Burt was one of the most prolific composers, writing such sophisticated music."

Working with lyricist Hal David, Bacharach changed the sound of mainstream '60s pop, chalking up numerous stylish hits. Beginning in 1962, with "Don't Make Me Over," the duo supplied Warwick with 39 charting records over ten years. "Going from one tune to the next the more I could see what she could do," Bacharach recalled before a Maui concert. "She's unbelievable, a perfect instrument. I could take more chances, more risks. Look at a song like 'Promises, Promises.' In the hands of anybody else, it's laborious. They're stressed out by the end of the song. It's a hard song to sing, but Dionne just floats through it."

After a long absence, Warwick reunited with Bacharach and David for the album *Friends Can Be Lovers* in 1993. The duo's contribution with "Sunny Weather Lover" featured their hallmark light melody combined with a tale of lost love. The album also marked Warwick's teaming with her famous niece, Whitney Houston, on the ballad "Love Will Find a Way." "Everyone was always asking when are you going to record together, and we kept saying when the right song comes along," she explains. "We felt this was the right one. The song is special to me because it was written by my son David."

Whatever she sings, Warwick adds her unique stamp. "I bring Dionne to a song whatever that is" injecting, "an understanding of what is trying to be said and an interpretation of the melody."

Dionne Marie Warrick grew up in a gospel family. Her mother was manager of a gospel group that gave her experience as an organist and occasional vocalist. Along with her sister Dee Dee and aunt Cissy (Whitney's mum), Warwick went on to found The Gospelaires Trio. "It's always been exceptionally helpful," she says of her gospel roots. "Gospel music teaches respect of the lyric and how to convey that lyric meaningfully. It centers you and lets you understand what you're singing about."

A tribute to her gift of interpretation, her hit "Alfie," from the movie starring Michael Caine, was released by more than 40 artists before it landed in the U.S. Top-20. "It was recorded first, of course, in England by Cilla Black," she recalls. "Then it was released in Australia as an instrumental from the film by Sonny Rollins. When it got to the States, Cher recorded it, and subsequently, it was recorded about 42 times before me. I thought, what was the point of me recording it. It had been done and done. The lovely thing about it was I was the only one to have a big hit record. It just goes to show when a tailor cuts a suit for you, no one but you can wear it. That's how I felt about Bacharach and David, they were my tailors, and I was the one who wore the garments."

In 1969, she released the terrific R&B album *Soulful*, covering soul and pop hits. Recorded in Memphis, it featured a brilliant interpretation of the Beatles' "We Can Work It Out," a jubilant gospel-flavored cover of "It's Been a Hard Day's Night," and Curtis Mayfield's classic freedom anthem "People Get Ready."

Warwick recorded one of her most personally rewarding songs, "That's What Friends Are For," with Gladys Knight, Stevie Wonder, and Elton John in 1985. The number one hit earned Song of the Year and Best Pop Performance by a Duo or Group at the 29th annual Grammy Awards and raised millions of dollars for AIDS charities. It had been composed by Burt Bacharach and his wife Carole Bayer Sager for the movie *Night Shift* and sung by Rod Stewart.

"I was doing a session with Burt and Carole, and I had been rehearsing with them," she explains. "The night before the film *Night Shift* was on, and I heard Rod sing this song and thought what a great song. I automatically knew it was Burt's melody. They thought it was appropriate for me knowing how vital friendships are to me. I wanted to include some friends, and Gladys, Stevie, and Elton were the friends available. Elizabeth (Taylor) was at the session, and she said it would be a great theme for AIDS foundations. We all agreed because we had all lost friends to the disease."

The legendary singer updated her songbook in 1998, recording a salsa version of "Do You Know the Way to San Jose?" joined by Latin stars Celia Cruz and Pete Escovedo, a funky take on "Reach Out for Me" with the Emotions and El DeBarge, and a South African twist on "Always Something There to Remind Me." "We're breathing a little fresh air into them, bringing them into the millennium with another tempo and treatment," she says.

In 2019, she released the R&B influenced *She's Back*, which included an updating of "Déjà vu," with rapper Krayzie Bone of Bone Thugs-n-Harmony, and a duet with Hawaii-based musician Fiji. A year earlier, she teamed with Fiji to record the Hawaiian Christmas favorite "Mele Kalikimaka."

While Warwick ranks among the biggest hitmakers of the entire rock era, it was only in 2021 that she was nominated for the Rock & Roll Hall of Fame. It's worth noting that in one year, she had more records in the Top Ten of the Hot 100 than inductees Ruth Brown and LaVern Baker had combined in their entire careers. She wasn't inducted.

Having earned so many hit records and won many awards over her long career, including a Grammy Lifetime Achievement Award, Warwick feels most proud of one particular honor - her old elementary school in New Jersey was renamed the Dionne Warwick Institute of Economics and Entrepreneurship in 1996.

"Aside from the birth of my two kids, that's the most incredible highlight of my life," she says. "It's such a monument. It's my grammar school which is even nicer because it's the beginning of my school career. It was quite an honor, one that my grandchildren will see and their grandchildren will see. It's quite something."

"SHINING STAR"

Earth, Wind & Fire

"Expanding awareness and uplifting spirits is so important."

"**P**eople come up and thank us for making the music, for having the fortitude of making the music," says Earth, Wind & Fire's founding bassist Verdine White. "We did a concert with Elton John, and Elton said, 'it's so good you guys are still here.' What we're keeping alive is good music."

With more than 90 million albums sold, Earth, Wind & Fire has enjoyed enormous success for five decades, forging a distinctive, infectious sound fusing R&B, jazz, funk, pop, gospel, and rock. Their many memorable chart-toppers include "Shining Star," "September," 'Let's Groove," "Boogie Wonderland," "Reasons," and "Sing a Song."

Miles Davis once described EW&F as his "all-time favorite band," while Alicia Keys proclaimed them as "the best band ever."

Formed in Chicago in 1969 by creative mastermind and spiritual visionary Maurice White, they evolved into one of the most musically accomplished, critically acclaimed, and commercially popular bands of the 1970s. With a name based on astrological elements in his birth chart (Sagittarius sun, Capricorn moon and ascendant, Venus & Jupiter in air signs), the band personified White's desire to mix a variety of musical styles into a unique sound disseminating positive lyrical themes of unity, empowerment, and universalism.

Channeling funk grooves blazed by James Brown, the progressive vision of Sly Stone, and the improvisatory spirit of jazz fusion bands like Weather Report, EW&F changed the face of popular music. "We just mixed a little of this and that appreciating all different forms of music," says Verdine White. "Our intention was just to make good music with good lyrics and be the best we could be."

White was initially captivated by the sound of an upright bass walking in on a high school orchestra class. "I walked into the room, and it just spoke to me," he recalls. "It said play me. You have a calling, and it has a calling." In time he would play with the Chicago Symphony Orchestra and later expand to playing jazz and helping form Earth, Wind & Fire. The transition from the classical world to the innovative fusion of EW&F "was like taking acid, like an out-of-body experience," he muses.

With their trademark horns, smooth, layered vocals, Philip Bailey's soaring falsetto, hook-laden melodies, and intricate arrangements, they became an unbeatable force. The band's imaginative brand of soul and funk first ignited the public in 1974, with the album *Open Our Eyes*, a gold-selling classic featuring gems like "Kalimba Song" and the superb "Devotion." But it was the brilliant *That's the Way of the World* that transformed them into multi-platinum superstars with funky hits like "Shining Star" and "Yearnin' Learnin,'" the gorgeous ballad "Reasons," and the powerful affirming title song.

With *That's the Way of the World,* they became the first Black group to simultaneously top the Billboard pop single and album charts. Then the brilliant live *Gratitude* catapulted the band into the stratosphere. It topped the Billboard pop album chart and earned them their first Grammy for the sensational live version of "Shining Star."

In his book *My Life with Earth, Wind & Fire*, Maurice White reported the band's songs expressed spiritual truths and transcendent spiritual wisdom with affirmations of positivity. Guided by White's metaphysical explorations, they referenced Kundalini energy on "Serpentine Fire," and sang about seeking spiritual solace on "Mighty Mighty." Walking in the light on "Spirit," they suggested a doorway to transcendence on "Getaway" and the importance of a higher path on "That's the Way of the World."

Ancient Egyptian imagery was often prominent on album covers, like the ankh eternal life symbol and the Eye of Horus symbol of protection on *Greatest Hits*. The Great Pyramid of Giza and the statue of Ramses the Great at Abu Simbel adorned the cover of *All 'n All*, while *I Am,* with a title referencing the divine Self, featured the mighty columns of Luxor's Karnak Temple.

Exploring the impact of ancient Egypt on the band, Trenton H. Bailey published a fascinating Ph.D. dissertation in 2017, on *Kemetic*

Consciousness: A study of ancient Egyptian themes in the lyrics and visual art of Earth, Wind & Fire, 1973-1983.

The release of 1983's *Powerlight* (with the chakra system on the cover) included a striking video for the single "Fall in Love with Me," which was rich in ancient Egyptian imagery. In a 1979 interview, Maurice White explained: "The group is very heavily into Egyptology. I truly feel that love is the better way, that when you can get inside and reacquaint yourself with yourself, you can make yourself a better life. Meditation is one way."

Visiting Egypt and the Pyramids with the band in 1979, he described it as a spiritual pilgrimage in *My Life with Earth, Wind & Fire*, and that he felt he was fulfilling his destiny. He told the *Chicago Tribune*, "I've always been interested in mysterious things. Stonehenge, the Mayans, the Incas, the Pyramids, and the Sphinx."

No other leading band explored such deep mysticism and focused on composing so many songs about uplifting humanity as Earth, Wind & Fire.

Besides creating memorable original material, they could take a Beatles' song like "Got to Get You Into My Life" and make it uniquely their own. They contributed this joyous cover to the *Sgt. Pepper's Lonely Hearts Club Band* film. "When I ran into George Harrison years later, he thought that was the best version he had ever heard," says Verdine White. "It was the biggest song in the movie. We had the only number one record out of the Bee Gees and Aerosmith and everybody." Paul McCartney also praised their version, calling it his favorite Beatles cover.

In concert, as captured on *Gratitude*, they were spectacular. Hiring magicians Doug Henning and David Copperfield to design their stage shows, they bedazzled audiences with band members levitating, disappearing, and emerging from Egyptian pyramids and spacecraft, while drum sets and synthesizer banks would flip upside down. "It was like Carnival, Mardi Gras, Broadway, Vegas, and Cirque du Soleil all at once," White remembers.

Not since Prince electrified Maui's A&B Amphitheater had the island experienced such an exuberantly energetic show as EW&F in 2007. With original members Verdine White, Philip Bailey, and Ralph Johnson fronting a superb 12-piece band, the funk collective delivered hit after hit repeatedly, drawing a near-capacity crowd to their feet in collective jubilation.

Known for his high energy on stage, White credits years of yoga practice and meditation with keeping him rejuvenated. "It's just something I like doing," he says. "I'm just one of the many who discovered it. There was a great section in *Vanity Fair* (magazine) about 20 yoga masters, and it just lets us know we are truly a one-world, multicultural society. I think Earth, Wind & Fire had a lot to do with that."

EW&F's more recent studio albums include the Grammy-nominated *Illumination,* which found them teaming with an ensemble of young, neo-soul stars like Raphael Saadiq, Black Eyed Peas' Will.i.am, and Brian McKnight. And *Now, Then & Forever,* evoked their brilliant sonic heyday - mightily jungle funking on "Dance Floor," cosmically tripping on "Splashes" (with a nod to Miles Davis), and heading Brazil way on "Belo Horizonte."

EW&F founder Maurice White died in 2016. In tribute, Lenny Kravitz posted: "King. Genius. Leader. Teacher. Producer. Arranger. Writer. Multi-instrumentalist. Motivator. Mystic. He is at the top of the list of all of the greatest masters."

"I'M EVERY WOMAN"

Chaka Khan

"Because of my skin color, I'm still trying to fight my way out of that box."

From her earliest days fronting Rufus, Chaka Khan became recognized as one of the greatest singers of our time. Over the course of a five-decade career, she has won 10 Grammy Awards, released more than 20 albums, and scored a bunch of timeless, number one songs.

Hailed as the "Queen of Funk," Chaka can effortlessly cross genres from R&B, pop, and rock to gospel, and country. This versatility is reflected in the range of leading musicians she has collaborated with, including Prince, Miles Davis (who once praised, "she sings like my horn"), Joni Mitchell, Stevie Wonder, George Benson, Eric Clapton, David Bowie, and B.B. King.

On her Grammy-winning *Funk This* album Chaka brilliantly re-imagined Prince's epic "Sign o' the Times." "Prince is a visionary, and those are some of my favorite lyrics," she explains. "It screamed about what's going on, and at the end, I did my own little adlib."

After first covering Prince's ballad "I Feel for You" in 1984 and turning it into a million-selling hit single, Prince contributed two songs, including "Sticky Wicked" with Miles Davis on trumpet to her *ck* album.

Signed to his NPG record label, they collaborated on *Come 2 My House* in 1998, with Prince co-writing and playing on most of the tracks. "We did the whole CD in two weeks," she recalls. "I'd write a poem and give it to him, and he'd come back the next night, and the music would be done, and I'd sing it. I would sing a song, and he'd say, 'we're done.' I said, are you sure? Are you kidding me? It was very fast."

Praising Chaka in a 1998 *Guitar World* interview, Prince reported: "One of the pleasures of my life is being able to work with some of my musical heroes." She later opened for his *Welcome 2 America* tour in 2011.

Chaka's *Funk This* album also included a cover of Jimi Hendrix's "Castles Made of Sand." "When I was a teenager, it was one of my favorite songs, the irony of it," she explains. "It really struck me, wow." She also covered a Joni Mitchell song.

A huge Mitchell fan, she once suggested the Canadian legend's album *Hejira* changed her life. It was Mitchell who suggested she record "Ladies Man." The two musicians had hung out after Mitchell was inducted into the Canadian Songwriters Hall of Fame, where Chaka performed with Herbie Hancock. "I was going to do 'Backstreet' or something like that, and she said, 'don't do that, it's depressing. Do something like 'Ladies Man.'"

The two musicians have shared a mutual admiration since working together on Mitchell's 1977 masterpiece *Don Juan's Reckless Daughter*. "She called me at like three in the morning to come to the studio to sing with her," Chaka recalls. "I was so excited. Finally, we got to sing together." At a tribute to celebrate Joni Mitchell's 75th birthday in 2018, Chaka sang a soaring version of "Help Me" and teamed with La Marisoul and Los Lobos for an epic Latin take on "Dreamland."

Whatever song she decides to cover, Chaka makes it her own. Take Fleetwood Mac's "Everywhere," included on the compilation *Epiphany: The Best of Chaka Khan*, which she transformed with a hint of reggae into a sensual soul classic. "There are some songs where I feel I wrote them," she explains. "'Everywhere' was one of those songs. I feel that way about almost every Joni song. I think songs are free agents. They don't belong to any one person. I just think they come from the heart or spirit of a person, but I don't think it makes them their song. They may get royalties and everything, but the song is not theirs."

Like Earth, Wind & Fire, she completely revamped a Beatles' song. With a grooving horn section backing, "We Can Work It Out" became a funky party that trumped the original.

While Chaka is known for classic funk hits, her musical tastes are far wider. At a Bonnaroo Music Festival, she teamed with the Tedeschi Trucks Band for a rocking take on Led Zeppelin's "What Is and What Should Never Be." "Besides jazz, rock 'n' roll and country are my first musics," she says. "I grew up on jazz, and when I first got with Rufus, we were doing rock 'n' roll and country, and then I walked into R&B. I love all music if it's good music."

Sometimes she feels people restrict her artistically by putting her in a box. "Because of my skin color," she says, "I'm still trying to fight my way out of that box."

Born and raised in Chicago, Yvette Marie Stevens (named after the Stan Getz song "Yvette") had a great-grandmother who was psychic and founded a spiritual church. Chaka reported at a *Variety* magazine Power of Women luncheon, that she predicted, "One day everybody's going to know your name."

One day at the Affro-Arts Theater, during a Yoruba ceremony, she was bestowed with the name Chaka, meaning "woman of fire." She was also given the other guiding spirit names Adunne ("loves to touch") Aduffe ("someone others love to touch") Yemoja ("mother of the waters") Hodarhi ("woman of nature"), and Karifi ("strength").

She began her singing career at eleven with the all-female group the Crystalettes, which later morphed into the Shades of Black. Youthful rebellion led her to become a brief member of the Black Panther Party. "I ran away from home at 16, and I was thinking how am I going to support myself," she recalls. "I had this voice; maybe I could join a band and make some money. I wanted to be an anthropologist, but I put that aside. I didn't know my main calling at the time."

At the age of 18, she became the lead singer for the Chicago-based Rufus. Stevie Wonder became such a fan he composed "Tell Me Something Good" for her. The single from the group's 1974 platinum-selling album *Rags to Rufus* earned Chaka her first Grammy. With Chaka as the group's dynamic center, Rufus dominated the airwaves and reviews began comparing her to Tina Turner and Aretha Franklin.

Before leaving Rufus, she released her debut solo album, the million-selling *Chaka*, featuring the enduring hit "I'm Every Woman" (with a young Whitney Houston on backing vocals). "That song and 'Ain't Nobody' are probably songs I'll be doing for the rest of my life," she notes.

As a solo artist paired with the late producer Arif Mardin, her catalog of hits grew with "Clouds," "Papillon," and "What Cha' Gonna

Do For Me?" It was during this period that Chaka began pursuing her love of jazz. With Mardin, she brilliantly re-worked the classic "Night in Tunisia," backed by Dizzy Gillespie on trumpet. She also recorded *Echoes of an Era,* an album of jazz standards with such jazz luminaries as Chick Corea, Stanley Clarke, and Lenny White, interpreting classics like Monk's "I Mean You" and Ellington's "Take the 'A' Train."

Then in 1982, she recorded her Grammy-winning "Be Bop Medley" on the album *Chaka Khan.* She calls it "my crowning achievement to date." The song prompted legendary jazz singer Betty Carter to proclaim Chaka the one female singer working outside jazz with legitimate improvising credentials.

Besides jazz icons like Dizzy Gillespie, she's also performed with Miles Davis, including joining him at the Montreux Jazz Festival. "After working with Miles, I was like, OK, I can go now," she says. "Arif Mardin was my producer in the '80s, and he was a great jazz aficionado like my dad was. I ended up working with a lot of the musicians that my father used to play with when I was a kid. That really moves me. My dad used to play a lot of horn players when I was growing up, and I fell in love with the sax and the trumpet."

Since her earliest days, many musicians have featured her vocal magic on their albums. Her voice electrified Steve Winwood's "Higher Love," and Quincy Jones teamed her with Ray Charles on his hit album *Back on the Block.* Herbie Hancock teamed her with Ravi Shankar's daughter, Anoushka Shankar, and saxophonist Wayne Shorter for an Indo-jazz fusion track on his *The Imagine Project,* and she was a guest vocalist on Eric Clapton's album *Old Sock.*

Chaka's most recent album, *Hello Happiness,* was lauded by the U.K.'s *The Observer* as "a vital calling card to remind everyone to come hear this unearthly voice, still sizzling with spice."

Besides performing a few times on Maui, Chaka has a strong connection to Hawai'i. "My sister was born and raised there," she says. "She's on the Big Island with my stepmother."

Having been honored with many awards over the years, she feels especially proud to have a street named after her in her hometown. "Chicago is my home where I was born and raised. It's a great place to be from, and it's also a pretty racist city. For a black person to have a street named after her is a big thing there. It's right on the same street I went to high school. So that was really cool. It was very meaningful for me. It was one of the times when I felt like I had accomplished something."

"PAPA WAS A ROLLIN' STONE"

The Temptations

"Sly and the Family Stone were our inspiration to getting into psychedelic soul."

One of the greatest soul/funk songs of all time, the Temptations' "Papa Was a Rollin' Stone" almost never happened. Certain it would flop, the musicians resisted their producer's attempts to get them to record it. Fortunately, he prevailed, and as a featured single on their album *All Directions*, the brilliantly arranged epic rocketed to number one on the charts and earned the Temptations a couple of Grammy Awards.

"At the beginning, we almost didn't record it," reveals Otis Williams, the last surviving original Temptation. "We were tired of singing psychedelic soul. We wanted to go back to ballads, the 'My Girls' and the 'Since I Lost My Baby's.' Our fans would ask, 'when are you going to go back to sing those ballads?' We had a strong debate about it, but (producer) Norman Whitfield was set on recording 'Papa Was a Rollin' Stone,' and we ended up recording it."

The last number one scored by the band, it's acclaimed as a masterpiece. "I would consider it one of the greats because Norman and (co-composer) Barrett Strong did a hell of a job on the production," Williams continues. "It's one of those songs I never get tired of hearing. *Rolling Stone* magazine listed the 500 Greatest Songs of All Time and we had three, 'Papa Was a Rollin' Stone,' 'Ball of Confusion,' and 'Just My Imagination.'"

The most commercially successful and critically acclaimed male vocal group of the 1960s and early '70s, the Temptations began their musical life in Detroit, an essential component of the original Motown "Hitsville" machine, invented by Berry Gordy.

"We had heard of Berry making a name writing songs for Jackie Wilson and then Smokey and the Miracles," Williams recalls. "As fate

301

would have it, he gave me his card at a record hop. I called him after a few weeks, and we auditioned, and he signed us up. In the early days before all the hits, Motown was a fun place to be. We would stay even when it closed up at 6 o'clock, and empty the trash and sweep the floors, whatever was needed for the next day. It was our Camelot."

The Smokey Robinson-produced "The Way You Do the Things You Do" gave the band their first chart hit. An avalanche followed, from "My Girl," "Since I Lost My Baby," and "Get Ready" to "Ain't Too Proud to Beg," and "Beauty Is Only Skin Deep."

The classic lineup was Melvin Franklin, Paul Williams, Eddie Kendricks, David Ruffin, and Otis Williams. Aside from their magnificent singing, the Temps became known for smooth stepping and flawless presentations.

In 1966, Norman Whitfield became the Temptations' primary producer, steering them towards a more harder-edged and brass-heavy soul sound, along with socially and politically charged lyrics that reflected the changing times and the influence of an explosive rising star from the West Coast, Sly Stone.

"Sly and the Family Stone were our inspiration to getting into psychedelic soul," Williams explains. "When I heard 'Dance to the Music,' it was such a departure from the sound that was happening at that time. I asked Norman if he had heard Sly, and he hadn't. I said they were doing something fresh and different, and maybe we should try that. Thus was the emergence of 'Cloud Nine.'"

It was the dawn of psychedelic soul at Motown, with the funky centerpiece of the group's landmark *Cloud Nine* album becoming a Top 10 hit. Referencing getting high as a way to escape inner-city woes, it won Motown its first Grammy for Best R&B Vocal Group Performance in 1969. The revolutionary album's highlights included the nine-minute warning to wayward city kids, "Runaway Child, Running Wild," with all five Temps sharing lead vocals backed by the incomparable Funk Brothers.

"My thing was to try and revolutionize the sound," Norman Whitfield explained in the liner notes to the Temptations' *Anthology*. "The vocal movement was accelerated, and the production heightened: swirls of electronic effects, lots of Latin percussion and congas, wah-wah guitars, echoes, sound effects, voices used like instruments, scatting." *Puzzle People* followed with such socially conscious anthems as "Slave" about prison injustice, the James Brown influenced protest song "Message From a Black Man," and the caution about conspicuous consumption on "Don't Let The Joneses Get You Down." The band's foray into psychedelic soul territory continued with epic songs like "Psychedelic Shack," the dreamy "Take a Stroll Thru Your Mind's" paean to getting high, and the magnificent "Papa Was a Rollin' Stone."

The Temptations originally recorded the political anthem "War" on their *Psychedelic Shack* album. But as Motown was reluctant to release it as single, fearing it might alienate more conservative fans, it was adopted by Edwin Starr. His version of the anti-war song soared to number one, remained at the top for three weeks, and sold more than three million copies.

Motown's head often shied from releasing songs he deemed too controversial. Gordy had assumed "Cloud Nine" was about drugs and tried to get the lyrics changed. Marvin Gaye's epic "What's Goin' On" was decried by Gordy, who thought it was career suicide and initially refused to release it. Gordy had only released the soul classic "I Heard It Through the Grapevine" as a single after radio stations began playing it.

Inspired by the Detroit riots, the Temps brilliant protest song "Ball of Confusion," with its potent, rapid-fire lyrics, sounds as relevant today as when it was first released in 1970. It condemned the Vietnam War, racism, white flight, drug abuse, air pollution, and high unemployment. "Every word on there was telling the truth about what was happening then," says Williams. "Thirty years later, that song is so apropos with what's happening in the world."

The group's glorious experimental period was captured on the double-disc *Psychedelic Soul.* Unbridled by time constraints, it included such gems as a 12-minute "Smiling Faces Sometimes," 13 minutes of "Masterpiece," about the trials of ghetto life, and an extended, 12-minute "Papa Was a Rollin' Stone."

After a long fallow period in the late 1990s, the Temptations scored a hit again with "Stay" on *Phoenix Rising*, their first million-selling album in more than 20 years. In later years they released the critically acclaimed album *Reflections,* which paid homage to Motown with covers of songs like Marvin Gaye and Tammi Terrell's "Ain't Nothing Like the Real Thing" and The Jackson 5's "I'll Be There."

Then on *Back To Front,* they paid tribute to classic soul with new recordings of Sam and Dave's "Hold On, I'm Comin'" and the Staple Singers' "Respect Yourself."

Their impressive collection of new material, *Still Here* in 2010, ran the gamut from sensuous ballads to social commentary, with one song, the inspirational "Change Has Come," honoring President Obama. Capturing their classic sound with a contemporary sheen, the track "Soul Music" paid tribute to the glory days of Motown. "We wanted to harken back to the way music used to be back then because when I listen to the radio and what's happening today, I'm not impressed," Williams explains. "The main focus has always been to come up with great music. Great music has stood the test of time, so we've always tried to have great songs."

And "Listen Up" echoed the activist lyrics of "Ball of Confusion." "One of our strong suits is being able to sing about what we are going through as a nation," he continues. "We just wanted the world to know this is what's happening today. We made 'Listen Up' for awareness sake."

In 2017, *Billboard* named the Temptations the most successful R&B act of all time, topping fellow legends like Aretha Franklin, Stevie Wonder, James Brown, and Michael Jackson.

Looking back over decades of performing with the legendary band, Williams concludes: "I had no idea that when we started out in 1960, I would be doing this for 50 years. I love what I do, and there are not too many people on this earth who can say that. I'm very blessed and thank God every day because this brings joy and happiness to a lot of people. Music is such a powerful force and a powerful influence, and it's great to be part of something that leaves positive feelings."

"THAT'S THE WAY GOD PLANNED IT"

Billy Preston

"Everything that's happened to me has been the way God planned it. Everything has been a blessing."

"I was treated as a Beatle, and it was wonderful," recalled Billy Preston in a 1990 interview on Maui. "I stayed with George (Harrison), and they were very nice to me. They said, 'just play whatever you feel.' It was great to watch them work in the studio. They were so creative."

Few musicians can claim to have played with so many superstars and to have inspired so many audiences as Billy Preston. Along with backing both the Beatles and the Rolling Stones, he was associated with Ray Charles, Aretha Franklin, Quincy Jones, Sly Stone, and Eric Clapton.

The composer of jubilant hits like "That's The Way God Planned It," "Nothing From Nothing," and "Will it Go Round in Circles" (and co-writer of Joe Cocker's biggest hit, "You Are So Beautiful"), Preston first met the Beatles when they opened for Little Richard at Hamburg's Star-Club.

Singing with his church choir, he had appeared locally playing organ with Mahalia Jackson when he was ten, and by 16, he was invited to play with Little Richard on a 1962 tour of Europe. In Britain, the Beatles opened one of the shows.

Little Richard had planned to play gospel on the tour, but the kids wanted to rock. "It was quite an experience," he remembered. "It was the first time I had ever played rock 'n' roll. In England, the kids were wild. They would have to call the guards."

He was initially unsure about playing the "devil's music." "It kind of worried me at first. But then I felt God was not narrow-minded, and he'd given me the talent, and I should use it as long as I put him first."

Playing with the house band on the TV music show *Shindig!*, in the mid-'60s, Preston's impressive imitation of Ray Charles caught the attention of the legend, and Charles hired him. "He's been my idol ever since I can remember," Preston said. "He's such a perfectionist, and he has a keen ear, and his vocals are just really touching. He was very kind to me and told me that I was the young man that he would like to carry on the work that he started."

After a London concert touring Europe with Charles, George Harrison invited Preston to attend a Beatles' recording session. "George came to the concert and he sent a note back for me to give him a call," he said. At the Abbey Road Studios, "they were working on *Let it Be*."

In the midst of recording "Get Back," the 22-year-old Preston was invited to join in on Fender Rhodes. His playing was so well received the Beatles credited his contribution – The Beatles with Billy Preston - the only time they allowed a co-billing with another musician, and thus began a fruitful collaboration.

"He got on the electric piano, and straight away there was 100 percent improvement in the vibe in the room," Harrison recalled in *The Beatles Anthology*. "Everybody was happier to have somebody else playing." Paul McCartney concurred in *Anthology*: "Billy was brilliant. We all said let's have him play on a few things."

Prominently featured in Peter Jackson's epic three-part documentary *The Beatles: Get Back*, all four Beatles lit up when Preston first begins playing keyboards on "I've Got a Feeling." At the end of the take, John Lennon announced, "you're in the group."

Buying up his old contract, the Beatles signed Preston to their Apple label. As the "fifth Beatle," he played on *Abbey Road* and *Let it Be* and performed with the group on their last live gig atop the roof of the Apple offices. John Lennon wanted him to join the Beatles, but Paul McCartney disagreed as the group was fracturing.

Harrison later produced the joyful, gospel-flavored "That's The Way God Planned It," bringing in friends like Eric Clapton, Keith Richards, and Cream's Ginger Baker to help out. The exuberant song, which became the highlight of the *Concert for Bangladesh*, was inspired during a Beatles' session. "It was inspired by 'Let it Be,'" he recalled. "One day, I was in the studio playing 'Let it Be,' and it kind of went right into 'That's The Way God Planned It.' It's a testimonial song for me because everything that's happened to me has been the way God planned it. I never expected to do the things I've done or had to be pushy. Everything has been a blessing."

Before releasing his own version of "My Sweet Lord" with Preston on piano, Harrison gave him permission to record his own rousing gospel version with the Edwin Hawkins Singers backing him.

The blessings continued following the breakup of the Beatles. Preston was asked to work on a number of solo Beatle projects, including John Lennon's *Plastic Ono Band* and *Some Time in New York City*, Harrison's *All Things Must Pass* and *Gone Troppo*, and Ringo Starr's *Ringo* and *Good Night Vienna*, as well as touring as a member of his All-Starr Band.

Traveling with Harrison on his 1974 *Dark Horse* tour, Preston often stole the show with his high-energy performances. "It was Billy who got the audience up on its feet," noted a *Rolling Stone* review. In the book *While My Guitar Gently Weeps: The Music of George Harrison*, drummer Andy Newmark recalls: "He could light the fuckin' place up, and get 20,000 people on their feet." Presenting concerts mixing rock, soul, jazz, and Indian music, Harrison closed each show with Preston's jubilant arrangement of "My Sweet Lord."

That same year Miles Davis paid tribute to him with the funky track "Billy Preston" on his worldbeat fusion album *Get Up with It*.

As a frequent player with the Rolling Stones, he helped ignite the Stones' massive 1975 tour of the Americas, rousing crowds with his joyful music. Reviewing the Stones' DVD *"From the Vault-L.A. Forum 1975, American Songwriter* praised Preston, "whose 10-minute mini-set is better, tighter and more exciting than much of the rest of the show."

With the Stones, he injected some authentic soul to *Sticky Fingers*, *Exile on Main Street* (especially the gospel-infused rocker "Shine a Light"), *Goats Head Soup*, and *Black and Blue*. His contribution to "Melody," playing keyboards and singing with Jagger, was a highlight of *Black and Blue*, though they neglected to give him co-composing credit.

In his book *Life*, Keith Richards commented: "Billy produced a different sound for us. If you listen to records like 'Melody,' he fit perfectly. He had all the talent in the world."

Preston's credits also included playing on Aretha Franklin's *Young, Gifted and Black*, Bob Dylan's *Blood on the Tracks*, Sly and the Family Stone's *There's a Riot Goin' On,* and Elton John's *Duets.*

Gospel was Preston's initial inspiration, and it imbued his playing with a spiritual root that kept his music vital. "There was always gospel music around, and it's been my foundation," he said. "Before I go on, I usually have a few seconds of prayer and meditation to put myself in the right spirit. I love to play, and when you see people enjoying themselves, it gives you inspiration, and I just lose it and go crazy. Even though we do the same songs each time, there's always something different. I like to work on inspiration and do what the spirit tells me to do."

Preston died in 2006 at the age of 59. Posthumously bestowed with a Musical Excellence Award at the 2021 Rock & Roll Hall of Hame induction ceremony, Ringo Starr, in a pre-recorded message, praised: "He was a Beatle and a Rolling Stone. He went on to play with me, George, and John on our solo records. He was an amazing singer, songwriter, and human being."

WHY I SING THE BLUES

"THE THRILL IS GONE"

B.B. King

*"The honor people give me, it feels so good
that sometimes I could cry."*

"I ain't sold my soul to the devil," B.B. King emphasized about his success. "I think I got lucky. This old myth of Robert Johnson selling his soul to the devil, if you believe that I've got a Brooklyn bridge, I can sell you."

A superb vocalist, powerful performer, and one of the most influential guitarists of his time, despite advancing age, King maintained his regal mantle as a prolific recording artist and vital entertainer.

Having accomplished so much during his rich life, this humble musician responded with a surprising answer when asked what he felt most proud about achieving. "I don't think I've ever made a perfect record," he reported, "but I think there's some good work in all of them. I always hear something like, why did you do that? What was that for? A lot of times, people praise me, and I thank them, but I don't always feel I deserve some of the things they praise me for. I started recording in 1949, but I don't think I've ever made a perfect record, and I don't believe I ever will. But each time I make a record, I do the best I can. One thing it does is make you try to do better even today."

The great-grandson of former slaves, Riley B. King, was born in 1925 to a farm-working family in the heart of the Mississippi Delta. As a child, he picked cotton and grew up through the Depression in a backbreaking regime of work from pre-dawn to long after sunset.

Buying his first guitar for $8, he would sneak out to the local town park to play for change as his aunt frowned on him singing the "devil's music."

At an early age, King discovered playing the blues proved far more lucrative than picking cotton. "I left the cotton fields thinking I wanted things to be better and make money and help my family and friends," he remembered. "I knew I had to be pretty good to make money, and the only thing I could do is try to wrap on Lucille and really work at it to make people like it."

Moving to Memphis, Tennessee, King worked part-time as a disc jockey for a local radio station, where he acquired the tag "The Beale Street Blues Boy," which was shortened to "Blues Boy King," and then the abbreviated form.

One of the keys to King's success lay in the wide range of ideas incorporated in his music. Raised on gospel, he cited his earliest influences as jazz guitarists Charlie Christian and Django Reinhardt, and he emulated the phrasing of blues guitarists like T-Bone Walker. But his distinctive, trilling guitar style came from a surprising source - Hawaiian steel guitar. Hearing that sweet island sound spurred him to practice. "It just sounds mellow," he emphasized. "I've never been a romantic guy, but I can enjoy having my girl on my arm when I hear those guys play. The Hawaiians playing with the slide and country players with the electric steel, oh man, that just goes through me. All these years, I've loved them."

During the 1950s, King established himself as a formidable hit-making force in the R&B field. Then the guitarist cut his seminal *Live at the Regal* album in 1964, and the same year he scored a hit with "Rock Me Baby." By the late '60s, King began playing huge rock festivals alongside the top acts of the day and finally achieved stardom in 1969, when the stately, violin-drenched "The Thrill Is Gone" became his biggest hit.

"It's been the stamp of approval of the people for B.B. King," he enthused. "I guess I play it nearly every night. I have to play it if I don't want tomatoes thrown at me, but I don't ever try to play it like I recorded it. Each night I play as if it it's the first night. I play it the best that I can, so I'm not trying to remember what I did 40 years ago.

That's what keeps it fresh and keeps me fresh because I'm not trying to repeat nothing. Each night it's like getting in your car and going for a drive in the air."

Showered with appreciation wherever he played, B.B. felt fueled by the genuine love of his audiences. "I feel so good people spoil me," he continued. "I can go on stage, and people will stand before I even sit down to play. The honor they give me, it feels so good that sometimes I could cry. That's the joy I get out of it, and it seems like these 50 some years of trying to play haven't been for nothing."

So did he have any thought to retiring and maybe relaxing by his Las Vegas pool? "Well, for one thing, I don't have a pool," he responded with a laugh, "and second, I'd get tired of going fishing every day. My fun when I'm home is getting in my El Camino and going up in the mountains, and I love to look at the wildlife. That's part of my fun, and I'm a TV freak, so those two things are my big enjoyments."

Teaming with Eric Clapton, King won a Grammy for Best Traditional Blues Album for *Riding with the King* in 2000. "We have a certain chemistry with each other where we connect when we're playing," said King, who first met Clapton in 1967 at a jam session that included Jimi Hendrix. "He's one of the nicest men I've ever met and one of the greatest musicians. In fact, in my book, he's number one. A few years ago, he worked on my CD *Deuces Wild*, and we hit it real good. He's been such a good friend that usually you don't want to impose on your friends. But one night, I heard him being interviewed by Larry King on *CNN*. Larry asked him a question about recording, and he said he'd like to do one with me. When he said that, I almost fell out of the chair."

Once their schedules were coordinated, King let Clapton arrange details. "My thing was, Eric, you pick the songs, you pick the musicians, you pick the studio, and if you get something I don't like, we'll talk about it," King continued. "He had two things I wasn't crazy about, doing a song 'Come Rain or Come Shine' and playing acoustic guitar."

Only once before in his long career had he unplugged, on the 1971 album *In London*, on a tune with British blues musician Alexis Korner. On *Riding with the King*, Clapton and King spun their acoustic

311

alchemy on two tracks. "I didn't want to do it," King said. "We talked about it, and Eric is more persuasive than my old lady. He can get me to do things without really asking me in a begging way the way my old lady does. He said, 'B, I know you don't like it, but do it for me.' I tried it, and it didn't sound so bad."

King also felt uncomfortable tackling the ballad "Come Rain or Come Shine," popularized by Ray Charles in the late 1950s. Complete with strings, soulful guitars, and muted horns, this sultry classic provided a fitting finale for the album. "I thought when Ray got through with it, there was nothing else I could do," King explained. "But we didn't try to do it like Ray did, we did it like Eric Clapton and B. B. King, and it came off all right."

Attracting many leading artists to record with him, he teamed with U2 on "When Love Comes To Town" in 1989, one of the highlights of the Irish band's *Rattle and Hum* album. "I wanted to record with them," he explained. "I was playing in Dublin, and U2 came out to see me. I knew about them because of the *Joshua Tree* album, and I liked some of the songs. That night I asked Bono, will you write a song for me? He smiled and said, 'yes.' I thought, oh yeah, same old thing again. But about a year later, he called and said he'd written a song and wanted to know if I'd open their show in Fort Worth, Texas. You're kidding, of course I would. I couldn't believe a guy his age could write such heavy words with such meaningful things. And they had me in the movie. They really did something for me. I'll never forget them. They're fantastic people."

Teaming with country legend Willie Nelson on the classics "The Thrill is Gone" and "Nightlife" on Willie's album *Milk Cow Blues*, King extolled Willie's guitar talent. "Everybody hear him singing and love that, but the man can play."

And he was grateful to the British rock legends who sang his praises early on. "Eric Clapton and a lot of the groups from the U.K. like the Rolling Stones all helped it (blues) be more popular than it would have been had they not played it," he noted. "The first time I heard someone talking about me was John Lennon. He was being interviewed, and he was asked, 'what would he like to do?' He said, 'play guitar like

B.B. King.' I couldn't believe it. No group has been like the Beatles. I was dumbfounded. It was one of the greatest (compliments) I've had."

As one of the last of the great living blues legends, one wonders how he felt? "It's scary," he revealed. "I lost my old friend John Lee Hooker not too long ago. I believe that I was left here for a reason, and after losing so many of the guys, I wonder when my day is coming. I hope I'm here for a while because I like looking at these pretty girls," he laughed. "I have three reasons for wanting to live as long as possible. It used to be ladies, ladies, and ladies. I changed a bit. Now it's ladies, friends, and music in that order. Without either one, I'd be very sad. I'm just glad to be alive."

B.B. King left us in 2015 in Las Vegas at the age of 89. His Grammy-winning final album, *One Kind Favor*, was released in 2008. "B.B. King was the greatest guy I ever met," posted Buddy Guy. "He could play so smooth, he didn't have to put on a show. The way B.B. did it is the way we all do it now." And President Barack Obama issued a statement, saying, "The blues has lost its king, and America has lost a legend. B.B. may be gone, but that thrill will be us forever."

"DAMN RIGHT I'VE GOT THE BLUES"

Buddy Guy

"If you're just playing for the dollar, it's not coming from your soul and body."

Only a handful of guitarists on the planet command as much respect as blues legend Buddy Guy. One of the greatest blues guitarists to emerge from post-war Chicago, Guy and his distinctive, searing sound influenced a legion of guitar stars ranging from Eric Clapton and Jimi Hendrix to Stevie Ray Vaughan and Gary Clark Jr.

Clapton hailed Guy as "the best guitar player alive," in a 1985 *Musician* magazine article, adding, "he really changed the course of rock and roll blues." Vaughan reported: "Without Buddy Guy, there would be no Stevie Ray Vaughan."

While many guitar greats sung his praises, Guy felt he still had to prove himself. "I appreciate it, but regardless of what they say, if you've never seen me play, you're going to come and say, well, if they said he was good, now let me see," Guy suggests. "Now I've got to see if I'm good enough to make them stay and listen. I can't live on what they've said. I've got to do what I've got to do."

Known for his boundless on-stage energy and blazing guitar style, this multi-Grammy-winning artist first stunned audiences in Chicago in the early 1960s, where he would play running up and down a bar countertop and lying flat on his back. "I saw the late Guitar Slim do that," he acknowledges. "I thought if I ever learn to play guitar, I want to play it excited. You have to entertain people. I'm not as fast as I was, but I'm still trying."

Raised in rural Louisiana by sharecropping parents, Guy made his first guitar out of a paint can, a stick, and "strings" from mosquito netting. Picking cotton on the weekends, he would earn enough money to buy one old 78 rpm record a week. "Nobody's ever sat down and showed me nothing on guitar," he emphasizes. "I didn't know what a guitar was, and my parents were sharecroppers. There was no way they could think about buying me a guitar at an early age. We didn't even have electric lights, so there were no fans. My mother would sleep with the window open at night, but she had to put up a piece of screen to keep the mosquitoes out. I would strip all that to make guitar strings."

Miraculous pivotal events seem to routinely crop up in his life. One involved blues icon Muddy Waters, who took Guy under his wing. Down on his luck having moved to Chicago and not having eaten in three days, Guy was strolling the streets with his guitar when a large man approached inquiring whether he could play the blues. Gaining an affirmative answer, Waters invited the starving 21-year-old to his home and later proudly introduced him at the famous 708 Club where Otis Rush was on stage. "I've got a black son of a bitch here that'll run you off stage," Waters announced.

Guy strapped on his guitar and was immediately hired. His prowess attracted the attention of the legendary Chess brothers who hired the guitarist to back some of the top names in blues, including Waters, Howlin' Wolf, Little Walter, Willie Dixon, and Junior Wells on recording sessions in the 1960s. "I was asked to play behind him in sessions," says Guy about working with Waters. "I just concentrated on what made him sound better. I was always a student like that. I would never go and try and blow someone like Muddy Waters off stage. I just concentrated on what they wanted. B.B. King called me up to play with him, and I said no, when you play, I'm supposed to listen."

Amazed that he was surrounded by such great players in Chicago, Guy says, "that's what I miss the most. I had seen B.B. King and T-Bone Walker, but I had never seen the giants like Muddy Waters and Howlin' Wolf. They never came through where I was brought up in Louisiana. When I arrived in Chicago, some of those guys were still living, and I just didn't even go to sleep because I thought I was going to miss something. Every night you would learn something."

In the early 1960s, when he wanted to blaze, Guy was advised to tone down as no one wanted to hear the "noise" he played. Chess Records wanted traditional blues. "They had the best blues people in the world, Howlin' Wolf, Muddy Waters, Sonny Boy Williamson, and they were successful with it. All these great guitar players in Chicago were sitting in chairs and standing still. I said I can't play that well, so I've got to do a flip or something for people to pay attention to me. I was trying to get Buddy Guy across to them, and they didn't understand that until the British kids brought it back. They thought I was too wild until all the wild rock guys like Jimi Hendrix came along."

The head of Chess realized his error at a meeting with Guy in 1967. Cream and Jimi Hendrix were enthralling millions at that time utilizing feedback and sustained techniques that Guy had pioneered years earlier. "He said, 'you've been trying to give me this all the time, and I was too dumb to accept it.'"

To his great surprise, Guy discovered the rising stars of British rock were paying careful attention to him. On his first tour of England in 1965, during which he shared a bill with The Yardbirds and Rod Stewart, guitarists like Eric Clapton and Jeff Beck sought him out backstage. "He gave us something to strive for," Clapton reported in the book *Damn Right I've Got The Blues*. "He really changed the course of rock and roll and blues."

And then, a couple of years later, a young Jimi Hendrix showed up one night to watch him in New York. Hendrix used to bring a tape recorder to Guy's club gigs and was inspired by Guy's explosive live performance. "I got some film that someone mailed to me, and I was surprised because he (Hendrix) was there on his knees at a club called Generation in New York. I didn't know who he was. I had the guitar behind my head, and he came up and asked if he could tape my show."

It is well-documented that Hendrix's favorite and most-listened-to records in the company of others included Guy's *Stone Crazy, First Time I Met The Blues*, and the 1963 *Folk Festival Of The Blues* album.

Just as Hendrix found approval in England before returning in triumph to America, the blues had to be recycled back home for popular digestion by British R&B rockers like the Stones, Animals, and Yardbirds. "Our music wasn't accepted at home until someone else brought it back, such as the Rolling Stones, Cream, and so on," he says. "White America was asking who was Muddy Waters? I'll never forget that. The Rolling Stones said, 'you mean you don't know who Muddy Waters is? We're named after one of his famous records.'"

And there was the time Eric Clapton acknowledged Guy's influence on the Cream hit "Strange Brew." "I was telling him how crazy I was about a line he was playing in that song, and he said, 'well you should be because it's yours.' We're the best of friends. Eric is responsible for me having the recording contract I've got now. He asked me to play at the Albert Hall.

"I got to the point that maybe I didn't have it, but it didn't make me stop playing the blues," he says about his previous lack of success. "When I learned how to play guitar, there was no Eric Clapton or the Beatles and all that, so I didn't look for a future in the guitar, and I didn't think about relaxing one day in a nice home with a nice car. I just wanted to be good at the thing because I love it for the love of music, not the love of money. If you're just playing for the dollar, it's not coming from your soul and body."

The revitalization of Guy's career was sparked by Clapton's request that Guy join an all-star lineup at London's Royal Albert Hall, captured on *24 Nights*. Guy's animated performance led to a recording contract and his Grammy-winning album *Damn Right I Got The Blues*. Propelled by a guest list that included Clapton, Jeff Beck, and Mark Knopfler, this scorching blues collection introduced his music to a new generation and cemented his reputation as a blues guitar giant. Up until then, he had never felt completely satisfied with his records because they rarely reflected his power. "I was never given a chance to record right, and I finally got that chance," he says.

Accepting a Grammy for his best blues album, Guy made sure America knew about Muddy Waters. "When I received it that night, I accepted it in honor of the great people who deserve it - Muddy Waters, Howlin' Wolf, Sonny Boy Williamson, Little Walter, names that were never mentioned on the Grammys during the height of their careers. I accepted in the name of the great people who were my teachers."

Barely slowing down, he loves to awe his audiences. "If it's raining, or it's hot, or there's snow, whatever the conditions if someone thinks enough of to come and see you, I think you should give 110 percent of everything you've got," he enthuses. "I want people to say, I can tell he was giving everything he had. If you're angry about something, I intend to make you forget about that for a while. And I'd love to get you tapping your feet with a smile on your face."

Famous friends who recently paid homage to him include Keith Richards and Jeff Beck on the track "Cognac" and Mick Jagger playing harmonica on "You Did the Crime," featured on Guy's Grammy-winning *The Blues Is Alive and Well*.

"It seems that everything I've gotten came to me in a spiritual way," he concludes. "That's what I call being blessed. That's why I'm not going to let nothing get in my way like what I have missed. If I went to the top in the '60s, who knows where I'd be now with the fast life and getting into drugs to keep up with the rest of them. I lived through that, and I'm still having joy today."

"ROCK AND ROLL, HOOCHIE KOO"

Johnny & Edgar Winter

"We used to sneak into tent revivals. We were the only white kids among black people there. It was amazing."

There's a legendary story about a time in 1962 when Johnny Winter and his younger brother Edgar talked their way into seeing B.B. King at a Black club in Beaumont, Texas. The 17-year-old was determined to play with the blues legend, and he didn't stop begging King to borrow his guitar and step on stage.

"I irritated the hell out of him," Johnny Winter recalled, laughing. "We were the only whites in an all-black club, and he thought we were from the I.R.S. He'd been having tax problems. He was so glad we weren't, so he decided to let me play. He didn't know if I could play or not. I got a standing ovation."

Growing up in Texas, Johnny felt inspired to play blues from a young age. "I was about twelve when I first heard blues. Before that, I'd just heard rock 'n' roll. As soon as I heard it, I thought this is great music; I've got to learn how to play this stuff. It was the sound, the guitar riffs of Muddy (Waters) and Robert Johnson. The list goes on and on. I loved it all."

The Winter brothers first formed an Everly Brothers style act playing 'ukuleles. "We were playing 'ukuleles when I was four," Edgar Winter recalls. "My dad played guitar and banjo and alto sax in a swing band, and my mother played beautiful classical piano. Johnny graduated to guitar, and it became apparent that he was going to be the guitar player. So I said I'll just play everything else."

The brothers' hometown had seen one of the worst race riots in Texas history. Months before Johnny's birth in 1943, mobs wandered the streets ransacking black homes and burning businesses. Martial law was declared, and the Texas State Guard and Texas Rangers sealed off access to the outside. In their segregated town, they would buy "race records" (music marketed to Black Americans) at a store that catered to all races.

"We used to sneak into tent revivals," Edgar recalls. "If you think rock and roll has energy, it pales in comparison to Pentecostal tent revivals. We were the only white kids among Black people there. It was amazing."

As teenagers, the brothers formed Johnny and the Jammers with Edgar on piano. "When I started playing jazz, it was like a parting of the ways for a while," Edgar explains. "I wanted to play sax and Johnny's, 'I don't want no sax in the band.' Ok, I'll get my own band. When horns got popular, all the R&B stuff like Otis Redding and Wilson Pickett, then we played together in some big horn bands. I loved jazz. I wasn't that interested in pop music or rock for a while.

"Johnny was the guy with the ambition. He was more extroverted, and I was more introverted. I was the weird kid who played all the instruments. Every time I walk on stage, I think of Johnny because we learned how to play together. There was almost a telepathic communication as brothers playing together. "

Johnny moved to Chicago in 1963 to check out the blues scene but wound up playing in twist music clubs. Returning to Beaumont, he began opening for major acts like Jerry Lee Lewis and the Everly Brothers. National acclaim arrived when a 1968 *Rolling Stone* magazine article described him as a "cross-eyed albino with long fleecy hair, playing some of the gutsiest fluid blues guitar you've ever heard."

He was soon signed to an unheard, at the time, $600,000 contract with Columbia Records. "It didn't feel so good," he reported. "I didn't like the pressure of it. I hated hearing about it."

Johnny's self-titled debut album was universally praised, and the follow-up, *Second Winter*, was met with equal acclaim in 1969. That summer, Johnny and Edgar performed at the Woodstock Music Festival.

"Woodstock really changed my life," Edgar explains. "When we played Woodstock, it was a transcendent moment. Looking out over this endless sea of humanity and seeing them united in a unique way, I realized music is a positive energy that can bring people together and transcend boundaries. Woodstock was like a spiritual awakening." (Unfortunately, the Winter brothers' performance was omitted from both the movie and the original live album, as their manager thought it wasn't going to help their careers)

When Johnny was looking for a band to back him, he hired The McCoys and launched *Johnny Winter And* in 1970. "We were so into blues and soul, and that's what Johnny Winter saw in our band," Rick Derringer explains. "At that time, people were starting to characterize the music we did as poppy bubblegum, so the record company was reticent to call it Johnny Winter and The McCoys. They said, 'we'll drop the McCoys and call it Johnny Winter And.' We were cheated out of our glory in some ways." The album featured the first recording of Derringer's signature song, the pile-driving "Rock and Roll, Hoochie Koo."

Johnny Winter blew away audiences with his incendiary take on classic blues, impressing the Rolling Stones and John Lennon. The Stones performed his song "I'm Yours and I'm Hers" at the free memorial concert for Brian Jones in London, and Winter recorded Lennon's unreleased song "Rock and Roll People" on his album *John Dawson Winter III.*

But personal demons sidelined the guitarist. Rumors of his heavy drug use were so widespread that Winter titled his 1973 album, *Still Alive and Well.* During this period, he was performing high energy rock shows in front of thousands with bandmate Rick Derringer, enthralling all with scorching versions of "Highway 61 Revisited," "Roll Over Beethoven," "Jumping Jack Flash," and the famous boogie number, "Rock And Roll, Hoochie Koo."

Johnny's true love, though, remained the blues, and the guitar virtuoso ended up putting his own career on hold to help out Muddy Waters. He produced and played on four Waters' albums, starting with *Hard Again* in 1977. Three of them won Grammy Awards. Waters affectionately called him "his adopted son." "My time with Muddy was the highlight of my career," Johnny said. "He was a good friend and a real classy guy. I received three Grammys for producing him, and I'm very proud of that."

After Waters died in 1983, Johnny began recording a series of more blues-oriented albums. Shifting between simple country blues in the vein of Robert Johnson to ferocious electric slide blues/rock, he remained one of the most respected singers and guitar players, linking the British blues/rock and American Southern rock movements.

Releasing *Roots* in 2011, it paid homage to some of the pioneering musicians who had influenced him. "It's songs I grew up being influenced by, songs that I loved when I first started," Johnny said. "I've been wanting to do something like this for a long time." The album included Robert Johnson's "Dust My Broom," Chuck Berry's "Maybellene," and Elmore James' "Done Somebody Wrong." Guests ranged from Gregg Allman and ZZ Top's Billy Gibbons to Derek Trucks, Susan Tedeschi, and his brother Edgar.

In 2011, Johnny made a surprise teaming with funk legend Sly Stone, playing guitar on a new version of Stone's classic "Thank You (Falettinme Be Mice Elf Agin)." "He's re-doing a lot of his old stuff," Winter reported. And who could forget his teaming with Captain Kirk. Winter was one of the musicians William Shatner enlisted for a covers project, unleashing his fiery guitar on an unusual cover of Deep Purple's "Space Truckin'." "He talks, he can't sing," Winter reported, laughing. "It's pretty cool. He did a good job."

Though hip surgery slowed him down, Winter was still able to amaze audiences. "It's not painful at all," he explained. "It's just that I get a little winded if I stand too long, so now it's better for me to sit and play. My love of music keeps me playing. I'll be playing till I die."

Johnny Winter died in Switzerland in 2014, at age 70. His last studio album, *Step Back*, was released posthumously. Friends helping out on the star-studded record included Eric Clapton, Billy Gibbons, Aerosmith's Joe Perry, and Dr. John. Gibbons posted: "We've lost another of the gifted guitar greats and a truly soulful spirit."

Edgar Winter released *Brother Johnny*, an all-star tribute to his brother in April 2022. *Ultimate Classic Rock* praised it as "a true labor of love, a musical love letter to his older brother."

"SHE CAUGHT THE KATY (AND LEFT ME A MULE TO RIDE)"

Taj Mahal

"I'm basically an example of the capacity of the human experience allowing oneself to really generate a positive energy."

When the Rolling Stones decided to film a TV special in 1968, with friends like John Lennon, Eric Clapton, and The Who, they paid tribute to their American blues influences by adding Taj Mahal to the bill. Titled *The Rolling Stones Rock and Roll Circus*, the resulting film was only released publicly in 1996.

Taj was amazed how the English rock royalty idolized American blues. "They championed the real innovators, and the result of what they learned was a much more powerful music," he says. "They jumped over the Elvis syndrome that kind of stunted the American growth where people were willing to take the substitute, whereas these guys landed on Elmore James' doorstep. They had heard the real records and then created something really good from it. In America, there was a mentality at the time to keep this music out of the mainstream because it would ruin everybody. White Protestant culture was the basic pattern, while in England, the music was heard without all the racial overtones."

Since hooking up with the Stones back in the late '60s, in subsequent years, this Grammy-winning musician has toured and or recorded with an extraordinary array of leading artists, including B.B. King, John Lee Hooker, Miles Davis, Bob Dylan, and Eric Clapton, along with jamming with Jimi Hendrix and Bob Marley.

A versatile artist who draws from a rich heritage, a move to the island of Kaua'i in 1981 led to Taj adding Hawaiian flavors to his music and incorporating the 'ukulele. "I love the sound of the harmony strings," he enthuses. "I've got the four-string, the six-string, and the eight-string ones. They're out all the time, so I can get my hands on them."

While living on Kaua'i, he formed the Hula Blues Band, which produced two memorable albums, *Sacred Island* in 1996 and *Hanapepe Dream* in 2003. A Caribbean/bluesy/Hawaiian stew accented with steel guitar, slack key guitar, and 'ukulele, *Hanapepe Dream* featured the classic "Stagger Lee" and Dylan's "All Along the Watchtower." Then *Live From Kauai* in 2015 included the classic "Moonlight Lady" recorded 40 years earlier by Hawaiian legend Gabby Pahinui.

Taj recalls being intrigued by Hawaiian music during his childhood. "I heard the music as a youngster, but so much of what they played was almost cartoonish. The situation with Hawaiian music was very similar to early attempts by Europeans to do Black music – make a caricature and downgrade the creativity. I was lucky enough to hear some real stuff on *Hawaii Calls*. I remember hearing this music one night on the radio in the '40s, and my brain went, wow, I hope I get to travel one day and see who those people are. The music was so pleasing. It really struck me as a very deep, resonating music."

"Playing a gig in California at a party later, someone played 'Moonlight Lady,' and it sounded so beautiful. I asked who it was by, and it turned out it was Gabby Pahinui, Ry Cooder, and Blah Pahinui, and all those guys. I picked up a couple of albums, and that's how I got in touch with Gabby Pahinui. To me, Gabby was similar to Charly Patton or Son House, someone from that deep in the culture. There's nothing that sounds like him.

"So many blues players have definitely been affected, and so many started out with a 'ukulele," he continues. "Chuck Berry has a great record called *Blues for Hawaiians*, and he's playing steel guitar on it. From the days of Andy Iona when Hawaiian music was very popular in the United States in the '20s and '30s, I have four recordings of Louis Armstrong and Andy's group along with Lionel Hampton on vibes, with Louis playing trumpet against a Hawaiian steel band. It's unbelievable."

A living music encyclopedia, over the span of time, Taj has enthusiastically expanded his vocabulary. On *Dancing the Blues,* he shone a light on exuberant, late-1940's jump blues, the precursor to rock 'n' roll. "This music gives you tremendous hope and energy to think of more positive ways of dealing with things," he suggests. "The natural progression from country blues to city blues, there's a link that's missing."

Black South Africans "refused to allow music to not be joyful in their soul. They've got a long way to go from where they could be, in terms of being aggravated, angry and sullen. With Afro-Americans, the spirit was broken, and it created a sorrowful sound, whereas when you listen to the original music it was generated from, it was never like that."

His passion for assimilating a vast inventory of styles while honoring the roots of American blues has kept him out of mainstream attention, yet he's gained pockets of loyal fans all over the globe. "Record companies say, 'we're trying to figure out what your core audience is,' and I'm flying across the country sitting next to the minister of agriculture from Mali, who asks me my name and says, 'oh, we know you'," says Taj. "Last time I was in England, a bunch of people from Zambia came up and were talking about how my records are priceless all over the continent. (Nigerian star) Sunny Ade said he was going to bring his records with him so I could autograph them, and his wife had told him, 'don't take the records, they'll never get back home.'"

Spreading joy wherever he travels, Taj's exuberance on stage never fails to captivate. "I'm just in it for the long haul," he concludes. "I've always been that way. I'm always playing music and trying to improve. I like playing and singing and showing people you can either go by the status quo or you can get busy.

"The music comes through me, so I'm basically giving an example of the capacity of the human experience allowing oneself to really generate a positive energy. And there's a tremendous amount of connection that happens when people see that. Every night's an experience compared to just a stroll around the block, an attitude a lot of musicians get after a while because they don't get the proper due."

"LOAN ME A DIME"

Boz Scaggs

"When things started happening, and radio started exploding, it was a wild ride."

O ne of the greatest R&B singers of our time, known for such smooth, soulful hits such as "Lido Shuffle," "Lowdown," "Georgia," and "Jo Jo," it took a few years for Boz Scaggs' popularity to soar after leaving the San Francisco-based Steve Miller Band. Before he found fame as a solo artist, Scaggs had helped revolutionize American rock as a member of Miller's band, recording the seminal albums *Children of the Future* and *Sailor.*

For his critically acclaimed major-label debut, Scaggs worked with the famed Muscle Shoals Rhythm Section (who backed Aretha Franklin). It included the smoldering, 12-minute epic blues of "Loan Me a Dime," with Scaggs trading lead with guitar legend Duane Allman. "It got a lot of critical acclaim, and it felt good to be recognized," Scaggs recalls.

Although it featured an infectious medley of soul, gospel, blues, rock, and country (including yodeling on a cover of Jimmie Rodgers' "Waiting for a Train") influences, the album failed to find an audience at the time. *AllMusic* would later praise it as "an enduring blue-eyed soul masterpiece."

"It was my first step into the wider world, and on one hand, I was very pleased, and on the other, I was wondering what the hell to do with myself," he continues. "I really didn't have a great perspective of what I was doing at that time. I was just sort of following what presented itself day to day. It gave me the courage to go on to the next stage."

He finally hit the jackpot with the multi-million selling *Silk Degrees,* which remained on the Billboard album charts for 115 weeks. Featuring three chart-topping singles, it earned a Grammy and became one of the most treasured albums of the 1970s.

"It didn't feel like such a big step," he suggests. "I had made four or five albums before that. I've always found that each stage of my career has been incremental. In a way, it was an enormous step in terms of the number of records I had sold. In those albums I'd made before, I had certain disappointments. I had thought they might reach a broader audience.

"I was pretty much living hand to mouth. Though I was selling a few hundred thousand records and playing quite a bit, I didn't get the breakthrough that I wished for. So when it came, it didn't come quickly, it was very slow. When things started happening, and radio started exploding, it was a wild ride. It was like OK, my number came up, and off I went."

After a couple more albums and further hit songs like "Jo Jo," he decided to take a sabbatical from music that ended up lasting almost ten years. "There had been a lot of pressure on me personally," he explains. "I had a family to take care of and two young sons. I decided to take a few months off, but that turned into a year, and a year turned into two. I just became involved with other things and stayed away from it for years."

Steely Dan's Donald Fagen helped bring him back to the spotlight, recruiting Scaggs for the Rock and Soul Revue. "It was a wonderful experience, and it put me in touch with some of my favorite contemporary musicians," he says. "I felt rejuvenated and started phase two of my career."

This fertile phase included a superb return to his R&B roots with *Come on Home*, where Boz interpreted classics by Jimmy Reed, Isaac Hayes, and Sonny Boy Williamson, backed by musicians from Little Feat and Bonnie Raitt's band. "That one wears particularly well with me," he notes. "We explored a lot of songs. Some were new I had not heard before, and some were old favorites, and I wrote a few new songs."

In more recent years, he released the brilliant concert recording *Greatest Hits Live*, and in 2003, he successfully embraced what he terms "sacred ground," reworking the Great American Songbook with a jazz quartet on the *But Beautiful - Standards Volume 1* album. *Jazz Times* lauded, "it came as no surprise that Boz Scaggs' first foray into jazz standards was an unqualified success."

He followed *Beautiful* with the exceptional jazz recording *Speak Low*, collaborating with musician/arranger Gil Goldstein. "It was a challenge to learn new areas of using my voice," he says. "There's a broad range of music I'm interested in."

Scaggs made his Maui debut in 2008, performing with the Honolulu-based Matt Catingub Orchestra. The unique concert marked only a handful of times that he had performed with an orchestra. "I've only done a few of these in my life," he explains. "It's another way of doing music that I don't do often." Asked whether he was going to play "Loan Me a Dime" on Maui, he suggested it was a possibility, and he closed his MACC concert with his brilliant version of the blues song, joined by Maui guitarist Jeff Peterson, stepping in for Duane Allman's part.

Between 2011 and 2018, he focused on a trilogy of covers albums from *Memphis* to *Out of the Blues*. Recording at Memphis' famed Royal Studios, where soul great Al Green cut so many hits in the 1970s, Scaggs has family roots in the city. "It felt like something of a homecoming," he offers. "My father grew up there, and my grandfather grew up there. We cut 13 songs in three days with no real rush. It's really keeping with the spirit of this kind of recording. It used to be that when you worked in Muscle Shoals or American Studios and you're Aretha Franklin or Wilson Pickett, you were given a week to do it."

Subsequent visits to Maui saw him co-headline with Michael McDonald and perform with fellow stars Donald Fagen and McDonald as the Dukes of September. "I feel very fortunate to be able to do what I do, to stay in music and have a career," he concludes.

During the 2020 pandemic, Scaggs joined legends like Willie Nelson and Neil Young for a live-streamed Farm Aid show and was part of "A Night for Austin" benefit with Bonnie Raitt and James Taylor. As a tribute to Covid frontline workers in his hometown, he posted a moving a capella version of "I Left My Heart in San Francisco."

ROUND MIDNIGHT

"A NIGHT IN TUNISIA"

Dizzy Gillespie

"No money, no job. We caught hell, but we stuck it out."

In the opening of Miles Davis' autobiography, the trumpet legend declared his indebtedness to his primary influence, John Birks "Dizzy" Gillespie. "The greatest feeling I ever had in my life - with my clothes on," Davis wrote, "was when I first heard Dizzy and Bird together in St. Louis back in 1944. If it hadn't been for Dizzy, I wouldn't be where I am today."

Acknowledged as one of the world's greatest trumpet virtuosos, Dizzy inspired countless musicians and fans since the early 1940s, when, along with Charlie "Bird" Parker, he founded the bebop movement, which revolutionized the course of jazz.

Trumpet great Wynton Marsalis once admitted in an interview, "His style is impossible to imitate. He's an innovator whose true accomplishments still have yet to be properly accessed, let alone digested."

Ever modest, Dizzy graciously accepted the accolades yet dismissed any notion that he deserved special attention. "It wasn't all that different from anything else," he said about his role as an innovator. "It's been going on for a long time – in astronomy, architecture. People get a new idea, that's great."

As the founders of bebop, Bird and Dizzy often endured scathing criticism and prejudice. Inventing a feverish, rhythmically, and harmonically complex sound, they were attacked for seeding the death of swing dance music. Bandleader Tommy Dorsey railed how "bebop had set music back 20 years." Even Louis Armstrong complained about bebop's "weird chords" and "no melody to remember and no beat to dance to." *Time* magazine referred to bebop as "a frantic, disorganized musical cult whose high priest was quid-cheeked Dizzy Gillespie."

How did Dizzy view this early criticism of his art form? "It didn't bother me at all," he responded philosophically. "Anything new coming out is going to hit some flak. So there is no problem. Any kind of art goes through that period. You just have to live it out."

"Charlie Parker was the designer (of bebop), but Dizzy was the cat who put it all down, like the architect," trumpeter Jon Faddis wrote in the liner notes to the Verve Records anthology Dizzy's Diamonds.

An abiding love for jazz kept him going even through the rough times. "We caught hell," he emphasized. "No money, no job. We caught hell, but we stuck it out, and now the fruits are coming forward."

Self-taught, Dizzy wrote his first arrangements at 18, and recorded two years later with the Teddy Hill Orchestra. By 1939, he joined Cab Calloway's band, performing regularly at New York's famed Cotton Club. Dizzy first met Charlie Parker while traveling with Calloway. A brilliant instrumentalist and showman, Dizzy learned early in his career how to charm audiences. His comic antics earned him his nickname. Often playing with gloves on or his back to the audience, he became known as the trumpet player who was as dizzy as a fox.

An irreverent prankster, in 1964, Dizzy jokingly announced his intention to run for president and take office in the Blues House. His cabinet would include Duke Ellington as Secretary of State, Miles Davis as CIA Director, Charles Mingus as Secretary of Peace, Louis Armstrong as Secretary of Agriculture, and Malcolm X as Attorney General.

For his campaign song, Gillespie reworked one of his most famous compositions, "Salt Peanuts," which he titled "Vote Dizzy." He summed up his escapades - "I used to have a lot of fun, that's all."

Dizzy's life was included in *Bird*, Clint Eastwood's movie tribute to Charlie Parker. Even though he owned a copy of the video, Dizzy never watched the film. "It gave an idea of what it was, but most everybody's idea is that it didn't do any great justice to Charlie Parker," he said, adding that the movie focused too much on dope and wild women and not enough on Parker's musical genius.

Managing to remain impervious to the lure of narcotics, Dizzy forged ahead as an innovator, while Parker descended into heroin and alcohol addiction, which cost him his life. "That didn't do anything to me," he said about drugs. "Some did, and some didn't," is all he revealed as to why he was never attracted.

An eternal optimist, he found inspiration in the Baha'i Faith, attracted by a universal philosophy that embraces all the major spiritual prophets. He formally converted on April 5, 1968, the night after the assassination of Martin Luther King, Jr. "Dizzy reached an inner strength and discipline that total pacifists call 'soul force,'" author Nat Hentoff reported in *Groovin' High: The Life of Dizzy Gillespie*. "He always had a vivid presence."

Dizzy wore a large quartz rock around his neck taken from Mount Carmel in Israel where Baha'i prophet Mirza Ali Muhammad is buried. He wrote in his autobiography, *To Be or Not to Bop*, "It all went along with what I had always believed. I believed in the oneness of mankind. I became more spiritually aware."

Having performed for so many years, one might assume playing came easy to this jazz giant. But no, he responded, "as the years go, the harder it gets, the more you know, the more you know what you can't do." And forget any notion that maybe he'd mastered his instrument. "You never master one," he concluded. "It will bring you down to its level any minute."

Playing up to 300 nights a year well into his seventies, to celebrate his 75th birthday, Dizzy played for four weeks at the Blue Note club in Manhattan, surrounded by one of the greatest selections of jazz musicians ever assembled.

He died in 1993. "We've lost one of the true giants; not just of music but of humanity," Wynton Marsalis pronounced. And Tony Bennett reported: "Once every 500 years a musician comes along who invents a new form of music. Dizzy Gillespie belongs in this category of rare musical genius."

"TAKE FIVE"

Dave Brubeck

"My quartet opened up more colleges to integration than before sports did."

T he first jazz single to sell a million copies, the landmark instrumental "Take Five," propelled Dave Brubeck and his group to international stardom. The biggest-selling jazz single ever, it was composed by Brubeck Quartet saxophonist Paul Desmond for an innovative project employing unusual time signatures. "I brought up the idea with my quartet of doing this experimental album," Brubeck recalled in 1986. "I said to Paul, write something in five."

The third track on the album *Time Out,* it was recorded in 1959, the same year that jazz giants Miles Davis produced *Kind of Blue* and John Coltrane released *Giant Steps.*

An iconic classic, "Take Five" still sounds like one of the coolest, sexiest jazz tunes ever, the kind that inspires one to light up a Gitanes and attempt to snap fingers to the unusual 5/4 rhythm.

As is often the case with unique works, his label, Columbia Records, was initially reluctant to release *Time Out,* fearing commercial failure. Brubeck had to assure Columbia that he would also record an album of standards - *Gone with the Wind.*

From a rugged childhood as a young cowboy on a California ranch, Brubeck rose to prominence as one of America's leading jazz musicians. One of the first modern jazz musician to grace the cover of *Time* back in 1954, he received commercial and critical acclaim with *Time Out,* which included stunning Brubeck compositions like "Blue Rondo à la Turk," in 9/8 time, inspired by Turkish street musicians.

A music career was a natural course for this child prodigy, who began composing tunes on the piano between the ages of four and five. These early compositions were dictated to his mother, who taught piano. From his earliest years, he was exposed to the music of Bach,

Chopin, Mozart, and Debussy, and this grounding in the classics served him later in life as he brought a classical sensitivity to jazz.

But his was no pampered artistic upbringing. His father was a cattle rancher and champion horseman, and Brubeck often toiled long hours on the range. "Fortunately, I had a balance of two opposite worlds," Brubeck recalled. "I think that was important. The years I worked as a cowboy, I figured, was the training that helped me to survive as a jazz musician."

While many of his jazz peers succumbed to drug addiction, he never felt tempted. "The endurance and a different set of values - you aren't going to get messed up with drugs," he noted.

After four years in the Army during World War II, Brubeck studied composition with the celebrated French composer Darius Milhaud, and by the early '50s, the Brubeck Quartet achieved national attention as a unique modern jazz combo. With a harmonically complex piano technique and often unconventional timing, his appeal became widespread.

But he didn't view himself as any special innovator. "I don't think you ever know you're choosing to be (a pioneer), you're just doing what you're doing, and someone else says you're a pioneer," he said. "When I was young, I was already branching out from being the typical player that just copies everything. I was thinking of original ways to express myself. Even back in the '40s, there was something going on, which was a little extension of the usual."

Fellow keyboardists who have praised his influence include jazz legends Herbie Hancock, Keith Jarrett, and Chick Corea, along with the Doors' Ray Manzarek. "We wouldn't be who we are if it weren't for Dave Brubeck," Hancock wrote in *Time* magazine. Billy Joel once commented that what *Sgt. Pepper* was to most other rock musicians, "Take Five" was to him.

Social injustice long concerned him. His second major work for chorus and orchestra, *The Gates of Justice*, was based on texts by Martin Luther King, Jr. and the Old Testament. This was followed by *Truth is Fallen*, which was inspired by the student massacres at Kent State University and Jackson State College.

"The social thing is very close to me," he emphasized. "I was always amazed that people could be judged by the color of their skin in any way inferior or superior. The injustices I've seen in my lifetime because people did that. They almost brought about the total destruction of Europe, thinking one race is different from another. We had it in the United States in our treatment of the American Indians, which from the beginning has been terrible. We keep making mistakes as a nation, such as with the Japanese in America during World War II."

Brubeck battled racism for many years. "I had maybe the first integrated band in Europe in World War II, when Black and white units were heavily segregated," he recalled. "There were problems because it wasn't part of the Army. A lot of officers were against it and tried to sabotage it. I learned first-hand about prejudice and how you stick out your neck and have to take chances."

During the 1950s, Brubeck's racially mixed group (bassist Eugene Wright was Black) toured the South challenging segregation policies. "My quartet opened up more colleges to integration than before sports did," he reported. "If they wouldn't accept the group, we'd cancel the concert." On one tour, he remembered 23 out of 25 concerts were canceled. Some colleges insisted he replace Wright with a white bass player.

The cancellations cost Brubeck $40,000 in lost revenue (worth nearly $400,000 today). When he canceled a show at the University of Georgia in 1959, which had banned integrated groups, a student wrote in the college newspaper *The Red and Black*, that all of Brubeck's records should be broken. "We cannot afford to be the least bit broad minded - not even for the sake of art." Brubeck also turned down a lucrative tour of South Africa because the apartheid government refused to allow Wright to enter the country.

It was not unusual for a college president to call a state's governor and refuse to allow them on stage. Often the group would need police protection. "We couldn't stay in hotels together and eat together, and it wasn't just in the South," he recalled.

Composing *The Gates of Justice*, during the '60s civil rights movement, Brubeck wrote in the program notes for its premiere: "Because of their long history of suffering, Jews and American blacks know better than any other people the consequences of hate and alienation."

Five years earlier, Martin Luther King, Jr. had written an essay on the significance of jazz, at the request of the organizers of the 1964 Berlin Jazz Festival.

"Everybody has the Blues," King wrote. "Everybody longs for meaning. Everybody needs to love and be loved. Everybody needs to clap hands and be happy. Everybody longs for faith. In music, especially this broad category called Jazz, there is a stepping stone towards all of these."

Always searching for new avenues for his music, Brubeck was one of the first jazz artists to improvise with a symphony orchestra. His performances and recordings of *Dialogues for Jazz Combo and Orchestras*, with Leonard Bernstein and the New York Philharmonic, are considered pivotal in opening new performance opportunities for jazz artists.

This pioneering legend continued to create up to his death in 2012 at the age of 91. Ideas would pop up in "airplanes, trains, cars, hotel rooms, even walking down the street," he explained, feeling inspired to "keep writing, keep improvising, and trying to get as good as I can."

Brubeck's last works included *Indian Summer*, a collection of solo piano ballads, and *Sacred Choral Works/Songs of Praise*, a combination of gospel, chant, and classical oratorio. "It is sure to enlighten, uplift, and entertain classical and jazz fans alike," noted *AllAboutJazz*.

"Dave Brubeck was a pioneer, so many of us sprang from his incredibly creative and daring work," Herbie Hancock posted on *Facebook* following his death. "He even proved that a song with 5 beats in it and one with 9 beats in it could become popular, with 'Take 5' and 'Blue Rondo à la Turk.'"

Wynton Marsalis had praised him back in 2014, at "The Life and Music of Dave Brubeck" concert in New York. "(Brubeck) is important because he stood up for Civil Rights, when many of us sat down."

Time OutTakes, featuring recently-discovered outtakes from the Brubeck Quartet's historic *Time Out* sessions, was released in December 2020. "An album of previously unheard recordings from the "*Time Out*" sessions in 1959 reveals the making of a masterpiece," praised *The New York Times*.

"WATERMELON MAN"

Herbie Hancock

*"I like variety, and I believe human beings like variety.
Unfortunately, the world doesn't support that."*

We can thank Sly and the Family Stone for inspiring Herbie Hancock to begin injecting some funk into his compositions. "The thing that really did the trick was Sly Stone's 'Thank You (Falettinme Be Mice Elf Agin),'" he explains during an interview in his Maui hotel room in 1989. "That killed me. It's still the funkiest record I've ever heard. It touched something so deep, so primal. How could he even conceive of something like that?"

Hancock also cites the impact of James Brown. "When I was a kid, I didn't like jazz," he continues. "I liked classical music and rhythm and blues. Once I started playing jazz, I became disinterested in any form of pop music. Then I heard James Brown's 'Papa's Got a Brand New Bag.' Even though there could be what one might call monotony, it didn't feel like monotony. It felt good, and I didn't want them to change the beat. The beat had a lot of internal, syncopated activity that was interesting."

An influential practitioner of modern jazz piano, Hancock's eclectic career has ranged from playing with Miles Davis and forming the funk-based Head Hunters ensemble to producing the Grammy-winning dance hit, "Rockit," releasing the Oscar-winning soundtrack to *Round Midnight*, and recording acclaimed tributes to George Gershwin and Joni Mitchell.

A piano prodigy who played Mozart with the Chicago Symphony at the age of 11, Hancock was attracted to jazz because of the freedom it offered. "The freedom and the personal element," he explains, "because it's your creation, your improvisation."

A couple of years after he released his debut solo album, *Takin' Off*, featuring the instant classic "Watermelon Man," Hancock was invited by Miles Davis to join a new group with Wayne Shorter, Tony Williams, and Ron Carter. This influential quintet dominated jazz for years. Davis taught Hancock the importance of teamwork. "I have the feeling that's what most people get from Miles," he says. "He's got big ears and a great ability to adapt moment to moment. He doesn't care that you sound perfect. He only cares that you're working on something, and he can tell when you're jiving. Trust is very important. You have to trust the caliber of the musicians and also your ability to be able to respond. It takes a lot of experience to do that well, and he has it."

During the '60s, Hancock, along with McCoy Tyner, dominated mainstream jazz piano. By the early '70s, after leaving Davis, instead of launching into jazz-rock fusion like many of his contemporaries, Hancock hit the funky streets. "The typical fusion thing really bores me," he says, "with the same pentatonic scales. The funny thing is that it used to have a lot of energy, then it spawned New Age music which is really bland."

In 1973, he re-recorded "Watermelon Man" with the Head Hunters, combining synthesizers with a Sly Stone/James Brown funk influence and a Pygmy-style whistle. Blending high-powered funk and jazz, Hancock's influential *Head Hunters* album became one of the biggest-selling jazz albums of all time. The album's "Chameleon" single became a pop hit, and Hancock was elevated to stardom.

Returning to Oahu to perform with the Head Hunters in 1988, at the inaugural Honolulu Jazz Festival, he recalled first playing Hawai'i at a Diamond Head festival. "There were 60,000 people. Sly Stone was on the show. It was the last concert of the Head Hunters band, and it was one of our best. It just had a wonderful spirit to it."

Hancock cracked the pop charts once again with an unlikely hit in 1983. The Grammy-winning "Rockit" had no vocals, it was a form of music unfamiliar to most people, and it was performed by a jazz artist. "The whole project was a speculative venture," he explains. Hancock had agreed to experiment with producers Bill Laswell and Michael Beinhorn, and the duo had just met a friend who had introduced them to scratching music through a tape of Malcolm McLaren's "Buffalo Girls."

"I didn't know that stuff well, and I said I'm willing to let them produce two things. A week before they were to bring what they had been working on to Los Angeles, I heard 'Buffalo Girls,' and I said, that's the kind of thing I want to do. When they came to play the tape, the first thing was the beginning of 'Rocket.' It was like they read my mind. How did they know I wanted to do that? I like variety, and I believe human beings like variety. Unfortunately, the world doesn't support that - it's the opposite fitting you into a pigeonhole. It took several years for people to realize I was going to do acoustic jazz and electric pop music."

Walking into his Kaanapali hotel room for our interview, Hancock had just finished chanting "Nam Myoho Renge Kyo" at his alter. He has been a follower of Nichiren Buddhism (Soka Gakkai International) since 1972, when he was introduced to by a musician friend. Hancock later introduced Wayne Shorter to the practice. Another SGI follower, Tina Turner, has reported Buddhist chanting helped save her life ("My personal practice has shown me, time after time, that it just works," she told *Tricycle*).

One day while chanting Hancock imagined creating funky jazz influenced by Sly Stone. He subsequently released the *Head Hunters* album, which included the tribute "Sly."

"People assume when you practice what's considered an Eastern religion, it makes you calm and peaceful," he says. "My religion makes you calm if that's what you need. If you need some fire and energy, that's what you're going to get."

This daily spiritual focus has positively impacted his music. "It makes it easier for me to concentrate and to develop the courage to persevere," he notes. "I'm not nearly as afraid of making a mistake or not having a perfect performance, so I'm a lot freer. A lot of things that were stressful don't affect you now until you're able to deal with them. People carry around all this baggage on their shoulders all the time, so they can't be where they physically are. But when you get rid of that stuff, you can observe more, make better decisions, and enjoy more. That's why I practice Buddhism.

"It helps to keep me in focus on what I believe in and develop the courage to persevere and a sense of hope that I can overcome challenges. Also, because of the strength of the practice, I think a lot of good things have come my way at the right time. Buddhism has helped me open up my viewpoint to see the whole forest and not just the trees. There's more clarity in my life about the things that happen to me."

Long known as an innovator, Hancock says he loves surprising people with new music. "I love it when people don't know what to expect. I try to write my music like that, too. I try to make it so they're sitting on the edge of their seats because they don't know what's going to happen next."

Few artists dare to propel themselves in new directions, preferring the comfort of the familiar. "Society supports you to find an area and stay," Hancock suggests. "It gives people stability if they know what you do. As soon as you start switching around, it gets chaotic, and you feel uncomfortable. But there's a dichotomy because the truth is, everybody's flexible."

Into the 21st century, Hancock's recordings included re-imagining Joni Mitchell's music on the Grammy-winning *River: The Joni Letters*, followed by the Grammy-winning *The Imagine Project*, where he collaborated with musicians from around the world, including Seal, Anoushka Shankar, the Tuareg band Tinariwen, and Malian kora player Toumani Diabaté.

"When I'm working on myself through my practice, it affects my music to make it function in a more constructive, positive direction," he says. "It doesn't necessarily mean the music is artistically better, but I sure hope that my music is encouraging."

"SPAIN"

Chick Corea

"The spirit of jazz for me always had with it a kind of honest, down-to-earth quality. It's the way I like to live."

"Every time I play and make music, it's a celebration," enthused Chick Corea, about his passion for creating. "It's what I dreamed of doing since I was a small lad watching my (trumpet playing) father. I love all aspects of creating music, and it's endlessly pleasurable."

Few pianists could equal Corea's stature and influence. A remarkably prolific composer and recording artist, he was the fourth-most-nominated artist in Grammy Awards history. Since embarking on a solo career in 1966, this pioneer had been at the fore-front of jazz, both as a renowned pianist forging new ground with his acoustic jazz groups and as an innovative electric keyboardist with the seminal fusion group Return to Forever and the Elektric Band.

Relishing creative independence, he explored an astonishing variety of music, with many of his compositions becoming jazz standards. Corea traversed vast stylistic ground while consistently enthralling audiences, from intense fusion and passionate flamenco-inspired pieces to majestic ballads. "I decided when I was a young man to make it my primary policy to always keep myself interested and challenged with music," he explained. "Freedom to create and use my imagination has been the most important thing for me and for my groups."

Brilliant on acoustic piano and a range of electric keyboards, Corea said, "I've always regarded my instruments as tools I use to make music. Until 1969, I never came across a keyboard other than a piano. But when Miles insisted I play an electric keyboard, I did the best I could with it trying to give him something that he was possibly looking for.

"Later, when I formed the first Return To Forever group, I chose the Rhodes as my sound rather than piano. I found that it worked really well with Joe Farrell's flute and soprano sax. It also allowed the band to play a more vigorous rhythm because the Rhodes sound and volume enabled Airto's drumming to explode. Then with the second Return To Forever band, I began exploring synthesizers - all new to me at that time. I found I could use some of the different sounds to enable the band to sound more orchestral. But it all finally comes down to choosing which instruments color and touch is best for the musical situation."

Over the years, Corea would perform with an astounding array of jazz greats from Sarah Vaughan and Stan Getz to Dizzy Gillespie and Miles Davis, playing on such influential albums as *In a Silent Way* and the groundbreaking *Bitches Brew*. One of jazz's greatest albums, the musical sketches of *Bitches Brew*, signaled the emergence of Miles' rock-influenced electric period. Along with Corea, the ensemble on the album included Joe Zawinul, John McLaughlin, Wayne Shorter, and Jack DeJohnette.

"Looking back, there was just a lot of change and exciting experiments with music," Corea recalled. "Miles encouraged and set the pace for this kind of experimentation. Miles never pandered to the status quo. He never waited for or asked for approval concerning what music to make. His artistic integrity was always fully intact. This was the biggest lesson I learned from him, not only playing with him and being around him, but by the whole legacy of great music he left us."

Since his formative days, Corea routinely dazzled his peers. "Even at an early age, Chick's ideas seemed to be original," Herbie Hancock told the Detroit Free Press. "And Chick really swung. There was kind of a lightness to it, like he was sprinkling magic dust on something."

"I learn so much playing with Herbie," said Corea, who last toured with Hancock in 2015. "Long ago, Herbie and I recognized that the thing that made our duet work was our ability to receive the other's ideas and always make something with them. It's easy to do with Herbie since I love everything he creates."

Scientology played a vital role in Corea's life, beginning in 1968 when he joined the church after reading books by founder L. Ron Hubbard. When he formed Return to Forever, bassist Stanley Clarke was also a member of the organization, and Flora Purim and Airto were taking Scientology courses. He later backed Hubbard's daughter, Diana, on her album *LifeTimes*.

Corea was reported to have achieved the Operating Thetan Level 8, the highest auditing level in the church. Influenced by Hubbard's science fiction writings, he released the albums *To the Stars* and the Grammy-winning *The Ultimate Adventure*.

"I've been a fan of L. Ron Hubbard's writing for years," he said. "When I finally decided to try to set a fiction story of his to music, it was with this background of being a long-time fan. I experimented by writing a piece of music that was described in (the novel) *To The Stars*, when the captain of a spaceship, played the piano in a bar in the future New Chicago.

"Hubbard's description of the music was so vivid I immediately envisioned what this piano music could sound like and composed a two-minute piece based on it. It was so much fun and challenging that I went ahead and completed a whole set of music based on the characters and places in the story. I basically tried to summarize in music what I'm portraying in the story. That's why eventually, I used the term tone poem to describe this music. *The Ultimate Adventure* was just a continuation of the game of portraying another one of Hubbard's great adventures. This time the story really fit my band Touchstone with its Spanish and Arabic musical flavors."

Corea said creating works he described as tone poems had become his favorite form of musical expression. "In one way or another, I have always worked best making music that told some sort of story - as a direct portrayal or something more conceptual with titles like 'Return To Forever,' 'The Leprechaun,' 'My Spanish Heart,' 'The Mad Hatter,' and many others."

Aside from being inspired by Hubbard to create musical works, one wondered how Scientology impacted his musical expression and life? "The application of Scientology has been a great help to me since I first read L. Ron Hubbard's book *Dianetics* in 1968," he responded. "Of course, one's musical expression cannot be divorced from one's attitude towards and abilities in life in general, and in both these areas, I have been continually refreshed by my study of Scientology."

Drawn to composing contemporary classical works, for the 250th anniversary of Mozart's birth in 2006, Corea composed his "Piano Concerto #2," which he first performed with the Vienna State Opera. "I enjoy working with an orchestra and have studied and revere some of the great orchestral works of Bartok, Stravinsky, Mozart, and many others," he said. "There is a thrill in working with that gorgeous sound and the joy of musicians all flowing together on stage."

Then in 2012, he released the marvelous double-disc *The Continents*, where he worked with an orchestra to conceptualize six continents. "I wanted to do something in the spirit of Mozart," he explained. "It's where jazz, Latin, and classical meet, and I really like the idea of jazz quintet with a chamber orchestra. It was one of those projects that I had dreamed of doing."

Having accomplished so much, did he ever feel proud of his varied achievements? "Unfortunately, in our modern society, it's become politically incorrect to ever admire yourself," he suggested. "I think we ought to admire ourselves and our own accomplishments as much as we do others. Salvador Dali's unabashed admiration for his own work and value as an artist is always looked upon as an insanity of some kind. I consider it refreshing. The truth is though, that I do acknowledge the positive things I've accomplished, but considering them only makes me re-double my efforts to improve and expand my abilities and accomplish even more and with a higher quality. I think it's spiritually a native impulse in all people to want to do better."

Corea's most recent group recording, *Antidote*, with The Spanish Heart Band, won the 2020 Best Latin Jazz Grammy. In September 2020, he released the wonderful solo piano work *Plays*, featuring impressionistic interpretations ranging from Stevie Wonder's "Pastime Paradise" and Scarlatti's "Sonata in D Minor" to Gershwin's "Someone to Watch Over Me." "Corea's way of paying tribute is to match his genius with that of other great composers, both playing and playing with what they've written," lauded *Downbeat*.

He died in February 2021 at the age of 79. In a message on *Facebook*, posted by his family, he wrote: "My mission has always been to bring the joy of creating anywhere I could, and to have done so with all the artists that I admire so dearly - this has been the richness of my life."

"GRAZING IN THE GRASS"

Hugh Masekela

"By the time I was nine, I was dreaming of New York and Duke Ellington and Count Basie."

" South Africa was hell," reported trumpet legend Hugh Masekela about his nation's brutal apartheid system. Interviewed before his Hawaii debut in 1994, he continued, "It's hell if you can't leave Maui to go to Honolulu without a permit, and when you get there, you have to have permission, and you're given only 72 hours. Every street corner, police are monitoring you. On one side, you're running away from police surveillance, and on the other side, you're running away from gangsters and mugging. There's amazing crime. In jail, people fall out of windows by accident or hang themselves. It was not human."

Performing what he called "jazz with a bone in the nose or a disc in the lip," Masekela was one of South Africa's greatest musicians, an anti-apartheid activist revered as the African nation's father of jazz. Among his accomplishments, he co-wrote the music for the Broadway hit and movie *Sarafina!*, featuring his powerful protest song "Bring Him Back Home (Nelson Mandela)," and scored an international number one with the instrumental "Grazing in the Grass," in the late '60s.

Playing at the legendary Monterey Pop Festival with the Byrds, he was among the musicians who performed at the historic Harlem Cultural Festival in the summer of 1969. Featured in the remarkable, Oscar-winning documentary *Summer of Soul (...Or, When the Revolution Could Not Be Televised)*, the festival included Sly and the Family Stone, Stevie Wonder, B.B. King, and Nina Simone. Called the "Black Woodstock," six free concerts attracted a combined attendance of around 300,000.

Masekela recorded with reggae icon Bob Marley (on *Natty Rebel*), Afrobeat legend Fela Kuti, and Paul Simon (*The Rhythm of the Saints*), and toured the world with Simon's *Graceland* project. Joining U2 on stage in Johannesburg before 98,000 in 2011, he played flugelhorn on "I Still Haven't Found What I'm Looking For."

Born in a coal-mining town near Johannesburg in 1939, Masekela knew from an early age that a better life beckoned beyond his country's border. "By the time I was nine, I was dreaming of New York and Duke Ellington and Count Basie," he recalled.

In school, he joined the Huddleston Jazz Band, South Africa's first youth orchestra, and when Louis Armstrong heard about the group, he sent one of his own trumpets as a gift. With Masekela on trumpet, the Jazz Epistles became the first jazz group in the country to record an album.

While the Epistles were on a national tour in 1960, 69 black protestors were shot dead at a massacre in the township of Sharpeville. Imposing a State of Emergency, the South African government made mass arrests, prohibited all public gatherings, and banned jazz from radio broadcasts. Bribing an official to obtain a passport, Masekela went into exile.

"Leaving South Africa was like how a Christian must feel when they go to heaven, but at the same time, it was heartbreaking," he said.

Encouraged by friendships developed with some famous entertainers, he arrived in New York in 1960. "Through the help of Miriam (Makeba) and through correspondence, I met people like Louis Armstrong, Miles Davis, Dizzy Gillespie, and Harry Belafonte. When I got there, I had five-star friends. They all believed in me. I had a very lucky and privileged life becoming successful right away."

Among his most famous songs, he composed "Soweto Blues," sung by Miriam Makeba, about a brutal police attack that killed many Black schoolchildren, and "Bring Him Back Home (Nelson Mandela)," which was inspired by a letter Mandela wrote to Masekela. It became an anthem of the anti-apartheid movement and was banned by the South African government. Mandela once said: "Music is a great blessing. It has the power to elevate and liberate us. It sets people free to dream."

It took 30 years for Masekela to attain his dream of being able to return to his homeland. Following Mandela's release from prison and the collapse of apartheid, he was able to record and tour with a band comprised entirely of South African musicians. He celebrated Black South Africans finally winning the right to determine their own destiny releasing *Hope*, recorded live in Washington, D.C.

A greatest hits package brimming with buoyant township jive, it included the extraordinary, 10-minute "Stimela/Coal Train," where Masekela narrated the plight of immigrant miners. "In 'Stimela,' Hugh Masekela wields trumpet and words like weapons, introducing a deeply political consciousness of class struggle and social justice," wrote Sharae Deckard in *World Literature, Neoliberalism, and the Culture of Discontent*. "Masekela's trumpet runs and spoken word poetry are by turns blistering and mournful, infused with the energies of resistance peoples."

"It's great to be touring with an all South African band," he enthused. "I don't have to explain anything, and I'm learning. It's exciting to be back home, but the damage that was done to a country and especially the impoverishment is disgusting. People think because we are free, we're riding into the sunset, but the work is just beginning. It's like how it must have felt in the mid-1800s, when a slave master said, OK, you can go now, you're free. Where do I go?"

At the time of the interview, Masekela was working on two new albums. *Johannesburg* featured "a lot of young South African singers and rappers. It's like a hip hop jazz album, an old direction with a new perspective." And *Note of Life* he described as "a mbaqanga dancehall reggae jazz album of love songs. During the struggle, we were obsessed so much with liberation that we never had a chance to sing about love. So I'm going to make a love album."

When Masekela died in 2018, South African president Jacob Zuma announced the nation would mourn a man who "kept the torch of freedom alive."

Released two years later, his last album, *Rejoice,* featured a collaboration with Afrobeat pioneer Nigerian drummer Tony Allen. *Jazz Journal* praised: "Ten years in the making, *Rejoice* was worth the wait. It's a celebratory, groove-laden, thoughtful, danceable, collection from two of the great figures in music."

"INSIDE THE TAJ MAHAL"

Paul Horn

*"The power of music is much more than entertainment.
You can see music as a way to raise consciousness
and spiritual awareness."*

"It's such a large dome, and the sound bounces off the marble so nicely," recalled legendary flutist Paul Horn, who recorded some sublime flute improvisations in India's Taj Mahal in 1968. "It was so perfectly constructed architecturally based on mathematical proportions."

While he had not intended to release the Taj Mahal recording commercially, *Inside* became a landmark album, selling more than one million copies worldwide and pioneering the contemplative field of New Age music.

Transporting listeners to serene realms, Horn became famous for his transcendent flute playing. Beginning with *Inside*, later renamed *Inside the Taj Mahal,* through recordings in Egypt's Great Pyramid, Peking's Temple of Heaven, and Tibet's Potala Palace, Horn recorded inside some of the world's most magnificent monuments.

A journey to Tibet in 1998, with Maui filmmaker Tom Vendetti and Tibetan Buddhist teacher Lama Tenzin, led to the renowned flutist gaining permission to record in Lhasa's majestic Potala Palace, the former winter home to many of Tibet's Dalai Lamas since 1649. This quest was captured in Vendetti's documentary *Journey inside Tibet*, narrated by Hana resident Kris Kristofferson.

Standing in the midst of the immense palace, Horn improvising soothing melodies, tuned in to the dormant presence of the great spiritual masters who had once inhabited the grand edifice. The first Western musician ever to record inside the palace he felt like he had completed a cycle. "This ends the trilogy," he noted. "The Taj Mahal was the first, the Great Pyramid was the second, and this is the third.

The Potala Palace has its own history, and it goes back about 1,000 years. Tibet has always been a very mystical country, and it taps something deep in me. Maybe I've had a past life there."

Born in New York in 1930, Horn was classically trained and later received a master's in music. Initially pursuing a successful jazz career, he toured with the Chico Hamilton Quintet in the mid-1950s, and cited Miles Davis as a primary influence. "Miles came out with a new approach to jazz, and this inspired me to get my first group. It was freer and expressive. It was like Ravel, the quality with a beat behind it. Every time he came out to Los Angeles, we'd hang out."

Horn later worked as a L.A. studio musician recording with Frank Sinatra, Tony Bennett, Duke Ellington, and Nat King Cole. Blending the jazz and classical worlds with hymns, his album *Jazz Suite on Mass Texts* earned two Grammy Awards in 1965.

As a studio musician, some of his notable contributions included working with Joni Mitchell on *Dreamland* and *Ladies of the Canyon*, the Beach Boys' classic *Pet Sounds*, Miles Davis' *Quiet Nights*, Duke Ellington's *Three Suites*, and Ravi Shankar's *Improvisations*.

In time he found the jazz life wasn't fulfilling a deeper need, and he began to realize it could destroy him. "I remember reading an interview in *Downbeat* with Bud Powell, who was a famous bebop pianist. It was a very sad picture of him sitting in a smoke-filled club in Paris, and he made the statement, 'I wish my father had taught me something else to do in life.' That was a mind-blower. Is this the sum total of this genius that he makes a statement like that? The energy and joy you experience as a young jazz musician, if you keep doing the same thing, it's going to kill you. It's a vicious circle after a while - the drug scene, even if it's just pot or maybe it's alcohol. I was so engrossed in my career, and it was not bringing me fulfillment. I found I had to deal with myself. I had to wake up."

Initiated into Transcendental Meditation in 1966, he studied with the Maharishi Mahesh Yogi and became one of the first TM teachers in the U.S. "It was a turning point, and meditation was the means and technique of discovery which enabled me to find out some important things," he said.

Then came *Inside the Taj Mahal*, which changed the course of Horn's life and led to his focus on music fostering tranquility. "A lot of things in life that happen to us that are supposed to happen are unplanned," he suggested. "We get in the way of our evolution and what we're supposed to be doing by projecting our own wants and desires, not knowing we're getting in the way. That gives rise to a lot of failure. I didn't plan any transition. As far as I'm concerned, I'm still a jazz musician, and I still play straight-ahead music, which I love, when the occasion presents itself. The solo flute thing came about because the *Inside* album was very successful, and it still sells. Many people didn't know about me before that, although *Taj Mahal* was my 14th album. I'd get on stage and start playing jazz, and people's introduction to me was through the *Inside* album, which was solo flute. So I started thinking how was I going to play solo flute in concert. It just evolved until that was what I was primarily doing."

Horn's association with the Indian sub-continent began back in the mid-1960s when he met Ravi Shankar in Los Angeles and was invited to play on the Indian sitar master's album *Portrait of a Genius*. "It was a great experience in many ways," he recalled. "I started to listen to more music from India, so when I was over there, it wasn't like a totally new thing, and I got to record a couple of albums in India (with some of Shankar's leading students) before the Taj Mahal recording."

In India featured classical ragas adapted by Ravi Shankar, performed by Horn with some of Shankar's students, while *Cosmic Consciousness - Paul Horn in Kashmir* included a group of musicians attending a Maharishi retreat, performing evening ragas and light classical pieces. The two albums were later compiled as *Paul Horn In India & Kashmir,* which *Jazzwise* praised as "two long-lost, semi-precious gems of Indo-jazz fusion."

Profoundly influenced by classical Indian music, he came to appreciate how music can serve as a source of healing. "The power of music is much more than entertainment," he emphasized. "When I became aware of that, there was no other way to look at music. You can see music then as a way to raise consciousness and spiritual awareness and as a tool of healing."

Deciding he wanted to make a film about TM and the Maharishi, he returned to the movement's Rishikesh ashram in 1968, arriving during the Beatles' famous pilgrimage to India.

"I found myself over there with a film crew and the Beatles," he recalled. "George Harrison, Paul McCartney, and John Lennon were there. Ringo had come and gone. We played a lot of music together and hung out."

The remaining Beatles were initially wary of Horn. "At first, they looked at me like an intrusion on their privacy. I got it real clear I'm here to do a film on the Maharishi, and I was here last year before you knew about meditation, and I totally respect your privacy. Maharishi set aside a hut by the Ganges for music. I would often be there with George playing sitar. Paul would play his guitar and sing, and Donovan would too. For them to sit back and be part of this group with this master was nice. All the celebrity stuff fell away."

Horn remembers a special night when, "Maharishi said, 'let's go for a boat ride on the Ganges on a full moon, and we'll have music with the Beatles, Donovan, and Paul.' So we all got excited and went down to the river, but no one had stopped to think you can't take a boat ride on the Ganges because of the rapids. The boat was on land, so we all sat in the boat and didn't go anywhere. But it was moonlight on the Ganges, and the Beatles were playing, strumming their guitars."

While filming at the ashram, after an L.A. producer showed up wanting to make a more slick production, Horn was dispatched to film at the Taj Mahal. That's what prompted him to explore the possibility of recording inside the magnificent mausoleum.

Interviewed in 2020, Horn's wife, Ann Mortifee, explains: "Paul had started to play his flute, and a guard stopped him and said, 'you can't do that here.' Paul, 'said why not, you sing here?' He said, 'we sing for God,' and Paul said, 'well I play my flute for God.' So the guard said, 'come back tonight when we close up, and it will be quiet.' That's how *Inside the Taj Mahal* was created. Paul always felt the Maharishi let him go all that way there so he would end up making the album." Unfortunately, the original film Horn shot of the Maharishi and the Beatles in Rishikesh has been lost.

Two decades later, with permission granted by India's Prime Minister, Horn returned to the Taj Mahal to record *Inside the Taj Mahal II*.

Playing soprano saxophone and a range of flutes, he almost abandoned the project because of obtrusive human and bird noise. Peace was only attained after Horn prayed and meditated. "The first time, there was no one else there, and it wasn't under strict guard like it is now," he continued. "It wasn't peaceful. There were so many pigeons and a lot of disturbances. Miraculously the meditation seemed to quiet everything down."

Horn's album *Inside the Great Pyramid* was another milestone, recorded in the 4,500-years-old King's Chamber. "To be alone in there was quite a different atmosphere," he marveled. "It's so still. It was similar to Haleakalā. You feel the power, and there's a lot of energy."

Within the stillness of Giza's ancient Great Pyramid, Horn was surprised to hear what sounded like a choir of beautiful voices in the distance, a phenomenon confirmed by a friend who was recording the session. "I have a theory on it. I think anything that's ever put out is there forever. A sound is emitted, its energy, and it's out in the universe diminishing, but it will never completely go away. There must have been chanting going on in the pyramid a long time ago. I think that's what I heard."

Horn cited the influence of Pythagoras' sublime understanding of the intrinsic value of music. Pythagoras believed that the whole universe could be reduced to harmonic principles, and these could be played. "He could go through the streets of the city and play a building on the lute. He knew how to reduce the building to harmonic elements and to actually play it. Pythagoras said that basically, it's the mood that's healing. Music has the power to raise the vibrations of man, and I think that's what New Age music stands for. The mood is one of peace and quiet because that's what I am feeling. I try to get out of the way and let the music come through me, and I know it does have a beneficial effect, and people feel less tension and stress and leave the concert hall feeling good."

A committed meditator for many years, he reported, "It's probably been the most wonderful thing I've come across as a tool for growth and to stabilize my life. It's really nice to have your life get simpler and clearer. My ego's been out of the way for a long time. I have no goals, and I'm really open to the moment. The only thing that is of value in life is service. Trying to get things for yourself or your life is really rather shallow."

Horn died in 2014 at the age of 84. Having contributed to the Tony Bennett and Lady Gaga duet album *Cheek to Cheek*, following his death, she tweeted: "You will hear his genius in the flute solo of our rendition of 'Nature Boy,' a solo that will echo through the world today. And forever."

He was heard posthumously on the enchanting CD *Himalayan Sessions*, which compiled various contemplative compositions by the flutist, along with Hawai'i's Keola Beamer, and Grammy-nominated musician Christopher Hedge, interspersed with inspirational words by His Holiness the 14th Dalai Lama.

REGGAE GOT SOUL

"MANY RIVERS TO CROSS"

Jimmy Cliff

"You can see that systems all over the planet are not working. They're breaking down. The new age that is coming is going to force us to think in new ways."

"I'm just playing the role I've always played, someone who tries to combine all the forms that have made what we now call reggae," says Jamaican icon Jimmy Cliff. "Reggae is based on the indigenous music of Jamaica like mento and calypso, and the music we were exposed to like Latin music, jazz, and rhythm and blues. I helped to create reggae music, and that's my roots. I'm an innovator, always trying to be one step ahead. I describe myself as a shepherd. I've been opening many doors all over the world. I think my mission is to innovate and clear the way and set things straight."

For decades Jimmy Cliff has helped enlighten the world with music, decrying injustice and oppression, and illuminating life's struggles while encouraging faith and love.

Like Ivan, the character he played in the cult hit movie *The Harder They Come*, Cliff left his country home for the city as a teenager. Arriving in Kingston in 1962, he scored his first local hit with "Hurricane Hattie," a song inspired by a storm that swept the Caribbean. A few years later, he broke internationally, first in Brazil and then in Britain.

Best known at that time as a songwriter - Bob Dylan once praised Cliff's composition "Vietnam" as "the greatest protest song ever written."

Cliff's sublime classic "Many Rivers to Cross" inspired Jamaican film-maker Perry Henzell to offer him the lead in *The Harder They Come*." The soundtrack, which included his songs "You Can Get It If You Really Want," "Sitting In Limbo," and "Many Rivers To Cross," turned the world on to reggae.

"I didn't know it would become a cult classic," he says. "I had a big fight with the director about my character. I thought the character shouldn't have died. So he froze the frame (as Ivan is shot at the film's close), so you half expected he died."

In 1986, the reggae star appeared in the movie *Club Paradise*, with Robin Williams and Peter O'Toole, playing a musician entertaining tourists with formula music.

Did he ever work the hotel circuit in his early career? "I did that," he says, laughing. "It's one way of earning a living in Jamaica if you're not doing well as a recording artist. In the early days, before I became established, I did that scene for quite a while. I didn't enjoy it because I couldn't expand or create. I had to do the same thing every night. It's like playing Las Vegas. When artists are established and not doing anything anymore on the recording scene, they go to Las Vegas."

Growing up in Jamaica, he heard calypso and mento, while on American radio, he soaked up Latin, blues, jazz, and country. "I was exposed to all these music forms," he says. "My first recordings were built upon those influences. After I left Jamaica, I lived in England and then South America, and those environments bring all their influences into my music. Basically, I've always had a global view."

Some of his most famous songs were composed while living in England. The epic ballad "Many Rivers To Cross" was composed when he was once stranded at the Channel port of Dover. "That was one of my tries going across the Channel to work in France and Germany. So something good came out of it."

In time Cliff's songs like "Many Rivers" would be covered by Cher, Joe Cocker, and Elvis Costello, while "Limbo would be covered by Willie Nelson, Jerry Garcia, and the Neville Brothers.

In the mid-1980s, he won a Grammy for *Cliff Hanger*, and a year later, he sang on the Rolling Stone's *Dirty Work* album. Continuing to address social and political themes, on *Hanging Fire*, the catchy

"Reggae Down Babylon" addressed apartheid, while the rousing title track of *Save Our Planet Earth* in 1989 urged global consciousness.

A decade later, Cliff released the superb *Journey of a Lifetime.* "It's about our journey as human beings on this planet," he explains. "The time we spend and all the things we go through – through trials and tribulations working for purification to be one with the source of creation making the journey of a lifetime. There are songs about social, political, and religious things."

"Let it Go" suggested contending with hardships through inner transformation, while "Democracy Don't Work," decried divisive "isms" fostering social conflict. With the sublime "Higher and Deeper Love," Cliff reminded how he was invited to the Earth Summit in Rio, where he warned the assembly the world needed to embrace divine love.

"People have to learn to love deeper and higher," he emphasizes. "What are we waiting for? Do aliens have to attack before we realize we're one human race? The basis of it is love. There's a lot of ignorance."

Including material with a spiritual focus in his albums, he says, "It's something that comes naturally. It's part of my evolution. I didn't start out writing like that. I started out writing love songs and songs about social things."

A few years back, Cliff wrote a song about the prophecies in the Bible's Book of Revelation. Entering the new millennium, he felt we would experience major global change. "Historically, we see every 2,000 years there's been changes in the world. We're coming to the close of 2,000 years, so we have to expect a change. On another level, every 6,000 years, there's a change. We're coming out of one cycle now, the silver or moon cycle, and we're going into a new 6,000 years golden or sun cycle (NASA scientists Mike Xapsos and Edward A. Burke posed 6,000 year cyles in the *Solar Physics* journal in 2009).

"That means the sun is going to become hotter and closer to the earth. It's a major change, and so we're seeing a lot of things happening. The systems as we know them today are going to change. If you observe closely, you can see that systems all over the planet are not working. They're breaking down. The new age that is coming is going to force us to think in new ways."

Along with Bunny Wailer, Jimmy Cliff is one of only two living musicians to receive the Order of Merit, Jamaica's highest honor for achievements in the arts and sciences. When he was inducted into the Rock and Roll Hall of Fame in 2010, Wyclef Jean announced: "There are two people in my entire lifetime that bring a certain level to the entire Caribbean people, and we look up to them. One is Bob Marley and the other is Jimmy Cliff."

A year after his induction, Cliff released the EP *Sacred Fire*, which featured a brilliant reggae cover of Dylan's "A Hard Rain's A-Gonna Fall." He followed up with the album *Rebirth*, which won the Reggae Grammy in 2012. A jubilant return to form it included covers of Joe Higgs' "World Upside Down" and The Clash's "Guns of Brixton," which referenced Ivan in *The Harder They Come*. *PopMatters* hailed it as "a magnificent return to the roots reggae he first brought to America in the '70s."

Having moved thousands with his inspirational music Cliff recalls being especially touched by meeting a Vietnam War veteran. "One of the greatest compliments I've had in my career I met someone who'd been through the Vietnam War, and he nearly shook my hands off. He said my songs were what helped him get through the war, to live through that war.

"I can remember one lady who came up to me and said, 'I'm a teacher now, and there was a time in my life when I dropped out of school. Then I listened to your music, particularly 'You Can Get It If You Really Want,' and now I'm teaching children and your music helped me do that.' It made me feel really good like I was doing something for humanity."

"REGGAE GOT SOUL"

Toots & the Maytals

*"One day I was singing, we were just playing around,
and I said to my friend, let's do the reggay."*

"The world says that me and Bob Marley, we are the two artists in Jamaica," Frederick Nathaniel "Toots" Hibbert affirmed on Maui in 1989. "We put the music where it was supposed to be."

One of the greatest vocalists in popular music, the Jamaican legend was compared with such soul greats as Otis Redding and Wilson Pickett. Known as Jamaica's Godfather of Soul, Toots represented the purest forms of Jamaican music for decades through ska, rocksteady, and reggae. He was unique, an originator.

Though he was lauded by critics and fans, widespread popularity eluded him. "I don't get enough push from the recording company," Toots suggested. "They love me a lot and know I'm talented, but they don't know what I can do."

Toots is credited with writing in 1968, the first song which employed the word reggae - "Do the Reggay." The term was a slang expression for "raggedy everyday stuff. One day I was singing, we were just playing around, and I said to my friend, let's do the reggay."

Raised in a Seventh Day Adventist home in rural Jamaica, where he sang in a church choir as a child, with his group the Maytals, Toots initially released ska songs like "Matthew Mark" and "Six and Seven Books," reflecting his religious upbringing.

Toots and the Maytals mid-60's hits included "Bam Bam," which won Jamaica's first Popular Song Competition in 1966, and the rocksteady single "54-46 That's My Number," his anthem against injustice, recorded after Toots spent time in prison for marijuana possession. Audiences outside of Jamaica first heard his music on the soundtrack to the seminal movie *The Harder They Come*, starring Jimmy Cliff.

The landmark release of the brilliant *Funky Kingston* album in 1975 featured three of the finest reggae songs ever recorded, "Pressure Drop," "Time Tough," and "Pomp and Pride." On "Time Tough," he addressed the economic hardships of impoverished Jamaicans, while "Pressure Drop" dispensed karmic justice on the corrupt.

Reviewing *Funky Kingston,* rock critic Robert Christgau wrote in his *Rock Albums of the Seventies* guide: "He's the nearest thing to Otis Redding left on the planet."

The album contained a fantastic (maybe best) cover of the rock classic "Louie Louie," as well as a lively reworking of John Denver's "Country Roads," which Toots thought was a Ray Charles' song. "Ray Charles is my favorite singer, and I heard him sing the song," he explained. "Believing that Ray Charles wrote it, I started singing it. Then I realized it was John Denver. I have a country and western voice. I can find that voice anytime."

With *Reggae Got Soul* in 1976, Toots delivered another seminal recording, with the infectious title song, "Living in the Ghetto's" indictment of exploitation, the soulful groove of "Everybody Needs Lovin'," and a funky cover of Van Morrison's "I Shall Sing."

In order to promote his broad stylistic range, Toots traveled to Memphis, Tennessee, in 1988 to record a tribute to the classic soul sound, entitled appropriately *Toots in Memphis*. Backed by reggae's greatest rhythm section, drummer Sly Dunbar and bassist Robbie Shakespeare, Peter Tosh band guitarist Mikey Chung, and with help from some of the Muscle Shoals Rhythm Section and The Memphis Horns, Toots created a memorable blend of soul and reggae. Highlights included covers of Al Green's "Love and Happiness," which rivaled the original, Anne Peebles' "Love the Rain," and "Love Attack," popularized by James Carr.

Obviously proud of the record, he enthused: "It was the best thing I've ever done, doing all these songs written by these good songwriters. It was fun to sing them my way," adding, "from time to time they've compared me with these American artists."

Toots love for American soul music stretched back to his child-hood, when he remembered listening to American radio, enjoying gospel and soul singers such as Mahalia Jackson, Sam Cooke, Jackie

Wilson, and Ray Charles. This gospel influence flavored his early music and was evident in "Redemption Song" (not Bob Marley's song) from the *Funky Kingston* album.

A legendary live performer, his concerts were exhilarating experiences. His 1989 concert at the Maui High School gymnasium was akin to watching an incendiary James Brown show. "It's like I'm stepping on stage every time, like the first time," he said. "If I play a place for a week, people keep coming back."

Island Records founder Chris Blackwell reported in the BBC documentary *Toots and the Maytals: Reggae Got Soul,* "The Maytals were unlike anything else... sensational, raw and dynamic." This magic was captured on the 1980 album *Live,* which included a jubilant, ten-minute version of "Reggae Got Soul," and the exuberant, crowd-sing-along "54-46 That's My Number." It ranks alongside such great concert albums as Otis Redding's *Live in Europe, James Brown at the Apollo,* and Bob Marley's *Live.*

When Willie Nelson recorded the reggae album *Countryman,* he invited Toots to sing on a cover of Johnny Cash's "I'm a Worried Man." "We decided to put it out, but it needed a remix," Willie recalls. "I did a record with Toots called 'Still Is Still Moving To Me,' and we liked the mix so much we let him and his engineer do the reggae album." Willie had previously worked with Toots on his Grammy-winning *True Love* album, where the reggae great was joined by the likes of Jeff Beck, Eric Clapton, Bonnie Raitt, and Keith Richards.

Toots joined the *Playing for Change* global family of musicians in 2014, recording a new live version of "Reggae Got Soul," with help from Taj Mahal, Jamaican guitarist Ernest Ranglin, and Cuban accordionist Alex del Sol.

In late August 2020, Toots And The Maytals released *Got to Be Tough,* his first album in a decade. Blasting out righteous rocking, funky, and soulful flavored reggae and ska songs, Toots encouraged perseverance, resilience, environmental activism, and spiritual rejuvenation in his last gift to the world. Co-produced by Ringo's son, Zak Starkey, *Got to Be Tough* included an energetic cover of Bob Marley's "Three Little Birds," joined by Ziggy Marley and Ringo on percussion. *Variety* praised: "Toots Hibbert, Jamaica's answer to James Brown, is still cranking out music that sounds as fresh as his original records in the mid-1960s."

The reggae legend died in September 2020, at the age of 77, after being placed in a medically induced coma. "I will miss his smile and laughter, his genuine nature," Ziggy Marley posted on Instagram. "(Toots) was a father figure to me, his spirit is with us, his music fills us with his energy." And Mick Jagger posted: "He had such a powerful voice and on stage he always gave the audience his total energy. A sad loss to the music world."

Closing the 2011 *BBC* Toots documentary, Bonnie Raitt noted, "when you think of him, can you even stop smiling." She covered Toots' song "Love So Strong" on her latest *Just Like That* album in 2022.

"LOVE IS MY RELIGION"

Ziggy, Sharon, Damian & Rita Marley

*"Where is the revolution that will cause love?
This is the revolution we speak about."*

"People don't believe that Bob Marley played here, especially the young kids," mused promoter Tom Moffatt about the reggae icon's Maui concert at the Lahaina Civic Center on May 5, 1979. "It was a good-sized crowd but not sold out. It was the first one where they wanted some Maui Wowie. Nobody had asked about it before. It was an easy show, though one of their guys was tough. I found out later he was the one who stepped in front of the bullet when they shot Bob Marley and saved his life."

Since that memorable night, Bob Marley's children have kept the reggae flame alight in the islands, with concerts paying tribute to their father. "I've been going to Hawai'i for a lot of years, not just coming for concerts, but to relax," says Ziggy Marley." "I like the vibe in Hawai'i. I like the people, and it's a good place to meditate. The nature, the ocean reminds me of Jamaica. Hawai'i is an inspirational place for me because it's so beautiful and has so much nature."

Hanging out in Hawai'i, Ziggy was inspired to celebrate the islands' natural beauty on his Grammy-winning album *Love Is My Religion,* singing about a favored "Beach in Hawaii," joined by 'ukulele virtuoso Jake Shimabukuro, strumming on the song.

A few years later, he gave Maui a plug on "Get Out of Town" from his 2011 album *Wild and Free,* singing about escaping the world's burdens to Maui or Fiji. "I keep coming back to Maui and Hawai'i," he says, chuckling.

Of all Bob Marley's offspring, Ziggy most resembles his legendary father in terms of raw talent, creative vision, and utopian spiritualism. From his earliest days fronting the Melody Makers, Ziggy's passionate idealism, penetrating perspective, and youthful optimism brought hope to those who had been galvanized by the revolutionary music of his father. He called for a revolution on *Wild and Free*, but he wasn't talking about storming the streets. The oldest son of Bob Marley suggested a quieter, yet no less profound, internal revolution.

Recalling the lyrical fire of his father and driven by a martial drumbeat, Ziggy urged a "Personal Revolution" on one of the album's most potent songs. "It's an evolution of the idea of what revolution is," Ziggy explains. "It's a consciousness. Throughout history, we've had revolutions, mostly political and social. But there's one revolution that seems to be not happening, and that's a personal revolution where human beings evolve and change from within their own selves. Why can't this world live in peace? Why can't we love each other? Where is that revolution that will have that effect on the world? Where is the revolution that will cause love? This is the revolution we speak about.

"The most important thing and the reason why we have not been able to solve the economic, social, and political thing is because we haven't had that spiritual revolution that we need," he continues. "There has to be a balance. We have to understand how to love each other before we can solve all the other problems in the world. Do you want us to keep on repeating history? Every few years, there's another dictator, there's another greedy Wall Street tycoon and corporations who don't care for the people. We're going to keep having these problems unless human beings change."

In his own unique way, Ziggy has furthered his father's legacy as a messenger of truth. Encouraging awakening consciousness, he has promoted unity through spreading uplifting messages of love. And not beholden to popular trends, he continues to craft what he calls "real music that grooves" with a spiritual element.

On *Wild and Free,* he also addressed the evolution of his life and family issues on the "Roads Less Traveled." I've done a lot of things outside of the box, even within my own family culture," he explains. "I left Jamaica and I lived by myself, and took some different roads. I think I've learnt from the mistakes of my father in terms of having a lot of women. I don't follow those roads. I follow my own path."

Ziggy has continued to expose exploitation and injustice, most recently condemning petroleum exploration in an ecologically sensitive region of Namibia. "The war against the planet and life itself is still being waged by greedy corporations who will stop at nothing and for nothing to fill their pockets," he posted on Instagram.

Years before Bob Marley rose to prominence, Ziggy's mother Rita Marley established her own successful music career in Jamaica with the female group The Soulettes. "They were the biggest, the Supremes of Jamaica," she enthuses. "We got reviews like The Soulettes top the Four Tops. We did a lot of covers, and people thought we were foreigners. As a female group, we were ahead of Bob. It was more of a struggle for them as rude boys trying to make an impression in Jamaica."

Born in Cuba and raised in Kingston's Trenchtown, Rita first met Bob when she was 18, and he was 19. They married in 1966 and began working together on stage in 1974. Rita teamed with Marcia Griffiths and Judy Mowatt, Jamaica's leading female vocalists, to form the famous I Three harmony trio who backed Bob and the Wailers. "We were all friends who had individual careers," Rita recalls. "We got a chance to meet, and Bob said, why don't we come and do this thing. It was a new sound, a new everything. We hit the road in '74, and it was continuous touring and having the reviews and crowds. We had a message that made sense."

Ziggy and the Melody Makers featuring his siblings Stephen, Sharon, and Cedella Marley, made their first record in 1977, with the Bob Marley penned protest song "Children Playing in the Streets." They reinvented themselves 20 years later with *Spirit of Music*, a radical departure from the band's familiar music, forging a more earthy, fundamental sound that at times was colored by the likes of Taj Mahal on harmonica, John Lennon band drummer Jim Keltner, and trumpeter Mark Isham. "It shows a new time and age," Sharon Marley explained. "It's like a metamorphosis. We're moving on. You have to grow. We had to grow up."

As a backup singer and dancer on the front line of the group, Sharon said, "I think of myself as a vessel which is being used to carry this message. People tell me you're a strong Black woman, and you can dance and sing, but that's all just a part of the outside. To me, what's on the inside is more important, the vibes that I need to get out."

Like their father, the Marley siblings imbued their music with a spiritual core, seeking to inspire and uplift. "I believe so much in God having things already arranged," said Sharon. "It's all planned, and we're just living on this sea of life that God has given us. You have to be open to this spiritual concept, otherwise, you're going to go through life so depressed and stressed, and trying to make things work, and disappointed that things didn't happen. You have to understand that you don't have 100 percent control. You have to let it flow. Just open your eyes and look within because there are so many distractions without.

"You never know what God has planned for you. Some people were born to be leaders and make changes, and they don't even know it. I'm sure Bob couldn't tell anybody he was going to be selling millions of records. Nobody from where he came from would have believed him. There were a lot of Jamaican radio stations that refused to play his songs in the '70s because he was a Rastafarian."

Damien "Jr. Gong" Marley was only two when his father died. Raised by his mother, Cindy Breakspeare, it was natural that he would follow in the footsteps of his father and siblings. At the age of 13, he formed his first band, The Shepherds, and by 2001, he had won his first Grammy. Then came the brilliant *Welcome to Jamrock*, which won him a Grammy for Best Reggae Album and another for Best Urban/ Alternative Performance. He was especially pleased to win a non-reggae award. "I want to be stepping toward, speaking about reggae winning Grammys outside of just the reggae category," he reports.

Armed with an air horn, an Ini Kamoze sample, and a gritty tale of life in Jamaica, Damian made a huge splash with his massive single "Welcome to Jamrock." The rough reggae-meets-hip-hop track dominated urban radio during the summer of 2005. Not since Shabba Ranks had a Jamaican artist made such an impact on mainstream American radio. "A lot of Jamaicans face struggle, and that's what it's about," he notes.

In 2011, he became part of the SuperHeavy project with Mick Jagger, Joss Stone, Dave Stewart, and Indian Bollywood composer A. R. Rahman. He was highly praised as the star vocalist of the ensemble.

Damian's *Stony Hill* album won him another Grammy. It was full of fierce, in-your-face reggae decrying the ills of the modern world. As a son of Jamaica's greatest artist, Damian says, "the biggest blessing is the family, the whole legacy and heritage. We have one of the greatest examples to follow. My father laid a foundation, an infrastructure that we could plug our thing into."

Just like his father, he feels a mission to inspire and uplift and provide a voice for the oppressed. "I use music as a means of communicating about what my thoughts and ideas are about the issues that face my generation today," he explains. "It's communication to learn from each other and uplift life globally. Music can transcend a lot of barriers. Ultimately people have to make the change, but music helps to influence people."

And like his father, Damian extols the virtues of the Rastafari culture. "Some think it's a religion, but it's really a lifestyle. So we're trying to communicate through music. Music influences the younger generation and the way they live, like with hip-hop, they dress like their favorite hip-hop artist. We try to look at things positively, but if you have someone listening to all this hardcore music and you come with too much flowers and daisies, it's not going to work. I hope people learn the message of Rastafari, and of course, good vibes to dance."

The life of Bob Marley was celebrated in the definitive biography of the reggae icon, *Marley*, which premiered at the Berlin Film Festival in 2012. It included newly unearthed performance footage, home movies, and some unreleased Wailers' music like a gospel rendition of "No Woman, No Cry," with Peter Tosh on piano.

Ziggy was one of the doc's executive producers and reports some of the material was even a revelation for him and his siblings. "There were things I wasn't aware of, especially in the early days, and some stuff in the latter days. Especially emotional for us was the period when he was sick and went to Germany. Us children didn't know much about that. It was definitely emotional and an eye-opening experience."

Still feeling a strong connection with his father, Ziggy reveals, "I talk to my father almost every day. As I grow, I learn more about him. I understand more things. I have a much closer relationship now. He left when I was 12, but the relationship didn't stop at that time. The more I've got into trying to explore spirituality, the more the relationship grew, and the more I realize the existence outside of the material and physical. So the relationship is very strong. I tell people it's a brother-hood now. It's not a child to a father. We're brothers now that come from the same mental state, that free-thinking mind."

BIBLIOGRAPHY

INTRODUCTION

Smith, Andrew. "Jeff Beck, solo voyager." *The Sunday Times*, Feb. 7, 2010.
https://www.thetimes.co.uk/article/jeff-beck-solo-voyager-gq58tc95z6p
"The Best Gigs Ever," *Q Magazine*, Sept. 1996. www.rocklistmusic.co.uk/
qlistspage2.html#Gigs
Townshend, Pete. "Gustav Metzger 1926-2017." *Pete's Blog*, March 2, 2017.
www.thewho.com/petes-blog/gustav-metzger-1926-2017/

MAUI NO KA OI

George Harrison

Harrison, George, Taylor, Derek, and Harrison, Olivia. *I Me Mine: The Extended
Edition,* Genesis Publications, 2017.
Harrison, Olivia. *Walking Down Rainhill,* liner notes. Hitchhike Records, 2004.
Thomson, Graeme. *George Harrison: Behind the Locked Door.* Omnibus Press, 2015.
Kahn, Ashley. *George Harrison on George Harrison.* Chicago Review Press, 2020
Brown, Mick. "A conversation with George Harrison."
Rolling Stone, April 19, 1979. www.rollingstone.com/music/
music-news/a-conversation-with-george-harrison-190204/.

Fleetwood Mac

Michaels, Sean. "Fleetwood Mac ready to begin recording?" The Guardian, Jan. 28,
2014. www.theguardian.com/music/2014/jan/28/fleetwood-mac-back-in-studio-2014
"Sounds of the 70s with Johnnie Walker." BBC2. Feb. 7, 2021.
https://www.bbc.co.uk/sounds/play/m000s1by

Willie Nelson

Nelson, Willie. *The Tao of Willie: A Guide to the Happiness in Your Heart.* Avery, 2007
Nelson, Willie and Ritz, David. *It's A Long Story: My Life.* Little, Brown and
Company, 2015.
Hall, Michael. "Willie's God! Willie's God! We love him!" *Texas Monthly,* May
2008. https://www.texasmonthly.com/arts-entertainment/willies-god-willies-god-
we-love-willie/
Gilmore, Mikal. "Willie Nelson's That's Life." *Medium,* Jan. 13, 2021.
https://legacyrecordings.medium.com/willie-nelsons-that-s-life-c0f1d0f0840

Prince

Shahidi, Afshin. *Prince in Hawaii: An Intimate Portrait of an Artist.* NPG Music Club, 2004.
"Interview with George Benson - Absolutely Famous." *Guitar.com*, March 9, 2010. https://guitar.com/features/interview-with-george-benson-absolutely-famous/

Paul Simon

"100 Greatest Songwriters of All Time." *Rolling Stone*, Aug. 6, 2017. www.rollingstone.com/interactive/lists-100-greatest-songwriters/

The Beach Boys

McCartney, Paul. *BBC Radio 1*, 2007 www.bbc.co.uk/programmes/articles/fVgTN 5Z7RF8xRztCmkHh3H/god-only-knows
The Beach Boys - *The Smile Sessions,* liner notes. Capitol Records, 2011. https://archive.org/details/the-beach-boys-the-smile-sessions-book-small-pages-deleted/page/n5/mode/2up
Sharp, Ken. "Al Jardine A Beach Boy Still Riding the Waves." Goldmine, July 28, 2000. https://troun.tripod.com/al.html
Kent, Nick. *The Dark Stuff: Selected Writings On Rock Music.* DaCapo Press, 2002.
Williams, Richard. "Beach Boys: A Reappraisal." *Melody Maker*, May 22, 1971.
Wilson, Brian. *Pet Sounds Box Intro.* Capitol Records, 1997. http://albumlinernotes.com/Pet_Sounds_Box_Intro.html
Wilson, Brian. *Friends*, liner notes. Capitol Records, 2001 reissue. http://www.albumlinernotes.com/Friends___20_20.html
John, Elton. *Carl And The Passions - So Tough,* liner notes. Capitol Records/Brother Records, 2000 CD reissue.
Perkins, Dave. *God Only Knows: Faith, Hope, Love, and The Beach Boys.* Cascade Books, 2015.
"The 50 Greatest Beach Boys Songs." *Mojo,* June 2012.
Leaf, David. "Brian Wilson Reissue" liner notes, 2000. http://albumlinernotes.com/Brian_Wilson__Reissue_.html

Santana

Santana, Carlos, and Kahn, Ashley. *The Universal Tone: Bringing My Story to Light.* Little, Brown, 2014.
"Africa Speaks" review. *Mojo*, July, 2019.
Grow, Kory. "Santana Explore New Musical Freedom." *Rolling Stone*, June 7, 2019. www.rollingstone.com/music/music-album-reviews/santana-africa-speaks-album-review-845131/

George Benson

Dingwall, John. "Jazz legend George Benson tells how a mysterious Scottish duke 'paid him for a recording session." *Daily Record*, June 17, 2016. www.dailyrecord. co.uk/entertainment/music/music-news/jazz-legend-george-benson-tells-8214815

Steely Dan

www.steelydan.com/#!/bio
sdarchive.com/grammymemo.html
Limbong, Andrew. "Remembering Walter Becker Of Steely Dan." *NPR*, Sept. 4, 2017. www.npr.org/2017/09/04/548415553/remembering-walter-becker-of-steely-dan
"Walter Becker - 1950 - 2017." *Guitarist*, Oct, 2017. www.magzter.com/article/ Music/Guitarist/Walter-Becker-1950-2017.
Steely Dan Induction. Rock & Roll Hall of Fame, 2001. www.rockhall.com/ inductees/steely-dan

Aerosmith

"100 Greatest Singers of All Time." *Rolling Stone*, Nov. 27, 2008. www.rollingstone. com/music/music-lists/100-greatest-singers-of-all-time-147019/steven-tyler-3-35332/.
Fujimoto, Lila. "Steven Tyler: 'I'm very grateful for being sober'." *The Maui News*, Feb. 16, 2018. www.mauinews.com/news/local-news/2018/02/steven-tyler-im-very-grateful-for-being-sober/

Alice Cooper

Weatherley, Mike. "Alice Cooper and Mike Weatherley MP Meet to Rock the House." Oct. 24, 2001. www.mikeweatherley.com/2011/10/24/alice-cooper-and-mike-weatherley-mp-meet-to-%E2%80%98rock-the-house%E2%80%99/.
"But Alice is a Clean Liver Mr. Abse." *Record Mirror*, June 2, 1973. www. alicecooperechive.com/articles/feature/remi/730602.
Sellers, Christian. "Public Animal #9 – When Mary Whitehouse Tried to Censor Alice Cooper." *Love It Loud*, Oct. 20, 2020. http://love-it-loud.co.uk/ public-animal-no-9-when-mary-whitehouse-tried-to-censor-alice-cooper/
Gordon, Shep. *They Call Me Supermensch: A Backstage Pass to the Amazing Worlds of Film, Food, and Rock'n'Roll*. Anthony Bourdain/Ecco, 2015.
Jeffries, Stuart. "Ban This Filth!" *The Guardian*, Oct. 26, 2012. www.theguardian. com/books/2012/oct/26/ban-this-filth-ben-thompson-review
Cooper, Alice. *Alice Cooper, Golf Monster: A Rock 'n' Roller's 12 Steps to Becoming a Golf Addict*. Three Rivers Press, 2018.

Sammy Hagar

Hagar, Sammy. *Red: My Uncensored Life in Rock*. It Books, 2011.

Jimi Hendrix

Mabbs, Valerie. "Hendrix Happy With U.S. Scene." *Record Mirror*, July 11, 1970.
"Hendrix Concert on Maui hummms." *Honolulu Advertiser*, July 31, 1970.
Cooper, Alice. *Nights with Alice Cooper*. Nov. 19, 2020.
https://bravewords.com/news/alice-cooper-eddie-kramer-and-billy-cox-discuss-jimi-hendrix-experience-live-in-maui-release-video
Knight, Curtis. *Starchild*. Inner Light - Global Communications, 1992.
Roby, Steve. *Straight Ahead Magazine,* October/November 1995 Vol. 79/80.
newyorkcityhendrix.gobot.com/whats_new.html
Wood, Ben. *Honolulu Star-Bulletin,* May 31, 1969
Glebbeek, Caesar. "Jimi Plays Hawaii 1969." www.univibes.com/Jimi_Plays_Hawaii1969.html
Johnson, Robert. "film crew expecting spaceships on Maui." *The Sunday Star Bulletin & Advertiser,* Aug. 2. 1970.
Perry, Shawn. "Jimi Hendrix Experience Music, Money, Madness . . . Jimi Hendrix In Maui & Live In Maui." *Vintage Rock*. https://vintagerock.com/jimi-hendrix-experience-music-money-madness-jimi-hendrix-in-maui-live-in-maui/
Cross, Charles R. *Room Full of Mirrors: A Biography of Jimi Hendrix*. Hachette Books, 2006.
Lawrence, Sharon. *Jimi Hendrix: The Man, the Magic, the Truth*. It Books, 2005.
Cox, Billy. *Guitar Player*, May 1989.
Nailen, Dan. "Life-Changing Experience." *Inlander*, Feb. 16, 2017. www.inlander.com/spokane/life-changing-experience/Content?oid=3005799
Shapiro, Harry, and Glebbeek, Caesar. *Jimi Hendrix: Electric Gypsy*. St. Martin's Griffin, 1995.

ROCK & ROLL MUSIC

Bo Diddley

Sullivan, Ed. www.edsullivan.com/artists/bo-diddley
Weingarten, Marc. *Station to Station: The Secret History of Rock & Roll on Television*. Gallery Books, 2000.
Farley, Christopher John. "Elvis Rocks. But He's Not the First." *Time*, July 6, 2004. http://content.time.com/time/arts/article/0,8599,661084,00.html
Fuentes, Jerry. "The Biggest Rock N Roll Show of '56." *A Rock n' Roll Historian*. Feb. 1, 2016. http://rnrhistorian.blogspot.com/2016/02/the-biggest-rock-n-roll-show-of-1956.html

The Legend of Bo Diddley. Directed by Gary A. Sherman. Mar Ken Enterprises, 1966.
Strauss, Neil. "The Indestructible Beat of Bo Diddley." *Rolling Stone*, Aug. 25, 2005.
www.rollingstone.com/music/music-news/the-indestructible-beat-of-bo-diddley-59117/
Leverenz, David. *Honor Bound: Race and Shame in America.* Rutgers University
Press, 2012.
Eder, Bruce. "The Duchess Biography." *AllMusic.* www.allmusic.com/artist/the-
duchess-mn0000212595
Wawzenek, Bryan. "When the Clash Finally Played Their First U.S. Show." *Ultimate
Classic Rock*, Feb. 7, 2019. https://ultimateclassicrock.com/clash-first-u-s-show/
"Bo Diddley, the guitarist who inspired the Rolling Stones, dies." *London Evening
Standard*, June 3, 2008. www.standard.co.uk/news/bo-diddley-the-guitarist-who-
inspired-the-rolling-stones-dies-6837140.html

Carl Perkins

Kornhaber, Spencer. "Did Rock and Roll Pacify America?" *The Atlantic*, July 11,
2015. www.theatlantic.com/entertainment/archive/2015/07/rock-and-roll-opiate-
of-the-masses-1964-atlantic-archive-piece/398180/
Surdam, David George. "Under the influence of rock'n'roll." *OUPblog*, April 14,
2015. https://blog.oup.com/2015/04/rock-and-roll-history/
"Frank Sinatra denounces rock n roll in 1957."
http://listserv.linguistlist.org/pipermail/ads-l/2012-July/120706.html
Cott, Jonathan. *Bob Dylan: The Essential Interviews.* Simon & Schuster, 2017.
"Matchbox." *Beatles Music History.* http://www.beatlesebooks.com/matchbox
McGee, David. "Stars Turn Out For Rockabilly King Carl Perkins' Funeral." *MTV.
Com*, Jan. 26, 1998. http://www.mtv.com/news/2805/stars-turn-out-for-rockabilly-
king-carl-perkins-funeral/
"Rock stars pay tribute to Perkins." *SouthCoastToday*, Jan. 25, 1998.
www.southcoasttoday.com/article/19980125/news/301259899

Johnnie Johnson/Chuck Berry

Schoemer, Karen. "A Diffident Rock Stylist Whose Just Starting at 67." *New York
Times*, Aug. 2, 1991. www.nytimes.com/1991/08/02/arts/pop-jazz-a-diffident-rock-
stylist-w ho-s-just-starting-at-67.html
Helmore, Edward. "'Johnny B Goode' takes his revenge." *The Guardian*, March 4,
2001. www.theguardian.com/world/2001/mar/04/theobserver
"Chuck Berry Sued By Pianist Over Royalties." *Chicago Tribune*, Dec. 6, 2000.
www.chicagotribune.com/news/ct-xpm-2000-12-06-0012070013-story.html
"Chuck Berry plays tribute to Johnnie Johnson." *CBC Arts*, April 15, 2005
https://www.cbc.ca/news/entertainment/
chuck-berry-plays-tribute-to-johnnie-johnson-1.559275

McDermott, Kevin. "Groundbreaking soldier and bluesman Johnnie 'B. Goode' Johnson posthumously awarded Congressional Gold Medal." *St. Louis Post-Dispatch*, Nov. 28, 2016.
Holliday, Art. *Johnnie Bee Good*. (in production) https://jjthemovie.com/

Yoko Ono & John Lennon

"Lennon's art showed a sick mind, said Yard." The Guardian, Jan. 26, 2001 www.theguardian.com/uk/2001/jan/26/freedomofinformation.thebeatles
The Beatles. *The Beatles Anthology.* Chronicle Books, 2000.
Ali, Tariq. "Power to the People!" *Red Mole*, March 22, 1971. Reprinted in Tariq Ali's 2005 book *Streetfighting Years*. www.beatlesinterviews.org/db1971.0121.beatles.html
Watts, Michael. "John and Yoko: A Press Conference at Apple." *Melody Maker*, Oct. 2, 1971. www.beatlesinterviews.org/db1971.1002.beatles.html
Graustark, Barbara. "The Real John Lennon." *Newsweek*, Sept. 29, 1980. http://www.beatlesinterviews.org/db1980.0929.beatles.html
Dolan, Leah. "Yoko Ono broadcasts global message of peace every night for a month." *CNN*, March 4, 2022. www.cnn.com/style/article/yoko-ono-imagine-peace-broadcast/index.html

Yes

Blaney, John. *John Lennon: Listen To This Book*. Paper Jukebox, 2017
Welch, Chris. *Close to the Edge: The Story of Yes*. Omnibus Press, 2003
"Tales from Topographic Oceans." http://yesworld.com/discography/tales-topographic-oceans/#ad29caa75aa81abd2

Neil Young

Brower, Andrea. "Hawai'i: GMO Ground Zero." *Capitalism Nature Socialism*, Volume 27, 2016. www.tandfonline.com/doi/abs/10.1080/10455752.2015.11 12420?journalCode=rcns20
Chow, Lorraine. "Neil Young and Monsanto Reignite War Over GMOs Since Release of 'Seeding Fear.' *EcoWatch*, July 25, 2015. www.organicconsumers.org/news/neil-young-and-monsanto-reignite-war-over-gmos-release-seeding-fear
Young, Neil. *Waging Heavy Peace: A Hippie Dream*. Blue Rider Press, 2012.

Gregg Allman

Allman, Gregg and Light, Alan. *My Cross to Bear.* William Morrow and Company, 2012.
Staunton, Terry. "Gregg Allman - Southern Blood album review." *Louder*, Sept. 6, 2017. https://www.loudersound.com/reviews/gregg-allman-southern-blood-album-review.

TROUBADOURS

Harry Belafonte

Hart, John (South Carolina senator). *The Index-Journal*, April 18, 1957.
Roosevelt, Eleanor. *My Day*, nationally syndicated column, Oct. 20, 1958.
Belafonte, Harry, and Shnayerson, Michael. *My Song: A Memoir of Art, Race, and Defiance*. Knopf 2011.
Hales, Larry. "Hip Hop and the Cuban Revolution." *Workers World*, Oct. 8, 2017.
www.workers.org/2007/world/hip-hop-1011/
Lynn Norment. *Ebony Magazine*, Sept. 1996.

Joan Baez

Baez, Joan. "Joan Baez's Rock Hall Speech." *Vulture*, April 8, 2017
www.vulture.com/2017/04/read-joan-baezs-powerful-political-rock-hall-speech.html
Hajdu, David. *Positively 4th Street*: The *Lives and Times of Joan Baez, Bob Dylan, Mimi Baez Fariña, and Richard Fariña*. Picador, 2011.

Buffy Saint-Marie

Zoladz, Lindsay. "Buffy Saint-Marie Illuminations." *Pitchfork*, Feb. 9, 2020.
https://pitchfork.com/reviews/albums/buffy-sainte-marie-illuminations/
Warner, Andrea. *Buffy Sainte-Marie: The Authorized Biography*. Greystone Books, 2018.
Locke, Jesse. "Buffy Sainte-Marie reflects on Illuminations." *musicworks*, issue 135.
www.musicworks.ca/profile/buffy-sainte-marie-reflects-illuminations
Statement from Morrissey, March 29, 2008. www.morrissey-solo.com/threads/
statement-from-mozzery.85571/
Powers, Ann. "Review: Buffy Sainte-Marie, 'Power In The Blood.'" *NPR*, May 3, 2015.
www.npr.org/2015/05/03/403277165/
first-listen-buffy-sainte-marie-power-in-the-blood
Warner, Andrea. "Is Buffy Sainte-Marie's Power in the Blood the defining record of our time?" *CBC Music*, Dec. 3, 2015. www.cbc.ca/music/is-buffy-sainte-marie-s-power-in-the-blood-the-defining-record-of-our-time-1.5402421

Crosby, Stills & Nash

Runtagh, Jordan. "15 Legendary Unreleased Albums." *Rolling Stone*, Aug. 30, 2019.
https://www.rollingstone.com/music/music-lists/15-legendary-unreleased-albums-67688/
"CSN Box Set Tracklist." AlbumLinerNotes.com. http://aln3.albumlinernotes.com/
CSN_Box_Set_Tracklist.html
Nash, Graham. *Wild Tales: A Rock & Roll Life*. Crown Archetype, 2013.

Crosby, David. *Stand and Be Counted: A Revealing History of Our Times Through the Eyes of the Artists Who Helped Change Our World.* HarperOne, 2000.

Bonnie Raitt

Richardson, Mark. "'Just Like That . . .' by Bonnie Raitt Review: Still Vital." *The Wall Street Journal*, April 18, 2022.

James Taylor

"100 Greatest Singers of All Time." *Rolling Stone*, Nov. 27, 2008. www.rollingstone.com/music/music-lists/100-greatest-singers-of-all-time-147019/james-taylor-2-41790/
McCartney, Paul. Rock & Roll Hall of Fame. www.rockhall.com/inductees/james-taylor

Jimmy Buffett

Feldman, Dana. "How Jimmy Buffett Turned Hit Song 'Margaritaville' Into A Multibillion-Dollar Empire." *Forbes*, Aug. 10, 2017. www.forbes.com/sites/danafeldman/2017/08/10/how-jimmy-buffett-turned-hit-song-margaritaville-into-a-multibillion-dollar-empire/?sh=6a1461ce6a49

Rickie Lee Jones

Coleman, Nick. "Rickie Lee Jones, Balm in Gilead." *Independent*, Nov.1, 2009. www.independent.co.uk/arts-entertainment/music/reviews/album-rickie-lee-jones-balm-in-gilead-fantasy-1813033.html
Williamson, Nigel. "Rickie Lee Jones – The Other Side Of Desire." *Uncut*, July 6, 2015. www.uncut.co.uk/reviews/rickie-lee-jones-the-other-side-of-desire-69530/

CALIFORNIA DREAMING

The Byrds

Dylan, Bob. *Chronicles: Volume One.* Simon & Schuster, 2004.
Fricke, David. *Sweetheart of the Rodeo,* liner notes. Sony Music Entertainment, 2003. http://albumlinernotes.com/Sweetheart_Of_The_Rodeo.html

The Doors

The Doors. "Honolulu International Center - 7/20/1968." *MildEquater. com.* http://mildequator.com/performancehistory/concertinfo/1968/680720.html

Davis, Stephen. *Jim Morrison: Life, Death, Legend.* Gotham Books, 2004.
The Doors. "Honolulu International Center - 7/4/1969." *MildEquater. com.*
http://mildequator.com/performancehistory/concertinfo/cancelled/690704-05.html
Hagen, Joe. "Maharishi Mahesh Yogi Obituary." *Rolling Stone*, March 6, 2008.
DiCillo, Tom. *When You're Strange.* Rhino Entertainment, 2009.

Jefferson Airplane

Slick, Grace. *Somebody to Love?: A Rock-and-Roll Memoir.* Virgin Books, 1999.
Wood, Ben. "Airplane picks up fare for 20,000 fans." *Honolulu Star-Bulletin,* March 12, 1969.
"Marijuana Charge Grounds Jefferson Airplane Crewman." *Honolulu Star-Bulletin,* Oct. 20, 1969. https://www.newspapers.com/clip/37378938/honolulu-star-bulletin/
Kaukonen, Jorma. "Damn Few Left." *Cracks in the Finish*, Jan. 29, 2016. http://jormakaukonen.com/cracksinthefinish/?p=5324
Kaukonen, Jorma. "Now We Are Three. *Cracks in the Finish*, Sept. 29, 2018. http://jormakaukonen.com/cracksinthefinish/?p=7426

Grateful Dead

Shapiro, Michael. "Back from the Dead." *Hana Hou!* December 2019/January 2020. https://hanahou.com/22.6/back-from-the-dead

Woodstock

Slick, Grace. *Somebody to Love?* Virgin Books, 1999.
Goodman, Barak. *Woodstock: Three Days That Defined a Generation.* PBS, 2019.

SUNDOWN IN NASHVILLE

Charley Pride

Cantwell, David. "What Country Music Owes to Charley Pride. *The New Yorker*, Feb. 22, 2019. www.newyorker.com/culture/culture-desk/what-country-music-owes-to-charley-pride.
Rader, Dotson. "Willie Nelson: 'Three Chords and the Truth - That's What a Country Song Is.'" *Parade*, June 27, 2010. https://parade.com/49964/dotsonrader/willie-nelson-2/
Dennis, Paul W. "Music in My Heart" review. *My Kind of Country*, Aug. 24, 2017. mykindofcountry.wordpress.com/2017/08/24/album-review-charley-pride-music-in-my-heart/.
Pride Charley, Henderson, Jim. *Pride: The Charley Pride Story.* William Morrow & Co, 1994.

Parton, Dolly. *Twitter* post, Dec. 12, 2020
https://twitter.com/DollyParton/status/1337864068821102592?ref_src=twsrc%5
Egoogle%7Ctwcamp%5Eserp%7Ctwgr%5Etweet
Yearwood, Trisha. *Twitter* post, Dec. 12, 2020.
https://twitter.com/trishayearwood/status/1337900133074219018?ref_src=twsrc
%5Egoogle%7Ctwcamp%5Eserp%7Ctwgr%5Etweet

Crystal Gayle

Jurek, Thom. "Crystal Gayle Sings the Heart & Soul of Hoagy Carmichael review."
AllMusic. www.allmusic.com/album/crystal-gayle-sings-the-heart-soul-of-hoagy-
carmichael-mw0000670931

Miranda Lambert

Paul, John. "Miranda Lambert The Weight of These Wings." *PopMatters*,
Dec. 7, 2016. www.popmatters.com/miranda-lambert-the-weight-of-these-
wings-2495406173.html
Dolan, Jon. "Miranda Lambert's Wildcard Is a Country-Rock Masterpiece." *Rolling
Stone,* Nov. 1, 2019. www.rollingstone.com/music/music-album-reviews/miranda-
lamberts-wildcard-is-a-freewheeling-country-rock-masterpiece-901904/
MacIntosh, Dan. "Hell of a Holiday." *Country Standrad Time*. www.countrystan
dardtime.com/d/cdreview.asp?xid=7428

Sara Evans

Erlewine, Stephen Thomas. "Slow Me Down." *AllMusic*. www.allmusic.com/album/
slow-me-down-mw0002609123
Tucker, Ken. "Sara Evans: Country Power Ballads With A Punch." *NPR*, March 20,
2014. www.npr.org/transcripts/291883955?storyId=291883955
Watson, Jada. "New Study: Gender Representation on Country Music Radio."
SongData, April 20, 2019. https://songdata.ca/2019/04/20/new-study-gender-
representation-on-country-music-radio/
Parton, Chris. "New Music: May 2020." *Nashville Lifestyles,* May 7, 2020.
https://nashvillelifestyles.com/entertainment/music/new-music-may-2020/

MELE O HAWAI'I

Henry Kapono

Chinen, Nate. "Hawaiian Music Star, Maker of Hybrid Hits." *The New York Times*,
Feb. 7, 2007. www.nytimes.com/2007/02/07/arts/music/07kapo.html

Willie K

Cooper, Alice. *Facebook* tribute, May 21, 2020.
www.facebook.com/nightswithalicecooper/photos/what-a-unique-privilege-to-have-known-the-late-great-willie-k-god-gave-him-the-h/2971381702916557/
Tyler, Steven. *Instagram* tribute, May 20, 2020.
www.instagram.com/p/CAZZQ-1hhJk/?utm_source=ig_embed

Kalani Pe'a

"2022 Grammy Awards: Complete live results and notable moments." *Riff Magazine,* April 3, 2022. https://riffmagazine.com/news/2022-grammy-awards-live-results/
Leger, Devon. "5 Stories from the 2017 Grammys You Might Have Missed." *Paste* magazine, Feb. 23, 2017. www.pastemagazine.com/music/grammy-awards/5-stories-from-the-2017-grammys-you-might-have-mis/

Jake Shimabukuro

May, Brian. "Brian May Praises Virtuoso Jake Shimabukuro." https://shorefire.com/releases/entry/brian-may-praises-virtuoso-jake-shimabukuros-exquisite-ukulele-playing1

TAKE ME TO THE RIVER

Smokey Robinson

Christian, Margena A. "Smokey Robinson, The Poet Laureate of Soul,' Celebrates 50 Years of Music." *Jet,* April 2, 2007.
Hunter, Charlayne. "Last Do-Wah Played by Smokey Robinson." *The New York Times,* June 1, 1972. https://www.nytimes.com/1972/06/01/archives/last-dowah-played-by-smokey-robinson.htmlObama, Barack. "Remarks by the President at 'In Performance At The White House: The Motown Sound.'" The White House, Feb. 24, 2011. https://obamawhitehouse.archives.gov/the-press-office/2011/02/24/remarks-president-performance-white-house-motown-sound
McCartney, Paul. *The Beatles Anthology.* Chronicle Books, 2000.
Kahn, Ashley. *George Harrison on George Harrison: Interviews and Encounters.* Chicago Review Press, 2020.
"The Soul of Smokey." *The Oakland Press*, April 18, 2004. www.theoaklandpress.com/2004/04/18/the-soul-of-smokey/
Robinson, Smokey and Ritz, David. *Smokey: Inside My Life.* McGraw-Hill, 1989.

The Supremes

Wilson, Mary & Bego, Mark. *Supreme Glamour.* Thames & Hudson, 2019.
"Rock 'n' Roll: The Sound of the Sixties." *Time*, May 21, 1965.
http://content.time.com/time/subscriber/article/0,33009,901728-6,00.html
Knight, Jack. "Ex-Supreme rejected in Motown suit." *Detroit Free Press*, Oct. 29, 1971.
http://tracy_prinze.tripod.com/atributetomotown/id24.html
Benjaminson, Peter. *The Lost Supreme: The Life of Dreamgirl Florence Ballard.*
Chicago Review Press, 2008.
Kisner, Ronald. "Florence Ballard: Ex-Supreme Fights To Get Off Welfare." *Jet*, Feb.
20, 1975.
Cosgrove, Stuart. *Detroit 67: The Year That Changed Soul.* Clayton Media and
Publishing, 2015.
Ross, Diana. *Twitter* post, Feb. 9, 2021.
https://twitter.com/DianaRoss/status/1359107845623455753?s=20
Staunton, Terry. "Mary Wilson - The Motown Anthology." *Ucut*, Jan. 14, 2022.

Earth, Wind & Fire

White, Maurice, Powell, Herb. *My Life with Earth, Wind & Fire.* HarperCollins, 2016.
Bailey, Trenton H. "Kemetic Consciousness: A study of ancient Egyptian themes in
the lyrics and visual art of Earth, Wind & Fire, 1973-1983." Ph.D. dissertation,
Dec. 2017. https://radar.auctr.edu/islandora/object/cau.td%3A2017_bailey_trenton
(a brilliant analysis of ancient Egyptian influences on the band's lyrics and imagery).
Kravitz, Lenny. *Facebook*, Feb. 4, 2016.
https://m.facebook.com/lennykravitz/posts/10153910565128390

Chaka Khan

Simonart, Serge. "The Artist in NYC." *Guitar World*, Oct. 1998.
https://sites.google.com/site/themusicinterviewarchive/prince/prince-1998-guitar-
world-interview
Wilman, Chris. "Chaka Khan: 'If I Can Inspire Anybody to Do Themselves,
I'm Happy.'" *Variety*, Oct. 11, 2019. https://variety.com/2019/music/news/
chaka-khan-speech-variety-power-women-luncheon-1203368199/
Morris, Damian. "Chaka Khan: Hello Happiness review – a consistent sizzler." The
Observer, Fe.17, 2019. www.theguardian.com/music/2019/feb/17/chaka-
khan-hello-happiness-review

The Temptations

Aletti, Vince. "Anthology" liner notes.
http://aln2.albumlinernotes.com/Temptations_Anthology.html

Kurlansky, Mark. *Ready for a Brand New Beat: How Dancing in the Street Became the Anthem for a Changing America.* Riverhead Books, 2013.
Mendizabal, Amaya. "The Temptations, Michael Jackson & Mary J. Blige Rule First-Ever All-Time R&B/Hip-Hop Rankings." *Billboard*, March 1, 2017. www.billboard.com/articles/events/greatest-of-all-time/7702136/rb-hip-hop-temptations-michael-jackson-mary-j-blige-all-time

Billy Preston

The Beatles, edited by Roylance, Brian. *The Beatles Anthology.* Chronicle Books, 2000.
Jackson, Peter. *The Beatles: Get Back.* Walt Disney Studios/Apple Corps Ltd. 2021
Leng, Simon. *While My Guitar Gently Weeps: The Music of George Harrison.* Hal Leonard Publishing Corporation, 2006.
Fong-Torres, Ben. "George Harrison: Lumbering in the Material World ." *Rolling Stone*, Dec. 19, 1974. www.rollingstone.com/music/music-news/george-harrison-lumbering-in-the-material-world-175017/
Horowitz, Hal. From the Vault-L.A. Forum 1975. *American Songwriter,* Dec. 19, 2014. https://americansongwriter.com/rolling-stones-vault-l-forum-1975-dvd/
Richards, Keith. *Life.* Weidenfeld & Nicolson Ltd, 2010.
"Billy Preston Earns Rock Hall's Musical Excellence Award." *Ultimate Classic Rock*, Oct. 30, 2021. https://ultimateclassicrock.com/billy-preston-rock-and-roll-hall-of-fame/

WHY I SING THE BLUES

B.B. King

Guy, Buddy. *Instagram*, May 14, 2015. www.instagram.com/p/2sgKSpq7f0/?utm_source=ig_embed
Obama, Barack. White House press release, May 15, 2015. https://obamawhitehouse.archives.gov/blog/2015/05/15/bb-king-blues-has-lost-its-king-and-america-has-lost-legend

Buddy Guy

Smyers, Daryl. "Buddy Guy: "If (Clapton) Says That I Am The Greatest Guitar Player Ever, Then Maybe I Am." *Dallas Observer*, Sept. 1, 2011. www.dallasobserver.com/music/buddy-guy-if-clapton-says-that-i-am-the-greatest-guitar-player-ever-then-maybe-i-am-7075792
Wilcock, Donald and Guy, Buddy. *Damn Right I've Got The Blues.* Duane Press, 1999.
T. Church. "Buddy Guy turns 74." *BFD*, July 30, 2010. http://thebigfootdiaries.blogspot.com/2010/07/buddy-guy-turns-74.html

Johnny Winter

Sepulvado, Larry, and Burks, John. "Tribute to the Lone Star State." *Rolling Stone*, Dec.7, 1968. www.rollingstone.com/music/music-news/tribute-to-the-lone-star-state-dispossessed-men-and-mothers-of-texas-242153/
Palmer, Robert. "Muddy Waters: 1915-1983." *Rolling Stone*, June 23, 1983.
Gray, Chris. "Billy Gibbons, Others, Remember Johnny Winter." *Houston Press*, July 18, 2014. www.houstonpress.com/music/
billy-gibbons-others-remember-johnny-winter-6781518

Boz Scaggs

Loudon, Christopher. "Boz Scaggs: Speak Low." *Jazz Times*, April 25, 2019.
https://jazztimes.com/archives/boz-scaggs-speak-low/

ROUND MIDNIGHT

Dizzy Gillespie

Davis, Miles, and Quincy Troupe. *Miles: The Autobiography*. Simon & Schuster, 1989.
Gillespie, Dizzy & Fraser, Al. *To Be or Not to Bop*. Doubleday, 1979.
Reich, Howard. "Remembering Dizzy in the centennial year of his birth." *Chicago Tribune*, May 8, 2017.
Fordham, John. "50 great moments in jazz: The emergence of bebop." *The Guardian*, July 6, 2009. www.theguardian.com/music/musicblog/2009/jul/06/50-moments-jazz-bebop
Shipton, Alyn. *Groovin' High: The Life of Dizzy Gillespie*. Oxford University Press, 2001.
Cole, Swinton. "The Papa of Bebop Dizzy Gillespie Dies at 75." *The Lewiston Tribune* (Associated Press), Jan. 7, 1993. https://lmtribune.com/northwest/the-papa-of-bebop-dizzy-gillespie-dies-at-75/article_e5d93657-72f2-505d-8f1f-d16ccb3752fb.html

Dave Brubeck

Klotz, Kelsey A. K. "Dave Brubeck's Southern Strategy." *Dædalus*, Spring, 2019. www.amacad.org/publication/dave-brubecks-southern-strategy
Ingram, Robert. "Letters to the Editor." *The Red and Black*, Feb. 26, 1959.
"The Gates of Justice." www.milkenarchive.org/music/volumes/view/swing-his-praises/work/the-gates-of-justice/
Zambito, Tony. "The Essay by Martin Luther King, Jr. That Lives Large In Jazz." *JazzBuffalo*, Jan. 21, 2019. https://jazzbuffalo.org/2019/01/21/the-essay-by-martin-luther-king-jr-that-lives-large-in-jazz/
Gioia, Ted. *West Coast Jazz*. University of California Press, 1998.

www.pbs.org/brubeck/talking/westCoastJazzBookExcerpt.htm

"Dave Brubeck: Take Five jazz pianist dies." *BBC*, Dec. 5, 2012. www.bbc.com/news/entertainment-arts-20609327

Hancock, Herbie. "Dave Brubeck Pianist and composer, 91." *Time*, Dec. 9. 2012. https://poy.time.com/2012/12/19/tributes-to-those-we-lost-in-2012/slide/dave-brubeck/

Hancock, Herbie. *Facebook*, Dec. 5, 2012. www.facebook.com/herbiehancock/posts/dave-brubeck-was-a-pioneer-so-many-of-us-sprang-from-his-incredibly-creative-and/10151114380971783/

Ricci, Michael. "Sacred Choral Works - Songs of Praise: The Sacred Choral Music of Dave Brubeck." *AllAboutJazz*, Jan. 27, 2010. www.allaboutjazz.com/news/sacred-choral-works-songs-of-praise-the-sacred-choral-music-of-dave-brubeck/

Russonello, Giovanni. "'Take Five' Is Impeccable. 'Time Outtakes' Shows How Dave Brubeck Made It." *The New York Times,* Dec. 7, 2020

Herbie Hancock

Strand, Clark. "Absolutely, Indestructibly Happy." *Tricycle: The Buddhist Review.* Winter 2020. https://tricycle.org/magazine/tina-turner-buddhist/

Chick Corea

Stryker, Mark. "Herbie Hancock & Chick Corea - 'a deep bond'." *Detroit Free Press*, April 14, 2015. www.freep.com/story/entertainment/music/2015/04/14/chick-corea-herbie-hancock-free-press/25802409/

Considine, J.D. "Chick Corea Plays." *Downbeat*, Oct. 2020. https://downbeat.com/reviews/detail/Plays

Corea, Chick. *Facebook*, Feb. 11, 2021. www.facebook.com/chickcorea/posts/10158422599898924

Hugh Masekela

Deckard, Sharae. *World Literature, Neoliberalism, and the Culture of Discontent.* Palgrave Macmillan, 2019

"Freedom Songs: How Nelson Mandela Used Music To Change The World." *NME*, Dec. 6, 2013. www.nme.com/blogs/nme-blogs/freedom-songs-how-nelson-mandela-used-music-to-change-the-world-21501

Burke, Jason. "Tributes paid to South African musician and activist Hugh Masekela." *The Guardian*, Jan. 23, 2018. https://www.theguardian.com/music/2018/jan/23/hugh-masekela-south-african-jazz-trumpeter-dies-aged-78

Lindsay, Bruce. "Tony Allen and Hugh Masekela: Rejoice." *Jazz Journal*, June 25, 2020. https://jazzjournal.co.uk/2020/06/25/tony-allen-and-hugh-masekela-rejoice/

Paul Horn

Hunt, Ken. "Paul Horn: In India/Cosmic Consciousness – Paul Horn In Kashmir." *Jazzwise*, 2013. www.jazzwise.com/review/paul-horn-in-india-cosmic-consciousness-paul-horn-in-kashmir
Gaga, Lady. *Twitter*. https://twitter.com/ladygaga/status/511743294305746944?lang=en

REGGAE GOT SOUL

Jimmy Cliff

Lindsay, James M. "The Twenty Best Vietnam Protest Songs." *Council on Foreign Relations*, March 5, 2015. www.cfr.org/blog/twenty-best-vietnam-protest-songs
McGuire, Collin. "Jimmy Cliff: Rebirth." *PopMatters*, July 17, 2012. www.popmatters.com/160886-jimmy-cliff-rebirth-2495833567.html

Toots

Christgau, Robert. *Christgau's Record Guide: Rock Albums of the Seventies*. Ticknor & Fields, 1981.
Toots and the Maytals: Reggae Got Soul. BBC Four documentary. Directed by George Scott. UK, 2011. www.bbc.co.uk/programmes/b00ymljb.
Bloom, Steve. "True to These 'Tough' Times, Toots and the Maytals' Latest Promises Things Will Be Alright." *Variety*, Aug. 28, 2020. variety.com/2020/music/reviews/toots-and-the-maytals-got-to-be-tough-album-review-1234751899/
Jagger, Mick. *Twitter*, Sept. 12, 2020. https://twitter.com/mickjagger/status/130478632126170316 9

The Marleys

Gardner, Claudia. "Ziggy Marley Objects To Oil Exploration In Namibia's Kavango Region." *DancehallMag*, April 12, 2022. www.dancehallmag.com/2022/04/12/news/ziggy-marley-objects-to-oil-exploration-in-namibias-kavango-region.html

Made in the USA
Middletown, DE
31 October 2022

13818241R00234